Christocentric Preaching Meets the Historical Jesus

Christocentric Preaching Meets the Historical Jesus

A Critical Analysis of Christology in N.T. Wright
and Wolfhart Pannenberg: Implications
for a Christocentric Homiletic

DEVON DUFFIELD

PICKWICK *Publications* · Eugene, Oregon

CHRISTOCENTRIC PREACHING MEETS THE HISTORICAL JESUS
A Critical Analysis of Christology in N. T. Wright and Wolfhart Pannenberg: Implications for a Christocentric Homiletic

Copyright © 2024 Devon Duffield. All rights reserved. Except for brief quotations in critical publications or reviews, no part of this book may be reproduced in any manner without prior written permission from the publisher. Write: Permissions, Wipf and Stock Publishers, 199 W. 8th Ave., Suite 3, Eugene, OR 97401.

Pickwick Publications
An Imprint of Wipf and Stock Publishers
199 W. 8th Ave., Suite 3
Eugene, OR 97401

www.wipfandstock.com

PAPERBACK ISBN: 979-8-3852-0281-2
HARDCOVER ISBN: 979-8-3852-0282-9
EBOOK ISBN: 979-8-3852-0283-6

Cataloguing-in-Publication data:

Names: Duffield, Devon, author.

Title: Christocentric preaching meets the historical Jesus : a critical analysis of Christology in N. T. Wright and Wolfhart Pannenberg : implications for a Christocentric homiletic / Devon Duffield.

Description: Eugene, OR: Pickwick Publications, 2024. | Includes bibliographical references.

Identifiers: ISBN 979-8-3852-0281-2 (paperback). | ISBN 979-8-3852-0282-9 (hardcover). | ISBN 979-8-3852-0283-6 (epub).

Subjects: LSCH: Wright, N. T. (Nicholas Thomas). | Pannenberg, Wolfhart, 1928–2014. | Christology. | Homiletics.

Classification: BT111.3 D85 2024 (print). | BT111.3 (epub).

Permission to use Price's (2018, 84) preaching comparative table published in *Trinity Journal* 39 (2018) was obtained from Dr. Dana Harris (editor, *Trinity Journal*).

Permission to use Clowney's (2003, loc. 432) relationship between symbolism and typology figure published in *Preaching Christ in All of Scripture* 2003 was obtained from Nicole Gosling (Licensing and Permissions Assistant – Crossway).

Scripture quotations marked (NIV) are taken from The Holy Bible, New International Version® NIV® Copyright © 1973, 1978, 1984, 2011 by Biblica, Inc. Used with permission. All rights reserved worldwide.

Scripture quotations marked (ESV) are from the ESV® Bible (The Holy Bible, English Standard Version®), © 2001 by Crossway, a publishing ministry of Good News Publishers. Used by permission. All rights reserved. The ESV text may not be quoted in any publication made available to the public by a Creative Commons license. The ESV may not be translated in whole or in part into any other language.

To the most courageous woman I know, my wife, Svenje Duffield, who continues to show me that it is better to dare mighty things—even though we might fail—than to live without passion. To our children, Lucas, Noa, and Hudson, may you come to know Jesus Christ historically, experientially, and eternally.

"I am [in your world]." said Aslan. "But there I have another name. You must learn to know me by that name. This was the very reason why you were brought to Narnia, that by knowing me here for a little, you may know me better there."

—C. S. Lewis, *The Chronicles of Narnia*

Contents

Preface | ix
Acknowledgments | xi
Abbreviations | xiii

1 Introduction | 1
2 N. T. Wright's Christology | 14
3 Wolfhart Pannenberg's Christology | 66
4 Critical Analysis of N.T. Wright's
  and Wolfhart Pannenberg's Christology | 119
5 The Embedded Christology
  of the Christocentric Homiletic | 174
6 Implications for a Christocentric Homiletic | 229
7 Conclusion | 273

Bibliography | 283

Preface

THE CHRISTOCENTRIC HOMILETIC IS considered one of the leading contemporary approaches within the evangelical hermeneutic and homiletic society. However, its popularity has not made this approach immune to criticism. This book seeks to point out that the Christocentric homiletic is embedded in a Christology from above, which contributes to its strengths and weaknesses. It explores the implications of the from below Christologies of N.T. Wright and Wolfhart Pannenberg on the Christocentric approach.

A unique research methodology is employed that consists of five literary tasks to address the research problem. The research project begins with examining the from below Christologies of Wright and Pannenberg, which encompasses the overarching tenets of their Christologies and the influences of other scholars upon their presuppositions and Christological developments. Then, the strengths and weaknesses of their Christologies are identified, described, and evaluated through critical analysis. Subsequently, the Christocentric homiletic is examined, and its underlying Christology and shortcomings are specified and assessed. It is argued that the Christocentric homiletic is embedded in a from above approach to Christology and that the presuppositions of a Christology from above contribute to the homiletical approach's shortcomings. The implications of the strengths of Wright and Pannenberg's Christologies on the Christocentric homiletic are then explored. These implications demonstrate that these two from below Christologies enrich and challenge the Christocentric method in various meaningful ways. This book suggests that if the Christocentric method takes the from below Christologies of Wright and Pannenberg seriously, it can address specific weaknesses and find resources to enhance some of its strengths without negating its central conviction of preaching Christ in every sermon. This book fulfills the profound need to place the current homiletical debate on Christocentric preaching in dialogue with Christology. It defends the unique proposal that the Christocentric method can address its criticisms without becoming more Theocentric.

Acknowledgments

I AM SINCERELY GRATEFUL to the South African Theological Seminary (SATS) for providing me with a robust theological foundation and an excellent PhD program. The guidance received from various SATS faculty members during this endeavor has been invaluable. I am forever indebted to my PhD supervisors, Dr Robert Falconer and Dr Michael Bartholomaeus, who have accompanied me on this academic journey. They have greatly encouraged me in lonely times and appropriately challenged me intellectually when required. I am deeply thankful to Prof Robert Vosloo, who baptized me into the field of Christology and exposed me to New Testament scholars such as N.T. Wright and Wolfhart Pannenberg. I also want to thank the pastors who have shaped my spiritual life over the last decade and a half and instilled a passion for preaching in me. Nick van Rensburg who allowed me to discover and cultivate my gift for preaching. Chris Gerber who challenged me to become a better communicator and exposed me to different audiences. And Cameron Roxburgh who introduced me to storytelling as an effective communication tool.

I want to thank my mother and greatest supporter, Alveda Bezuidenhout, who remained interested in my project throughout. She has shown her support in various ways, and her positive attitude has been contagious. I am grateful to my wife, Svenje Duffield, and our three children for allowing me the opportunity to embark on this journey. I wish to give my deep appreciation for your sacrifices over years to make this possible. I want to thank my friends and family who have supported me in some fashion throughout this project: Louis Uys, Justin Duffield, Jannie Steenkamp, Deon Els, Willy Wright, Stian le Roux, Darren Bouwer, and Craig Bosnick. My conversations with you motivated me to stay the course during this project. Lastly, I express my gratitude to my Lord and Savior Jesus Christ, who has allowed me to study him historically.

Abbreviations

COQG	Christian Origins and the Question of God Series
E	Event or institution
ESV	English Standard Version
FCF	Fallen Condition Focus
JVG	Jesus and the Victory of God
NT	New Testament
NTPOG	The New Testament and the People of God
OT	Old Testament
Tn	Truth fulfilled in Christ
T1	Old Testament truth

1

Introduction

Definitions

CHRISTOCENTRIC HOMILETICS: CHRISTOCENTRIC HOMILETICS can be defined as a model of preaching that seeks to integrate the original meaning of a text of Scripture with the culmination of God's revelation in the person and work of Jesus Christ (Greidanus 1999, 10). Peppler (2012, 120) asserts that it is an approach by which all doctrinal formulations and preaching find their focal point in the person, life, and teaching of Jesus Christ. Scholars such as Clowney (2003, loc. 98) and Chapell (2018, loc. 236) state that this homiletical model expresses the meaning of both the human and divine authors by placing the text within the unifying theme of all of Scripture, namely, human need and the divine provision of redemption through Christ.

Christology "from above": Christology from above is a method of Christology that commences its exploration of the meaning of Jesus Christ for our day with the confession of faith in the deity of Christ as received from the New Testament (NT) writers (Kärkkäinen 2016, 4). Welker (2013, 75) shows that the from above Christological approach takes the divine Christ, as confessed by the early church, as its point of departure. Qin (2015, 39) adds that the from above approach to Christology focuses on Jesus from an ontological perspective; that is, it perceives Jesus through his ontological identity rather than through his actions or words.

Christology "from below": Christology from below is a method of Christology that commences its exploration of the meaning of Jesus Christ for our day with an inquiry into the historical Jesus of Nazareth (Kärkkäinen 2016, 4). This undertaking goes behind the texts of the New Testament writers to investigate the historical and factual grounds of Christological claims. Baker (2006, 77) and Qin (2015, 39) show that Christology from below is functional in nature as it focuses on the functions of Jesus, namely, his works and words through which it concludes his identity.

1.1 Review of Scholarship

The Christocentric homiletic, occasionally referred to as the redemptive-historic approach, is considered one of the four main contemporary approaches within the evangelical hermeneutical and homiletical society (Gibson and Kim 2018, 4).[1] The main contributions to the Christocentric homiletic, as shown by scholars such as Chapell (2018, loc. 143), Prince (2011, 87), and Gibson and Kim (2018, 4), have been made by North American scholars Sidney Greidanus, Edmund Clowney, and Bryan Chapell. The contribution of these scholars to the Christocentric approach centers on providing theological justification, practical guidance, and demonstrative examples of Christocentric sermons.

The work of Greidanus (1999) has had such a formative effect on the Christocentric model that he is considered representative of the approach and one of its pioneers (Price 2018, 70; Chapell 2018, loc. 143). Greidanus' (1999, 10) main argument is that a preaching text must be understood in its historical context and the context of the larger canon and redemptive history. In this way, Greidanus builds his redemptive-historical approach on the foundation of the classical expository method, which limits its understanding of the text primarily to its historical context (Allen 2011, 85). Practically, Greidanus provides numerous ways of preaching Christ from the Old Testament.

Another pioneer of the Christocentric homiletic is Clowney (Chapell 2018, loc. 143). Like Greidanus, Clowney's (2003) main argument is that only when we see the text in relation to Christ do we truly see the larger context of God's purpose in revelation (Clowney 2003, loc. 98). Clowney provides a unique contribution in terms of the theological justification of this approach, namely, that the purpose of the Hebrew Scriptures is to reveal God's plan for human redemption, which centers on God's presence in his incarnate Son (Clowney 2003, loc. 500).

---

1. The other three homiletical approaches presented by Gibson and Kim (2018, 5) are the christiconic (pericopal) theological approach, the theocentric approach, and the law-gospel approach.

More recently, Chapell (2018) established himself as one of the foremost contemporary representatives of the Christocentric homiletic (Gibson and Kim 2018, 4). Like the others, Chapell argues that sermons must explore how the gospel unfolds through all Scripture. Chapell (2018) emphasizes that redemptive-historic sermons motivate and enable Christian obedience without becoming moralistic.

There has been regular engagement with these works and the Christocentric approach as a whole within the evangelical hermeneutical and homiletical society, especially in North America. Keller (2015), who taught with Clowney on "Preaching Christ in a Postmodern World" at Reformed Theological Seminary, expands Clowney's work by providing a philosophical argument as to why Christocentric preaching is beneficial and essential. He shows that the convictions of a culture must be confronted in preaching and that people must be shown that only in Christ can the culture's most significant aspirations for good be met. For Keller, this aspiration is embodied in Christocentric preaching. Similarly, there have been various dissertations that have engaged with the Christocentric approach. Allen (2011) completed his PhD on the Christocentric homiletics of Edmund Clowney and Sidney Greidanus in contrast to the human author-centered hermeneutics of Walter Kaiser. This work provides a critical comparative study of these two approaches.

Similarly, Prince (2011) engages with Greidanus and Clowney in his dissertation on the necessity of Christocentric kingdom-focused preaching. Prince's main contribution was to show how Christocentric kingdom-focused preaching is genuinely biblical, exposing the meaning of both the human author in the historical context of the text and that of the divine author in the broader canonical context. Likewise, Lee's (2016) dissertation focused on Christ-saturated preaching. His dissertation identified, defined, and analyzed the Christocentric hermeneutics and homiletics of Edmund Clowney, Sidney Greidanus, Graeme Goldsworthy, and Bryan Chapell before presenting his own "Christ-saturated" approach to preaching, which addressed particular hermeneutical and homiletical challenges of the Christocentric method.

Although the Christocentric approach to preaching has gained a significant following, it has also received a fair amount of criticism. Chou (2016) criticizes the Christocentric approach for making alterations to the classical grammatical-historical hermeneutical method that are not scripturally permitted. He argues that the classical approach is sufficient to reveal the glories of Christ without preaching Christ from every text. Likewise, Price (2018, 84–85) criticizes the Christocentric approach for delivering repetitive sermons that overlook the text's unique details and for avoiding the biographical studies of biblical characters. Furthermore, scholars such as Kuruvilla (2008, 138) and Gibson and Kim (2018, loc. 3377) critique this approach for its significant duplication of sermon goals and for operating on a general level. However, Gibson and Kim's (2018, loc. 3377) most significant criticism toward the Christocentric approach is that the sermon application process of this approach very often becomes, "Jesus accomplished everything for us; we cannot obey on our own," which, in their view, discourages the Christian from pursuing Christlikeness.

It must be conceded that these critiques raise some serious challenges for the Christocentric approach, which must be addressed if this approach is to thrive. A potentially profitable avenue for bolstering the Christocentric model opens if we focus on the relation between Christology and homiletics. Scholarship at the intersection between Christology and homiletics has been irregular. This is mainly indicative of the fact that homiletical models are primarily embedded in a from above Christology, as can be observed in the assumptions and arguments made by the pioneers of the Christocentric homiletic (Clowney 2003, loc. 2601; Greidanus 1999, loc. 225–61). While more general discussions have made meaningful connections between theological presuppositions, hermeneutics, and homiletics (Gibson and Kim 2018, 4; Hyun 2015), which include the Christocentric homiletic, these discussions do not make explicit mention of how hermeneutics and homiletics relate to Christology. This is a significant omission as our views of Jesus significantly influence how we interpret the canon and, ultimately, what we preach (Peppler 2012, 117; Steven Smith 2008, 141; Kevin Smith 2012, 157). There is recognition of this in homiletical scholarship more broadly. For example, Busch (1998) produced a dissertation on the link between these two issues that focuses on the liberation Christology of Jon Sobrino and the implications thereof on preaching. However, in relation to Christocentric preaching, the connection between Christology and homiletics has not yet been thoroughly investigated.

In particular, the instinctive tendency of the Christocentric homiletic for a Christology from above raises the question of whether a Christology from below could provide resources that might strengthen this homiletical model. Typically, because of the excessive historical criticism and liberal presuppositions of the from below Christologies in the past (Kärkkäinen 2016, 4), these Christologies have not been appreciated by the homiletical societies, including the Christocentric model. However, recent developments suggest that this caricature is no longer accurate. In the mid-late twentieth century, more historical data became available through various literary discoveries and archaeological findings, such as the dead sea scrolls at Qumran in 1947, which gave greater insight into the social-political context in the timeframe and setting of Jesus (Wessels 2006, 44). Consequently, certain from below Christologies arose that are not characterized by excessive historical criticism or liberal presuppositions but by affirming and even arguing historically for the deity of Jesus Christ. This development potentially provides a pool of resources from which the Christocentric model could draw without betraying some of its fundamental convictions.

Two Christologies from below present themselves as valuable dialogue partners for the Christocentric model, namely, the work of British New Testament scholar N.T. Wright and German theologian Wolfhart Pannenberg. A brief overview of their contributions should indicate the appropriateness of these scholars for the present thesis. Wright's (1996) work in *Jesus and the Victory of God* (*JVG*) insists that historical research and theology belong together, especially regarding the study of Jesus. Following this conviction, Wright presents a from below Christology, which seeks to describe the historical Jesus as an eschatological prophet announcing and inaugurating the long-awaited kingdom of God. However, because of Wright's commitment to joining history and theology in his Christology, his historical research and theological methodologies have both been criticized. Casey (1998) claims that there are severe issues with Wright's presentation of the historical Jesus, most of which proceed from his presuppositions, namely the Christian tradition to which he belongs. For Casey, Wright's quest for the historical Jesus makes the same mistake as the first quest for the historical Jesus, to replace the historical Jesus with the Christ of faith. Furthermore, Casey criticizes Wright's interpretation of the Gospels, which according to him, stems from a hermeneutical circle that seeks to replace the historical Jesus with an infallible Christ of faith. Likewise, Marsh's (1998) most fundamental criticism of Wright's work is the continuity of his conclusions about the historical Jesus with the confessions of the Christian church. He argues that Wright uses historical data to defend theological assertions and concludes that Wright's work is firmly grounded within the idealist tradition. In response to Casey and Marsh, Wright (1998) indicates that the main themes within which he places Jesus were not provided by his Christian background or training but from a historical study of first-century Judaism. Stein (2001, 210) critiques Wright for using a theological methodology constructed from his historical research through which he forces various texts to fit his overarching system. Consequently, this tendency leads to a one-sided view of Jesus' ministry (Stein 2001, 212).

With a similar interest in the relationship between history and theology, the main objective of Pannenberg's (1977) initial Christological work, *Jesus—God and Man*, is the defense and application of the from below methodology to Christology. Pannenberg's fundamental conviction for providing a from below Christology is that Christology needs to offer rational historical support for belief in the deity of Jesus Christ rather than presuppose it (Kärkkäinen 2016, 5). Wildman (2007) provides a helpful assessment of Pannenberg's Christology. He shows that Pannenberg's emphasis on Christology within the context of universal history is due to Hegel's philosophy of history. However, he critiques Pannenberg for linking an ascending Christology with the resurrection, as this is a suspect endeavor.

Nevertheless, Wildman still places Pannenberg with Moltmann as one of the most significant contributors to universal historical Christologies. Similarly, Kärkkäinen (2016) presents and assesses Pannenberg's work as a contemporary European Christology. Significantly, he identifies the anthropological foundation of Pannenberg's Christology, whereby Jesus' humanity is presented as the fulfillment of human destiny (Kärkkäinen 2016, 117). This clarifies why certain scholars, such as Wildman (2007) and Kärkkäinen (2016), refer to Pannenberg's Christology as universal in nature. On the other hand, Peters (2014) investigates the roots of Pannenberg's commitment to historical inquiry by producing a biographical work on Pannenberg's theological education and theological influences. Peters engages with Pannenberg's historical approach to Christology and concludes that it provides a more objective public platform for theological debate. However, Pannenberg's universal historical Christology has not gone without criticism. Macleod (2000) provides a thorough presentation and critical assessment of the significant components of his Christology. He questions why Pannenberg believes in the historicity of the resurrection but denies the historicity of other occurrences described in the Gospels, attributing them to legendary influences, such as the virgin birth and Jesus' baptism.

While Wright and Pannenberg's from below Christologies have been criticized, especially regarding the processes they have utilized in linking history and theology, these two European from below Christologies have specific strengths that can enhance the Christocentric model in various ways. Therefore, research at this underexplored intersection is imperative.

1.2 Research Question

Main Research Question:
What are the implications of a critical analysis on Wright and Pannenberg's Christology for a Christocentric homiletic? This problem requires answering the following subsidiary questions.

Subsidiary Questions:

(1) How has N. T. Wright developed his historical Jewish-embedded Christology in light of the "Third Quest" for the historical Jesus?

(2) How has Wolfhart Pannenberg developed his universal anthropological Christology in light of the "No Quest" and "New Quest" for the historical Jesus?

(3) What might a critical analysis of the Christology of N. T. Wright and Wolfhart Pannenberg reveal?

(4) What is the embedded Christology of the North American modern development in Christocentric homiletics?

(5) How do the strengths of N. T. Wright and Wolfhart Pannenberg's Christologies enrich and challenge the Christocentric homiletic?

1.3 Hypothesis

My hypothesis in this research project is that a critical analysis of Wright and Pannenberg's Christology will enhance and challenge the Christocentric homiletic in various ways. (1) I expect that these European from below Christologies, with their focus on historical first-century Jewish convictions, will challenge the Christocentric method to preach the kingdom of God theme from the Gospels. (2) It will provide helpful ways of linking Christ to the Old Testament. (3) They might supply historical tools with which the Christocentric homiletic may operate in apologetic spaces. (4) I expect these functional Christologies to challenge a significant weakness of the Christocentric homiletic, namely, its flawed application process.

1.4 Delimitations

I wish to make the following delimitations: (1) I will research the Christologies of N.T. Wright and Wolfhart Pannenberg for the following reasons: (i) Wright and Pannenberg are and were both European scholars who began their Christology from below in the historical Jesus. (ii) Both affirmed the deity of Christ through historical argumentation rather than relying on the early church's preaching. (iii) They have developed their theology on Christ differently; Wright focuses on Jesus as an eschatological prophet announcing and inaugurating the kingdom of God, while Pannenberg emphasizes a universal anthropological Christology that focuses on Jesus' humanity as the fulfillment of human destiny.

(2) There are various mainstream homiletical approaches in contemporary evangelicalism; however, I have chosen to engage with the Christocentric homiletic for the following reasons: (i) it is one of the main homiletical approaches in contemporary evangelical scholarly debate. (ii) It emphasizes the person, work, and teachings of Jesus, which is the subject of Christology.

1.5 Presuppositions

My convictions align with the council of Nicaea, that Jesus is of one substance (*homoousios*) with the Father, and with the Chalcedonian creed, that Jesus was truly God and truly man, with two unchangeable, indivisible, unified, inseparable natures in one person (Kärkkäinen 2016, 61). However, I consider particular contemporary from below Christologies that place Jesus in the first-century Jewish context helpful. I do not consider these as an alternative to a from above Christology but complementary, assuming these Christologies conform to the boundaries of the Christological creeds. Concerning homiletics, I appreciate integrating the text's message with God's ultimate revelation in the person, work, and teachings of Jesus. Therefore, I would consider myself an advocate of the Christocentric approach but acknowledge the various critiques against this position and argue that it should be applied with caution and prudence.

1.6 Purpose and Significance of the Research

1.6.1 Purpose

Various scholars such as Kärkkäinen (2016, 1), Williams (2018, 250), and Bonhoeffer (2009, 332) have shown that Christology is a continuing task of the church. Others such as Migliore (2014, 169) and Welker (2013, 12–13) agree, stating that Christology is not merely a repetition of Christological creeds but a contextualization of the person and work of Jesus Christ in every generation in the light of biblical and historical developments. In other words, Christology is not stagnant nor theorized in a vacuum but is continuously developing and changing. With that in mind, this research is essential for two reasons. First, it seeks to critically analyze two different contemporary European from below Christologies, which use a historically skeptical method to describe who Jesus is without denying his deity. This critical analysis aims to identify their strengths, which will be applied to the Christocentric homiletic. Second, it endeavors to assess the implications of the strengths of these Christologies for the contemporary North American Christocentric homiletical model. This research project hopes to enhance the Christocentric homiletical approach by indicating how more functional-orientated Christologies might strengthen its ability to preach Christ and address specific weaknesses of the approach, such as its application process.

1.6.2 Theological Significance

This thesis is theologically significant for the following reasons. First, it seeks to clarify how two very prominent theologians have developed their from below Christologies as well as the strengths and weaknesses of these Christologies. Second, it endeavors to indicate how theological presuppositions influence homiletical models, particularly how Christological convictions affect the hermeneutical process, which directly impacts homiletics. New perspectives on Jesus' character, values, words, and deeds will affect the hermeneutical approach. Scholars such as Peppler (2012, 117), Steven Smith (2008, 141), and Kevin Smith (2012, 157) show that our views of Jesus have a significant influence on how we interpret the canon. Third, research on the implications of European from below Christologies on the North American Christocentric homiletic will provide a unique contribution to current scholarship on the Christocentric homiletic, which has been chiefly confined to comparisons with other homiletical models. It will provide recent scholarship on Christocentric homiletics with ecumenical and interdisciplinary considerations. In other words, how European Systematic Theology informs North American Practical Theology, specifically homiletics.

1.6.3 Practical Significance

Practically this thesis is significant for the following reasons. First, by emphasizing the humanity of Jesus, it will provide the Christocentric homiletic with ways of addressing its major criticism, namely, its lack of adequate application in its sermons. The Christocentric homiletic is embedded in a from above Christology, showing how the eternal Son acted in redemptive history by becoming a man, living the life we could never live, and dying on the cross for the sins of the world. Conversely, scholars such as Baker (2006, 77) and Qin (2015, 43) argue that a from below Christology is functional rather than ontological in nature as it places the emphasis not on the personhood but on the works and words of the historical Jesus, which could assist the church in identifying with the historical Jesus and therefore could cultivate Christian discipleship. Second, this project will provide the Christocentric approach with historical means with which it might operate in more apologetic spaces. Third, with its emphasis on first-century Jewish convictions, the project will provide helpful ways the Christocentric homiletic might link Christ to the Old Testament.

1.7 Research Design

The nature of this research is a development from a literary type of theological research to a conceptual construction. The nature of the data involved is literary and has no empirical component. This thesis will consist of five literary tasks related to the key questions. These are as follows: (1) An examination of the Christology of N.T. Wright. This will be done through a literary exploration of his Christological works, sermons, and the works of other scholars who have engaged with him. (2) An examination of the Christology of Wolfhart Pannenberg. This will be done through a literary investigation of his Christological works and the works of other scholars who have engaged with him. (3) A critical analysis of the two Christologies wherein the strengths and weaknesses will be explored. Whilst literary, this task is predominantly conceptual, using conceptual analysis. (4) A summary and analysis of the embedded Christology of the Christocentric homiletic. This will be based on a literary exploration of the literary works of current scholarship on Christocentric homiletics. This task examines the literary works of theologians who are advocates of and opponents of the Christocentric homiletical approach and explores its embedded Christology. (5) A conceptual analysis that highlights the implications of these from below Christologies on a Christocentric homiletic. It will seek to demonstrate these implications.

1.8 Research Methodology

This research project is a study primarily in systematic theology, with implications for practical theology, namely homiletics, which employs a unique research methodology. There are various research methodologies within systematic theology; however, none adequately fits this project. The Osborne (2006) research methodology is primarily concerned with theological formulations; the Lewis and Demarest (1996) research methodology is suitable for apologetic research. However, these methodologies do not adequately address the research problem of this study. Therefore, a unique research methodology will be employed, which includes specific steps from different methodologies. The first and second steps are taken from the Dialectical Inquiry Methodology, which will assist with describing the Christologies of Wright and Pannenberg (Berniker and McNabb 2006). Subsequently, the third step of the Dialectical Inquiry Methodology will assist with critically analyzing their Christologies, whereby their works will be placed in conversation with other scholars and Scripture. Likewise, a combination of steps one and three of the Dialectical Inquiry Methodology will assist with describing and analyzing the Christocentric homiletic. Finally, the last stage of the Osborne research methodology will enable the project to explore the practical implications of the critical analysis of homiletics. The following methodological steps will be followed in addressing the research problem.

Step 1: Examining N.T. Wright's Christology

In this step, Wright's from below Christology will be examined. This will be undertaken primarily through a literature review of Wright's Christological works and sermons. Secondarily, a literature review of other scholars who have engaged with Wright's Christology will be set forth. Based on this literature review, the following will be considered and analyzed: (1) the overarching tenets of his Christology, which will include, amongst others, Jesus' mindset, aims and beliefs, self-awareness, Jesus' crucifixion, and resurrection, (2) the influences of other scholars upon Wright, his presuppositions, and his Christological developments.

Resources to be consulted in this examination of N.T. Wright's Christology will, among others, include the following: Wright (1996), Wright (1998), Wright (2003), Allison (2009a), Casey (1998), Herzog (2000), Johnson (2013), Jonker (1977), Loke (2009), Marsh (1998), Newman (1999), Newman (2005), Perrin (2015), Stein (2001), Stewart (2006), Welker (2013), Wells (2012), Wessels (2006).

Step 2: Examining Wolfhart Pannenberg's Christology

In this step, Pannenberg's from below Christology will be examined. This will be attained primarily through a literature review of Pannenberg's Christological works. A literature review will also be conducted, focusing on the works of other scholars who have engaged with him. Based on this literature review, the following will be considered and analyzed: (1) the overarching tenets of his Christology, which will include, amongst others, the virgin birth, incarnation, Jesus' works, Jesus' message, Jesus' self-awareness, and the resurrection, (2) the influences of other scholars upon Pannenberg, his presuppositions, and his Christological developments.

Resources to be consulted in this examination of Wolfhart Pannenberg's Christology will, among others, include the following: Pannenberg (1966), Pannenberg (1994), Allison (2009a), Braaten and Clayton (1988), Harvie (2008), Hendrickson (1998), Herzog (2000), Jonker (1977), Kärkkäinen (2016), Macleod (2000), Peters (2014), Rosok (2017), Welker (2013), Wessels (2006), Wildman (2007), Wright (1996).

Step 3: Critical Analysis

Here a critical analysis of the overarching tenets of Wright and Pannenberg's Christologies will be conducted based on the findings of steps 1 and 2. This step will identify, describe, and evaluate the strengths and weaknesses of these two Christologies by placing them in conversation with secondary sources and by engaging with Scripture. A critical analysis is needed to ensure that strengths and weaknesses are not merely assumed and that accurate conclusions are reached.

Resources to be consulted in this critical analysis section will, among others, include the following: Braaten and Clayton (1988), Casey (1998), Harvie (2008), Hendrickson (1998), Johnson (2013), Kärkkäinen (2016), Loke (2009), Macleod (2000), Marsh (1998), Newman (1999), Newman (2005), Pannenberg (1966), Pannenberg (1994), Perrin (2015), Peters (2014), Stein (2001), Stewart (2006), Wells (2012), Wildman (2007), Wright (1996), Wright (1998), Wright (2003).

Step 4: Summary and Analysis of the Christology of the Christocentric Homiletic

The Christocentric homiletic and its embedded Christology will be examined in this step. This will be conducted through a literature review of the homiletical works of the pioneers of the approach—Sidney Greidanus and Edmund Clowney—as well as a contemporary representative, Bryan Chapell. These scholars' homiletical works and sermons will be analyzed, and their theological reasoning and practical guidance will be compared. This literature review will be extended to include the works of other scholars who have engaged critically with them or their approaches. Based on this literature review, the weaknesses of this homiletical approach will be identified, described, and explored. Subsequently, based on the literature review, the underlying Christology of the Christocentric homiletic will be identified and analyzed.

Resources to be consulted in this review of scholarship section will, among others, include the following: Allen (2011), Busch (1998), Chapell (2018), Chou (2016), Gibson and Kim (2018), Clowney (1998), Clowney (2003), Greidanus (1999), Johnson (2007), Keller (2015), Kuruvilla (2008), Kuruvilla (2013), Lee (2016), Moore (2010), Price (2018), Price (2019), Prince (2011).

Step 5: Implications for a Christocentric Homiletic

This step will explore the implications of the critical analysis of Wright and Pannenberg's Christologies upon the Christocentric homiletic. I will apply the strengths of these Christologies to the Christocentric homiletic and explore how it might benefit the homiletical approach. I will consider specifically how these Christologies' strengths might address the Christocentric approach's weaknesses, as identified in step 4. Furthermore, the strengths of the Christocentric homiletic that these two Christologies might enhance will also be identified. Finally, this step will demonstrate the implications for the Christocentric homiletic by providing sermon examples.

Resources to be consulted in this assessment of the implications on a Christocentric homiletic will, among others, include the following: Allen (2011), Busch (1998), Chapell (2018), Chou (2016), Gibson and Kim (2018), Clowney (1998), Clowney (2003), Greidanus (1999), Johnson (2007), Keller (2015), Kuruvilla (2008), Kuruvilla (2013), Lee (2016), Moore (2010), Price (2018), Price (2019), Prince (2011).

2

N. T. Wright's Christology

2.1 Introduction

My first task is Christological in nature. Every generation, from the first century until now, has endeavored to answer the question Jesus posed to his disciples in Matthew 16:15, "But *who* do you say that I am?"(italics mine; ESV).[1] This figure has continually occupied the thinking of some of the greatest minds over the past two millennia. Considered more prominent than even Socrates (Pelikan 1985, xxi), the story of Jesus of Nazareth has been told and retold through the centuries. Consequently, the meaning and significance of his person and work have been interpreted in several ways in numerous contexts through various ages. Each epoch of history provides a continuity and discontinuity of images and titles for Jesus according to their historical contexts and fundamental questions (Moltmann 2015, 113; Pelikan 1985, 2), which leads Kärkkäinen (2016, 1) to ask, how are we to speak of Jesus Christ in the third millennium?

Kärkkäinen (2016, 1) shows that before the Enlightenment, the from above approach was predominantly used to describe Jesus Christ. Conversely, since the Enlightenment, scholars have mostly sought to describe Jesus using a from below approach that focused on the historical human, Jesus of Nazareth, rather than the so-called Christ of faith, and often resulted in positions at odds with traditional claims regarding the divinity

---

1. The English Standard Version (ESV) is the primary translation utilized throughout this thesis, unless otherwise stated.

and person of Christ. This tendency of the from below approach raises the question: should conservative Christians advocate a historical approach to Jesus when so many of these prominent from below historical portraits conflict with what the church believes about Jesus Christ? For example, consider two scholars Wright (1996a, 3–4) refers to as theological giants, Albert Schweitzer and Rudolph Bultmann. On the one hand, Schweitzer described Jesus historically as a prophetic genius who was wrong about his end of the space-time world prediction.

On the other hand, Bultmann argued that Jesus was a mistaken hero who hoped for a kingdom that never arrived. For Bultmann, the gospels' stories of Jesus are merely expressions of the early church's faith. These conclusions have tarnished historical research on Jesus of Nazareth and encouraged the suspicion that such research will not benefit the church, the result of which is that historical research is ignored by many (Wright 1996a, 16). This has led scholars such as Allison (2009a, 34–35) and Migliore (2014, 172) to suggest that the aim of Christology should not be to satisfy historical curiosity but to affirm Christ and, correspondingly, that Christology is not ultimately dependent upon historical validity.

However, this is not the position Wright takes. For Wright (1996a, 8–11), history and theology belong together, especially when describing Jesus Christ. He argues that theology without history leads to icons of Jesus, which are supported by ahistorical readings of the gospels. In contrast, history without theology leads to irrelevant and misleading portraits of Jesus. According to Wright, Christology cannot ignore history as it relies on history to build its case. For him, historical research is part of the church's God-given mandate and mission to the Enlightenment world; it has tremendous apologetic value (Wright 1998a, 50). He disagrees with Bonhoeffer (2009, 328), who argues that historical research on Jesus is unnecessary because Jesus is the Lord of history. Instead, Wright (2019a, 4) believes that history is real knowledge and follows the accepted methods of natural science whereby true knowledge of Jesus Christ can be obtained. And yet, Wright identifies as an evangelical Christian and holds to what would broadly be recognized as an orthodox Christian faith. The question remains, how does Wright then use a historically skeptical approach to describe Jesus Christ yet remains orthodox?

This chapter will examine how Wright developed his from below Christology. It is descriptive in nature and does not provide a critical analysis of Wright's Christology, which will be performed in chapter 4 of this thesis. It will explore where Wright belongs within the different quests for the historical Jesus, his influences, and the framework he uses to conduct his historical Christological study. This framework includes Jesus' mindset within the first-century Jewish worldview, his aims and beliefs, why he died, how the church came into being, and why the gospels are what they are. The purpose of this chapter is to understand Wright's from below Christology to ultimately apply its strengths to the Christocentric homiletic in chapter 6.

2.2 Wright and the Quests for the Historical Jesus

2.2.1 Introduction

The eighteenth-century Enlightenment can be summed up by its slogan, "Have courage to use your own reason!" (Kärkkäinen 2016, 73–74). This movement encouraged people to use their reason independently from the opinions of other people, institutions, and particularly the church. That which could be proved by reason was considered the only form of valid knowledge. According to philosophers such as Immanuel Kant, whatever opinions were based on faith were considered illusions that needed to be "cleared up" (Aufklärung). This age of independent reason also saw an increase in biblical criticism, which led to a re-evaluation of central Christian doctrines, especially in Christology (75–76). Arising from this reconsideration of Christology in light of biblical criticism and critical history was an endeavor called the "Quest for the Historical Jesus." The foundational idea around this quest was to discover the historical truth about Jesus of Nazareth independently from the church's creeds and theology. The quest has been an ongoing endeavor that has gone through different phases since its inauguration.

This section will explore the different quests for the historical Jesus, where Wright fits within this spectrum, and, consequently, what the fundamental questions are that he uses as his framework to describe Jesus historically. This section will conclude with Wright's methodology and hypothesis, which the subsequent sections of the chapter will analyze.

2.2.2 The First Quest for the Historical Jesus

Although there is consensus among many scholars that the quest for the historical Jesus started with Hermann Reimarus in the eighteenth century, Wright (1996a, 13–15) believes that the seeds of the critical movement initiated by Reimarus came as a result of the Reformers' inadequate treatment of the gospels, their failure to understand Jesus' career, and their reluctance to compare the Christ of the church to history. In reaction to this deficit, the quest for the historical Jesus commenced as an explicitly anti-theological and anti-Christian movement that sought to prove European Christianity wrong by showing it relied on a failed Messiah and a misleading gospel sustained by historical distortions (16–17).

The "First Quest" provided three significant directions for discovering and defining the historical Jesus. First, Jesus must be approached as "either purely historical or purely supernatural"; second, the gospel sources used in the endeavor must be "either the Synoptics or John"; third, Jesus must be seen as "either eschatological or un-eschatological" (Herzog 2000, 4). The eschatological category issued from Albert Schweitzer, who, like Reimarus, placed Jesus within the first-century Jewish context; however, instead of considering Jesus as a failed revolutionary, Schweitzer positioned Jesus within an apocalyptic framework (Wright 1996a, 19). Subsequently, much twentieth-century scholarship has offered variations on Schweitzer's view of an eschatological Jesus, of which Wright is one such variation (Allison 2009a, 91). The eschatological approach proves foundational to Wright's Christological endeavor insofar as Wright maintains that there are two main approaches to follow in historical inquiry into Jesus, either thoroughly skeptical or thoroughly eschatological (Wright 1996a, 20).

However, in 1906 Schweitzer, who felt that the definitions of Jesus produced during the First Quest conformed Jesus to the canons of modern philosophy, published a work that summarized and criticized this quest in such a compelling manner that it discouraged two generations of scholars from continuing the search (Wright 1996a, 18; Herzog 2000, 6–8). This discreditation of any further attempts to write a biography of Jesus started a new era in the quest for the historical Jesus, known as the "No quest" period, which lasted until around 1953 (Herzog 2000, 8).

During the "No Quest" period, serious New Testament scholars placed their focus elsewhere, focusing on early traditions about Jesus rather than attempting to reconstruct a historical Jesus (Dunn and Wright 2004, 2). Scholars such as Rudolf Bultmann sought to change the approach by focusing on the kerygma of the early church rather than using the gospels as historical sources to reconstruct the life of Jesus (Herzog 2000, 8–9). For Bultmann, the personality of Jesus could not be retrieved from the gospel records, which, according to him, were statements of the faith of the early church (Wright 1996a, 22). These scholars were convinced that the distance between the historical Jesus and the Christ of faith, between the preaching of Jesus and that of the early church, was just too great and that no bridge could connect the two.

2.2.3 The New Quest for the Historical Jesus

After the "No Quest" period, Ernst Käsemann, who was one of Bultmann's students, launched the "New Quest" for the historical Jesus on the conviction that unless Jesus Christ is grounded in history, people can re-invent Jesuses to suit their ideologies (Wright 1996a, 23). This conviction, Wright argues, stems from what Käsemann observed during the 1930s in Germany when, because of the lack of historical study on Jesus during the "No Quest" epoch, an opportunity presented itself for the Nazis to invent a Jesus that would suit their political program (Dunn and Wright 2004, 2). Wright (1998a, 49) agrees with Käsemann that even the church is not immune to self-delusion, often creating Jesuses according to all kinds of fantasies that reflect its interests.

The "New Quest" started in 1953. It focused on demythologizing the kerygma of the gospels to arrive at the actual words of Jesus by using such methods as Ernst Käsemann's criterion of dissimilarity (Herzog 2000, 13). This quest aimed to validate the authentic sayings of Jesus and treat them as timeless truths rather than actual events (Wright 1996a, 24). Generally, they followed Schweitzer's understanding of the apocalyptic as the literal ending of the space-time universe. However, like the previous two quests, the New Quest did not last and eventually stalled in 1970.

Although there is consensus among some scholars that the New Quest ended, Wright interestingly argues that the New Quest has subsequently been revived. Wright (1996a, 21) identifies two main streams within which late twentieth-century historical research on Jesus can be categorized and describes them as the path of thoroughgoing skepticism of William Wrede (*Wredestrasse*) and the path of thoroughgoing eschatology of Albert Schweitzer (*Schweitzerstrasse*). For Wright (28), the continuation of the New Quest can be located in those critical thinkers who follow what he refers to as the *Wredebahn* or *Wredestrasse*. According to the *Wredestasse*, the gospels consist of theologically motivated fiction of the early church; therefore, little can be known about Jesus. Alternatively, the *Schweitzerstrasse* places Jesus within Jewish apocalyptic eschatology and regards the gospels as the records of his kingdom proclamation (21). There are three reasons why Wright regards the *Wredestrasse* as a new wave of the "New Quest": (1) the primary sources for their historical reconstruction of Jesus are his sayings, which Wright considers a continuation of Bultmann (79),[2] (2) like

---

2. Wright (2011c, 159), speaking about Bultmann's legacy states, "The legacy of this movement has been a nervous belief among many to this day: the belief that the New Testament can only tangentially, as it were, give us access to Jesus himself." Although Wright (2011c, 158–59) disagrees with Bultmann's view that Jesus' career was

Käsemann these scholars assess the sayings of Jesus through a set system of criteria, and (3) they present a demythologized non-Jewish Jesus who taught timeless truths.

The most prominent scholars Wright engages with who form part of this renewed "New Quest" are Robert Funk, Burton Mack, Dominic Crossan, and Markus Borg. Funk gathered North American scholars and founded the Jesus Seminar in 1985, who, in Bultmannian style, voted on the authenticity of several different sayings of Jesus (Wright 1996a, 29). Their approach consisted of three features: (1) all relevant material of Jesus must be included in the historical study, not merely the sayings in the gospels. (2) The sayings would then be voted on by these scholars by using a 4-color system, and (3) the results of the process would be published as widely as possible (Funk, Scott, and Butts 1988, 21).[3] Wright (1996a, 32–33) criticizes this approach because of its heavy reliance on the gospel of Thomas and Q as the grid through which the sayings of Jesus are judged, in addition to its questionable claim of objectivity.[4] He points out that, because of its dependence on the gospel of Thomas and Q, a common thread in the renewed New Quest has been associating Jesus' sayings with the Cynic philosophy rather than Judaism (66). Wright points out that the Cynics were popular philosophers who emphasized the corruption of human societies and called people to reconsider their lives and worldviews.[5] Others, such as Downing (1992, 154), have chosen the middle ground by concluding that Jesus was a Jewish Cynic who drew from both traditions.[6]

Burton Mack and Dominic Crossan are two of the most prominent scholars of the new wave of the New Quest. Mack (1988, 323) prefers Q for his reconstruction, claiming that Mark's gospel is theological fiction written to legitimize second-century Christianity (376). Mack argues that Jesus was a Cynic teacher rather than a Jewish eschatological figure. Wright (1996a, 36) points out that Mack's treatment of Mark corresponds with that of

---

non-political, that Jesus transcended Judaism and therefore taught timeless truths, he remains sympathetic towards Bultmann as someone who thought deeply in difficult times.

3. The Seminar sought to arrive at the authentic sayings of Jesus through applying critical scientific methods (Funk, Hoover, and the Jesus Seminar 1993, 34). However, this approach was based on a predetermined criterion of authenticity which dictated the results and yielded little insight into who Jesus was historically (Perrin 2011b, 127).

4. Snodgrass (2009, loc. 688–89) affirms Wright's avoidance of critically attempting to arrive at a bundle of authentic sayings.

5. Wright (2013:490) points out that Cynicism was more a mood than a movement.

6. Although other scholars such as Meyer (1972) and Sanders (1985) attempted to work around the standard criteria of authentication that marked the New Quest, it was Wright's methodology that made the break altogether (Perrin 2011b, 128).

Wrede. Like Funk, Mack relies heavily upon Q, which according to Wright, presents a vastly different version of Christianity than the gospels and Paul (Wright 2000, 86). Wright (1996a, 43) heavily criticizes the use of Q for a historical reconstruction of Jesus as it stems from the "mythology of the counter-cultural movement" of the 1960s. For him, a historical hypothesis based upon Q must be verified according to the accepted canons of historiography, and it is unclear whether Q can bear this weight.

Similarly, the main argument in Crossan's historical reconstruction is that Jesus was a peasant Jewish Cynic who opposed the brokerage systems of the Mediterranean by rebuilding a community through his miracles and meals (Crossan 1991, 422). Although Wright (1996a, 65) has high regard for Crossan's work, he does critique Crossan for underplaying the Jewishness of Jesus. He argues that if Crossan's historical reconstruction is all that there is to Jesus, then the Jewish authorities would never have opposed him (59). Although Crossan also contends that the gospel of Mark is theological fiction, he disagrees with the Bultmann line that we cannot know much historically about Jesus due to the nature of the gospels (45). According to Wright, Crossan's work on Jesus represents the most significant contribution to this renewed New Quest (44). Lastly, there is Marcus Borg. Wright describes him as a middleman between the New Quest and the Third Quest for the historical Jesus (75). He considers Borg an apologist for the Jesus Seminar who denies the deity of Jesus; however, he does place Jesus in his Jewish context, a trademark of the Third Quest.[7]

Unfortunately, the consequences of the skeptical approach to historical Jesus research, especially as conducted by this new wave of the New Quest, have been that various scholars have abandoned and rejected any further historical research on Jesus (Wright 2019a, 3). Conversely, others such as Wright (2019a, 4) and Allison (2009a, 5), designating the work of the New Questers as the low point of historical study on Jesus, have continued to encourage historical research on Jesus because, for them, an unexamined Christ is not worth worshipping.

2.2.4 The Third Quest for the Historical Jesus

The discovery of archaeological findings, especially the Dead Sea Scrolls, invigorated historical research on Jesus once again (Welker 2013, 74; Dunn and Wright 2004, 2). Allison (2009a, 54) observes that these discoveries have given scholars an improved tool kit to manufacture better historical

---

7. For other critiques of the Jesus Seminar and their methods see Hays (1994, 43–48), Pearson (1995, 317–38), Witherington (1995), Johnson (1996), and Evans (2006).

products insofar as these literary findings gave significant insight into Jesus' first-century Judaism. Correspondingly, one of the most significant factors that separate the Third Quest from those that go before is that it takes Jesus' Jewish context extremely seriously (Wright 1996a, 89; Welker 2013, 77; Herzog 2000, 24). Davies (1968, 344–47) points out that the New Quest followed the Bultmann line, arguing that Jesus' career was not politically laden but rather his ethical call focused on timeless truths and personal piety. This line contends that the kingdom of God has already arrived with Jesus; therefore, Jesus' career transcended Judaism and is marked by disinterest in Israel's national agendas (Perrin 2011b, 122–23).

Conversely, the Third Quest followed the Dodd and Caird line, which held that Jesus' kingdom message did not focus on personal ethics that transcended Judaism but on an impending national crisis (Davies 1968, 347–53). Caird (1968, 8–10) contends that Jesus' ethical call was sociopolitical in nature and occurred within an eschatological framework according to which unless there were corporate national repentance, an impending catastrophic event would overtake the nation. Perrin (2011b, 124) points out, "It is the conflict between the post-Bultmannian New Quest of the Historical Jesus, on the one side, and the so-called Third Quest, on the other. Whereas the Bultmann-Bornkamm line has tended to see Jesus as a politically innocent sage declaring timeless and universal truths that transcend Jewish particularity, the so-called Third Quest has, above all, been characterized by taking Jesus very seriously as a socio-politically minded Jew, one who spoke forthrightly into the political arena of his day." Wright grounded his Christology firmly within this Cairdian trajectory (124).

According to Herzog (2000, 1) and Wright, who coined the phrase the "Third Quest," the Third Quest commenced in the 1970s (Dunn and Wright 2004, 2). For Wright, the work of Ben Meyer, who worked extensively on the Dead Sea Scrolls and produced a Jewish eschatological reconstruction of Jesus, was the catalyst for the "Third Quest." Meyer (1979) emphasized the aims of Jesus within an eschatological Judaism of the first century, which significantly impacted Wright and his reconstruction of Jesus. Where the "New Quest" was renewed by the scholars following the *Wredestrasse*, the "Third Quest" renewed the position of Schweitzer, that is, scholars who insist on placing Jesus within the eschatological context of first-century Judaism (Dunn and Wright 2004, 3). According to Wright (1996b, 405), placing Jesus within this context addresses the historical challenge posed by Reimarus and takes the apocalyptic proposal of Schweitzer seriously.

Apart from its serious focus on the complete Jewish context of Jesus, Wright (1996a, 89) contends that the two other advantages of the Third Quest are that its participants don't have a united agenda, like the Jesus

Seminar[8], and that it focuses its study on key historical questions. There are five, sometimes six, historical questions that have emerged explicitly from the Third Quest, which, according to Wright, all serious historians of the first century must ask (Wright 1998d, 107; Wright 1996a, 90). Put together, these questions address a major over-arching question, namely, "how do we account for the fact that, by 110AD, there was a large and vigorous international movement, already showing considerable diversity, whose founding myth was a story about one Jesus of Nazareth, a figure of the recent past?" (90). The Third Quest is interested in this, and Wright in particular.

To answer this overarching question, one must begin with the first of the six questions, namely, how does Jesus fit into the Judaism of his day? Wright (1996a, 91–93) contends that scholarship falls into three categories when placing Jesus within first-century Judaism: (1) some elevate his Jewishness to such an extent that he becomes camouflaged within his Jewish context (Vermes and Brandon), (2) others minimize his Jewishness to the extent that he becomes a teacher of timeless non-Jewish truths or even a Cynic (Bultmann, Downing, Mack, and the Jesus Seminar), (3) and yet there are others, like Wright, who argue for a very Jewish Jesus who was nevertheless opposed to certain vital features of first century Judaism.

The second question follows closely: what were the aims of Jesus? Put differently, what was Jesus trying to accomplish within Judaism? Again, it was Meyer's (1979) work that pioneered this avenue of thought. To establish what any historical figure tried to accomplish, Wright (1996a, 100–101) argues, one must understand the worldview of the person's culture and the mindset of that individual. Three sub-questions derive from this: the consistency of Jesus' aims during his life, the main objective of his journey to Jerusalem, and his sense of vocation. The third question addressed by the Third Quest is, why did Jesus die? This question can be approached from a historical perspective and a theological perspective. Wright argues that the superficial idea that Jesus was only a revolutionary and therefore crucified must be rejected (107). For him, the consensus among the Third Quest is that Jesus was given over to the Romans by the Jewish authorities (109). In other words, political and theological elements offended the Romans and his Jewish contemporaries. Another aspect that is essential to the Third

---

8. Robert Funk, who spent at least 20 years of his life promoting the views of the Jesus seminar believed that their work was of critical importance to set the world free from orthodox Christianity (Funk 1996). He believed that critical study has revealed that Jesus was not born of a virgin, was not God's only Son, and did not rise from the dead. Therefore, Christians are caught up in a false religion based on orthodox fairytales (Allison 2009a, 6–7).

Quest and influences the answer to this question is Jesus' attitude towards the temple and its connection with his death (Sanders 1985, 309–18).

Fourth, serious historians of the first century must ask, how and why did the early church begin? (Wright 1996a, 109). According to Wright, a proper understanding of any event includes understanding its sequel. The bottom line of this question is why did the early Jewish Christians, who were Jewish monotheists, start worshipping Jesus Christ?

Fifth, and closely related, why are the gospels what they are? For Wright, the gospels are a new genre of literature within which the historical Jesus is found (Wright 1996a, 112). The gospels are a critical source for the Third Quest because the gospels answer the first three questions and were written by the early church that grew out of question four (115).

Finally, how does the historical Jesus relate to the contemporary church and world? (Wright 1996a, 117). Sanders (1985, 334) and Wright (1996a, 119) argue that if historical research is done correctly, it will have theological consequences; therefore, it is important to explore these theological and practical opportunities. Wright laments that such contemporary reflection in the Third Quest has not been thoroughly done (118).

These six questions can be summarized as (1) Jesus' relation to Judaism, (2) Jesus' relation to the early church, and (3) Jesus' relation to the contemporary church and world (Neill and Wright 1988, 398–401). These six questions are significant for Wright as this is the framework he uses for his historical research on Jesus of Nazareth. In what follows, we will discuss his Christology from below under this structure.

2.2.5 *Method and Hypothesis*

Another significant difference between the renewed New Quest and the Third Quest for the historical Jesus relates to presuppositions and methods (Wright 1997, 360; Wright 1998b, 106–7). The scholars from the renewed New Quest divided the sayings of Jesus into smaller units, assessed these sayings according to their criteria, and then combined the so-called authentic sayings of Jesus to form a whole. However, as Wright points out, the portrait of Jesus they came up with corresponded to a presumed picture of Jesus because they used this picture as the criteria for judging the smaller sections of his sayings (Dunn and Wright 2004, 7–8).

Conversely, the Third Quest prefers the method of hypothesis and verification, whereby the hypothesis of the scholar is presented and then tested against the analysis of material on Jesus (Wright 1998b, 106–7; Wright 1997, 366). Herzog (2000, 43) suggests that this prevents taking smaller literary units and deducting certain conclusions that might conflict with the whole. Wright's (1997, 365) hypothesis, put simply, is that "Jesus of Nazareth was a Jewish eschatological prophet who believed that the climax of Israel's history was occurring in and through him, his work, and his approaching fate."[9] For Wright (1998b, 108), eschatology means that Israel's history was reaching its climax as opposed to the end of the space-time universe, as argued by Schweitzer. The significance of this climax is that it is when Israel comes out of exile, YHWH returns to Zion and defeats her enemies.

Furthermore, Wright states that there is an intertwined connection between these three aspects and the grand narrative of Scripture, namely, that God is going to be king, which is summed up in the phrase the "kingdom of God" (Dunn and Wright 2004, 9–11). The concept of the kingdom of God divides into three strands: (1) Israel's return from exile, (2) the return of YHWH to Zion, and (3) the defeat of evil. In other words, according to Wright's hypothesis, this is what Jesus believed was occurring in and through him, his work, and his imminent death. Correspondingly, Jesus' eschatological belief is communicated through apocalyptic language (Wright 1998b, 108). Wright (1997, 368) highlights the fact that apocalyptic language, with its metaphorical imagery, was one way of effectively expressing eschatological hope. Wright's from below Christology aims to validate this hypothesis, which, according to him, addresses the key questions of the Third Quest (Wright 1996a, 132).[10]

Lastly, in terms of validating literary material, Wright uses the criteria of double similarity and dissimilarity as opposed to a predetermined portrait of Jesus (Wright 1996a, 132). For him, something is historically probable when it is credible to both the first-century Jewish context and the early church world as opposed to when something conforms to pre-set ideas as applied by the Jesus Seminar.

2.2.6 Conclusion

From the context in which Wright's work is located, it can be concluded that he had various influences that shaped the way he presents his Christology. Reimarus set the stage for Wright. Although Wright disagrees with

---

9. Allison (2009b, 90–96) argues that the quantity of eschatological sources in our primary sources around Jesus necessitates that Jesus was an eschatological prophet.

10. Blomberg (2009, loc. 100–102) simplifies Wright's hypothesis by claiming that it can be drawn down to the idea that Jesus came announcing the longed for "end of exile," through his person and deeds, without meeting the characteristic expectations held by the Jewish nation, such as the defeat of the Romans.

Reimarus' skeptical approach, it drew his attention to history's importance. Similarly, Käsemann pointed out to Wright the importance not only of history but of historical research on Jesus of Nazareth to prevent fake portraits of Jesus, which support ideologies. However, the most significant influences on Wright's Christological approach came from Schweitzer and Meyer. Schweitzer's emphasis on placing Jesus within an eschatological Jewishness was formative for Wright, even though he differs from Schweitzer regarding what eschatology meant for Jesus. Likewise, Meyer's work on the Dead Sea Scrolls and his focus on the aims of Jesus led Wright to inquire into the worldview of first-century Judaism as well as into the mindset and beliefs of Jesus of Nazareth. These elements form the crux of his from below Christology.

Wright belongs within the Third Quest for the historical Jesus as opposed to the earlier quests. Consequently, the key questions that form the framework through which he investigates Jesus historically are: (1) how does Jesus fit into first-century Judaism? (2) What were his aims? (3) Why did he die? (4) How did the church come into being? (5) How were the gospels formed? And (6) how does the historical Jesus relate to the contemporary church and world? Wright addresses these key questions through his hypothesis that Jesus was a Jewish eschatological prophet who believed that the climax of Israel's history—her return from exile, the return of YHWH to Zion, and the defeat of her enemies—were occurring in and through him, his work, and his imminent death on the cross. To these key questions, I will now turn.

2.3 Jesus' Mindset within the First-Century Jewish Worldview

2.3.1 Introduction

The first question Wright seeks to address in answering the broad-stroke question of who Jesus of Nazareth was historically is how Jesus fit into first-century Judaism. Wright (1996a, 139) believes that a historian must gather evidence regarding a person's worldview, mindset, aims, and beliefs to understand a historical person. This is the approach that Wright follows in researching the historical person of Jesus.[11] Wright (1996b, 404) laments the idea that other biblical figures have been granted permission by modern

---

11. Blomberg (2009, loc. 106–7) points out that Wright "recognizes the false dichotomy, perpetuated by so many, that pretends committed theologians cannot also function as serious and careful historians."

historians to think theologically, act symbolically, and reflect a self-understanding of personal vocation. In contrast, the historical Jesus has been denied this privilege. For Wright, however, Jesus must be approached in the same manner as the others and granted the same privileges. Jesus also had specific habitual actions; he told stories, he acted symbolically, and he had particular answers to the questions of his historical, cultural, and social context (Wright 1996a, 138). These four characteristics, according to Wright, constitute the four quadrants of a worldview or, to use a synonymous term, mindset (Wright 1992, 109–12; 122–26; 1996a, 138).

To understand Jesus' mindset, Wright studies the praxis, stories, symbolical acts, and questions and answers of Jesus. To understand the worldview or mindset of Jesus characterized by these factors is to understand how Jesus fit into first-century Judaism. However, Wright is adamant that in no way is he applying modern methods of psychology to understand the psyche of Jesus. Instead, he seeks to understand the worldview of Jesus from his public life (Wright 1998b, 108; Wright 1996a, 143). This section investigates how Wright develops his understanding of Jesus' mindset within first-century Judaism by exploring how he comprehends the four quadrants of Jesus' worldview: his habitual praxis, stories, symbolic acts, and the answers he gave to basic worldview questions.

2.3.2 *The Praxis of a Prophet*

The first quadrant within the worldview of Jesus that Wright investigates is the habitual praxis of Jesus. Wright (1996a, 147–50) believes that some of the elements of Jesus' public career were thoughtful habitual practices and that Jesus acted intentionally; therefore, they must not be considered irrelevant to his mindset but are the lenses by which his worldview comes to the fore. Bearing this in mind, he hypothesizes that Jesus' praxis points to that of a Jewish prophet with an urgent eschatological and apocalyptical message from the God of Israel to his people (150). According to Wright, although the writing prophets had ceased after Daniel, other prophets and prophecies of various sorts continued well into the first century (150–54). Additionally, he points out that, within first-century Judaism, there was an undercurrent of revolution stemming from these prophets and that these prophecies created an expectation that Israel's exile was coming to an end, that their sins were being forgiven, and that their enemies were going to be defeated.[12] Wright relies upon Robert Webb's discussion of the types of

---

12. These prophets were sometimes violent and at times compared to bandits and protesters (Wright 1997, 371).

prophets that could be distinguished during the second temple period to specify which type of prophet he believes Jesus was. Webb (1991, 326-31) provides three categories with which we might understand the prophets of this period. The Clerical prophets were those who were considered prophets because of their positions, like those who held priestly or royal offices. The Sapiential prophets were considered prophets due to their inspirational wisdom, like the Essenes and Pharisees. The third type of prophet within second temple Judaism was the Popular prophet, who appealed to the ordinary people without position or scribal learning. This group of prophets was further divided into Leadership Popular, prophets who used the promises of salvation, of which they made themselves the central characters, to lead their movements, and Solitary Popular prophets, who, like the old Hebrew prophets, proclaimed a message of warning against imminent destruction (333-46). Wright (1996a, 160) also refers to the Solitary prophets as "Oracular" prophets because they announced oracles of woe upon the nation if it did not repent.

According to Wright (1996a, 154), both John the Baptist and Jesus belong among those who proclaimed salvation and imminent disaster. He observes that John the Baptist's prophetic style and theology were in many ways formative for Jesus. Wright considers both John and Jesus to have been "Oracular" and "Leadership" prophets (160-62).[13] Both announced through their proclamation and symbolic acts, as was customary for Leadership popular prophets, that Israel's checkered history was finally reaching its climax.[14] Wright (1996b, 407) points out that Jesus was known as a prophet, spoke of himself as a prophet, and that Jesus' prophetic career grew out of John's.[15] Consequently, Jesus must be seen at a foundational level to have stood in the prophetic tradition of the Old Testament, bringing a word from Israel's God, warning the nation that her current way of life was leading to destruction, and summoning her to a new path (Wright 1996a, 163).[16] For

---

13. Wright disagrees with Horsley and Hanson (1985, 175-81) that John was only an oracular or solitary prophet. He points to the continuation of John's disciples to make his argument.

14. Wright (1996a, 162) makes a very compelling argument about the validity of the sayings about Jesus as a prophet. He argues that, by the time the gospels were written, the followers of Jesus considered him to be more than a prophet, yet they refer to him as a prophet in the gospels. From this, Wright concludes, we can see that while his followers saw him as more than a prophet, they never saw Jesus as less than one.

15. Matt 11:7-19; Luke 7:24-35; Mark 9:11-13; Luke 16:16; Mark 11:27-33; Matt 21:23-27; Luke 20:1-8.

16. Blomberg (2009, loc. 180-81) points out that Wright's description of Jesus' profile as a prophet is more extensive than any of the other Third questers.

Wright, the portrait of a prophet is the clearest point upon which to ground his study of the historical Jesus.[17]

Furthermore, Wright identifies that Jesus went further than John the Baptist in three distinct ways: (1) he had an itinerary ministry, traveling to villages to proclaim his message (Wright 1996a, 169), (2) he gave extensive teaching through which he was cryptically redefining the term the kingdom of God (173, 185), (3) he engaged in a regular healing program through which he was restoring membership to Israel and indicating that the time of great renewal had arrived (194). Considering the significance of these actions, Wright concludes that Jesus, most fundamentally, was aware of his vocation as a prophet commissioned by God to bring a message to Israel (196–97).[18] However, he agrees with Sanders (1985, 237–41) that Jesus did not see himself as only a prophet but as the one through whose praxis, words, and symbolic acts the history of the Jewish nation was being brought to its climax. Jesus believed that he was inaugurating the kingdom of God, which consisted of three threads, a return from exile (forgiveness of sins), the return of YHWH to Zion, and the defeat of Israel's enemies (Wright 1996b, 406). To see why this is so, we turn to Wright's second quadrant, Jesus' stories of the kingdom.

2.3.3 Stories of the Kingdom

The second quadrant of the worldview of Jesus that Wright investigates is his characteristic stories. Wright (1996a, 199–201) contends that part of Jesus' prophetic work was to explicitly and implicitly retell the Jewish nation's story. He indicates that the retelling of the national story was a central part of any renewal movement, and as a Leadership prophet, Jesus made himself the main character of Israel's renewal. His analysis of Jesus' characteristic stories is presented in 5 stages. First, he argues that Jesus' kingdom announcement was reminding Israel of her history, calling, and destiny and that the fulfillment of this destiny was imminent. Second, he indicates that this story summoned the nation of Israel to embrace this new way of being the people of God through following Jesus. Third, this story included a climactic ending in the form of judgment for the unrepentant and vindication

---

17. Wright (1996a, 166–67) believes that Jesus was modelling his career not only on John the Baptist but on other Old Testament prophets such as Ezekiel, Jeremiah, Jonah, Amos, and, above all, Elijah. Considering this, Wright concludes that Jesus was bringing this great prophetic line to its climax.

18. Eddy (2009, loc. 430–32) believes that this claim has a significant historical plausibility and is held widely within the current Quest, apart from certain Jesus Seminar scholars.

for the followers of Jesus. Fourth, Jesus' story generated a new version of Israel's traditional symbols which led to conflict. Finally, this story generated renewed answers to first-century Jewish worldview questions.

2.3.3.1 Announcement

Three aspects of Jesus' announcement are essential to follow Wright's argument: (1) what is meant by the "kingdom of God," (2) the nature of Jewish eschatology, and (3) the character of apocalyptic language. First, what did Jesus mean when he proclaimed that the kingdom of God was at hand?[19] In a sermon, Wright (2019b) highlights that some have said that the kingdom of God meant going to heaven, whereas others have argued that it meant the end of the space-time universe (Wright 2019b). Wright disagrees with both these views. He believes that the kingdom of God had nothing to do with a place one goes to when one dies or the end of the world and everything to do with the God of Israel becoming king and addressing every wrong in the space-time world (Wright 1996a, 202-3).[20] Additionally, three themes from Israel's history were implicitly implied within this kingdom of God meta-narrative When the kingdom of God came, and God became king, that would mean: (1) Israel was coming out of exile, (2) YHWH was returning to Zion, and (3) Israel's enemies would be defeated (206). These were the characteristics of many of Jesus' kingdom announcements (Wright 1996b, 407).

According to Wright (2019a, 5), unless we understand historically what Jesus meant by his kingdom stories, we cannot understand Jesus historically. Correspondingly, these three themes were deeply embedded in Israel's hopes for the future. Their hopes stemmed from the promises of Israel's prophets and were guaranteed by the covenant between themselves and their God (Wright 1997, 367). However, Wright (1998f, 146) points out that at the time of Jesus, the Jews believed that these promises were still unfulfilled. Most first-century Jews did not believe that the exile was over even though they had returned geographically to Israel and occupied Jerusalem (Wright 1998b, 111). In the first century, Jews were still under pagan rule, this time under Roman power, just as they were under Persian, Greek, and Syrian rule before. Furthermore, Wright believes that the Jews connected their exile and the forgiveness of their sins. When the exile ended, the sins that caused the exile would be forgiven (Wright 2016, 114).[21] From this per-

---

19. Matt 4:17; Mark 1:15.
20. This is an example of how Wright's Christology from below shapes his sermons.
21. Johnson (2009, loc. 2877-879) highlights that the notion that most Jews

spective, Wright (1998f, 146) argues that the most appropriate metaphor used by the first-century Jews for this return from exile and forgiveness of sins was the new exodus.

Alongside the return from exile hope was the hope that YHWH would return to Zion. Wright argues that, with the destruction of the first temple by the Babylonians, the Shekinah glory departed, and heaven and earth were separated (Wright 1996a, 205). In this context, the kingdom of God language implied that the God of Israel would become king of the whole world, that he would return to Jerusalem, and reside once again in the Jewish temple. Accompanying these two hopes was the hope that the enemies of Israel, referred to as the pagans, would be defeated and the Davidic monarchy re-established (205). According to Wright (1996b, 406), nobody in Jesus' day would have claimed that these promises from prophets like Ezekiel, Jeremiah, or Isaiah had been fulfilled.

According to Wright (1996a, 203), this hope and expectation contained within the kingdom of God's announcement are what Jewish eschatology means. Eschatology in the first-century Jewish context never meant the end of the space-time world, as believed by traditional readings or Schweitzer (207–9). Wright contends that "eschatology is the climax of Israel's history, involving events for which end-of-the-world language is the only set of metaphors adequate to express the significance of what will happen, but resulting in a new and quite different phase within space-time history" (208).[22] For Wright, this understanding of first-century Jewish eschatology takes Jesus' Jewish apocalyptic language seriously.

Now, as much as Jesus was reaffirming these Jewish eschatological hopes—return from exile, YHWH's return to Zion, and the defeat of her enemies—that would usher in a new phase in space-time history, he was also redefining this Jewish expectation of the kingdom of God (Wright 1996a, 225). For Wright, a critical element of Jesus' prophetic career was the telling and acting out of Israel's story reaching its climax (226). Jesus believed that the long-awaited kingdom of God had come, Israel was coming out of exile, YHWH would return, and evil would be defeated.[23] Therefore, he claimed

---

believed themselves still to be in exile and their hope of restoration is central to Wright's entire reconstruction.

22. Allison (2009c, loc. 1645–647) claims that "Wright correctly insists that apocalyptic eschatology is at the very center of what Jesus was all about. He is also on the mark when he refuses to dissolve eschatology into atemporal or existential categories. He rightly sees that, in Jesus' proclamation, eschatology is first the conclusion of a narrative and that this narrative is the story of God's dealing with Israel."

23. When YHWH became king, he would be king over all the nations and would right all wrongs over his entire creation (Wright 2012b, 33).

that through his sayings and works, this national expectation was now being fulfilled in a new fashion through himself (243).[24] Using this framework, Wright explains Jesus' kingdom announcement in a way that makes historical sense in the first-century Jewish context (226-27).

2.3.3.2 Invitation, Welcome, Challenge, and Summons

For Wright, the coming of the kingdom that Jesus envisaged radically differed from what his contemporaries imagined. Jesus' contemporaries expected a sudden violent revolution that would overthrow the Roman powers. Conversely, Jesus announced that the kingdom of God would come like a seed that grows secretly. The new creation would come through the slow process of sowing and eventually reaping. This was the narrative that Jesus was telling by which he was affirming the hopes and expectations of Israel whilst radically redefining it. Wright highlights that Jesus' kingdom announcement came with an invitation to both benefit and share in Jesus' work and that the invitation came with a challenge to conduct oneself in a certain manner. This kingdom announcement narrative required characters to form a new type of community that would be the real Israel (Wright 1996a, 244-46). Therefore, Wright contends that Jesus' kingdom announcement came in the form of invitation, welcome, challenge, and summons (245).

Wright (1996a, 247, 259) indicates that Jesus' kingdom of God story generated an invitation to repent and believe.[25] This repentance was required from Israel to end the exile and therefore was a condition for entry into the kingdom. Wright refers to this as eschatological repentance, a return to YHWH so the exile would end. Furthermore, he argues that this call to repentance, which was part of the coming of this new age, implied loyalty to Jesus (252). Jesus offered membership to this renewed Israel by his authority apart from the temple and its sacrificial system (257). Along with the call to repentance, Jesus issued a call to believe as part of his invitation to partake of the coming kingdom he was inaugurating. Wright finds it imperative that Paul's Christian understanding of belief or faith is not pressed upon Jesus here (259). According to Wright, Jesus' call to believe and repentance fit together. The faith Jesus called for was a belief that Israel's God was acting climactically, as hoped for by Israel, through the career of Jesus (262).

---

24. Matt 12:28; Luke 11:20; Matt 8:17; Matt 11:2-6; Luke 7:18-23; Matt 15:29-31; Mark 7:37; Matt 9:1-8; Luke 5:17-26; Matt 14:15-21; Mark 6:35-44; Luke 9:12-17.

25. Mark 1:15; Matt 4:17.

Similarly, Jesus' kingdom of God story welcomed sinners to be part of the renewed Israel (Wright 1996a, 274). Jesus' welcome extended to ordinary, non-Pharisaic Jews and sinners, such as tax collectors and prostitutes (267).[26] Additionally, Wright highlights that Jesus offered forgiveness. However, he points out that this forgiveness of sins was not primarily a gift to individuals but was the unrepeatable eschatological forgiveness of sins that Israel longed for (Wright 1996a, 271–72; 2016, 177). This forgiveness of sins was another way of saying the end of the exile has occurred, the time of covenant renewal has come, and the kingdom of God has come. The great offense, Wright observes, is that Jesus offered this return from exile or eschatological forgiveness of sins outside the official temple structures to the wrong people by his own authority.[27]

Likewise, Jesus' narrative of the kingdom included a call and challenge to his audiences to live like the renewed Israel according to the new covenant (Wright 1996a, 275).[28] This, Wright argues, is because Jesus was concerned about the renewal of the covenant, Israel, the fulfillment of promises, and the realization of hope. For him, Jesus' ethics must be placed within this eschatological framework (Wright 1996b, 407). He is adamant that Jesus was not setting up a kingdom movement against Israel but was challenging Israel to be the true Israel now that the kingdom has arrived (Wright 1997, 376). He was reforming Israel by establishing groups of followers who followed his praxis and vision of the way of being Israel and who would therefore be different from the others in their communities (Wright 1996a, 276–77). This was how God's kingdom was to spread slowly.

With the invitation, welcome, and challenge, Jesus' kingdom story also issued a summons to his hearers to be his helpers and associates (Wright 1996a, 298). Jesus summoned all to be loyal to him and to live as characters in his kingdom story, implying that they lived as renewed people who came out of exile. However, he also summoned some to follow him with specific tasks to help him accomplish his agenda. Wright illustrates that the twelve received such a summons which was intentional because they represented the twelve tribes of Israel, and that Jesus was thinking in terms of the eschatological restoration of Israel (300). The few summoned to follow Jesus were given the responsibility to be his agents and extend his work of announcement (303).[29]

26. Mark 2:15; Matt 9:10; Luke 5:29; Matt 11:19; Luke 7:34; Matt 21:31.

27. Matt 9:1–8; Mark 2:1–12; Luke 5:17–26; Luke 7:48.

28. Mark 3:31–35; Matt 12:46–50; Luke 8:19–21.

29. Wright observes that adhering to Jesus' summons came with political danger because following him meant one subscribed to his new and radicalized version of Torah observance (Wright 1996a, 307).

2.3.3.3 Judgment and Vindication

Wright observes that Jesus' story of the kingdom included a climactic conclusion with judgment befalling the unrepentant Israel and vindication coming for those who followed Jesus' way. He states that Jesus was warning Israel of an imminent national catastrophe that would lead to Jerusalem's destruction if they continued their path of violent revolution.[30] Wright (1997, 372–73) contends that during most of the first century, there was a nationwide spread of revolutionary tendencies among various social classes of the people of Israel. This resulted from the agenda and influence of the Shammaite Pharisees who, out of zeal for the Torah, wanted to guard Israel against paganization and were bent on a militant revolt to overthrow Roman rule (Wright 1996a, 384). Accordingly, the issue between the Pharisees and Jesus was not about the fine details of the Torah but operated at the level of agendas (Wright 1996b, 408). According to Wright (1998f, 148–49), Jesus believed that God had elected Israel—one of the twin beliefs held by Judaism—as his agent to bring forth his saving purposes for the world through its suffering and vindication. This, he argues, is the climax of the story told by Moses, the psalms, and the prophets, the story of how God would save the world through Israel and their Messiah (148–49).

According to Jesus, then, Israel's vocation was to be the light of the world instead of bullying the other nations of the world to become the world rulers. Therefore, Wright (1996b, 407–8) states that Jesus warned his contemporaries that failure to repent of this ruling ambition and failure to follow his way of peace would ultimately lead to their destruction at the hands of the Romans. Indeed, Jesus (like Amos and Jeremiah) warned that God's wrath would be poured out on Israel through Rome because of this nationalist revolutionary agenda. Wright (1996a, 323) argues that Jesus ironically compared Jerusalem with Babylon and that the nation would call the wrath of God upon herself because she failed to fulfill her vocation. Put differently; God was intentionally abandoning Israel to their fate and using the Romans as his instruments of wrath, just like the Assyrians and Babylonians before (336). This disaster would bring destruction to the nation, Jerusalem, and the temple.

At various stages, Wright (1996a, 335) points out, Jesus implicitly declared the temple system redundant and explicitly declared the same through symbolic action.[31] Furthermore, Jesus' warnings were aimed at his genera-

---

30. Matt 5:20; Luke 12:58–59; Mark 11:25; Matt 26:52; Luke 13:24; Matt 7:19; Matt 8:11–12; Luke 13:28–29.

31. Matt 7:24–27; Luke 6:46–49; Matt 12:43–45; Luke 11:24–26; Luke 13:1–5; Matt 23:38; Luke 13:35; Matt 21:13; Mark 11:17; Luke 19:46; Mark 11:12–14; Matt 21:18–22;

tion of Jews and were about actual events. Although Jesus used apocalyptic language to describe these events, Wright insists that they should not be taken to mean the end of the space-time universe nor are they to be taken to be only metaphorical (321). He emphasizes that the apocalyptic language Jesus used referred to real-life events that would occur within the space-time universe and for which "cosmic language" was the only fitting metaphor system (Wright 1997, 369). These warnings of impending judgment placed Jesus well within the profile of the prophets of the Old Testament.

Conversely, Wright (1996a, 336–38) observes that Jesus' kingdom announcement contained the assurance that the God of Israel would vindicate his people. However, although Jesus reaffirmed the eschatological hope of vindication, he radically redefined this expectation. Wright suggests that Jesus' kingdom story communicated that those who followed him and his way of being Israel, a way of peace, would escape the coming disaster and be vindicated thereafter as the true renewed Israel. By this, Jesus declared the temple redundant and claimed he would build a new temple. The followers of Jesus, like in the days of Noah and Lot, were to flee when the destruction came upon Jerusalem, after which they would be vindicated as the true Israel (366). When Jerusalem is destroyed, the followers of Jesus would be liberated, YHWH would become king, and a new world order would be established through his followers (364).

2.3.4 Symbols and Controversy

So far, Jesus' kingdom announcement delivered through praxis and story made a double positive claim, the time for the return from exile and YHWH returning to Zion has come through his ministry, and a single adverse claim, that YHWH's judgment was going to befall the disloyal Israelites. While this kingdom announcement had a mixed reception among his contemporaries, his confrontation with the treasured symbols of Israel ignited real hostility towards him (Wright 1996a, 369). Wright argues that Jesus implicitly and explicitly confronted the traditional symbols of second-temple Judaism with his own kingdom symbols. This attack on and redrawing of Israel's national symbols was considered disloyal.

Wright (1996a, 384–85) identifies a significant connection between the widespread agenda of the Shammaite Pharisees—who taught that Israel had to be protected against paganization—and Israel's purity codes. These purity codes, namely, the temple cult, Sabbath, food laws, and circumcision, were all symbols that marked Israel out from the pagan nations. But even

---

Mark 11:23; 14:58; 15:29–30; John 2:19.

more importantly for his argument, these codes maintained and reinforced the political agenda of the Shammaite Pharisees. Sanders (1983, 102) points out that although Jewish monotheism set the Jewish nation apart, the purity codes of the Sabbath, food laws, and circumcision created a social distinction between Israel and the Greco-Roman world. Wright (1996a, 385–87) agrees, stating that these purity codes shaped the national identity of Israel, an identity that was to be kept separate from other nations. Therefore, without these symbols, the Jewish nation lost its identity. These badges of identity were used to reinforce the agenda of the Pharisees to guard Israel against paganization through revolutionary zeal.

According to Wright (1996a, 393–95), Jesus confronted the Sabbath by comparing himself to David, claiming that Israel's great Sabbath day was being inaugurated through his career.[32] The significance of this can be seen if we follow Wright's thought that the Sabbath was to time what the temple was to place (Wright 2019a, 7). In other words, the temple was the place where heaven and earth met, whereas the Sabbath was where the present age and the age of rest and celebration that was to come were held together. This is what Jesus claimed had come through him and his career. Likewise, Jesus confronted the issue of handwashing and food, which, to Wright (1996a, 396–98), was about the concept of purity.[33] Moreover, at the root of the idea of purity was a particular interpretation of the Torah (Wright 1996b, 408).[34] Jesus confronted the Pharisees' customary purity laws, which were generated from their understanding of the Torah, by arguing that the purity the Torah requires is not the washing of hands but the cleansing of the heart. He claimed that his interpretation of the Torah was more in line with the ancestral interpretation than that of the Pharisees.

Additionally, Jesus confronted a national symbol that proceeded from Israel's election, namely, the symbol of nation or family (Wright 1996a, 398–401).[35] For Wright, a significant part of Israel's identity was their common ancestry with Abraham, Isaac, and Jacob. However, for Jesus, family identity and national pride were secondary to himself and his kingdom movement, which offered an alternative family. Wright argues that Jesus did not dismiss the God-givenness of Jewish symbols but cut across them (403). Similarly,

---

32. Mark 2:25–26; Matt 12:3–4; Luke 6:2–4; 14:5.

33. Mark 7:1–23; Matt 15:1–20.

34. Wright (1996a, 389) agrees with Sanders (1985, 260–64) that Jesus' challenge of these purity codes was not an attack on Torah but rather a reinterpretation that, according to him, stemmed from an alternative political agenda generated from alternative eschatological beliefs.

35. Mark 3:21; 3:31–35; Matt 12:46–50; Luke 8:19–21; Matt 8:21–22; Luke 9:59–60; Luke 11:27–28; Matt 10:34–39; Luke 12:51–53; Mark 10:29–30; Matt 19:29; Luke 18:29.

Jesus challenged his audiences to be less concerned about their possessions, including their land (403–4).[36] The Jewish people inherited their land from their ancestors, who received it as an inheritance from YHWH. As such, it had significant theological meaning. Nevertheless, Jesus challenged his hearers that being part of his kingdom movement entailed being prepared to renounce their inherited possessions.

Most significantly, Jesus confronted the central symbol of Judaism, the temple (Wright 1996a, 406–7). Wright points out that scholarship toward the end of the twentieth century, mainly due to work done by Sanders (1985), reached somewhat of a consensus about two things: that Jesus performed a dramatic action in the temple and that this was one of the main reasons for his death (Dunn and Wright 2004, 7). Wright (1996a, 406–7) observes that the temple was significant to the Jewish worldview for three reasons: (1) It was the place where YHWH chose to dwell, (2) it was the place where sacrifices were made for the forgiveness of sins and cleansing from defilement, and (3) it had tremendous political significance and was connected with the royal house of Israel. According to Wright (2019a, 5–6), the temple in first-century Judaism was the place where heaven and earth met and held a significant promise of a new creation. However, by Jesus' day, it was also a symbol of oppression for the villagers and peasants who disliked and distrusted the ruling class and its chief priests (Wright 1996a, 413). When it comes to Jesus' actions in the temple, Wright observes a spectrum of interpretations of what those actions meant (413). Chilton (1992, 155) and Lang (1992, 470) argue that Jesus only sought to reform or cleanse the current temple system. Others, such as Crossan (1994, 202) and Borg (1994a, 125), have interpreted Jesus' temple action as a symbolic act of judgment to come whereby the temple would be destroyed. Then there is Sanders (1993, 254), who has taken the middle ground, arguing that Jesus symbolically enacted the temple's destruction but without any sense of judgment, which was a necessity for rebuilding a new temple.

Wright approaches Jesus' temple action against the backdrop of Jesus' entire prophetic career. He contends that Jesus saw himself and conducted himself as a prophet in continuity with the Hebrew prophets of the Old Testament, who at various times acted symbolically and at certain times did so to predict the destruction of Jerusalem and the temple, as we see in Isaiah, Jeremiah, and Ezekiel (Wright 1996a, 415).[37] He believes that because Jesus pronounced judgment on an unrepentant Israel and predicted

---

36. Matt 6:19–21; Luke 12:13–15, 33–34; Matt 6:19–21; Luke 14:33; Mark 10:21–22; Matt 19:21–22; Luke 18:22–23.

37. Mark 11:12–14; Matt 21:18–19; Luke 13:6–9; 19:41–44; John 2:19; Mark 14:58; Matt 26:61; Mark 15:29; Matt 27:40.

the destruction of the nation, Jerusalem, and the temple if they continued on their current path of revolutionary zeal, his symbolic actions against the central symbol of Israel would have been the climax of Jesus' prophetic career. Correspondingly, two of the main threads within Jesus' kingdom of God announcement were the return of the nation from exile, and the return of YHWH to Zion, both of which Wright argues are related to the temple (415). When the return from exile occurred, the temple would be rebuilt, and YHWH would come to the temple. He argues, in agreement with Bauckham (1988, 87), that Jesus' kingdom announcement implicitly meant that the current temple, which would be rebuilt, was under divine judgment. Likewise, Jesus' invitation, welcome, challenge, and summons to follow his new way of subversive wisdom to be the true Israel rather than the course of his Jewish contemporaries, with the promises of vindication and warnings of judgment, was a threat to the temple which, according to Wright (1996a, 416) drew together the themes of Israel's identity.

Jesus' attack on Israel's nationalistic symbols indicates that he considered them icons which fueled and energized the political agenda of revolutionary zeal. Consequently, when Jesus' entire career is considered, Wright (1996a, 416) contends that the natural reading of the incident is that Jesus was symbolically and prophetically enacting the judgment upon the temple and Jerusalem that he had communicated verbally as part of his kingdom story. This action made the message clear; the temple was under divine judgment unless Israel repented of her nationalistic revolutionary tendency and followed Jesus' true way of being Israel, a way of peace. Wright argues that in Jesus' day, just like in Jeremiah's day, the temple had become the motivation for nationalist violence because it assured Israel that YHWH would assist them in conquering her enemies (420). For Wright, then, Jesus' action in the temple, which brought a temporary halt to proceedings at the temple, was intended to be a dramatic symbol of its imminent destruction.

Wright (1996a, 428) indicates that Jesus challenged the existing symbols of his contemporaries and offered different Jewish variations on them, and added other alternatives, all of which were signs of the great renewal for which Israel had longed. These alternative symbols were creative non-violent alternatives to the Jewish revolutionary symbols of his contemporaries (Wright 1997, 375). Wright observes that the healings, forgiveness of sin, choosing of the twelve disciples, creating a surrogate family with an open table fellowship, the promise of blessing the Gentiles, the feasts instead of the fasts, and the destruction and rebuilding of the central symbolic figure of Israel (the temple), all declared in symbol that the time of fulfillment of

Israel's hope had come. All of this pointed to the return from exile and time of renewal, inaugurated through Jesus.[38]

2.3.5 Worldview Questions and Answers

Within his discussion of Jesus' mindset within first-century Judaism, Wright (1996a, 443) provides what he believes to be Jesus' answers to the five main questions of a worldview. First, who are we? Jesus and his followers are the true returned-from-exile-Israel whose sins are forgiven, the remnant, the small flock, the chosen people (Wright 1996b, 409; Wright 2015, 177). Second, where are we? Jesus and his followers are back in the land, although still enslaved people; however, they will inherit the earth (Wright 1996a, 445). Third, what time is it? For Jesus and his followers, it is the time of great crises through which the kingdom will come when Israel's exile ends, YHWH will return to Zion, and evil will be defeated (Wright 1996b, 409). Fourth, what is wrong? According to Wright, what is wrong is that evil is rampant in the land. This is not only the case among the pagans because evil has even infiltrated the nation of Israel, which is evident through the oppressive regime of the priestly order and the widespread violent revolutionary zeal that consumed Jews from various social classes (Wright 1996b, 406). Finally, what is the solution? Wright's (1996a, 463–64) answer is twofold. On the one hand, the kingdom of God was the solution through its three threads of return from exile, the return of YHWH to Zion, and the defeat of evil. On the other hand, the solution to evil was most fundamentally Jesus himself, through whom the kingdom was being revealed (Wright 1996b, 409).

2.3.6 Conclusion

In answering the broad stroke question of who Jesus of Nazareth was historically, Wright first addresses how Jesus fits into first-century Judaism. According to the layout of this section, he argues, first, that Jesus was an "Oracular" and "Leadership" prophet, which he considers to be the clearest portrait upon which to ground his study of the historical Jesus. Additionally, he contends that Jesus did not see himself as only a prophet, but as the one through whose praxis, words, and symbolic acts the history of the Jewish nation was being brought to its climax. Jesus believed that he was inaugurating

---

38. Wright's conclusion is aided by Meyer (1992, 257) and Freyne's (1988, 47) deduction that Jesus' claim to forgive sins independently grossly undermined the temple system and its control over Israel.

the kingdom of God, which consisted of three threads, a return from exile (forgiveness of sins), the return of YHWH to Zion, and the defeat of Israel's enemies. Second, Wright investigates Jesus' characteristic stories and points out that the kingdom of God announcement of Jesus provided a new variation of the basic Jewish story and worldview. Jesus reaffirmed her most basic hopes—namely, the return from exile, a return of YHWH to Zion, and the defeat of evil—but radically redefined them, claiming that these hopes were being realized through him. Wright states that this kingdom story presented an invitation well beyond the borders of Israel to whoever would follow him and his way of being Israel. It presented a welcome to all sinners to become part of the renewed Israel through the forgiveness of sins he offered. It presented a challenge to be loyal to Jesus and to live according to the praxis fitting of this kingdom movement through a renewed heart, and it issued a summons to be his helpers and associates. Furthermore, he points out that Jesus' kingdom story came with a warning for those who refused to repent of their revolutionary zeal and a promise of vindication for those who followed him. Third, Wright indicates how Jesus and his movement opposed the purity codes and the temple, which supported the violent revolutionary political agenda of the Shammaite Pharisees and offered alternative symbols, all of which declared the time of fulfillment of Israel's hope had come.

2.4 The Aims and Beliefs of Jesus

2.4.1 Introduction

From his discussion of the worldview of first-century Judaism and, more specifically, Jesus' mindset within that context, Wright moves on to an analysis of Jesus' aims and beliefs. This approach of emphasizing Jesus' aims originated with Meyer (1979), who produced a Jewish eschatological reconstruction of Jesus, concentrating on the aims of Jesus within the context of the first century.[39] For Wright, an essential benefit of investigating the aims of Jesus—or what he calls the controlling theme—is that it manages to reconcile the facts that, on the one hand, Jesus lived as a Jewish moral example, healed some people, loved and welcomed people, taught about the kingdom of YHWH and, on the other hand, that Jesus died on a cross for the sins of the world (Dunn and Wright 2004, 5-6). Wright (1996b, 409) believes that studying the aims and beliefs of a historical figure is by no

---

39. Meyer's work had a profound influence on Wright, according to whom much error could have been avoided if Meyer's work were taken more seriously within scholarship (Wright 1998a, 49).

means something that would be categorized as psychology today. Applying psychological methods to a historical figure to understand their psyche is impossible and would also not be credible grounds for drawing historical conclusions (Wright 1998b, 108). Rather, Wright (1996a, 409) argues that a historian can move naturally from a worldview or mindset to a historical person's specific aims and beliefs insofar as these aims and beliefs are regarded as a network of motivations. Wright (1996a, 479–80) understands these motivations as the foundation for a person's sense of vocation. This section then focuses on Wright's understanding of Jesus' sense of vocation and identity and his attitude toward his death. It will address the second and third key questions of the Third Quest, namely, the aims and beliefs of Jesus and the reasons for his death.

2.4.2 Messiahship

According to Wright (1998b, 106–7), the Third Quest prefers the method of hypothesis and verification, whereby the hypothesis of the scholar is presented and then tested against the analysis of material on Jesus. He uses this same historical method in his discussion on the messiahship of Jesus. Wright hypothesizes that Jesus believed that his task was not only to announce the kingdom of God—by which Wright means all three threads within the kingdom of God announcement, namely, the return from exile, the return of YHWH to Zion, and the defeat of evil—but also to enact, embody, and apply it to himself (Wright 1996a, 481). These aims and intentions shaped Jesus' messages and praxis. An essential move in Wright's argument is to connect the aspect of Israel's return from exile with messiahship. He states, "Jesus saw himself as the leader and focal point of the true, returning from exile Israel" (477). "He was the king and not just a prophet through whose work YHWH was, at last, restoring his people, he was the Messiah" (Wright 2018, 301–2). In other words, Jesus believed that he was embodying and symbolizing in himself the long-awaited return from exile. Wright (1996b, 409) observes that various people were regarded as messiahs by certain Jewish societies before, during, and after Jesus' lifetime and presumes that they also regarded themselves as such. Correspondingly, Wright highlights that it would not have been strange for Jesus to regard himself as the Messiah within a first-century Jewish context. Also, Wright is adamant that Jesus must be seen as a theologian in his own right, just like the gospel writers. In other words, Jesus also had the capability of reflecting and thinking about Israel's God, the Scriptures, Israel's history, her hopes and expectations, and his role in bringing these hopes to pass as her Messiah (Wright 1996a, 479).

To corroborate this, he points to Jesus' temple action, whereby he claimed authority over the temple, which, in itself, was a claim to royalty, and to the titles on his cross, which suggest that Jesus did believe himself to be Israel's king, the Messiah.[40]

Wright (2018, 297–99) indicates that during the first century, there was no singular picture of what the Messiah would look like because there was no "one-size-must-fit-all" messianic text. This meant that would-be Messiahs and their movements had freedom within a broad concept. For instance, it would have been easy enough for the Herodians in Jesus' day to find proof-texts to accommodate themselves as messianic (Wright 1996a, 482). However, messiahship had to do with Jewish kingship, as the Messiah was the king of the Jews by definition. Wright points out that what all messianic understandings had in common was that when the Messiah appeared, he would bring Israel's history to its climax, he would usher in a time of renewal, a return from exile, would bring national liberty, and he would be Israel's king who would fight her battles just like David (482–84). Moreover, Wright contends that this Messiah would be called the son of God because he would be the true representative of Israel, who, as a nation, was referred to as the son of YHWH (486). According to Wright, this was what the early church had in mind when they believed that Jesus was the Messiah.

Yet claims to be the Messiah are not equivalent to claims to be divine. Wright (1996a, 478) emphasizes that none of these would-be Messiahs, nor Jesus, claimed themselves to be the second person of the Trinity. The word Messiah in the first century did not refer to divinity in itself but was a theological reference to the coming king who was going to exercise restorative justice by which the entire world would be filled with YHWH's glory (Wright 2018, 297–98).[41] Certain scholars, such as Moltmann (2015, 116), contend that the name Jesus must be seen as "who" is meant, whereas the titles referring to Jesus, such as Messiah, refer to what is meant. In other words, the titles are used to speak about the eternal or divine side of Jesus, whereas the name Jesus is for his temporal or human side. However, Wright (1998b, 110–11) strongly opposes the use of the title Messiah as a means of referring to Jesus' divinity, which he argues stems from a de-Judaized Christian tradition. According to Wright, first-century Jewish evidence demands that the title Messiah be interpreted not according to trinitarian theology but according to its Jewish roots from Old Testament texts like the Psalms

---

40. Borg (2009, loc. 3155–158) disagrees with Wright regarding Jesus' self-awareness as Israel's Messiah. According to Borg, Mark's silence on any explicit messianic claims is deafening.

41. Here Wright follows the thinking of Schweitzer rather than Wrede and Bultmann (Wright 1996a, 478).

and Isaiah. He indicates that, according to these Jewish texts, the Messiah was the anointed one who was to be the ruler not only of Israel but of the world. Jesus believed himself to be this ruler (Wright 2018, 300–301).

Wright (1996a, 529–30) observes that Jesus' disciples regarded him as the Messiah while still in Galilee (Mark 8:27–30). Although Jesus prevented them from telling anyone, Wright observes that he did accept the title. For Wright, Jesus either received this self-knowledge of his vocation as Messiah, or it was confirmed at the beginning of Jesus' ministry when he was baptized at the hands of John (537). This deep-rooted knowledge of his messianic calling, Wright points out, can be seen in Jesus' very act of announcing the kingdom of YHWH (530–32). According to the Qumran scrolls, the person who proclaims the arrival of the kingdom of YHWH is the Danielic Messiah. Therefore, Wright states that Jesus' praxis of announcing the kingdom were themselves signs of messiahship. Furthermore, he adds that Jesus' choosing of the twelve disciples who would constitute the renewed Israel likewise points to Jesus' belief that he was the Messiah. Again, Jesus' messianic awareness is also evident in his sayings throughout his ministry. In particular, Wright highlights Jesus' reference to himself as the great shepherd (John 10:11), which was messianic imagery, his comparisons to David (Mark 2:25) and Solomon (Matt 12:41), and his claims to being YHWH's anointed (Isa 61; p. 534–36).

Although Jesus' sayings and praxis throughout his ministry point to him believing that he was Israel's Messiah, for Wright, it is Jesus' actions in the temple[42] and his parables around that event[43] that most reveal Jesus' belief in his messiahship. According to Wright (2018, 299–300), what one said about the temple was closely related to what was said about the Messiah.[44] He claims that the temple was one of the central symbols of royal vocation; therefore, Jesus' temple action was his most apparent messianic act (Wright 1996a, 485). The temple was linked to a long line of royalty in Israel's history. Wright (2018, 299–300) points out that King David planned it, his son, King Solomon, built it, King Hezekiah and Josiah reformed and restored it, and King Zerubbabel was supposed to rebuild a new temple. Even the would-be messiahs had a close relation to the temple; they either cleansed it, rebuilt it, or intended to do so.

---

42. Matt 21:12–13; Mark 11:15–17; Luke 19:45–46; John 2:13–22.

43. Mark 14:58; Matt 26:61; John 2:19; Mark 11:23; Matt 21:23–27; Mark 11:27–33; Luke 20:1–8; Matt 21:33–46; Mark 12:1–12; Luke 20:9–19; Matt 22:15–22; Mark 12:13–17; Luke 20:20–26; Mark 12:35–37; Matt 22:41–45; Luke 20:41–44.

44. Bock (2009, loc. 1434–436) indicates that whether one interprets Jesus' temple actions as a call to reform or a prophetic symbol of its destruction, it certainly was a strong challenge to the authority of Israel's current leadership.

Wright (1996a, 490–91) suggests that through this temple action, Jesus was claiming a kind of authority over the temple which only belonged to the ruler of the temple, namely, Israel's king. Wright points out that in the richly symbolic world of first-century Judaism, Jesus' Jeremiah-like warning and pronouncement of judgment over the temple were explicit royal claims.[45] To strengthen his argument, Wright investigates Jesus' parables, what he calls "royal riddles," and concludes that Jesus also made implicit messianic claims which pointed back at the temple event (493–510). In particular, Mark 13 consolidates Jesus' claim to messiahship through his temple action, prophetic judgment, and future vindication (511). From this text, Wright suggests that, according to Jesus, when the temple is destroyed, as predicted in symbolic action and announced in prophetic judgment, he will be vindicated as both prophet and Messiah.

Wright argues by the criterion of double similarity and double dissimilarity that passages about Jesus' messiahship were not later inventions because Jesus' portrait as Messiah, as portrayed in the gospels, differs from the Jewish expectation of the Messiah and the writings of the early church (Wright 1996a, 488–89). Finally, according to Wright (2018, 302–3), the Jewish Messiah had to partake in the messianic battle wherein he had to deliver Israel from her enemies. With that in mind, we move on to the third question, why did Jesus believe he had to die?

2.4.3 Reasons and Intentions of Jesus' Crucifixion

Wright approaches the question of why Jesus died from three perspectives, the perspective of the Romans, the Jewish authorities, and Jesus himself. For Wright (1996a, 540), the crucifixion of Jesus and his own intentions with his death form the heart of historical studies on Jesus. According to Wright, it is essential not to follow the default position of the Enlightenment, namely, to separate history and theology on this issue. Nor is it reasonable to criticize the historicity of the gospels just because there are traces of theology (541). Unlike Crossan (1996), who argues that the passion account has been "prophetically historicized," Wright uses the gospels to inform his historical understanding of Jesus, even if there are traces of theology because he is convinced that to understand Jesus' death historically his entire career, that

---

45. Blomberg (2009, loc. 148–49) shows that Wright agrees with Sanders regarding using the temple action as a reliable historical event from which to reconstruct Jesus; however, due to the interrelation between temple and king, the issue of Jesus' messiahship cannot be avoided in discussing this action.

is—his praxis, stories, symbolic actions, and belief of his messianic vocation—needs to form the backdrop of the investigation.

From the perspective of the Romans, Jesus was crucified as a rebel against Rome (Wright 1996a, 543). Wright highlights that Jesus would not have been perceived as a standard revolutionary leader who typically sought to overthrow Roman power through militant revolutionary action. Nevertheless, he would have been seen as another failed would-be Messiah and was, therefore, considered a would-be rebel king. However, Wright agrees with Sanders (1985, 329) that neither the Romans nor the Jewish authorities felt Jesus posed a serious violent revolutionary threat.

Then there are the Jewish authorities. To understand the Jewish charge against Jesus, Wright (1996a, 547) explores Jesus' temple action and his charge before Pilate. Ultimately, the Jewish authorities accused Jesus of leading Israel astray, which, according to Deuteronomy 13, was a crime punishable by death. He contends that although the Romans crucified Jesus as a would-be Messiah, the Jewish rulers accused him of being a would-be prophet who was leading Israel away from the temple and her national life (549). As far as his contemporaries were concerned, Jesus was acting and speaking in opposition to the agenda of the Shammaite Pharisees, which stemmed from the ruling interpretation of the Torah and was sustained by the temple, and he was encouraging others to do the same. Additionally, he suggests that because Jesus perceived himself as the Messiah, it posed a threat of possible revolutionary activity, which could attract the unwanted attention of Rome upon the nation (551–52). Wright points out that at the hearing, Jesus did not deny or recant his belief that he was the Messiah and blasphemously placed himself alongside YHWH.[46]

Wright confirms the position of Schweitzer (2016, loc. 7183), although only in outline rather than the details, that Jesus intentionally went to Jerusalem to die.[47] The central symbolic action that confirms this suggestion is the Last Supper.[48] Wright draws from the fact that the Last Supper was a sort of Passover meal, which celebrated the deliverance of Israel from the tyrant bondage of Egypt, the conclusion that Jesus intended the meal to symbolize the new exodus that he was about to accomplish through his impending fate (Wright 1996a, 556–57). He indicates that, for the first-century Jews,

---

46. Bock (2009, loc. 1310–311) points out, "The movement in the trial from questions about the temple to Messiah is perfectly natural in a first century Jewish setting, since the Messiah was associated with the temple in Jewish eschatological hope."

47. Borg (2009, loc. 3193–194) disagrees with Wright and Schweitzer by arguing that Jesus' death was not part of his vocation but rather something that happened to him because of his career.

48. Matt 26:17–19; Mark 14:12–16; Luke 22:7–15.

Passover meals were more than commemorating what happened in the past. These meals pointed to the new exodus, which was synonymous with the return from exile and YHWH's return to Zion to deliver his people. Wright contends that Jesus' last supper drew on this symbolism to indicate that this new exodus was occurring in and through Jesus himself. Wright believes that Jesus accomplished this through his prophetic symbolic actions with the bread and the cup. Thus, he proposes that Jesus was weaving together the Passover story, first-century hopes, his own story, and his fate (559).[49]

Wright (1996a, 563–65) indicates that just as Jesus' temple action was surrounded by riddles that explained the event, there are parables that indicate what Jesus thought would happen next. Wright believes that Jesus' symbolic actions and clarifying statements during the Last Supper strongly suggest that Jesus knew that he was about to die and that his death was part of the eschatological plan to usher in the kingdom of YHWH (559–62). For him, the parables around the last supper indicate that Jesus envisaged a great messianic battle, although radically redefined from the predominant Jewish expectation, after which the kingdom of YHWH was to come (563–65). This battle, Wright believes, was against the real enemy, the Satan or Accuser who had infiltrated Israel. This infiltration manifested most clearly in violent revolutionary zeal.

Moreover, Wright points out that these riddles show that Jesus intended to live out Israel's calling, namely, to be the salt of the earth and the light of the world. The "double revolution"—a revolutionary way of being revolutionary—that Jesus was calling the true Israel to embody, he was going to embody himself. In other words, Wright deduces that Jesus aimed to embody the true Israel, that he would defeat evil by allowing it to do its worst to him, and, in doing so, YHWH's kingdom would be launched in the world. To test this proposal, Wright investigates several sources that would have been available to Jesus and allowed him to arrive at the mindset that his suffering could bring forth hope for vindication (Wright 1996a, 576).

For Wright (1996a, 576–77), the overarching story of first-century Judaism was one of exile and restoration. The Jewish people were longing and hoping for a new exodus, which consisted of the return from exile and the forgiveness of the sins that caused the exile in the first place. Wright points out that this is the controlling story that Jesus wanted to evoke in what he calls Jesus' "last great prophetic and symbolic action." Furthermore, he points out that this controlling story included a pair of sub-plots, making it highly probable that Jesus would think this way. First, Wright (1992, 277)

---

49. Eddy (2009, loc. 536–538) highlighted the fact that for Wright the temple action and last supper are "mutually interpretive" because in both occurrence Jesus replaces the temple with himself.

highlights the fact that some second-temple Jews believed that their liberation would come after a time of intense suffering. Following Schweitzer (2016, loc. 6826), Wright maintains that this expectation of the "messianic woes" is essential to understanding what Jesus believed about himself and what his death would accomplish. Second, he demonstrates, by drawing on Old Testament prophetic texts as well as extra-biblical literature such as The Wisdom of Solomon, Qumran, and 2 Maccabees, that there was a widespread tradition during the second temple period according to which the redemptive plan of YHWH to free his people from the oppressive pagans could be brought into effect by the suffering and potential death of certain Jews (Wright 1996a, 583–84).

Wright (1996a, 588–91) contends that although Daniel, the Psalter, Zechariah, and Ezekiel all evoke the notion that through the suffering of Israel, the kingdom of YHWH would dawn, it is Isaiah 40–55 that led certain Jews to believe that the suffering of Israel would be taken upon a specific individual, namely, the Suffering Servant. Furthermore, Wright points out that there is evidence that certain second-temple Jews interpreted this suffering servant as the Messiah (588–91). Although this deduction was not as widely spread as the general idea of Israel suffering before her vindication, nevertheless, Wright contends that there was a wide spread belief among the first-century Jews of Jesus' day that their suffering in exile was due to their sin and that this would come to an end after a period of intense tribulation of the nation or, as some believed, of her representative. Wright concludes that, within this controlling story and its sub-plots, Jesus' symbolic act, statements during the Last Supper, and the riddles that surround them indicate that he believed that he would die, that his death would be representative and redemptive for Israel and that it would usher in the new exodus (591–92).

According to Wright, Jesus' mindset and his aims as the suffering servant of Israel were two-fold. First, Jesus envisaged his death on the cross to be a prophetic and symbolic act of what would happen to his contemporaries because of their violent revolutionary agenda and refusal to follow his kingdom's way of peace (Wright 1996a, 595–96). Wright believes that Jesus was enacting what he had announced would happen to his fellow Jews who compromised with pagan politics. Jesus would, therefore, undergo the same fate he announced over the temple, Jerusalem, and the nation. Second, Jesus evoked Israel's martyr tradition, according to which his death would be representative of exilic Israel, whereby her suffering would bring forth their vindication (596–97). According to Wright (1996b, 410), Jesus believed that great tribulation was coming upon Israel and that it was his vocation to go ahead of them and take it upon himself. Jesus believed his death would be an eschatological event leading to the new exodus, a return from exile, the forgiveness of sins, and the new covenant.[50] Moreover, Wright believes that it is highly probable that Jesus considered Isaiah 53 informative to his vocation and formative. Jesus intended not only to share in Israel's suffering but also believed that his suffering was part of YHWH's redemptive plan for Israel and the world. This redemptive plan would liberate Israel from evil, release them from exile, and forgive their sins. For Wright (2017a, 60–61), Jesus believed the cross would achieve the kingdom.

Ultimately, as the Messiah, Jesus was required to perform two crucial tasks, (1) cleanse, restore, and rebuild the temple, and (2) engage in the messianic battle and defeat the enemies of Israel (Wright 1996a, 604–6). According to Wright, Jesus set out to accomplish these two tasks, albeit radically redefined, through his death. Wright illustrates that through his temple action and Last Supper, Jesus intended his death to function sacrificially and thereby accomplish what the temple typically provided and ultimately replace the temple. He believes that Jesus drew on the context of Isaiah 53 and uniquely considered his death part of the sacrificial system whereby Israel would be cleansed and purified. This event would usher in the new exodus. This was how sins were to be forgiven. Additionally, he contends that Jesus intended to fight the real enemy of Israel, which, according to Jesus, was not the Romans but the Accuser, Satan (Wright 1996a, 605–7). Ultimately, Wright believes this battle occurred in two places, (1) during Jesus' hearing before Caiaphas as his accuser, and (2) when Jesus endured the power of Rome on the cross. He argues that Jesus fought this battle in the same way he challenged his followers to live, namely, by being the salt and light of the world and following the way of peace. Wright (2006, 87–88) believes that Jesus went into the heart of evil, took its full weight, and exhausted it. He went into chaos to bring order, into death to bring new life. Moreover, Wright contends that this was the climax of Jesus' career, whereby he would decisively defeat evil through love. The way of love would be the way of victory, the victory of God (Wright 1996a, 610). For Jesus and the New Testament writers, his death is the victory over the bondage of evil that entangled Israel and the world, a victory that was confirmed through his resurrection (Wright 2019a, 9).

This historical understanding of Jesus' intentions informs Wright's atonement theology. Wright (2017b) preaches that without the reality of Jesus' death on the cross and his victory over evil, the principalities and powers would still be ruling the world unhindered. It is evident, then, that

---

50. Wright argues, along with scholars such as Dunn, that Schweitzer was incorrect to state that Jesus' death was a disaster and only paradoxically a success (Dunn and Wright 2004, 6).

Jesus' victory over evil was not an abstract idea or atonement theory for Wright but an event that launched a new world order. He believes that the atonement theories and models are too often played off against one another (Wright 2017b). Falconer (2013, 88–89) indicates that, for Wright, the *Christus Victor* motif and penal substitutionary atonement theory are complementary. Wright regards the *Christus Victor* motif as the overarching theory within which the penal substitutionary atonement theory makes sense. Falconer (2017, 296) observes that for Wright, the penal substitutionary element of Jesus' atoning death, by which our sins are forgiven, is made possible only because of Jesus' victory over evil. Wright (2017b) preaches that the atonement theories are interpretations of the real-life events regarding Jesus as contained in the gospel stories. Therefore, he argues that no atonement theory must be created unless we understand what is meant by Jesus dying for our sins "in accordance with the Scriptures" (2017b). To understand what it means that Jesus died for our sins, we must understand the overarching narrative of Israel's Scriptures and how the Messiah's death fits into that story (Wright 2017c). Wright warns that unless the overarching narrative of Israel is used as the backdrop for the cross, proof-texts are utilized, occasionally leading to docetist conclusions about Jesus' death (Wright 2017b).

Wright calls his atonement theory "representative substitution." Wright (2017b) preaches that some have paganized their soteriology by depicting God as an angry God punishing an innocent victim. He contends that this stems from the medieval church that sought to over-simplify things and thereby presented an angry God and a loving and innocent Jesus, which can be summed up as "God so hated the world that he killed his only son" (Wright 2007a). Instead, Wright (2006, 82–83) argues that the biblical penal substitution is that God punished sin through the representative flesh of the Messiah. Sin was condemned, and the powers of evil were thereby defeated. Wright sums it up as follows, on the cross, it is not only the wrath of God that was satisfied, but the love of God was satisfied (Wright 2007a). Falconer (2013, 240) highlights that Wright seems somewhat Anselmian because he believes that God's forgiveness of sin not only releases people from guilt but also releases God from being angry with the world. Although certain scholars, such as MacArthur (2020), have criticized Wright for not believing in penal substitutionary atonement, it is evident that he does, albeit slightly nuanced. He hypothesizes that Jesus' death was how the evil power over this world was overthrown by the greater power, the revolutionary power of God's love. What is vital for Wright is not refined theories of atonement but an understanding of the greater biblical narrative within which Jesus understood his vocation and acted. In answering the question, what had changed in the world that first Good Friday? Wright (2017c) states that the victory over evil is won through the representative substitution of the Servant, the Son, the Image, and the foot-washer in whom God's glory is revealed. Through this victory over evil, the new Passover took place by which the creator had rescued humanity and the world from sin and death (Wright 2016, 348).

2.4.4 YHWH's Return

Up to this point, Wright (1996a, 612) has painted the portrait of Jesus as one who saw himself as a prophet, who was announcing and inaugurating the kingdom of Israel's God, as well as the Jewish Messiah who, through his death, would bring this kingdom about. It is evident that Wright is not interested in surveying titles given to Jesus to ascertain who he was historically. Instead, he investigates Jesus' praxis, sayings, and symbolic actions. So far, he has assessed two symbolic actions with their accompanying sayings, which have revealed a great deal about Jesus' aims and beliefs. These were, first, Jesus' temple action and its accompanying riddles, by which Wright deducts that Jesus was pronouncing judgment on the temple establishment and declaring himself as Messiah. Second, concerning the Last Supper and its related sayings, Wright points out that Jesus was drawing the judgment pronounced against the temple and nation upon himself, by which he intended to defeat evil and accomplish the new exodus and the new covenant. Wright believes that there is a third symbolic action Jesus performed that draws these previous two together, namely, Jesus' journey to Jerusalem (614–15).[51] This symbolic action embodied the last thread within his kingdom announcement, namely, that YHWH was returning to Zion. Wright indicates that for Jesus to announce that YHWH was returning to Zion was insufficient; rather, he enacted and symbolized this event.[52]

To understand this third symbolic action, Wright (1996a, 615) suggests that three issues are essential to grasp within the Jewish context of Jesus' day. These are: (1) that there was a widespread hope that YHWH would return to Zion within second temple Judaism, (2) that some deducted that YHWH's agent would share his throne, and (3) that second temple Jews had symbolic language to refer to YHWH's activities in the world. To this

---

51. Matt 21:1–11; Mark 11:1–11; Luke 19:28–44; John 12:12–19.

52. In a sermon, Wright (2011b) compares Jesus' entry into Jerusalem with the story of the boat, *Andrea Gail*, sailing into the famous "perfect storm." Jesus' entry was a risky action because of the political, social, and militant presence of Rome and the violent revolutionary zeal of the Jews, drawing dangerous attention to himself.

discussion, we now turn. First, Wright (1996a, 615–16), in agreement with scholars such as Chilton (1984, 124–27) and Meier (1994, 299), maintains that there was a general hope deep within second-temple Judaism that YHWH would return to Zion and would dwell with his people as he did during the exodus. Additionally, Wright (1996a, 623) suggests that when YHWH did return, he would come to act among his people through his agent. This thread of the kingdom of YHWH was intertwined with the ideas of Israel coming out of exile and her enemies being defeated.[53] However, this expectation was still unfulfilled by Jesus' day.

Second, Wright points out that certain Old Testament and extra-biblical texts state that YHWH's agent would be vindicated and exalted uniquely (Wright 1996a, 624–25). He argues that Jesus drew on some of these texts in terms of his understanding. Wright contends that although this belief was not as widespread as the belief that YHWH would return to Zion, it was nonetheless possible for second-temple monotheistic Jews to legitimately believe that the Messiah could share the throne of YHWH (629). Third, Wright (1992, 248–59) highlights that within Jewish thought, YHWH was both transcendent and actively involved in their history in specific ways for which they assigned particular symbols such as Shekinah, Torah, Wisdom, Logos, and Spirit. He argues that although the Messiah was not considered divine, he would nonetheless embody these symbols as he was the agent for YHWH. It is through his agent that YHWH himself would act to judge and save (Wright 1996a, 630).

By referring to various parables,[54] Wright (1996a, 633–44) concludes that Jesus aimed to symbolize and embody YHWH's return to Zion and believed he would be vindicated and exalted as YHWH's agent to share YHWH's throne. He contends that it was this belief that was considered blasphemy by Caiaphas. From this, Wright deduces that within his prophetic and messianic vocation, Jesus believed that he had a more profound vocation that remained hidden until the end of his career (645). In other words, Jesus did and said things that not only fell within his prophetic and messianic vocation but were attributable to YHWH himself. Wright agrees with Sanders (1985, 271–74) that Jesus claimed loyalty to him meant loyalty to Israel's God (Wright 1996a, 646).[55] Furthermore, Wright (1998a, 53) shows that Jesus embodied the incarnational symbols of YHWH to such an extent that in Jesus, we see a biblical portrait of YHWH come to life.

---

53. Wright is largely indebted to Webb (1991) for this understanding of YHWH's return.

54. Luke 12:35–48; Matt 24:36–51; Matt 25:1–13; Mark 13:33–37.

55. Matt 19:21; Mark 10:21; Luke 18:22.

The self-awareness of Jesus' vocation shapes an important part of Wright's understanding of Jesus' aims and beliefs. Wright (1996a, 653) emphasizes that Jesus did not "know" that he was God in the same way that he "knew" he was hungry, thirsty, or tired. For him, to assume that Jesus was fully aware that he was God incarnate would not do justice to the full humanity of Jesus as observed in the New Testament and as declared at the council of Chalcedon (Wright 1998a, 51). Wright argues that the view that Jesus knew he was the second person of the Trinity trifles with the Apollinarian heresy. Migliore (2014, 172) contends that scholars must not merely repeat the Christological creeds but interpret them and use them as their points of departure. That seems to be what Wright does. For Wright, Jesus was aware of his vocation given to him by Israel's God to enact what the Old Testament promised God would accomplish by himself. He believed that Israel's God had called him to evoke and enact the tradition that YHWH would return to Zion and that he would share his throne (Wright 1996a, 651). Jesus believed that his vocation was to do and be what only Israel's God did and was (Wright 1998a, 53).[56] Wright (1996b, 410) resists the thought that Jesus was aware of being the second person of the Trinity and argues rather that Jesus is thought of as:

> A young Jewish prophet telling a story about YHWH returning to Zion as judge and redeemer, and then embodying it by riding into the city in tears, by symbolizing the temple's destruction, and by celebrating the final Exodus. I propose, as a matter of history, that Jesus of Nazareth was conscious of a vocation, a vocation given him by the one he knew as "Father," to enact in himself what, in Israel's Scriptures, Israel's God had promised to accomplish. He would be the pillar of cloud for the people of the new Exodus. He would embody in himself the returning and redeeming action of the covenant God.

Certain scholars, such as Marsh (1998, 86), criticize Wright for avoiding the question of Jesus' divinity. However, Wright (1998b, 108) believes it would be premature to ask if Jesus was divine at this stage of his historical portrait of Jesus. Instead, he emphasizes that the historical Jesus was aware of this vocation (Dunn and Wright 2004, 13). In an interview, Wright (2017d) argues that this is most clearly revealed during Jesus' agony in the garden of Gethsemane, where he is depicted not as one who knew himself to be God but as one wrestling with a difficult vocation.

---

56. Hays (2011, 69) contends that although Wright followed a Christology from below approach, the self-knowledge of his vocation to enact YHWH in himself unexpectedly opens the door to a very high Christology.

2.4.5 Conclusion

Wright moves smoothly from discussing Jesus' mindset within the first-century Jewish context to Jesus' aims and beliefs. The answer he gives for the second historical question of the Third Quest, namely, what were Jesus' aims and beliefs, is that, first, Jesus believed that he was the Messiah. Wright shows that although Jesus' sayings and praxis throughout his ministry indicate that he believed that he was Israel's Messiah, for Wright, it is Jesus' actions in the temple and the surrounding riddles that most clearly reveal this belief. Furthermore, he connects the aspect of Israel's real return from exile with messiahship. According to Wright, then, Jesus saw himself as the leader and focal point of Israel's return from exile and believed that he was embodying and symbolizing this return from exile. Second, Jesus believed that through his impending fate, he would accomplish the new exodus by overthrowing the evil power of this world with the greater power, namely, the revolutionary power of God's love. Wright contends that Jesus' Last Supper drew on the symbolism of the Passover story and intended to indicate that this new exodus was occurring in and through Jesus' death. According to Wright, Jesus knew that he was about to die and that his death was part of the eschatological plan to usher in the kingdom of YHWH. He believed his death would be an eschatological event leading to the new exodus, a return from exile, the forgiveness of sins, and the new covenant. This, along with the Roman charge and that of the Jewish authorities, is Wright's answer to the third historical question of the Third Quest, namely, why did Jesus die? Third, Jesus aimed to symbolize and embody YHWH's return to Zion, and he believed that he would be vindicated and exalted as YHWH's agent to share YHWH's throne. Wright contends that the symbolic action of Jesus' journey to Jerusalem was meant as an embodiment of the last thread within his kingdom announcement, namely, YHWH was returning to Zion. According to Wright, Jesus believed that he had a vocation given to him by Israel's God to enact in himself what the Old Testament promised God would accomplish by himself. Jesus believed that his vocation was to do and be what only Israel's God did and was.

2.5 The Rise of Early Christianity

2.5.1 Introduction

When Jesus was crucified in Jerusalem, the general impression would have been that he was another failed Messiah who tried to lead a revolutionary movement, albeit an unorthodox one (Wright 1996a, 543). Bearing in mind that, according to Wright, there was no such thing as a failed yet revered Messiah, Wright's fourth question asks, "how then did the early Christians who were Jewish monotheists come to worship Jesus of Nazareth?" (658). According to Wright, the broad answer to this question is that the resurrection of Jesus provided the foundation of this worship (659). Wright (2003, 587) states that early Christianity is inexplicable without their belief in the bodily resurrection of Jesus. Where other Third Quest scholars have chosen to ignore the resurrection historically, Wright believes that the resurrection of Jesus has the same historical probability as the fall of Jerusalem in 70AD and, therefore, cannot be ignored (710). In other words, it has the same degree of historical validity. His historical investigation of the resurrection is critical to understanding why he believes in a high early Christology. He states that the "only credible line of explanation runs from resurrection to Christology" (Wright 2008a, 46). Wright provides an in-depth investigation of why the early Christians believed that Jesus rose from the dead, the implications of this belief on their Christology, and how their Christology interlocked with their monotheistic faith. These are the three aspects this section will investigate.

2.5.2 *Reasons for Belief in the Resurrection of Jesus*

The belief that Jesus of Nazareth was bodily raised from the dead was fundamental to the origin of early Christianity, which is why Wright (2003, 587–88) refers to the early Christians as a "resurrection movement." According to Wright, it is also because of the belief in the resurrection of Jesus that early Christianity remained a "messianic movement" even though Jesus was a crucified, failed Messiah in the eyes of his contemporaries. But where did the belief in the resurrection of Jesus of Nazareth come from? Wright suggests that if we were to ask the early Christians why they believed that Jesus rose from the dead, they would answer because of the stories of Jesus' empty tomb[57] and the stories of his appearances to various people (686).[58] He argues that these two things must and can be securely established historically by investigating the earliest traditions. According to Wright, these stories were told repeatedly through ancient oral traditions before being written down in the gospels and other versions, such as the gospel of Peter (587–88). While he maintains that each of these five written versions,

57. Matt 28:1–10; Mark 16:1–8; Luke 24:1–12; John 20:1–10.
58. John 20:11–18; Matt 28:9–10; Luke 24:34; Luke 24:13–31; John 20:19–29; John 21:1–14; Matt 28:16–20; 1 Cor 15:6–7; Luke 24:50–51.

with their differences in details and emphasis, was generated from related oral and written traditions, he nevertheless limits his investigation of the resurrection accounts of Jesus to the four gospels, claiming that the gospel according to Peter was a secondary addition which relied on the canonical sources and which reflects signs of later theological convictions (591).[59]

For Wright (2003, 614-15), then, the canonical gospels are the key to understanding the early church's accounts of the resurrection of Jesus because, despite their surface differences, they tell the same tale that Wright attributes to the earliest oral tradition stories. He contends that these oral traditions, as the primary testimony of what happened, were considered too important to be significantly altered (Wright 2005, 221). He believes that although the evangelists had the freedom to tell the well-known story in their ways and with their emphasis, they never had the freedom to invent a new one (Wright 2003, 660). Indeed, Wright highlights that the outline of their accounts seems basic and underdeveloped (680). They intended to refer to actual events that occurred. Although these accounts are not photographic descriptions of what happened, Wright (2008a, 48) argues that they challenge the historian to either accept them or come up with a better reason for Christianity's beginning. What emerges clearly from each of the canonical gospel accounts is the empty tomb and Jesus' appearances, which in turn formed the foundation for what the early Christians believed happened to Jesus (Wright 2003, 629).

Wright (2003, 686) explains that neither the empty tomb nor the appearances would by themselves constitute a necessary and sufficient condition for belief in the resurrection of Jesus. In other words, an empty tomb without the appearances would have been tragic, whilst the appearances without the empty tomb could have been interpreted as visions or hallucinations (688-89). Wright points out from Luke and John that Jesus' resurrected body necessitated an empty tomb (691-92). Although when considered independently, the first two factors are deemed inadequate to have generated belief in the bodily resurrection of Jesus, Wright argues that combined; they provided a sufficient condition for such a belief (692-93). Furthermore, he is convinced that when both these conditions were encountered together, it gave birth to early Christianity.

Correspondingly, Wright (2003, 693-96) contends that the empty tomb and Jesus' appearances were not only sufficient for belief in his resurrection but also necessary conditions. He builds his argument upon the notion that, according to Jewish and pagan belief, resurrection never meant

---

59. On the issue of sources, Wright indicates that he does not take the omission of the resurrection in the Q source seriously nor those who use it to argue against the resurrection (Wright 2000, 96-97).

merely going to heaven in a bodiless form. Instead, resurrection always implied embodiment; therefore, the claim that Jesus rose from the dead necessitated an empty tomb. Additionally, he also argues that the appearances were a necessary condition for belief in Jesus' resurrection. He views them as a necessary supplement to the empty tomb, without which the empty tomb would have been an insufficient condition.

Wright (2003, 696–705) is convinced that no explanation for this belief in Jesus' resurrection is more convincing than the empty tomb and Christ's appearances. Wright points out that even if the early Christians searched the Jewish Scriptures, they still would not arrive at this type of belief. Nobody expected these events, which would have been difficult to invent regardless of how many hours they mulled over the Scriptures. For Wright, this distance from the general Jewish expectation provides damning evidence against the "cognitive dissonance" theory, according to which the disciples lived in a fantasy world because they could not come to grips with reality. What the early Christians described as having transpired was entirely unexpected (699).

In conclusion, Wright (2008a, 49) proposes that historical investigation brings us to the point where we must conclude that the tomb that contained Jesus' body was empty and that someone whom the early Christians were convinced was Jesus was seen to be bodily alive again in a renewed manner. Additionally, because all other explanations for why early Christianity arose are less convincing, Wright argues that the best explanation must be followed, which is that of Jesus' followers, namely, that Jesus did rise bodily from the dead, leaving an empty tomb behind, for which the four gospel accounts are the best expression we have (Wright 2008a, 49). Without this basis, the rise and shape of early Christianity cannot be satisfactorily explained (Wright 1998e, 125). Therefore, Wright (1996b, 412) concludes that the only way he can make sense of the entire picture historically and theologically is to agree with the deduction made by the early Christians.

2.5.3 *The Consequences of the Resurrection*

2.5.3.1 Jesus as Messiah

According to Wright (2003, 577), the resurrection of Jesus played a pivotal role in establishing the Christology of the early church. However, Wright (2015, 79–80) emphatically argues that in the first-century context, there is no suggestion that the resurrection by itself implied that Jesus was in some sense divine. Instead, he suggests that there was a progression of thought about Jesus after his resurrection. The understanding of Jesus' personhood progressed from the mighty prophet to the Messiah to the *Kyrios* (lord of the world) to YHWH himself.

Wright (2003, 576) argues that the resurrection led Jesus' followers to conclude that this eschatological Jewish prophet was indeed Israel's Messiah. He points out that the resurrection by itself would have been insufficient for anyone to conclude that Jesus was the Messiah; however, because of Jesus' messianic career, filled with implicit and explicit messianic references and his messianic execution, this was the first obvious conclusion his followers reached (Wright 1998d, 114). The resurrection of Jesus was fundamental to the early church's belief in Jesus' messiahship. Although there were glimpses of belief in Jesus' messiahship among his followers during his ministry, that belief was shattered at his crucifixion. Wright (2003, 557–59) describes the Jewish expectation of its Messiah as one who would defeat Israel's enemies, rebuild the temple, and bring peace and justice to the world.

Conversely, Jesus was executed at the hands of the pagans, acted symbolically in judgment against the temple, and was crucified unjustly and violently instead of bringing justice and peace (Wright 2008a, 45). According to the Jewish expectation, Jesus was a failed, would-be Messiah because no Jewish interpretation presented a Messiah who would be killed at the hands of the pagans. Wright points out that not even the two key figures of the first and second Jewish revolts, Simon bar-Giora and Simeon ben Kosiba, were hailed as Messiahs because of their executions. Nevertheless, Wright (2003, 554–56) indicates that within 20 years of Jesus' resurrection, the title Messiah was so frequently used to describe Jesus of Nazareth that it became a name. Moreover, other non-believing Jews like Josephus described Jesus as the "so-called Messiah" (556). It was through the resurrection that Israel's God validated Jesus' messiahship.

In Wright's (1992, 309–10), *The New Testament and the People of God* (NTPOG), he contends that the early Christians were a thoroughly messianic movement. He suggests they accomplished this by redrawing the Jewish models of the Messiah around Jesus himself (Wright 2003, 563). In other words, although they reaffirmed the biblical roots of messiahship, they developed it further in four ways: (1) the Messiah now belonged to the world and not only to Israel, (2) the messianic battle was now defined against evil itself rather than the pagan nations, (3) the Messiah's followers would now be the rebuilt temple, (4) the justice and peace of God was the aim rather than that of Rome. Therefore, Wright (2008a, 45) believes that the early Christians remained a Jewish messianic movement because they showed complete loyalty to whom they considered Israel's Messiah. He states that this redefinition of messiahship around Jesus occurred because of the resurrection by which Jesus' was vindicated as Messiah (Wright 2003, 563). A reversal of the Jewish and Roman charges against him that he was a messianic pretender. Additionally, it was a validation of Christ's messianic claims.[60] For Wright (1998e, 139), the resurrection of Jesus is primarily about eschatology. In other words, it is about the dawning of the new creation, the renewal of the covenant, the end of the exile and the forgiveness of sins, which Jesus as the Messiah had accomplished for Israel and the world.

2.5.3.2 Jesus as *Kyrios*

The early Christian belief did not end with the messiahship of Jesus but extended into other positions of honor as they contemplated the meaning of his Messiahship. Wright (1998d, 122) believes a clear line of early Christian thought can be traced from believing in Jesus as the Messiah to believing in Jesus as the world ruler (see Psalm 89 and Daniel 7). Wright (2003, 728-30) illustrates from these passages that Israel's Messiah would be not only the king of the Jews but also the entire world. Therefore, according to Wright, early Christians' view of Jesus as the *Kyrios* stemmed from their understanding of the Jewish Scriptures. Correspondingly, Wright maintains that belief in Jesus as the Lord of the world was a function of his messiahship and not a departure from his messiahship (563-66). He strongly refutes the arguments suggesting that the Jewish messianic category was replaced by the Gentilic lordship category when the gospel spread into the Hellenistic regions; therefore, Christ's lordship has no socio-political relevance. Conversely, Wright (2012a, 398-99) points out that even though Paul's ministry was predominantly to the Gentiles, the standard Jewish expectation of the Jewish Messiah being the lord of the world, as seen from the Psalms, Isaiah, and Daniel, is evident within his thought and writings. Wright suggests that Paul never lost the Jewishness of his mission which promised that through the Messiah, the God of Israel would fulfill his purposes by bringing both Israel and the world under his saving rule (399). For this reason, the early Christians referred to Jesus as the lord of the world, the *Kyrios*. It was the natural and biblical consequence of his messiahship, albeit a redefined messiahship. Therefore, Wright concludes that Jesus' lordship category must not be seen as an abandonment of Jewish categories for Greek ones but as embracing the function of his Jewish messiahship.

---

60. Wright (2003, 726-28) argues that Jesus was referred to as the "son of God" in the Davidic sense of 2 Samuel 7:14; Psalm 2; and Psalm 89, which was a reference to the Messiah.

According to Wright (2003, 726), because Jesus had been raised from the dead and therefore vindicated by Israel's God, the early Christians believed that the kingdom of God had arrived. Thus, they acted as though they were the returned from exile remnant, the new covenant people, the new temple. Wright (1998d, 117–18) contends that according to the Jewish tradition, the resurrection from the dead was a metaphor for the dawn of the new age, that the exile had ended, and their sins had been forgiven. The early Christians lived as if this had happened by redefining their worldview, praxis, stories, and theology. Wright (2003, 568–70) suggests, using various New Testament texts[61], that by proclaiming Jesus as *Kyrios*, the early Christians implied, albeit implicitly, that Caesar was not. The title "son of God" given to Jesus, which in the Jewish world meant the Messiah, was a direct challenge to Caesar because, in the pagan Greco-Roman world, it was a title ascribed to him (729). According to these early believers, the lordship of Jesus confronted the kingdoms of the world. It demanded a rival loyalty to Jesus and his kingdom movement as opposed to the rest. For Wright (2008b, 31), the resurrection of Jesus should not be seen as a sign of his uniqueness or even divinity but as the launching of the new creation: God's kingdom in the space-time universe under Caesar's nose. Therefore, being a follower of Jesus' kingdom movement entailed political and social dangers. He proposes that the early Christians maintained their loyalty to Jesus as *Kyrios* because he rose from the dead, which validated his messianic career and death. Because Jesus was demonstrated to be Israel's Messiah, he is the lord of the world and summons it to allegiance (Wright 2003, 660).

2.5.3.3 Jesus as YHWH

Wright (2003, 563) argues that the progression of thought of the early Christians did not stop with Jesus being the Messiah and, therefore, *Kyrios* but continued until he was identified with YHWH himself. However, if we are to call Jesus God, like very early Jewish Christology, Wright (2015, 70–72) warns that it is vital that we define who this "God" is and, more importantly, who this God is within the first-century Jewish world. He contends that what first-century Jews implied by the word "God" can be summed up as "creational and covenantal monotheism" (Wright 1998a, 44–45). Wright indicates that monotheism was never an internal analysis of the personhood of YHWH but was always a way of saying that there is only one true God,

---

61. Rom 1:3–5; 1:16–17; 15:12; Phil 2:6–11; 3:19–21; 1 Cor 15:20–28; 1 Thess 4:15–17.

YHWH, the God of Israel. Wright highlights that this was the meaning of the Jewish prayer: "YHWH our God YHWH is one!"

Additionally, Wright (1991a, 46) points out that attached to this belief in only one true God was the belief that this God had chosen Israel to be his special people through whom God would accomplish his purposes. This central belief formed the apex of what it meant to be Jewish. Wright (2015, 75–76) observes that this one God was believed to be integrally involved in the affairs of his special people and, consequently, that they referred to him metaphorically in five different ways. These five metaphors are Glory (Shekinah), Spirit, Law, Word (Logos), and Wisdom (82–85). Wright (1998a, 46) contends that second-temple Jews could speak of YHWH in these ways without compromising their monotheism. So Jewish monotheism was never a numerical analysis of the personhood of God. He suggests that early church Trinitarian theology was not a tri-theistic abandonment of their Jewish monotheistic worldview but a fresh perspective from within this framework (47).[62]

According to Wright (2013, 1226–227), Richard Bauckham is one of the most important contributors to the study of early Christology. Bauckham (2008, 3) argues that "the New Testament, Paul included, offers a Christology of divine identity in which Jesus is included 'in the unique identity of this one God.'" According to Bauckham, this high Jewish Christology was foundational to the early Christians' faith long before it was committed to writing and it did not require them to denounce their Jewish monotheism (Bauckham 2002, 1–4; 2008, 17–19). Wright (2013, 1229–230) agrees with Bauckham's hypothesis and appreciates the tension he maintains between a high Jewish Christology and Jewish monotheism.[63] Wright (2003, 576–77) contends that the early Christians had a remarkably high yet very Jewish Christology that originated from a progression of thought after the resurrection. He points out that the early Christians spoke of Jesus alongside the creator God and as his self-expression without compromising their Jewish

---

62. Blomberg (2009, loc. 165–67) argues that many other historical Jesus scholars, including some from the Third quest, do not adequately address the reasons why the Jewish monotheistic followers of Jesus began to worship him when their monotheism would have prevented them from doing so.

63. Wright (2013, 1441) suggests that Bauckham's proposal of a high early Christology and its compatibility with Jewish monotheism be placed on the noticeboards of many theological or biblical studies faculties.

monotheism (576–77).⁶⁴ This "Christology of divine identity" comes to the fore, especially when we consider the writings of Paul (Wright 2013, 1230).⁶⁵

According to Wright (1998a, 47), Paul is the earliest biblical writer and, therefore, the clearest reflection of the earliest Christian tradition. Within this early tradition, he points to three passages within Paul's earliest works that indicate how Paul placed Jesus within explicit Jewish monotheistic themes and texts (Wright 1991a, 50). 1 Corinthians 8:6 is, according to Wright (1991b, 136), possibly the earliest and most significant pioneering moment in the history of Christology. In this text, Paul presents a unique and ground-breaking theology that Wright refers to as "Christological monotheism." Wright (1998a, 47) observes that what Paul accomplished with this revolutionary Christological formulation was to place Jesus within the heart of Jewish monotheism by expanding the formula of the Shema to include Theos and *Kyrios*.⁶⁶ He points out that the most explicit monotheistic statement from the Old Testament is the Shema, a confession of Jewish faith and a widespread prayer at the time of Jesus. Paul redefined the Shema Christologically by placing Jesus within this confession (Wright 1991a, 48). Wright (1991b, 132) argues that by doing this, Paul issued a theological statement about Jesus of the highest possible Christology.⁶⁷

Similarly, Wright (1998a, 47) demonstrates that in Philippians 2:5–11, Paul also uses Jewish monotheistic theology to indicate Jesus' significance.⁶⁸ This time Paul uses Isaiah 40–55 to proclaim Jesus' universal lordship. Wright believes, with Bauckham (2002, 12–15), that Paul equates Jesus' status to that of the Father because he accomplished what the prophet Isaiah proclaimed only the God of Israel could accomplish, namely, the defeat of pagan idols (47). Wright indicates that within this Jewish monotheistic

---

64. Wright (2013, 1441) agrees with Bauckham (2008, 58), that "it was actually not Jewish but Greek philosophical categories which made it difficult to attribute true and full divinity to Jesus." Therefore, Wright believes that the Nicene and other creeds were attempting to reaffirm the Christological Monotheism of the New Testament, whilst guarding against Greek philosophy.

65. Wright (2013, 1230) agrees with Bauckham (2008, 184) that Paul ascribes a triple divine identity to Jesus which contain the three aspects of Jewish monotheism: creational, eschatological, and cultic.

66. The distinction between Jesus as *Kyrios* and the Father as *Theos* is upheld by Paul in this passage, and it is an important distinction to maintain. These titles are Paul's way of preserving the distinctiveness within the Trinity (Fee 2007).

67. Fee (2007, 113–14) points out that fulfills the role of Messiah, and as the reigning *Kyrios*, the one God is now all in all.

68. Newman (2009b, loc. 3853–54) writes, "Given the liturgical constraints of Jewish-style monotheism—Yahweh is only one true god; only worship him—the question 'when was Jesus first worshiped?' and 'what precipitated his worship?' and 'was the worship of Jesus a legitimate development of Judaism?' become all the more intriguing."

theology, Jesus is the one who defeats the pagan powers. Furthermore, he argues that, according to Paul, although Jesus possessed divine equality with the Father, he did not exploit that as a human being but rather interpreted that as a vocation to humiliation and death, which the Father honored by exalting him to share his divine glory (Wright 1991b, 97).

Although Wright (1998a, 48) argues that there are differences between 1 Corinthians 8 and Philippians 2, he believes the poem in Colossians 1:15–20 belongs firmly on the same Jewish monotheistic map. Wright (1991b, 113) contends that Paul's poem takes the form of Jewish wisdom theology, a characteristically Jewish way of proclaiming covenantal and creational monotheism. However, instead of attributing creation and redemption to Wisdom, Paul assigns them to Jesus, whereby Paul introduces his Christological monotheism again, similarly to Philippians 2 (99). This time Paul places Jesus within an explicit Jewish monotheistic statement in which the Messiah is the dwelling place of Wisdom (Wright 1991b, 118). Paul redefined his Jewish monotheism around Jesus himself (Wright 2013, 1216).

Now, according to Wright, the reasons why the early Christians arrived at a Christology of divine identity are twofold: First, Wright (2013, 1225–226) contends that the experience of the risen Jesus led the early church to worship him. Wright learned this from Hurtado (2003), who proposes that it was "the sense and experience of the personal presence of the exalted Jesus, in the way that one might expect to experience the presence of the living God, that led Jesus' earliest disciples first to worship him."[69] Subsequently, Jesus' followers re-read Israel's Scriptures in such a way as to find him in the texts that were about the one God, which in turn led to new ways of describing him (Hurtado 2003). For example, Wright (2003, 571–74) points out that, from the earliest moments of Christianity, the title *Kyrios*, which was utilized in the Greek translation of the Old Testament as a translation of the name YHWH, was deliberately assigned to Jesus. This move, he argues, stemmed from scriptural reflection on what was accomplished in Jesus the Messiah and who the God was in whose new world they were participants (Wright 2012a, 399). Similarly, Wright highlights that Paul interpreted Old Testament texts about YHWH as referring to Jesus the Messiah, for example, in Romans 10:13.[70]

However, according to Wright (2013, 1226–230), an element is missing from Hurtado and Bauckham's proposals for why the early Christians

---

69. Wright (2013, 1223–26) considers Larry Hurtado and Richard Bauckham's Christological work to be of the highest quality within recent decades.

70. Wright (2013, 1227–28) agrees with Tilling (2012, 256) that the Old Testament relationship between God and Israel is matched by Paul's description of the relationship between Jesus and his followers.

included Jesus in their Jewish Monotheism. So, the second reason Wright believes the early Christians made this move, which he considers "the hidden clue to the origin of Christology," is because of the long-awaited return of YHWH to Zion (1232). According to Wright, the early Christians believed that Israel's God had done what he had long before promised: to return in person as the rightful king to save his people (1232–233). This, they believed, occurred in and through the person of Jesus. Wright contends that "in his life, death and resurrection Jesus had accomplished the new exodus, had done in person what Israel's God had said he would do in person" (1233–234). Wright (1998a, 53) observes that in Jesus, the early church found the biblical portrait of YHWH come to life. The creator God came to do in person what only he could do. Put differently; Wright suggests that Jesus personified the Old Testament portrait of YHWH. However, Wright again emphatically argues that Jesus was not aware of being God but rather of the vocation he had to do and be for Israel and the world, what only YHWH could do and be.

Wright (1998a, 46) argues that from serious theological reflection on the Jewish traditions and Scriptures, the early church arrived at the language with which they described Jesus' divinity. They did not allocate titles of honor to Jesus from other contexts but used familiar ways of speaking about Jesus as they contemplated the one true God, YHWH. Wright maintains that by using Jewish God language, the early church communicated everything they needed about Jesus and found a coherence between the nature of God and Jesus (46). Additionally, the early church utilized the five metaphorical ways of referring to YHWH's activity in the world by linking them to Jesus (46). He argues that the central Christological passages of the New Testament offer an early high Jewish Christology that is dependent upon this line of thought. The early Church utilized the language and imagery of Glory (Shekinah), Spirit, Law, Word (Logos), and Wisdom and developed them concerning Jesus (47). From John, Hebrews, and Revelation, Wright concludes that the earliest Christian traditions used the Jewish monotheistic categories; they already had to think about Jesus as the personal embodiment and revelation of Israel's God (49). In other words, the fact that the God of Israel had raised Jesus from the dead, seen in the light of all that Jesus said and did and in the light of the Jewish Scriptures, led the early Christians to conclude that Jesus was the unique "Son of God" as opposed to anyone else (Wright 2003, 731).[71]

71. The early Christians, then, referred to Jesus as the son of God in the messianic sense, the son of God in the sense that he was the true ruler of the world, but also as the Son of God in the sense that he was the personal embodiment and revelation of Israel's God (Wright 2003, 731).

Because of the resurrection of Jesus, alongside his messianic career and death, the early Christians believed that Jesus was the Jewish Messiah. Consequently, he was seen as the *Kyrios*, the lord of the world, which was implied by Jewish messiahship. However, the early Christians extended the lordship of Jesus even further by stating that Jesus made present and visible what the Old Testament said about YHWH himself. And if early Jewish Christology believed that Jesus was somehow divine, Wright insists that they did so within the Jewish framework of monotheism.[72]

2.5.4 Conclusion

Wright's answer to the fourth historical question of the Third Quest, namely, "how did the early Christians who were Jewish monotheists come to worship Jesus of Nazareth?" can be summarized as follows. The early Christians believed that two actual events occurred; namely, Jesus' tomb was empty on the third day after his execution, and he appeared bodily, similar yet different, to various eyewitnesses after that. These two events led them to conclude that Jesus rose bodily from the dead. The resurrection by itself did not mean that Jesus was the Messiah or that he was divine. However, the resurrection considered in the light of Jesus' messianic career and death, along with theological reflection, led the early Christians to conclude that Jesus truly was Israel's Messiah. Consequently, because of Old Testament promises that the Messiah would be lord of the world, Jesus was considered the *Kyrios*. Additionally, considering that Jesus accomplished what the Jewish Scriptures promised only YHWH could accomplish, their train of thought led them to conclude that Jesus as the *Kyrios* was the personification and embodiment of YHWH. Wright argues that this early high Christology remained Jewish in the sense that the church did not abandon their Jewish monotheism but, through reflection on the God of Israel, their Scriptures, and the five metaphorical ways of describing YHWH's activity in the world, they concluded that Jesus personified the Old Testament portrait of YHWH.

2.6 Concluding Remarks

From this chapter, it is evident that Wright's Christology has been informed and shaped by scholars, such as Reimarus and Käsemann, who convinced

---

72. Jesus Seminar scholar Borg (2009, loc. 3089–3110) places Wright within the conservative traditionalist camp because of his belief in Jesus' messianic awareness, salvific death, and bodily resurrection and shows that, because of these convictions, Wright differs from the moderate to liberal Jesus scholars.

him of the importance of historical study around Jesus of Nazareth. However, in terms of the historical inquiry process, none were more influential to Wright's Christology than Albert Schweitzer and Ben Meyer. Schweitzer imparted to Wright the conviction that the historical study of Jesus of Nazareth must place him firmly within an eschatological Jewishness. Meyer taught him a unique way of approaching the study of the historical Jesus by placing the focus on the Jewish worldview of the first century, Jesus' mindset within that worldview, and, ultimately, Jesus' aims and beliefs. Additionally, it is abundantly clear that Wright belongs to the Third Quest for the historical Jesus. He was the one who gave this quest its name. Consequently, the way he develops his Christology is under the six key questions of the Third Quest: How does Jesus fit into first-century Judaism? What were his aims? Why did he die? How did the church come into being? Why are the gospels what they are? And how does the historical Jesus relate to the contemporary church and world?[73] Wright addresses these key questions through his hypothesis that Jesus was a Jewish eschatological prophet who believed that the climax of Israel's history, her return from exile, the return of YHWH to Zion, and the defeat of her enemies, were occurring in and through him, his work, and his imminent death on the cross.

First, Wright's answer to the question, "how does Jesus fit into first-century Judaism?" is that Jesus was most fundamentally an "Oracular" and "Leadership" prophet. However, Jesus did not see himself as only a prophet, but as the one through whose praxis, words, and symbolic acts the history of the Jewish nation was being brought to its climax. Wright argues that Jesus' announcement of the kingdom of God provided a new variation on a basic Jewish story and worldview. That is, this announcement reaffirmed her most basic hopes—namely, the return from exile, a return of YHWH to Zion, and the defeat of evil—even as it radically redefined them by declaring that these hopes were being realized through Jesus himself. Additionally, Wright contends that Jesus' announcement came with a warning for Israel if she refused to repent of their violent revolutionary zeal and a promise of vindication for those who followed him. Correspondingly, Jesus opposed the purity codes and the temple, which supported the violent revolutionary political agenda of the Shammaite Pharisees and offered alternative symbols, all of which declared in symbol that the time of fulfillment of Israel's hope had come.

Second, Wright addresses the question, "what were Jesus' aims and beliefs?" by arguing that Jesus believed that he was Israel's Messiah and that

---

73. Wright's answers to the fifth question and the sixth question will be discussed in chapter 4.

this belief is most clearly demonstrated in Jesus' actions in the temple and the surrounding riddles. Included in this belief of his messiahship, Wright shows that Jesus saw himself as the leader and focal point of Israel's return from exile as he believed that he was embodying and symbolizing in himself this return from exile. As the Messiah, Jesus was required to perform two crucial tasks, namely, cleanse, restore, and rebuild the temple and engage in the messianic battle, and defeat the enemies of Israel. According to Wright, Jesus set out to accomplish these two tasks, albeit radically redefined, through his death. Furthermore, Wright highlights that the symbolic action of Jesus' journey to Jerusalem indicates that Jesus aimed to symbolize and embody YHWH's return to Zion. He believed he would be vindicated and exalted as YHWH's agent to share YHWH's throne. Jesus believed that his vocation was to do and be what only Israel's God did and was.

Third, Wright answers the question "why did Jesus die?" which also formed part of his aims and beliefs, by pointing out that Jesus believed that through his impending fate, he would accomplish the new exodus by overthrowing the evil power of this world by a greater power, namely, the revolutionary power of God's love, which, according to Wright, is explicitly and implicitly implied by Jesus' symbolic action of the Last Supper. According to Wright, Jesus knew that he was about to die and that his death was part of an eschatological plan to usher in the kingdom of Israel's God. He believed his death would be an eschatological event leading to the new exodus, a return from exile, the forgiveness of sins, and the new covenant.

Fourth, Wright believes that the answer to the question, "how did the early Christians who were Jewish monotheists come to worship Jesus of Nazareth?" is that the early church believed that two actual events occurred; namely, Jesus' tomb was empty on the third day after his execution, and he appeared bodily to his followers after that. These two events led them to conclude that Jesus rose bodily from the dead. Although the resurrection by itself did not prove Jesus' messiahship nor his divinity, Wright believes that, along with Jesus' messianic career and death and through theological reflection, the early Christians concluded that Jesus truly was Israel's Messiah. As part of his messianic profile, they considered him the *Kyrios*, lord of the world. Furthermore, Wright suggests the progression of thought about Jesus after his resurrection did not end there; the early Christians' train of thought led them to conclude that Jesus as the *Kyrios* was the personification and embodiment of YHWH. In this way, Wright concludes that, although early Jewish Christology believed that Jesus was somehow divine, they did so within the Jewish framework of monotheism.

3

Wolfhart Pannenberg's Christology

3.1 Introduction

WOLFHART PANNENBERG WAS CONVINCED that theology must be informed by historical facts and interact with the social sciences. For Pannenberg, something is only true if it is true for everyone, regardless of whether everyone believes it. Therefore, the concepts of truth and universality formed the basis of his theological method. This point of view proved fundamental to his approach to Christology. Truth, especially when it comes to Jesus of Nazareth, must be grounded in history and have a universal significance to be worth pursuing. This is what he believed could be attained through systematic historical research.

Pannenberg's Christological work focused on the defense and rigorous application of the from below methodology. He dealt with Christological issues right from the commencement of his theological career in works such as *Revelation as History* (1968b) and *Jesus—God and Man* (1977a), which brought about his international fame (Kärkkäinen 2016, 115). Pannenberg was critical of Christological approaches that commenced with the incarnation as its presupposition. Rather, the incarnation should be the conclusion of Christology and not its starting point. He was adamant that a from below approach was the only way in which the divinity, humanity, and unity of Christ could be persuasively maintained.

Although Pannenberg appeared cynical in some ways—for example, he declared some stories in the Gospels as mythical and legendary and claimed that the Chalcedon creed was a Christological compromise—he was adamant that our faith cannot rest upon the preaching of the early church but should rely on historical facts. Pannenberg was very careful about what he meant by the term "historical." Pannenberg acknowledged that history cannot be reconstructed according to the limitations of present reality (Pannenberg 1996, 64–65). Therefore, Christian historians must not accept this method, as many secular scholars employ, as it excludes God from its presuppositions and forces a secular reading of the Christian story (64–65). For Pannenberg, historical studies must be open to the supernatural and miracles. Historical research, then, is how the proclamation of the contemporary and early church is legitimized. But the question remains, how did Pannenberg use a historically skeptical approach to describe Jesus Christ while staying Christian?

This chapter will examine how Pannenberg developed his from below Christology. It will explore where he commenced his approach, what he believed the task of the endeavor was, and the method he employed. It will investigate his arguments concerning the relationship between Jesus and Israel's God, which he believed needed to be the starting point. This includes his thoughts around the resurrection of Jesus, the mode of God's presence in Jesus, and Jesus' essential unity with God. Then, it will assess his views on the humanity of Jesus with a particular interest in how he employed his anthropological understanding of what it means to be human. It will explore Pannenberg's claims about Jesus as the ultimate man, his office, and the meaning of his death. Lastly, it will examine how he avoided the two-natures dilemma, his views on the unity of Jesus with God, and the lordship of Jesus. This chapter is descriptive in nature. Chapter 4 of this thesis will provide a critical analysis of Pannenberg's Christology, and in chapter 6, the strengths of Pannenberg's Christology will be applied to the Christocentric homiletic.

3.2 The Point of Departure

3.2.1 *Introduction*

Pannenberg's (1974a, 139) central claim is that the Christian faith, unlike any other religion, depends entirely on the career and fate of Jesus of Nazareth. Consequently, the significance of Jesus must be developed from what Jesus was historically in his own religious, political, social, and cultural context rather than what his significance is for us in our contemporary context. But why did he approach the study of Jesus in this way when so many prominent theologians of his day, including some of his influences like Karl Barth, did not follow that same trajectory, particularly at a time when the quest for the historical Jesus had lost its momentum? Some scholars are skeptical about whether his endeavor to approach Christology from below is even possible because he was a Christian before he was a theologian, but Pannenberg (1977a, 34) was resolute that it is not only possible for Christology to be approached from below but necessary (Macleod 2000, 20).

This section will explore Pannenberg's views on the task and purpose of Christology. It will examine his Christological methodology and arguments as well as Christology's relation to soteriology. I will then conclude with the structure and sequence of his Christology, which the subsequent sections of the chapter will analyze.

3.2.2 The Task of Christology

Pannenberg made his Christological contribution during the "No Quest" and "New Quest" periods, which means that he would have been confronted with the dialogue of whether to start one's Christology with the preaching of the early church or with Jesus himself. According to Herzog (2000, 8–13), focusing on the kerygma of the early church rather than using the gospels as historical sources to reconstruct the life of Jesus was the fundamental characteristic of the "No Quest" period.[1] Likewise, the attempt to demythologize the kerygma of the gospels to arrive at the actual words of Jesus was a distinctive mark of the "New Quest."[2] This was the situation in which Pannenberg found himself when he did his Christological work.

Pannenberg began from the conviction that it makes a fundamental difference whether Christology starts with the historical Jesus or the kerygma of the early or contemporary church (Pannenberg 1966, 15). Calvin (1960, loc. 12886) contended that it is essential that the church understands who it is that they proclaim, lest they be criticized for speaking of a name of which they know nothing. Pannenberg would agree but emphasize that we can only understand who we are preaching about if we have studied Jesus historically. Pannenberg (1966, 16) agreed with the work of Martin Kähler to the extent that Kähler finds continuity between the life and message of

---

1. Herzog (2000, 8–9) shows that the "No Quest," which lasted until around 1953, was led by scholars such as Rudolf Bultmann who sought to change the approach of Christology by focusing on the kerygma of the early church rather than using the gospels as historical sources to reconstruct the life of Jesus.

2. The "New Quest" started in 1953 and focused upon demythologizing the kerygma of the gospels to arrive at the true words of Jesus by using such methods as Ernst Käsemann's criterion of dissimilarity (Herzog 2000, 13).

Jesus and the preaching of the apostles; for him, Christology must start with the historical Jesus. He agreed with Kähler that driving a cleft between Jesus and the apostles' preaching was unwarranted. Kähler (1964, 66) wrote, "The real Christ, that is, the Christ who has exercised an influence in history, with whom millions have communed in childlike faith, and with whom the great witnesses of faith have been in communion—while striving, apprehending, triumphing, and proclaiming—this real Christ is the Christ who is preached."[3] Pannenberg (1966, 17) insisted that "the historical reconstruction of the figure and the proclamation of Jesus is always required to explain how the early Christians' proclamation of Christ could arise from the fate of Jesus."[4] However, he criticized Kähler's idea that what can be known about Jesus is limited to the apostles preaching and that Jesus' effect (*persönliche Wirkung*) on them is historical (16).

The continuity between the life and message of Jesus and the kerygma of the early church was essential for Pannenberg because it was on this premise that he built his argument that going behind the New Testament writers to get to the historical Jesus is not only possible but necessary. Pannenberg (1966, 17) agreed with Herrmann (1892, 253) that if the church based its faith solely on the preaching of the early church, then it based its faith on something that was itself a product of faith. Instead, in siding with Ebeling (1961, 46), he proposed that faith must be supported by an understanding of the historical Jesus himself (*am historischen Jesus selbst*). Although Pannenberg agreed that historical study alone could not lead one to an ultimate faith commitment in Jesus, it nonetheless provides the foundation that makes faith possible (Kärkkäinen 2016, 116). Pannenberg (1974a, 140) held that "faith presupposes something upon which it is grounded, something which confirms itself as real again and again in the face of all doubting: it is the information about the events which constitute in their context the career of Jesus." Therefore, he contended, "the Christian faith cannot be disconnected from the knowledge of past events and its verification" (Pannenberg 1994a, 318).[5] The foundation, which binds the witnesses together, can be seen by going behind the New Testament text (Pannenberg 1966, 18). This, he maintained, occurs when they are seen as a historical source about Jesus himself rather than what was once believed and preached.

---

3. All German translations into English are my own unless otherwise stated.

4. "Die historische Rekonstruktion der Gestalt und der Verkündigung Jesu ist immer verpflichtet zu erklären, wie vom Geschick Jesu her die urchristliche Christusverkündigung entstehen konnte."

5. "Der Christliche Glaube läßt sich nicht trennen von der Kenntnis vergangenen Geschehens und seiner Vergewisserung."

Similarly, just as Christian faith in Jesus should not be based on the kerygma of the early church, Pannenberg (1966, 19) argued that it should also not solely rest on current Christian experience ("gegenwärtigen Christlichen Erfahrung"). The idea of basing a Christology on contemporary experience brought about by the church's kerygma was prevalent in his context. It originated with Schleiermacher (1928), who formulated his Christology on the experience of redemption and a God-consciousness (Pannenberg 1966, 19). Similarly, scholars such as Bultmann, Weber, and Althaus insisted that faith is not based on who Jesus was but on who Jesus is as he encounters us in contemporary experiences (19–20). Bultmann claimed that Jesus meets us in the kerygma of the Church (Bultmann 1953, 117). For Weber (1962, 36) it is an encounter with Jesus which establishes and supports faith ("den Glaube begründende und tragende Begegnung mit Jesus Christus").

Similarly, Althaus (1962, 423) contended that "faith does not primarily have to do with who Jesus was, but rather with what he is as he encounters us in the proclamation."[6] However, Pannenberg (1966, 20–21) indicated that similar to the faith based on the kerygma of the early church, faith based on the contemporary experience of proclamation is also based on the product of faith rather than historical facts.[7] Moreover, historical research is how the proclamation of the contemporary and early church is legitimized ("legitimation des Kerygmas selbst").[8]

Pannenberg (1966, 21) also opposed the idea of certain scholars, like Koch (1959, 302), Künneth (1962, 286), and Bonhoeffer (2009, 329–30), who argued that because the risen and exalted Lord is experienced in his Word, sacrament, and Church community he existed historically.[9]

---

6. "Der Glaube hat es nicht primär zu tun mit dem, was Jesus war, sondern mit dem, was er, wie er uns in der Verkündigung begegnet, ist."

7. Pannenberg used the same critique for faith based on contemporary experience and proclamation as Hermann (1892, 253) used to criticize the grounds for faith *(grund des glaubens)* that rests solely on the kerygma of the early church.

8. If ever someone had a contemporary experience of Jesus Christ worth building a Christology upon, it was Pannenberg, who had an experience like Paul on the Damascus Road (Peters 2014, 366). Pannenberg (1981, 261) described his own encounter with Jesus on 6 January 1945, as America was bombing Berlin and the Russians were advancing from the East. He recalled, "I was suddenly flooded by light and absorbed in a sea of light which, although it did not extinguish the humble awareness of my finite existence, overflowed the barriers that normally separate us from the surrounding world."

9. According to Koch (1959, 302), "Nun offenbart sich im Mahl zu Ostern der Kyrios" (Now the Lord reveals himself in the Easter meal). For Künneth (1962, 286) because the resurrected Jesus shows himself effective in faith ("im Glauben wirksam erweist"), faith believes his historical existence. Bonhoeffer (2009, 330) suggested that historical research can neither affirm nor deny any historical fact, in other words, Jesus'

Bonhoeffer (330) insisted that the past is that which is present and that the historical validity of something is affirmed by its existence here and now. This conclusion, he maintained, is made possible only through faith in the resurrection of Christ (330). Since the Risen Christ is present, we have absolute certainty that this Christ also existed historically. However, Pannenberg (1966, 22) criticized such an argument as being susceptible to self-delusion (*Selbsttäuschungen*).

Conversely, we know that Jesus lives as the exalted Lord not due to recent experiences but because of what happened in the past. Our current experiences in the world are validated by what occurred in the past, which led Pannenberg to go as far as to say that history reveals God's presence in his creation (Pannenberg 1981, 261).[10] Therefore, Pannenberg (1966, 22) wrote, "Christology does not merely deal with the development of the Christian community's confession of Christ, but above all with establishing it from the works and fate of Jesus."[11] In other words, Christology cannot use the dogmatic confessions of the church as its starting point but should be formulated in light of who Jesus was historically.

Pannenberg (1966, 22–24) contended that this task of Christology has two components: (1) it entails obtaining systematic historical insights about Jesus from his history, and (2) it must assess how the early church arrived at the statements they made about him in the light of the historical knowledge obtained about him. Therefore, the term "Christology" is apt since he was adamant that it should demonstrate that Jesus is the "Christ" of Israel's God (24–26).

3.2.3 *The Method of Christology*

The from above and from below methods of Christology have different focus points at their core (Pannenberg 1966, 26). Although Weber has sought to follow an alternative approach to the from above or from below approaches to Christology by starting with the "encounter of Jesus," Pannenberg remained unconvinced that the issue of the humanity and deity of Jesus has been adequately addressed by such an approach (26). The from

---

existence cannot be denied nor affirmed with absolute certainty by using historical research methods. For Bonhoeffer this is too much to ask of historical research.

10. Karl Löwith's lectures on theology and philosophy of history and Gerhard von Rad's writings on the Old Testament were formative for Pannenberg's understanding of linking God and history (Pannenberg 1981, 261).

11. "Die Christologie hat es also nicht nur mit der Entfaltung des Christusbekenntnisses der Gemeinde zu tun, sondern vor allem mit seiner Begründung aus dem Damals des Wirkens und Geschickes Jesu."

above method has the incarnation at its core, whereas Jesus' career and fate form the center of the from below method. In contrast to the from above approach, the from below approach only arrives at the issue of the incarnation toward the end of its endeavor. However, Pannenberg's preference for the from below approach to Christology was not shared by many of the influential theologians of his time, such as Brunner (1949), Vogel (1949), and Tillich (1957). He hinted that this was due to a mistrust of historical research (Pannenberg 1974a, 142).[12]

Karl Barth insisted on a "from above to below" approach that sought to describe how God the Son entered humiliation by becoming a human through uniting himself with the man Jesus of Nazareth (Barth 2009a, 59). This union was simultaneously the exaltation of the man Jesus, in whom humanity itself was taken up into covenant fellowship with God. Pannenberg (1966, 27) believed that Barth combined two doctrines previously held apart in traditional Protestant dogmatics, namely the two natures and two states of Jesus Christ. By doing this, he was convinced that Barth identified with the "Gnostic redeemer myth," which argues for the descent of the redeemer from heaven and his return to heaven.[13] However, Barth's position is unique because he believed that the redeemer did not come to redeem himself but humankind.

Pannenberg (1966, 28–29) contended that this approach to Christology is invalid for three reasons: (1) It presupposes the divinity of Jesus ("setzt die Gottheit Jesu schon voraus") and thereby avoids what he thought to be the actual task of Christology, namely, to present the reasons for belief in the deity of Jesus. Rather than presuppose it, he argued that the Christological task is to inquire about how the historical Jesus became recognized as divine. (2) It does not take the actual historical context of Jesus seriously. Pannenberg (1966, 28–29; 1970, 26–27) insisted that when the discussion around Jesus commences with his divinity, the relationship between Jesus and his Jewish context, which is essential to understanding his life and message, is not given enough prominence. Inevitably, the offices and states of Christ then receive more attention than placing Jesus within his real historical Jewish context. The neglect of Jesus' relationship to Israel and the Old Testament inevitably means that even Jesus' death loses much of its significance. (3) It ignores our human limitations. Pannenberg pointed out that we cannot see through God's eyes to follow the way of God's Son into the world

---

12. Pannenberg (1966, 27–28) did credit Tillich (1957, 148) for providing a from above approach that was unique, the "New Being"; however, he thought that this approach achieved the from above from the perspective of humanity.

13. Macleod (2000, 20) believes that comparing Barth to the Gnostic Redeemer myth was harsh and unfounded.

(29). In other words, as human beings, we are compelled to think from the context of historically determined situations. Therefore, the starting point of Christology must be the man Jesus of Nazareth, and only from there can we ask about his divinity.[14]

But while the starting point of Christology should be the historical man, Jesus of Nazareth, the first question must be concerned with his unity with God (Pannenberg 1966, 30). Pannenberg warned that if Jesus' life and message are taken independently from an understanding of his relationship to God, the history of Jesus will be inaccurate. Instead, he argued that the total characterization of his appearance must be investigated, which includes Jesus' life and proclamation and decisively his relationship to Israel's God (30). Pannenberg insisted that Jesus' life, sayings, and fate are to be understood and evaluated in this context. This omission, he suggested, is quite prevalent within the quests for the historical Jesus. For instance, he pointed out that rationalism investigates Jesus without his unity with God. Likewise, others, such as Schleiermacher, thought of Jesus' relationship to God merely as his God-consciousness (30).[15] Although Pannenberg had reservations about this, he nevertheless agreed that the relationship between Jesus and God must be investigated so that the church's confession of the divinity of Jesus could be substantiated rather than simply considered self-explanatory (31).

3.2.4 *Christology and Soteriology*

Before the fundamental Christological question about Jesus' relation to YHWH can be developed, Pannenberg (1966, 31) believed that the relationship between Christology and soteriology must be explained. He proposed that soteriology and Christology "*Sind als verschiedene aufeinander bezogen*" (are related to each other as distinct) (32). Jesus' saving significance is the real reason why interest is given to his divinity, and his saving significance presupposes his divinity. In other words, soteriology and Christology are inseparable because of our interest in salvation; the gospel leads us to

---

14. In Pannenberg's later work, he seems to have become more sympathetic towards the from above approach: "Hence we cannot regard a Christology from below as ruling out completely the classical Christology of the Incarnation. It is simply reconstructing the revelatory historical basis that classical Christology has always in fact presupposed, though never properly explained."

15. Although Jonker (1977, 85–86) has shown that, for Schleiermacher, the person of Christ is reduced to a historical person, devoid of any divinity, he understood Christ's works, and particularly his "God-awareness," as something to be imitated in human religiosity.

ask about the figure of Jesus (41). Nevertheless, the divinity of Jesus does not merely consist of his saving significance for us.

Pannenberg criticized the Christologies that are based on a soteriology. He questioned whether they had spoken about Jesus himself at all (Pannenberg 1966, 41). Moreover, he demonstrated that if Christology is approached from a soteriological perspective as its starting point, specific characteristics that derive from humanity's desire for salvation and deification are projected onto Jesus. This was the case even as far back as patristic theology (33–34). Starting with deification through the incarnation, he illustrated that the early church's Christology was motivated by soteriological concerns.[16] For these church fathers, humanity was created to participate in the divine Logos, whereby they would be rational beings and related to God. Salvation meant restoring participation with the divine Logos, by which humanity's rationality would be returned, death defeated, and immortality obtained. Therefore, by emphasizing the incarnation, they explained how Jesus had fulfilled that destiny. In other words, they projected their human desire for, and understanding of, salvation upon Jesus.

Likewise, Pannenberg (1966, 36) demonstrated that preconceived ideas of salvation have significantly shaped other significant Christologies. For instance, Luther's Christology of God's grace alone is based on the soteriology in which Jesus passively endured God's judgment on our sins so that we might share in his righteousness through faith (38). This theology of faith and grace is fundamental to Luther's understanding of Jesus. Luther saw Jesus as humanity's representative who neither strove for good nor offered works of satisfaction on our behalf but humbled himself under God's wrath against sin and thereby was seen as righteous before God (37). Furthermore, Luther considered Jesus the prototype of God's actions, wherein the hiddenness of his grace is revealed.[17] Pannenberg found that Luther and the reformers' soteriology led them to prefer to speak about the office of Jesus rather than his person (38).

Even the more critical scholars' Christologies have been influenced by their view of soteriology or their lack of interest therein. For Schleiermacher, salvation can be summed up in the phrase "consciousness of God" (Pannenberg 1966, 38). The more one becomes conscious of God as opposed to other types of knowledge; the greater salvation is experienced. From this understanding, Schleiermacher saw Jesus as the prototype to be imitated.

---

16. Pannenberg (1966, 34) referred to Irenaeus in the second century, Athanasius and Gregory of Nazianzus in the fourth century, Apollinaris of Laodicea in the fifth century, and Origen and Cyril of Alexandria.

17. For Luther, the general rule of divine action was that it was hidden, it is not recognized when it happened (*theologia crucis*) (Pannenberg 1966, 37).

Pannenberg pointed out that, for Schleiermacher, Jesus' strength of his God-consciousness indicates something of his divinity. Likewise, Kant and Ritschl also considered Jesus a prototype, albeit somewhat different from Schleiermacher (38–39). Kant (1960, 54) saw Jesus as the prototype for moral perfection spreading good in the world. Ritschl (1902, 449–51) also saw Jesus as the prototype for moral perfection; however, he emphasized Jesus' awareness of a vocation to find a moral community. Because of the alignment of Jesus' will and God's will in establishing such a moral community, he considered Jesus divine in that sense. Pannenberg (1966, 39) indicated that the neo-Protestant Christologies of Schleiermacher, Kant, and Ritschl have relatively little interest in soteriology and limit it to life on earth; nevertheless, it is clear how their soteriological interests have shaped their Christologies.

Pannenberg (1966, 41) highlighted that many significant Christologies are guilty of this projection, often without realizing it. Others, such as Tillich, have seen no issue with this sort of projection, unreservedly claiming that "Christologie ist eine Funktion der Soteriologie" (Christology is a function of soteriology) (42). But, Pannenberg opposed Christologies based on the experience of salvation. He acknowledged that all soteriological motifs have one common aspect critical for Christology: they explicitly express that in Jesus, the destiny of humanity has found its fulfillment (43). However, the soteriological outworking of Christology must follow the historical reality of Jesus of Nazareth.

Fundamentally, Pannenberg (1966, 42) sided with Luther and Bonhoeffer (2009, 314–15) that Jesus is to be understood in terms of the personal ontological "pro-me" structure. Bonhoeffer believed so strongly in this pro-me structure that he argued that all theology and Christology must start with acknowledging this assertion and that any scholar who denies this truth practices a theology that has deserted its God (314–15). By this, it is meant that the being of Christ's person is his relatedness to me; his "being-Christ" is his "being-for-me."[18] However, Pannenberg (1966, 42) maintained that "Jesus has importance for us only as far as this significance is inherent in himself, his history, and his person constituted through this history."[19] Moreover, only when Jesus is defined in these terms can we be sure that we are not projecting our desires onto his figure. Pannenberg (2002, 612) differed from Moltmann (2015, 260–67) by claiming that Jesus being "for us"

18. Williams (2018, 190) shows that, for Bonhoeffer, Christ's ultimate identity is contained in being *pro nobis* and *pro me*. Christ, therefore, is who he is as the one whose existence is for our individual and corporate church community's sake.

19. "Jesus hat Bedeutsamkeit für uns nur, sofern ihm selbst, seiner Geschichte und seiner durch sie konstituierten Person diese Bedeutsamkeit innewohnt."

must be based on the context of Jesus' history rather than on the Christian proclamation that through Jesus' suffering, death, and resurrection he was "for us." In other words, it must be shown from history rather than projected onto Jesus based on our soteriological interests (Schwöbel 2005, 131). Therefore, although Christology and soteriology are inseparable, the question of Jesus himself as a person of history must receive preference before all other questions regarding his significance to the salvation of humanity. Simply put, soteriology must follow Christology and not the other way around; otherwise, our faith in salvation loses its foundation (Pannenberg 1966, 42).

3.2.5 Conclusion

Pannenberg strongly emphasized that Christology must be based on historical facts rather than the early church preaching or our contemporary experiences of Jesus. It must be based on systematic, historical insights and on the reasons why the early church made the statements they did. Jesus' significance for us must be determined by who he was in the past. Additionally, he was critical of the from above method of Christology because it has the incarnation at its core. In contrast, he claimed that Jesus' message and fate should form the center of one's method. In contrast to the from above approach, his from below approach only arrives at the issue of the incarnation toward the end of its endeavor.

In terms of how one should determine Jesus' significance for us, he insisted that it should be based on who Jesus was historically rather than on our soteriological needs. For Pannenberg, although Christology and soteriology are inseparable, man's need for salvation must not determine who Jesus of Nazareth was.

3.3 The Knowledge of Jesus' Divinity

3.3.1 Introduction

The structure of Pannenberg's Christology follows the following sequence: (1) the knowledge of the divinity of Jesus Christ (the relationship of Jesus to God), (2) the fulfillment of human destiny through Jesus (Jesus as a man), (3) the relationship of his divinity to his humanity (Jesus as the fulfillment of human existence). The first concept Pannenberg sought to address was Jesus' relationship with Israel's God. Pannenberg (1966, 28–29; 1970, 26–27) was adamant that Christology cannot begin with the presupposition that Jesus was divine. However, although the starting point of Christology should be the humanity of Jesus, the first question must be concerned with Jesus' relationship with God. He contended that taking Jesus' actual historical context seriously entails investigating Jesus' relation to Israel's God. Additionally, if one examines Jesus' life and message independently from his relationship to YHWH, the historical conclusions would be inaccurate (Pannenberg 1966, 30).

This section investigates how Pannenberg developed his understanding of Jesus' relation to the God of Israel, particularly based on his assessment of the historical probability of the resurrection. It examines the implications of the resurrection in his argument, which include the mode of God's presence in Jesus and his essential unity with God. It also investigates his views on the retroactive power of the resurrection and, consequently, his understanding of the virgin birth and incarnation of Jesus.

3.3.2 The Resurrection as the Ground of Jesus' Divinity

Pannenberg (1966, 47) observed that for most from below Christologies of his day, the ultimate indication of Jesus' unity with God was his claim to authority in his proclamation and work. For instance, Elert (1956, 303) believed the decisive argument for Jesus' divine sonship was his claim to be the Son of God, which was most clearly revealed through his addressing God as his Father ("wenn er von seinem Vater sprach").[20] Althaus (1962, 431) suggested that "the authority that Jesus claimed presupposes a proximity to God, a solidarity with him, that no other person has."[21] He argued that Jesus implicitly, through his proclamation and work, and explicitly called himself the Son of Man. Although Pannenberg (1966, 48) was not convinced that Jesus explicitly claimed such authority, he conceded that the implicit claims to this authority have greater argumentative power concerning their historical validity. Both Gogarten (1948, 124–27; 1952, 263) and Diem (1959, 115) based their Christology on the sufficiency of Jesus' claim to authority, considering the words of Jesus as "Der unmittelbare Anspruch Gottes an uns" (the immediate claim of God on us). For these theologians, Jesus'

---

20. Elert (1956, 303) agreed with Bornkamm (1995, 169–71) that the Christological titles assigned to Jesus by his disciples were because of their faith in him which came as a result of the resurrection, however, Jesus made implicit claims through his words and works which preceded that faith.

21. "Die Vollmacht, die Jesus in Anspruch nimmt, setzt eine Nähe zu Gott, eine Verbundenheit mit ihm voraus, die kein anderer Mensch hat."

testimony about himself is enough, as there is no higher form of legitimization of authority.²²

For many of these scholars, finding continuity between Jesus' proclamation and that of the early church gave reasonable confidence in Jesus' implicit and explicit claims to authority. Consequently, these claims were enough on which to build their Christologies. This, however, was not the case for Pannenberg. He argued that although the early church's idea that Jesus was the preexistent Son of God emerged from his teachings, insofar as in him the eschatological kingdom of God became present, this implicit claim needed validation (Pannenberg 1991a, 31). Therefore, he (1968a, 105) proclaimed that: "For the early Christians the resurrection of Jesus was the foundation of salvation, and it is highly probable that it was the starting point of all Christological confessional statements."²³

The resurrection made it possible to believe in a crucified messiah; historically speaking, it was the point of departure for early Christian theology (Pannenberg 1994b, 343–44; 1972, 96). Pannenberg (1966, 55–56) believed that Jesus' claim to authority comes in the form of what he calls a "proleptic structure" *(Proleptische Struktur)*, which means that it comes with the anticipation of a future verdict.²⁴ Moreover, although Jesus' career was unique compared to other apocalyptic visionaries, he nonetheless made predictions that needed to be confirmed. This confirmation of Jesus' claim to authority was required in the same sense that the words of the prophets needed to be confirmed through them coming about (Deut 18:21–22; 1 Kgs 22:28; Jer 28:9; p. 55). Although Jesus validated his claim to authority through certain mighty deeds, Pannenberg acknowledged that these could only validate his claims to a certain extent (58–59). Pannenberg argued that, in light of the Jewish apocalyptic context, Jesus' claim to authority was aimed at a future validation by God himself, which was bound up with the coming of the proclaimed end event (60–61). Correspondingly, Jesus' apocalyptic proclamation indicated that he expected an imminent end to the space-time universe with the universal resurrection and that through this event, God would validate Jesus' claim to authority.

22. They would disagree with Funk (1996, 41) that "Jesus had nothing to say about himself, other than he had no permanent address, no bed to sleep in, no respect on his home turf."

23. "Für das Urchristentum ist die Auferstehung Jesu das Fundament des Heils und mit hoher Wahrscheinlichkeit der Ausgangspunkt aller christologischen Bekenntnisaussagen gewesen."

24. Owen (1966, 57) writes, "Pannenberg points to the historical context of Jewish apocalypticism, in which Jesus' claim to assure men of eschatological salvation must have looked forward to future confirmation."

Pannenberg (1966, 61) proposed that Jesus and the disciples probably did not expect an individually experienced resurrection but an imminent, universal resurrection. However, when the disciples encountered the resurrected Jesus, they would undoubtedly have interpreted that as an eschatological event signifying the beginning of the end of history (Pannenberg 1984, 125). Pannenberg (1966, 62–69) argued that in the Jewish apocalyptic tradition, Jesus' resurrection had inherent significance, which he summarized as follows: (1) Jesus' resurrection signified the end of the space-time universe had begun. Within Jewish tradition, it would have meant that the universal resurrection and judgment were at hand.[25] The expectation of the resurrection from Jewish tradition was the presupposition to understanding Jesus' resurrection (Pannenberg 1974a, 145; 1973, 64–65). (2) For the Jews, Jesus' resurrection could only mean that the God of Israel had validated his pre-Easter activity. This would have been considered a validation of Jesus' claim to authority. (3) It meant that the Son of Man who was to come was none other than the man Jesus of Nazareth. By the resurrection, Jesus stepped into the role of the Son of Man, which meant that it would have been improbable for a second figure to fulfill the same function (Pannenberg 1973, 64).

(4) If Jesus had been raised from the dead, ascended into heaven, and if the end of the world had begun, then Jesus is the ultimate revelation of God.[26] Pannenberg believed that God could only be revealed in his divinity at the end of all of history (Pannenberg 1966, 64; 1977a, 69). He deduced this idea from the Old Testament's concept that God's divine activities were performed to reveal God's divinity. Moreover, because Israel's history is a single historical unity, the full knowledge of God will only be obtained as this history comes to an end (Pannenberg 1977a, 128–29). It is when all the world events come to an end that we will know his divinity. Therefore, since the end of the age has already begun with the resurrection of Jesus, God himself is revealed in Jesus.[27] (5) The eschatological character of the resurrection of Jesus motivated the Gentile mission. Pannenberg (1966,

25. Pannenberg (1966, 62) contended that the indwelling Spirit of the early church was a vivid reminder that the end was at hand as the Spirit had eschatological significance (Rom 1:3; 2 Cor 13:4; 1 Tim 3:16; 1 Pet 3:18; Rom 8:11).

26. Chiavone (2009, 229) writes, "Pannenberg believes that history and the eschaton have met, and that therefore God has been revealed, in the resurrection of Jesus Christ."

27. Kilcrease and Ziegler (2018, 158) point out that "there must be a final and universal revelation of God's deity at the end of history. The apocalyptic tradition of the prophets and of late second temple Judaism understood that this ultimate verification would be tied up with the resurrection of the dead. For this reason, Jesus demonstrates the universal lordship of God in his resurrection."

65) contended that the beginning of the end, signified in Jesus' resurrection, revealed that the time had come for the inclusion of the Gentiles into the eschatological salvation promised through the Jewish tradition.[28] (6) The resurrection event and the words of the risen Jesus are essential for establishing faith in him. Although the words of the resurrected Jesus added nothing unique to the event itself, they did verbalize its significance. Without this explanation of the inherent significance of the resurrection, faith in this event would not have been reasonable.

Pannenberg was convinced that the resurrection of Jesus could be affirmed through a historical investigation (Peters 2014, 367).[29] In dealing with the resurrection of Jesus as a historical event, Pannenberg discussed two events that formed the basis for the belief in Jesus' resurrection. These two events are the appearances of Jesus and the empty tomb wherein Jesus was placed after his crucifixion (Pannenberg 1966, 85). He proposed that each event should be investigated separately to assess these two traditions historically.

Pannenberg maintained that early church traditions remained the decisive authority for judging the resurrection's historicity. He stated, "the investigation of the early church Easter tradition remains the decisive authority for the decision over the historicity of the resurrection of Jesus" (Pannenberg 1968a, 111).[30] Pannenberg commenced his discussion with the tradition of appearances. He based his investigation of the appearances of Jesus mostly on the Pauline report (Pannenberg 1966, 85–86).[31] Pannenberg agreed with Grass (1962, 88,107) that the Gospels' accounts of Jesus' appearances are heavily influenced by "legendary character" (*Die Evangelischen Berichte sind stark legendär*), which makes them less useful for historical research. Moreover, the Gospels' accounts tended to emphasize the physicality of Jesus' resurrected body, which he felt was one of the most significant legendary elements in their reports.[32] In contrast, Paul's

---

28. Ps 2:8; Isa 2:2; Mic 4:1; Zech 9:10; Gen 12:3; Matt 25:34; 8:11; Luke 13:29.

29. In fact, whilst others shied away from the resurrection because of the possible problems regarding its historicity, Pannenberg considered the resurrection of Jesus to be the only adequate foundation for statements about Jesus (Tupper 1974, 68).

30. "Die Prüfung der urchristlichen Osterüberlieferungen die entscheidende Instanz für das Urteil über die Historizität der Auferstehung Jesu."

31. Paul's report of the resurrected Jesus' appearances is recorded in 1 Cor 15:1–11, which forms the foundation of Pannenberg's discussion.

32. Pannenberg (1977a, 88–89) contended that the Gospel's overemphasized the physicality of the appearances of Jesus in an effort to draw it closer to the empty tomb tradition. But that the earliest traditions kept these two traditions separate, namely, Mark only refers to the empty tomb tradition and Paul only refers to the appearances tradition.

account seems to contain the core of the tradition of appearances, which began with Peter and was later experienced by Paul (Pannenberg 1996, 67). Additionally, Paul's experience in Acts 9 paralleled that of the earlier witnesses (Pannenberg 1994a, 320).

Through an exegesis of 1 Corinthians 15:1–11, Pannenberg (1966, 85–86) showed that Paul documented the appearances of the resurrected Jesus and that the purpose of this was to provide proof of witnesses to his resurrection. Pannenberg highlighted that Paul was trying to provide credible evidence of Jesus' resurrection by referring to Jesus' appearance to more than five hundred people at once, most of whom were still alive at the time of his writing (Pannenberg 1974a, 141). Paul wanted to convince the people of his time and context with the methods available to him then, rather than being concerned with convincing modern historians who are negatively predisposed (Pannenberg 1966, 86). The two elements that Pannenberg dealt with in assessing Paul's reports, namely, the time-lapse between the events and when Paul wrote about them, and Paul's use of formulated traditions, gave him a firm conviction that the appearances stories were real. The birth of the church itself was another contributing factor to this conviction. He agreed with Leipoldt (1948, 737) that the primitive church was convinced that they had encountered the resurrected Jesus, without which the origin of the early church is a riddle.[33]

Subsequently, Pannenberg discussed the empty tomb tradition. Pannenberg (1966, 97) emphasized that both traditions be considered independently if they are to give any historical probability to the resurrection of Jesus. He showed that, for Paul, the empty tomb was not of as much concern as it was for the disciples in Jerusalem, where Jesus was buried. He agreed with Althaus (1940, 22) that the early Christians' preaching would have been disproved within a day if it could not be established that Jesus' tomb was empty (Pannenberg 1996, 69). The preaching of the resurrection of Jesus necessitated the assumption of an empty tomb ("Vorausgesetzt das Grab Jesu leer war"; Pannenberg 1994a, 327). Pannenberg critiqued the view that the Jewish authorities would not have bothered to check the grave, much less would they have done a scientific examination to establish whether the corpse in the tomb was not Jesus.

Conversely, he emphasized that the Jewish authorities would have checked Jesus' grave in response to the proclamation of the early Christians (Pannenberg 1966, 98). Additionally, the Jews and Christians validated this as it has been shown historically that both shared the conviction that

---

33. "Sonst wird der Ursprung der Jerusalemer Gemeinde und damit der Kirche zu einem Rätsel."

Jesus' tomb was empty, even though they disagreed about why (Pannenberg 1994b, 357–59). Pannenberg (1994a, 324) contended that Mark's account of the discovery of Jesus' empty tomb by the women indicates that this account was not an apologetic legend (*Apologetische Legende*). He preferred the empty tomb account in Mark 16 for historical inquiry, claiming that it is in its most original form, whereas Matthew and Luke added dogmatic deviations (Pannenberg 1977a, 102). The empty tomb is vital in Pannenberg's argument, for if the resurrection account were ahistorical, it would not have involved the empty tomb, an event that implies historical time and space (Pannenberg 1994b, 360). Nevertheless, the empty tomb tradition was of secondary importance to the idea that Jesus rose from the dead because it is the appearances that formed the foundation of the proclamation and establishing of the apostles (Pannenberg 1996, 70).

The relationship between the empty tomb tradition and the tradition of appearances is significant to Pannenberg's argument. Additionally, given that the appearances were in Galilee and the empty tomb was in Jerusalem, the whereabouts of the disciples are a vital consideration that sheds light on the relationship between these two events (Pannenberg 1966, 101–2). He argued that the disciples returned independently to Galilee before they knew about an empty grave (102–3). They left Jerusalem after Jesus was taken captive and, therefore, would not have been in Jerusalem when the empty tomb was discovered. He agreed with Grass (1962, 119–21) that the disciples might have only come to know about the empty grave upon their return to Jerusalem after the appearances in Galilee. All these observations, he claimed, point to the probability that these two events occurred independently from each other. Pannenberg (1994a, 328) insisted that "the Galilean appearances tradition alongside the Jerusalem grave tradition provides considerable weight for the verdict of the historical judgment."[34]

Pannenberg (1994a, 319) contended that the relationship between faith and historical experience (*Glaube und Geschichte erfahren*) is especially problematic when it comes to the resurrection of Jesus. Moreover, he argued that conclusions drawn from historical inquiry are never incontestable and should be revisited as discoveries are made (Pannenberg 1974a, 142–43). Nevertheless, the resurrection is so fundamental to his Christology that he suggested that if the resurrection were ever proved to be incorrect, Christianity would no longer exist.[35] However, he was convinced that

---

34. "Galiläa Erscheinungstradition mit der Jerusalemer Grabestradition erhebliches Gewight für die historische Urteilsbildung."

35. For Pannenberg, a historical study must have an openness to the supernatural and miracles, therefore, it can accept the concept of the resurrection (Kärkkäinen 2016, 116).

all the objections to the resurrection were a-historical; therefore, based on his historical inquiry, the probability of the resurrection seemed the most convincing conclusion and the best explanation for the origin of Christianity (143). However, because Jesus was truly human, there will always be historical doubt about his identity and works (144).

In conclusion, Pannenberg (1966, 104) emphasized that among the early Christians, the significance of Jesus' resurrection was bound to the fact that it started the beginning of the universal resurrection and, therefore, the end of the world. Therefore, only because Jesus is the beginning of the end, which leads to the judgment of the Son of Man, could his pre-Easter claim to authority be validated.[36] Because Jesus had been the presence of the end, he had become the one in whom God had appeared. Pannenberg's main point about the resurrection account of Jesus is that it is the basis for the perception of his divinity, as will be discussed below. He was adamant that neither Jesus' pre-Easter claims to authority implicit in his teaching nor his resurrection by itself could be sufficient grounds for faith (Pannenberg 1974a, 139–40; 1966, 108). Instead, the pre-Easter claims were confirmed by the resurrection as being accurate, and the resurrection was given its meaning by Jesus' pre-Easter career (Pannenberg 1975b, 92).

3.3.3 *The Mode of God's Presence in Jesus*

In Pannenberg's Christology, Jesus' relation to God has two key aspects: his unity with God and the presence of God in him. Pannenberg proposed that although not all theories about God's presence in Jesus implied unity with God, the debates throughout church history about Jesus' divinity were necessary to provide a link between God's presence in Jesus and Jesus' unity with God. Pannenberg (1966, 113) argued that the presence of God in Jesus was "*Für uns*" (for us) and that the issue of Jesus' unity with God cannot be settled without this presupposition. Ultimately, for Pannenberg, the most proper understanding of God's presence in Jesus is what he called "Revelational Presence" (114–31).[37] By this, Pannenberg meant that God's presence in Jesus was not only a mere appearance but the essential identity of Jesus with God (*einer Wesensidentität Jesu mit Gott*; 124–25).[38] He insisted

---

36. Although much time had lapsed between the resurrection and the coming end of the world, Pannenberg (1966, 103–4) warned that the church must keep the unity of these two events intact.

37. Alternatively God's presence in Jesus is referred to as the Presence of the Spirit, Substantial Presence, Mediator Christology, and Presence as Appearance.

38. Pannenberg (1968a, 108) wrote, "Offenbarung der Gottheit in ihrer

that the concept of self-revelation sums up appearance and essence.³⁹ His revelational presence view differs from the heretical substantial presence view, according to which God is present in Jesus to such an extent that he is no longer a mere man (Pannenberg 1977a, 121). This is the aspect that Pannenberg attempted to protect.

Pannenberg relied on Barth's (1936a, 362)⁴⁰ understanding of revelation, as primarily God's self-disclosure, which he traced back to Hegel and, more broadly, *Deutschen Idealismus*, or German Idealism (Pannenberg 1982, 7–8).⁴¹ Pannenberg highlighted that although there were differences among theologians of his time regarding the meaning of the term revelation (*Offenbarung*), there was a consensus that revelation is fundamentally the self-revelation of God (*Offenbarung wesentlich Selbstoffenbarung Gotte ist*). He agreed with Barth that God in his eternal essence must be envisioned to be consistent with his historical revelation in Jesus Christ (Pannenberg 1991a, 29).⁴² From this foundation, Pannenberg (1977a, 128–29) made use of three steps to explain the divinity of Jesus from the concept of revelation: (1) Since he considered Jesus' resurrection as the beginning of the end from a Jewish apocalyptic perspective, he argued that this was the actual event of the appearance of the glory of God through revelation. Pannenberg deduced from the Old Testament that the Jewish apocalyptic expectation was that God would be fully revealed at the end of time. YHWH has revealed himself in different ways throughout Israel's history, but at the end of time, the full revelation of his divinity would be perceived. In other words, God revealed himself in and through Jesus only to the extent that this event was the beginning of the end of the world.⁴³ (2) Pannenberg contended that

---

Letztgültigkeit gehört in der Wurzel zusammen mit dem Thema der Inkarnation als der nicht nur fragmentarischen, sondern ganzen und endgültigen Erscheinung Gottes in dieser unserer Wel" (The revelation of divinity in its ultimate validity is fundamentally due to the complete and final appearance of God in this world of ours, along with the theme of the incarnation, rather than as the fragmentarily).

39. Chiavone (2009, 263) clarifies, "Because Christ is God's self-revelation, he is in fact God. Therefore, in the case of Christ, revelatory presence is not set against, but actually includes, the idea of genuine deity."

40. Barth (1936, 362) stated, "Revelation in the Bible means the self-unveiling, imparted to men, of the God who according to His nature cannot be unveiled to man."

41. The Barthian emphasis on God's sovereignty in his revelation is what convinced Pannenberg to become a theologian rather than a philosopher (Pannenberg 1981, 261).

42. Pannenberg (1982, 9) showed that Barth, like Hegel, formulated his doctrine of the Trinity around the concept of revelation (*Offenbarungsbegriffs*).

43. In this way, Pannenberg modified the Hegelian philosophy of history by reference of biblical eschatology (Wildman 2007, 291). MacDonald (2016, 35–36) points out that Pannenberg was more directly influenced by Wilhelm Dilthey's view of history, who held Hegel's Chair in Philosophy at Berlin University. Dilthey's philosophy of

God's self-revelation was limited to a single revelation. The whole concept of self-revelation implies that there can only be a single revelation. By this, he means that if someone has ultimately revealed themselves in a decisive event, they cannot reveal themselves in the same sense in occurrences that differ from this ultimate revelation. Pannenberg's reason for this conclusion is that if this were not true, it would mean that his first revelation was incomplete. Moreover, God cannot disclose himself in another way if he has already disclosed himself entirely in the first event. He suggested that "the claim of a plurality of revelations means discrediting each and every one of them" (Pannenberg 1982, 10).[44] (3) Pannenberg argued that within the concept of God's self-revelation is the idea that the revealed and the Revealer are the same. In other words, God is as much the content of the revelation as the author. He agreed with Barth that "if there is only one God there can only be a single and unique revelation in which God is at the same time author and medium of revelation" (Schwöbel 2005, 130). Moreover, self-revelation is only possible if the medium through which God revealed himself is consistent with himself rather than something unfamiliar to himself. This again demonstrates Pannenberg's commitment to history and his conviction that it is within history that divine revelation occurs (Pannenberg 1981, 262; 1977c, 85).

For Pannenberg, Jesus' identity in essence with God makes sense in the light of the revelatory event, namely, the resurrection. Pannenberg (1994b, 345) contended, "Only the Easter event determines what the meaning was of the pre-Easter history of Jesus and who he was in his relation to God." Pannenberg (1966, 127–29) stated that to speak of a self-revelation of God in the resurrection of Jesus means that Jesus belongs to the essence of God himself. Consequently, if God is revealed through Jesus, then God must only be defined by the Christ event, as Jesus belongs to his essence. Linking God's self-revelation to Jesus' divinity was, according to Pannenberg, one of Barth's (1936a, 358) most significant theological contributions. Pannenberg (1982, 11) agreed with Barth that "the revelatory unity of Jesus with God must therefore be the root of all Christological statements on the deity of Jesus Christ."[45] He pointed out that the concept of revelation has become significant since the *Aufklärung* (Enlightenment), wherein the existence of God was no longer pre-supposed, and the experience of reality has become the ultimate foundation for dialogue (Pannenberg 1966, 129). It has become

---

history placed a greater emphasis on ontology rather than epistemology.

44. "Die Behauptung einer Mehrzahl von Offenbarungen bedeutet die Diskreditierung jeder einzelnen von ihnen."

45. "Die Offenbarungseinheit Jesu mit Gott muß daher die Wurzel aller christologischen Aussagen über die Gottheit Jesu Christi sein."

the only credible basis for speaking about God. Therefore, only if God has revealed himself in the experience of reality can a correct knowledge of God be obtained.

Although the reality of experience is a prerequisite to speaking about God in a modern enlightened era, Pannenberg (1966, 130–31) suggested that the primitive church likewise thought in new ways about YHWH in the light of their experience of Jesus. The early Christians did not consider it self-evident that God was in Jesus; nonetheless, through the course of the historical development of the early church traditions, it became more apparent that the primitive church started to think about God more from the perspective of Jesus' history. Therefore, the early church's Christology was done from a from below perspective, commencing with Jesus' pre-Easter claims to authority which were confirmed through the resurrection.

The only appropriate way to speak about God's presence in Jesus is to speak about it as the revelatory presence of God in Jesus and a revelatory identity of Jesus with God, which includes an identity of essence (Pannenberg 1966, 130–31). Pannenberg contended that the idea of revelation and its implied identity of essence can deal with the concept of the substantial presence of God in Jesus, which other centuries could not address. Moreover, the idea that God's presence was in Jesus solely by his eternal Spirit is inadequate, for then God remains distinct from his appearance in Jesus. This view often led to an adoptionist view of Jesus, whereby either at his birth, baptism, or resurrection, Jesus became the Son of God only by adoption (119).[46] Conversely, Pannenberg believed that the presence of the Spirit is correctly seen when God's revelation is seen in the humanity of Jesus (131).

3.3.4 Jesus' Essential Unity with God

After Pannenberg's discussion concerning the mode of God's presence in Jesus, he continued to explore the scope of God's presence in Jesus' life to bring further clarity regarding the meaning of God's revelatory presence in Jesus and how it includes Jesus' essential unity with God. Pannenberg (1966, 131) indicated that the early church expressed Jesus' unity with God in different ways and that the various titles assigned to him were connected to definite events. However, the earliest Christians considered the resurrection the ultimate defining point of Jesus' relation to God (132). Due to the

---

46. Pannenberg (1966, 118–19) showed that in periods when the doctrine of the Trinity was neglected, adoptionism (*Adoptianismus*) was advocated. In more recent times, the eighteenth and nineteenth centuries, variants of adoptionism have appeared in Kant, Schleiermacher, Ritschl, and von Harnack.

resurrection, they were convinced that Jesus was the future Messiah and Son of Man who would return in judgment in the future (Pannenberg 1984, 125). Pannenberg (1966, 132–33) repeatedly contended that Jesus rejected the title of Messiah on earth but had been exalted to Lord and Messiah through the resurrection. Consequently, the significance of the resurrection can be seen in the two-stage Christology of the early Church.

Pannenberg was adamant that the title "Son of God" was not assigned to the earthly Jesus; instead, it was attributed to him only based on the resurrected and exaltation (Pannenberg 1966, 133). Although, as Son of David, Jesus had been set apart on earth for a future reception of divine sonship, this establishment only occurred at the resurrection (133). On the other hand, Jesus was also called the Son of God because he was already preexistent as the Son of God.[47] In other words, Jesus was installed as the Son of God through the resurrection; however, he was also understood as the preexistent Son of God (*Präexistenz des Gottessohnes*; p. 117). Moreover, Jesus' preexistence formed the basis of the trinitarian concept of God.

Accordingly, Pannenberg (1966, 134) disagreed with Künneth (1965, 114) that Jesus only received his divinity because of his resurrection. Rather, the resurrection confirmed Jesus' pre-Easter claims to authority (Pannenberg 1994b, 45). Consequently, the resurrection event has "retroactive power." Pannenberg (1966, 134) emphasized that Jesus did not become something different than he always had been through the resurrection, but God confirmed his divine Sonship through it.[48] Pannenberg said, "The resurrection truly is the divine confirmation of Jesus' earthly claim to authority, it therefore judges with retroactive power that Jesus as a person has always been the Son of God" (Pannenberg 1968a, 108).[49] Pannenberg (1966, 134–35) insisted Jesus' identity is established retrospectively from the viewpoint of the end of his life, particularly from his resurrection. Since Jesus was confirmed to be one with God through the resurrection, he had always been one with God before that.[50]

47. Rom 1:3; Gal 4:4; Rom 8:3; Phil 2:5.

48. Pannenberg (2003, 240) argued that the resurrection was not only a confirmation of the divinity of the Son, but also the divinity of the Father and his rule over Israel ("Bekräftigung der Gottheit des Vaters . . . und seiner Königsherrschaft").

49. "Vielmehr bedeutet die Auferstehung ja die göttliche Bestätigung des irdischen Vollmachtsanspruches Jesu; sie entscheidet also mit rückwirkender Kraft, daß Jesus als Person immer schon 'Sohn Gottes' gewesen ist."

50. Pannenberg (1966, 376–78) proposed that the resurrection not only confirmed the claims of authority Jesus made, but also his sinlessness. He stated that the concept of Jesus' sinlessness could not be affirmed through investigating the ambiguous conduct of Jesus, but rather through the resurrection God's judgement of Jesus is pronounced as sinless.

Pannenberg (1966, 138–40) was also critical of the idea that Jesus' unity with God occurred at his baptism, as argued by Seeberg. Seeberg (1924, 159) referred to the baptism of Jesus as "*es ist der Moment der Menschwerdung*" (it is the moment of incarnation). Pannenberg emphasized that even if Jesus received the eschatological Spirit at his baptism, it is incorrect to assign that experience as his moment of incarnation. Rather, at most, what occurred at Jesus' baptism was a prophetic consecration and perhaps where he received a spiritual self-awareness which led to his claims to authority (Pannenberg 1966, 138–40). Pannenberg remained adamant that God is revealed in Jesus only based on his resurrection. He agreed with Althaus (1962, 440) that the resurrection of Jesus establishes retroactively (*so gild von der Auferweckung her rückwirkend*) that he should not be separated from God at any moment in time.[51] It is only because of the resurrection of Jesus that the early Christians even included the baptism account as part of their tradition (Pannenberg 1966, 137). Significantly, this retrospective significance (*Rückwirkenden bedeutung*) of the resurrection stretches back further than Jesus' baptism account to the very origin of his earthly life (139–40).

Surprisingly, Pannenberg (1972, 71–77) referred to Jesus' virgin birth as the "legend of his virgin birth." Macleod (2000, 21) points out that for Luke and Matthew, the virgin birth accounts are the symbols of a Christology from above, but Pannenberg did not share this view. In contrast to the baptism tradition, Pannenberg claimed that the virgin birth legend began solely in the development of traditions through history (Pannenberg 1994b, 315–19). He contended that the virgin birth was unfamiliar to John and Paul and most likely invented by later theologians from the Hellenistic Jewish community who sought to elevate the person of Christ above other Old Testament characters. Consequently, Luke and Matthew both included the virgin birth account to make a theological point (Luke 1:26–38, Matt 1:18–25; Pannenberg 1966, 141–42). Furthermore, the virgin birth legend was formed to preserve the idea of the incarnation against Gnostics. However, Pannenberg felt that the incarnation is better preserved through normal birth (145–46). Pannenberg (1973, 23) highlighted that early Christianity was more prone to mythology than ancient Judaism because of its strict monotheism. However, for Paul, there is a coherence between Jesus' public instantiation of his sonship through the resurrection and his preexistence as the eternal Son of God that is not upheld in the virgin birth account (Pannenberg 1966, 142).

---

51. Althaus (1962, 440) stated that, "Jesus war das, was er ist, ehe er darum wußte" (Jesus was what he is before he knew about it).

Barth was praised for his connection between the divinity of Jesus and the concept of revelation; however, when it comes to Barth's view on the virgin birth of Jesus, Pannenberg remained highly skeptical. He critiqued Barth's (1936b, 172–202) argument that there is perfect unity between the incarnation of Jesus and the "sign" that points towards it, namely, the virgin birth of Jesus (Pannenberg 1966, 142–43). Pannenberg spurned Barth's attempt at placing the virgin birth on the same footing as the resurrection (Macleod 2000, 21). In contrast, he insisted that the virgin birth legend does not point to the incarnation but contradicts it (Pannenberg 1972, 63). In other words, the virgin birth implied that God created his Son in Mary, which meant that he could not have been his Son in pre-existence (76).[52]

Pannenberg (1966, 150) believed that "the unity of Jesus with God in the revelatory event of his resurrection from the dead, as we saw, can only be understood as his unity with God's eternal essence, so that the eternal divinity of God cannot be thought of apart from in relation to Jesus of Nazareth."[53] Pannenberg viewed God as being transcendent to his creation, yet at the same time immanent within the space-time universe (Pannenberg 2005, 106). He would have agreed with Cilliers (2016, 15–17) that God is the "cosmic Migrant" who moves through time and space. God has always been separate from his creation, but in the incarnation, he became a physical component of the world through the person Jesus of Nazareth (Pannenberg 2005, 101). It is through Jesus that the eternal Father is present in history (Pannenberg 2000, 12). Therefore, Pannenberg (1977b, 83) believed God is not detachable from history (*Gottes nicht schlechthin von Geschichte ablösbar*). He highlighted that God's revelation through Jesus not only provides the language for trinitarian doctrine but also formulates the relationship between God and history in general (86). Jesus' essential unity with God compels us to consider his eternality and, therefore, his preexistence.[54] He contended that since the Father was there before the coming of Jesus,

---

52. Even though Pannenberg (1997, 212–13; 1970, 4–5) opposed the Reformers' idea of a literal inspiration and infallibility of the Scriptures, and though he viewed the virgin birth as myth, he did affirm the inspiration of the Scriptures in the sense that the apostolic gospel was impregnated by the Spirit of God.

53. "Die Einheit Jesu mit Gott im Offenbarungsgeschehen seiner Auferweckung von den Toten läßt sich, wie wir sahen, nur als Einheit Jesu mit dem ewigen Wesen Gottes verstehen, so daß die ewige Gottheit Gottes nicht anders gedacht werden kann als in bezug auf Jesus von Nazareth."

54. For Pannenberg (1975a, 164) a significant issue with a Christology from above is that "Sie bringt es nicht dazu, die historische Gestalt Jesu von Nazareth aus der Gottheit Gottes selbst als seine Offenbarung zu denken" (It does not lead to thinking of the historical figure of Jesus of Nazareth from the divinity of God himself as his revelation).

the Son must also have been there before Jesus; otherwise, the Son and the Father cannot be of one essence (Pannenberg 2000, 12).

Pannenberg (1966, 150) showed that the preexistence of the Son was a critical part of Christology for Paul.[55] This can be observed from his descend-ascend schema. In other words, Jesus, as the Redeemer, came down from heaven, accomplished humanity's salvation, and then returned to heaven. Pannenberg indicated that although this schema had some resemblance to other ideas in the history of religions, such as the Hellenistic concept of gods occasionally being active in the world, it is deeply embedded in the Jewish tradition (151). According to certain Jewish traditions, the Son of Man and Messiah was occasionally thought of as one that was preexistent, who would descend from heaven.[56] Therefore, Jesus' preexistence was primarily connected to the idea of the Son of God being "sent" to earth.[57] The Son of God designation was given to Jesus after the resurrection as he was identified as the one who would come again in messianic lordship (152). Subsequently, it was used to describe Jesus' lordship in heaven and his entire earthly activity from his birth. Pannenberg explained that it was due to the revelatory character of the resurrection that Jesus was thought of as belonging to the sphere of God (152–53). Consequently, because his claims to authority were confirmed through the resurrection and, therefore, he was one with God, his divinity meant that he was one with God even before his birth. If God has revealed himself in Jesus, then his Sonship belongs to eternity. Therefore, Jesus cannot be separated from God's essence if Jesus is God's self-revelation (158–59). Nevertheless, Pannenberg pointed out that Jesus did distinguish himself from God the Father, for if this is not the case, then Jesus would not be the one revelation of God in person.

Pannenberg (1966, 152) suggested that due to Jesus' oneness with God and because he was seen as God's representative in creation, we can no longer think of God in his eternal divinity without Jesus. Jesus' preexistence was developed from the resurrection and the accompanying idea that he was God's Son, the coming Messiah (153). Also, for the New Testament writers, referring to Jesus as the "Son" was a way of designating his relation to the Father, which was one of obedience and mission (159). It was used figuratively; in Romans 8:3, Galatians 4:4, John 3:17, and 1 John 4:9. The divine Logos, the eternal Son of God, became incarnate according to the

---

55. Gal 4:4; Rom 8:3; Phil 2:6–11.

56. Enoch 39:6; 40:5; 48:3–6; 62:7; 4 Ezra 13:26, 52; Prov 8:22; Sirach 24:3; Enoch 42:1–3.

57. Pannenberg (1966, 152) pointed out that the concepts of Jesus as the Logos and the image of God contributed to the idea of his pre-existence but was not the primary cause.

preordained plan of the Trinity to fulfill the "mission" of the Father (Pannenberg 2000, 12–13).⁵⁸ Therefore, Pannenberg (1975a, 159) argued that if knowledge about God can be obtained without Christology, then one must ask whether Christology has not become irrelevant. However, he believed that Christology informs what we know about God because Jesus is the one revelation of God in person.

3.3.5 Conclusion

In addressing how Jesus related to the God of Israel, Pannenberg commenced his argument by investigating the resurrection. For him, the pre-Easter claims to authority of Jesus are not a sufficient basis for faith in his divinity; instead, the resurrection formed the basis for any faith in the deity of Christ. Pannenberg was adamant that through the resurrection, God validated the pre-Easter claims of Jesus. Consequently, he proposed that Jesus' relation to God must be expressed as God's self-revelation and, therefore, that Jesus was part of the essence of God himself. Moreover, the only appropriate way to speak about God's presence in Jesus is as revelatory presence. Therefore, the identity of Jesus is established retrospectively from the end of his life, namely, through the resurrection. Pannenberg noted that this unity with God, or incarnation, was not something that occurred at Jesus' baptism but took place right at the origin of his earthly life. In other words, Jesus did not become what he not already was. Although he considered the virgin birth of Jesus to be a myth, he argued that the essential unity with God points to the eternality of Christ. For Pannenberg, then, Jesus' divinity is found in his revelational unity with God, which makes it possible for him to be one in essence yet distinct from God as Father.

3.4 The Man Jesus of Nazareth

3.4.1 Introduction

When it came to the humanity of Jesus, the historical myths of Gnosticism, which claimed that Jesus was merely the appearance of a man, or Monophysitism, which showed that Jesus was entirely permeated by divine immortality, were almost unthinkable for Pannenberg (1966, 193). He insisted that

---

58. Pannenberg (1991a:28–29) showed that critics who argue against the concept of the Trinity, by claiming that it is a Hellenization of Christianity, used Logos Christology and incarnation language in the argument. Nevertheless, he maintained that language to a certain degree throughout his Christology.

all statements about Jesus, whether inside or outside the church, presuppose his humanity. Therefore, the only question to investigate was how Jesus is distinct from other people (*die historische Besonderheit und Individualität Jesu*; 193). Furthermore, the only reason why the uniqueness of Jesus will matter is if it has universal significance, which would only be the case if it has saving significance (*Heilsbedeutung*). Pannenberg believed the saving significance stems from Jesus' particular relation to God (194). Therefore, he approached the question of Jesus' universal significance from the perspective that Jesus is the revelation of God. He suggested, "As the revelation of God, Jesus is also the revelation of the human essence and the destiny of mankind" (195).[59]

3.4.2 *The Ultimate Man*

In Jesus, the ultimate destiny of humanity, namely, our destiny to be raised from the dead, had been fulfilled (Pannenberg 1966, 195–96). This destiny is not only for the individual but extends to humanity because Jesus is the new Adam who has fulfilled this destiny of all humankind (Kärkkäinen 2016, 118). This life of resurrection, which is the destiny of humanity (*die Bestimmung des Menschen*), has been fulfilled by Jesus (Pannenberg 1974a, 147; 1978a, 110; 1973, 68). Therefore, the revelation of God in Jesus and the revelation of humanity's destiny are closely related. Hence, Pannenberg (1966, 196) claimed that one must not separate the revelation of God in Jesus and the revelation of salvation for men.

The concept of salvation is essential in Pannenberg's reasoning. He claimed that salvation is a concept that refers to the fulfillment of the ultimate human destiny for which human beings long. Moreover, it is an ultimate destiny that can never be obtained during earthly existence. People are driven by a focus on the future but are also reminded of the shortcomings of their present experience over their preferred future (Pannenberg 1978a, 104). Therefore, salvation is obtained when a man is united in his present with his past and future, which can only come after the resurrection from the dead (Pannenberg 1966, 197).

Moreover, Pannenberg (1966, 197) contended that the essence of man, which must not be sought in what is already experienced by man but must still come to him from his future, is revealed through Jesus in two ways, namely, through Jesus' deeds and his fate. Through his deeds, Jesus promised community with himself and, therefore, eschatological salvation, and

---

59. "Als Offenbarung Gottes ist Jesus zugleich die Offenbarung des menschlichen Wesens, der Bestimmung des Menschen."

through his fate, humanity's destiny has been revealed by his resurrection. Second, the essence of man, what it means to be fully human, consists of openness for God (197). Pannenberg sought to show that belief in God is not a strange idea to the structure of a human being (Kärkkäinen 2016, 117). He pointed out that the anthropology of his day, what he called *Weltoffenheit* (cosmopolitanism), argued that man has an openness to the world and beyond (Pannenberg 1976b, 9–10). This, in his view, is because "the family tree of modern anthropology points back towards Christian theology" (12).[60] Although cosmopolitanism did not refer to God directly, Pannenberg proposed that man's openness to the world and beyond implied man's openness to God (13). And this openness to God is part of humanity's essence.[61] The concept of "an openness for God" plays an important role in his understanding of Jesus' vocation. Pannenberg proposed that Jesus' office was to call people into the kingdom of God and, therefore, he could impart salvation to them, which consisted of an "openness for God." Pannenberg (1966, 198) preferred to refer to Jesus' office rather than his vocation because he felt it emphasized Jesus' commissioning and service to the Father rather than giving the idea that he fulfilled a free-choice vocation. He showed that the office by which Jesus imparted salvation underwent a development process consisting of three periods (199). The first period consisted of his dedication to the office given to him by God. Next, he was obedient in accepting his fate and, lastly, his resurrection, by which he glorified God. Pannenberg claimed that Jesus is humanity's representative in all three areas before God, through which he brought man's destiny to fulfillment in his person (202).

Pannenberg (1966, 202–4) highlighted that through various periods in the church's life, the concept of Jesus as man's representative had been presented in many ways. These different descriptions of how Jesus is man's representative led him to suspicion that theologians have projected various anthropologies upon Jesus. In other words, as pointed out by Schweitzer (2016, loc. 7352), scholars have projected their ideal images of man upon the historical figure Jesus of Nazareth. However, Pannenberg (1966, 205–9) contended that this application of reinterpreted traditional anthropology upon the figure of Jesus is an age-old phenomenon and is not to be negatively perceived. He showed that Paul used the Genesis understanding of man, the old Adam, to argue that the resurrected Jesus, through the new life that appeared in him and his obedience, is the "Last Adam."

60. "Der Stammbaum der modernen Anthropologie weist zurück auf die christliche Theologie."
61. The idea of eternal value of humanity in cosmopolitanism was largely due to the contribution of Christianity (Pannenberg 1977c, 14).

Similarly, the New Testament's use of the image of God and John's concept of the Logos reveal the same application of reinterpreted traditional anthropology upon Jesus. Similarly, Luther's image of humanity in the doctrine of justification by faith, Schleiermacher's idea that full consciousness of God is what characterizes full humanity, as well as the more modern Christologies that argues that to be truly human means that one has an openness to God and the future or is living in loving dedication towards one's neighbor, all have their roots in biblical tradition (Pannenberg 1966, 207–8). He criticized Schleiermacher's concept as too abstract, contending that too little information can be obtained about God in human existence (208).

Pannenberg (1966, 208) argued that our understanding of humanity is profoundly shaped by biblical thought (*Biblischen Denkens*), especially by the works and words of Jesus. Therefore, it is appropriate to highlight the fundamental elements of what we understand about humanity in Jesus' behavior. Based on this, Pannenberg concluded that the ideal of the truly human should not be projected upon Jesus at random without any historical reality, as perhaps Schweitzer would have argued (209). He believed that the church is obligated to highlight the universal significance of his human individuality, with the caveat that all theological statements about the man Jesus be grounded in the earliest traditions about Jesus. In other words, the historical reality of Jesus must be interpreted rather than replaced by anthropological conceptions derived from elsewhere.[62]

3.4.3 The Office of Jesus

The Protestant Christology of the seventeenth century usually consisted of the discussion of three things; the two natures of Christ and how they relate to each other, the office of Jesus, which consisted of prophet, priest, and king, and the two states of Christ, that is, his humiliation and exaltation (Pannenberg 1966, 214). However, since Schleiermacher, the separation between Jesus' person and work was questioned. In addition, Pannenberg (1966, 214–15), along with other theologians of his time, such as Ritschl (1902, 387,452) and Althaus (1962, 462), affirmed that the office and person of Jesus Christ belong closely together. For Pannenberg, both Jesus'

---

62. An example Pannenberg (1966, 209) provided that illustrated how an anthropological conception was projected onto Jesus that was not in conformity to what has been revealed about him historically is Anselm's concept that Jesus accomplished some ethical tasks before God.

historical works or office, which was the commissioning he believed himself to stand under, and his crucifixion and resurrection must be considered.

Pannenberg provided a lengthy discussion of the Reformed concept of the threefold office of Christ (*Munus Triplex*), which was the framework used to discuss the office or works of Jesus.[63] Pannenberg (1966, 218) saw particular strengths in this concept, such as providing a systematic framework (*Systematische Zusammenfassung*) to organize an extensive scope of Christological material. Therefore, scholars such as Welker (2004, 213) and Wainwright (1997, 109) show that the *munus triplex* has enjoyed broad ecumenical consensus. However, Pannenberg also had several severe criticisms of this approach. First, Pannenberg (1966, 218–21) criticized the theological justification that because Jesus is called the Christ, in other words, since he was given the title of "Anointed One," he fulfilled all three offices believed to have received special anointings in the Old Testament. Second, Pannenberg insisted that the functions the prophet, king, and priest fulfilled in the Old Testament did not fit Jesus' work (221–30). For instance, the office of the prophet, Calvin (1960, loc. 12886), quoting from John 4:25, showed that even the Samaritans, who were not considered pure Israelites, expected that the Messiah would make the way of salvation clear. Therefore, the Messiah was to fulfill this prophetic office. However, Pannenberg argued that the entirety of Jesus' activity and his self-understanding did not fit either the profile of a prophet in the ancient Israel sense or the contemporary Jewish expectation (Pannenberg 1966, 221). Likewise, Jesus did not fit the royal function as he never sought nor practiced the kingly office (223–25). Calvin (1960, loc. 12998) stated that because the Spirit chose Christ and rested upon him, it is to him to which believers must turn and from whom they may partake in heavenly riches. However, Pannenberg claimed that the pre-Easter Jesus never took such an office for himself.

With regards to the priestly office, Calvin (1960, loc. 13035) stated that under the law, the priests themselves required blood to enter the sanctuary, as they had sins that needed to be expiated before they could stand as an advocate between God and the people of God. But this was not the case with Christ because he was the spotless lamb. The priestly office, therefore, belongs to him, for by his very own blood he blotted out our guilt and made propitiation for our sins (Calvin 1960, loc. 13035). Of the three offices, this is the one that Pannenberg critiqued most severely. Pannenberg (1966, 225)

---

63. Pannenberg (1966, 218–19) pointed out that the origin of this structure originated from Andreas Osiander and not from Luther or Calvin as is often thought, which Jonker (1977, 49) and Wainwright (1997, 99) affirm. Osiander suggested that because Jesus was the "anointed one," all three of the anointed offices in the Old Testament, namely, the prophets, kings, and priests, belonged to him (Gussmann 1911, 302).

questioned both the New Testament grounds for Jesus' priestly office, namely, his designation as High Priest and his atoning sacrifice on the cross. He believed that the Father is better suited for the priestly office as it relates to Jesus' sacrifice (226). For it was the Father who fulfilled the priestly office by presenting his only Son's sacrifice.[64] Furthermore, somewhat contentiously, Pannenberg claimed that the Synoptic Gospels projected the messianic office of the resurrected Christ back onto the historical Jesus, which made his death on the cross appear thought out and premeditated (*Planmäßig bedachten und vorausgesehenen*; p. 226).

The earthly Jesus only partly fits one of these three offices, namely the prophetic office, because in Protestant dogmatics, Jesus Christ, the God-man, was the bearer of these offices rather than the historical man Jesus (Pannenberg 1966, 227).[65] In contrast to this approach, Pannenberg argued that Jesus appeared at the beginning as a human who knew himself to be under a mission, an office, an assignment from Israel's God, and not as a God-man (*Gottmensch*; p. 229). This office of Jesus was to call humanity into the kingdom of God (218). Rather than presuppose Jesus' divinity in the discussion of his office, Pannenberg preferred to presuppose Jesus as merely a man with an assignment from God.

Jesus proclaimed the imminent kingdom of God just like John the Baptist (Pannenberg 1966, 232). For Pannenberg, there was no doubt that Jesus' prediction about the end of the world was wrong. The lordship of God did not begin in his generation nor the generation of his followers as announced. Nevertheless, Pannenberg insisted that Jesus' imminent expectation was fulfilled differently (232–33). He argued, "It was fulfilled by himself, insofar as the eschatological reality of the resurrection from the dead appeared in Jesus himself." Likewise, Pannenberg (1978a, 111) contended that "the resurrection of Jesus is therefore the completion of his message of the kingdom." However, although Jesus' resurrection justified this imminent expectation, it was not fulfilled universally but re-established the eschatological expectation of the resurrection from the dead.

Pannenberg (1966, 232–33) contended that the imminent expectation of the kingdom of God, fulfilled through Jesus' resurrection, provides one of the most significant understandings of humanity ever discovered. Jesus' announcement of the imminent kingdom of God meant that the lordship of God was near, which summoned humanity out of their securities and exposed the insufficiencies of this world to fulfill human destiny. The message

---

64. Rom 4:25; 5:8–9; 2 Cor 5:21.

65. In the time of Luther and Calvin the concept of the God-man occupied the intellectual world whereas in Pannenberg's time it was regarded a mythological concept (Pannenberg 1966, 228).

of the nearness of God's lordship revealed the destiny of humanity, which is never fulfilled in this life (233). Pannenberg (1984, 121) emphasized that there can be no human self-understanding without eschatology. He argued that Jesus' proclamation gave humanity an openness to God (*Offenheit für Gott*) and God's future by creating an expectation of a future-transformed world and the resurrection from the dead, which radically reduced the significance of worldly commitments (Pannenberg 1966, 234). The expectation Jesus created was confirmed through his resurrection, by which the divine and human are already reconciled in the person of Jesus Christ (Pannenberg 1984, 123). Jesus Christ is thus the future of humankind (*Jesus Christus die Zukunft des Menschen*; Pannenberg 1978a, 105). Pannenberg held, "What occurred through Jesus Christ is not only for the Christians and their future significance, but rather for the future of humanity generally" (105).[66]

Unlike John the Baptist, Pannenberg (1966, 234) thought that Jesus' message not only called men to repentance for future salvation but also granted this eschatological salvation. Pannenberg argued that the proclaimed immanence of the kingdom of God was salvation for those who took notice of it. In other words, those who looked to God's future rather than to themselves and their possessions already experienced salvation. Therefore, salvation, which is the fulfilled destiny of humanity and which consists of openness to God, is already present in the message of Jesus (234). Pannenberg explained that Jesus' healing ministry fits the understanding of the imminent kingdom of God as the nearness of God because it likewise emphasized the present effectiveness of this salvation (234–35). Humanity, therefore, needed to come to Jesus and seek communion with him since he is the revelation of the future salvation (*Heilszukunft*) and can promise salvation directly (Pannenberg 1978a, 110).

Consequently, Pannenberg (1966, 239) contended that anyone who heard and believed Jesus' message about the nearness of the kingdom of God, thereby coming into a right and humanly natural relation to God, and anyone who received the forgiveness of sins would be willing to live for the fulfillment of God's rule. This forgiveness of sins and openness to God and his future also demanded certain conduct toward others. Pannenberg saw a close relationship between the love for God, forgiveness, and the love for neighbors. He suggested that Jesus' call to love one's neighbor and thereby create community also reveals the essence of humanity, namely, its destiny in community (240–41). Pannenberg (1976b, 59) stated, "*Die Menschen suchen Gemeinschaft*" (People seek community). Pannenberg (1966, 240)

---

66. "Was durch Jesus Christus geschehen ist, das ist also night nur für die Christen und ihre Zukunft bedeutsam, sondern für die Zukunft der Menschheit überhaupt."

argued that the message that Jesus proclaimed, which bestowed the promise of salvation and the forgiveness of sins, empowered the hearer to love his neighbor. In this, the universal significance of Christ's activities became apparent because part of the essence and destiny of humanity is to strive for community, which Jesus made possible through his message of salvation and the forgiveness of sins (240–41).

Pannenberg (1966, 246), along with Von Campenhausen (1960, 180), criticized Jaspers' (1957, 223) argument that because Jesus preached the imminent kingdom of God, "there can no longer be any interest for construction in the world." In other words, the early church was only focused on the world to come, and the church's subsequent engagement with the world on a political, economic, and social level was a compromise to Jesus' message. In contrast to Jaspers, Pannenberg and Von Campenhausen insisted that Jesus, his message, and his disciples did not intentionally evade the issue of public responsibility and civil participation (*Bürgerlich-politisches*) but were not confronted with it directly. He pointed out that Jesus' message was not an expression of private devotion. Still, he argued that "with his announcement of the coming kingdom of God he stood in the tradition of the political expectations of the Jewish nation" (Pannenberg 1978b, 23).[67] However, the church's circumstances changed as it was confronted with different situations to which it needed to respond. Pannenberg (1966, 246) was adamant that the church does not overlook the differences between the present and Jesus' situation. In other words, one needs to consider principles rather than interpreting and applying Jesus' story literally today.[68] Nevertheless, Pannenberg insisted that we can live in continuity with Jesus' imminent expectation, as has been fulfilled by Jesus' resurrection from the dead, by maintaining the hope and expectation of the universal resurrection (249).

3.4.4 The Meaning of Jesus' Death

Pannenberg also addressed the fate of Jesus, which according to him, includes both the crucifixion and resurrection of Jesus. Contrary to Jesus' activity, Pannenberg (1966, 251) demonstrated that Jesus' fate was something that happened to him rather than something that he actively did. However, Pannenberg believed that although critical scholars since Wrede

---

67. "Mit seiner Verkündigung des kommenden Gottesreiches stand er in der Tradition der politischen Erwartungen des jüdischen Volkes."

68. For Pannenberg (1986, 80–81), the only way that Christianity could be connected to politics is if it contained a theocratic element ("theokratische Element") and a Christian social justice theory ("eine christliche Theorie sozialer Gerechtigkeit").

have denied that the passion predictions in the gospels' accounts belonged to Jesus, he did not think that Jesus' crucifixion came as a surprise to him (251–52). Pannenberg (1988, 167; 1969, 133) argued that Jesus' suffering and death were not his primary mission but the consequence of his primary vocation, namely, to proclaim the imminent kingdom of God. To understand Jesus' crucifixion, Pannenberg maintained that his previous activities need to be considered.

Pannenberg (1988, 167) pointed out that this is where nineteenth-century historical Jesus scholars such as Schleiermacher and Ritschl went wrong in that they never considered the link between Jesus' fate and the ambiguity of his activities. Although Jesus never claimed messianic titles, Pannenberg emphasized that by proclaiming that the kingdom of God had arrived in his teaching and actions, Jesus was making the implicit claim that he was the mediator of the presence of God (167). Jesus not only spoke about the kingdom of God in the sense that John the Baptist had, but he also claimed that through his message it became a present reality in the lives of those who accepted it. Thereby, he is the mediator of God's presence. Pannenberg (1991a, 30) highlighted that the early church's incarnational language proceeded from the idea that Jesus was the presence of the kingdom of God.[69] Other ambiguous actions included Jesus' claim to authority, for example, the sermon on the mount, the forgiving of sins, the sayings against the temple, and his temple actions which led to the Jewish authorities' rightful accusation that Jesus made himself equal with God (Pannenberg 1966, 257–58).[70] Pannenberg suggested that Jesus' statement that blessed are those who do not take offense at him indicates that he was aware of the ambiguity around his career (Pannenberg 1988, 168). These accusations against Jesus were not raised due to his explicit claims to be the Messiah or the Son of God but because of different incidents.

The concept that Jesus was making himself equal with God through his activities was considered blasphemous, hence the actions taken against Jesus (Pannenberg 1966, 258). Pannenberg showed that the charges of blasphemy (*Gotteslästerung*) against Jesus were not without legitimate grounds since his activities clashed with the Jewish traditions head-on (259). Jesus' interpretation and explanation of the law, the promise of salvation, and the forgiveness of sins were an outgrowth of Jewish tradition. Moreover, Jesus' activities had called into question the traditional authority of the law;

---

69. Pannenberg (1991a, 29–30) used this idea to argue for the doctrine of the Trinity. Although many scholars contended that Jesus never claimed himself to be God, Pannenberg showed that although he did not explicitly say it, his career implicitly made this claim in various ways.

70. Matt 5:21–22; 27–28; 31–32; Matt 9:1–8; 2:5; Matt 12:5–6; 23:16–35; 21:12–13.

therefore, it was not some troublesome individuals who condemned Jesus but the Jewish law (260–61). Pannenberg argued that when Jesus' sinlessness and purity are overemphasized, his opponents are viewed as only evil and not rightly as Jews who were faithful to their Jewish traditions (260–61). Therefore, Pannenberg agreed with Moltmann (2015, 182,197) that Jesus was crucified as a blasphemer and a rebel.

When it comes to the interpretation of Jesus' crucifixion, Pannenberg (1966, 252) claimed that it must be seen through the light of the resurrection because the resurrection of Jesus was an event that is easier to interpret than the meaning of the cross. When the meaning of Jesus' death is approached from the perspective of the resurrection, Pannenberg pointed out, "it revealed that he died a righteous man, not as a blasphemer" (266).[71] Moltmann (2015) considered "the cross of Christ as the foundation and criticism of Christian theology," however, Pannenberg considered the resurrection to fulfill that role.[72] For Pannenberg, the meaning of the cross is correctly deduced from the perspective of the resurrection. From this angle, God, whom Jesus had allegedly blasphemed, confirmed that he had not done so (Pannenberg 1974a, 140; 1975b, 92) through the resurrection, which means that Jesus' pre-Easter claims, implicit in his teachings and actions, were confirmed by God (Pannenberg 1988, 170). Therefore, his accusers deserved the punishment he endured, and, in that sense, he bore their penalty. Pannenberg (1966, 266) highlighted that the Jewish leaders were the real blasphemers because they condemned the one whom God legitimized and therefore deserved death. But it was not only their punishment that Jesus took upon himself but that of the entire Jewish nation (267). Pannenberg contended that the intention of the Jewish law was decisive for Jesus' rejection; therefore, any law-abiding Jew would have acted the same as their Jewish leaders. Hence, anyone who lived under the law was a blasphemer; as a result, "the death penalty borne by Jesus is, therefore, that of the whole people" (267).[73]

However, because Pannenberg was concerned about the universality of Jesus' fate, as this is closely related to the divinity of Jesus, he moved beyond Israel to investigate the universal meaning of Jesus' death. Pannenberg (1966, 267) proposed that Jesus' death only has vicarious significance if all men can be shown to be blasphemers by Jesus' cross. However, this idea

71. "Von der Auferweckung Jesu her ist offenbar, daß er als ein Gerechter starb, nicht als ein Gotteslästerer."

72. This difference is an interesting development considering that Pannenberg and Moltmann were colleagues at the same institution, *Kirchliche Hochschule* in Wuppertal (Schwöbel 2005, 129).

73. "Die Todesstrafe, die Jesus getragen hat, ist mithin die dem ganzen Volke."

cannot be justified merely by the argument that the Romans who crucified Jesus or Pilate, who sentenced him to death, represent the Gentiles (267). Moreover, the universal significance of Jesus' vicarious death cannot be deduced from Jesus' conflict with political powers (268). Pannenberg emphasized that Jesus' conflict with the political powers of Rome only occurred superficially in his trial and was characterized by various misunderstandings (267–68).

For Pannenberg (1966, 269), the "universal anthropological presupposition" (*Allgemeine anthropologische Voraussetzung*) under which the vicarious significance of Jesus' death extends beyond the Jews to all of humanity is the idea of human mortality as the consequence of sin. He referred to Paul to build his argument, according to whom Jesus' death associates with human death in general, which is a result of their sins.[74] Pauline soteriology is based on the universality of sin (Pannenberg 1988, 170). Paul links the Jewish law with the relation between sin and death (Rom 5:13, 7:8), which is relevant for all humanity, thereby relating Jesus' fate to all humankind (Pannenberg 1966, 269). Additionally, the relationship between sin and death and the connection between Jewish law and universal anthropological conditions still retain their validity today (269–70). Due to the universality of the Jewish law, which described the relationship between sin and its consequences which are still experienced universally, Pannenberg contended that the Jewish people represented humanity in general when they rejected Jesus as a blasphemer (270).

Pannenberg (1966, 268) indicated that only if it can be shown that Jesus experienced the abandonment of God (*Gottverlassenheit*) in death, and has removed that sense of abandonment, then his death was for all humankind. He believed that by dying as a blasphemer, which all have incurred, Jesus died for us and our sins (270). However, since humanity still experiences death today, he was concerned about the vicarious significance of Jesus' death. Pannenberg agreed with Moltmann (2015, 212–14) that Jesus died as one who was excluded and expelled from the community with God, whose nearness he proclaimed. Because Jesus did, nobody else has to die in complete rejection as Jesus did. Everyone who believes in Jesus dies but dies with the hope of the resurrection from the dead, which already appeared in Jesus.[75] Pannenberg (1978a, 112) said, "Whoever dies with Christ will also be resurrected with him." [76] Although for Pannenberg, resurrection as an

74. 2 Cor 5:14; Rom 5:6, 12; 6:10, 23.

75. Pannenberg (1995, 71) insisted that no other Christian doctrine confronts the spirit of secularism *(dem Geist des Säkularismus)* more squarely than Christian eschatology.

76. Marheineke (1827, 398) pointed out that Jesus was not humanity's representative

entrance into the new life of God means more than just the consummation of our early lives, it signifies the glorification and transformation of our lives in the light of the glory of God (Pannenberg 1974b, 177).[77]

Although certain scholars such as Ritschl (1902, 268–69), in line with the concerns of the Enlightenment, have questioned the concept of substitution as it relates to the sphere of personal life, Pannenberg (1966, 272–74) argued that this was mainly because of modern thought rather than Jewish understanding. The two concepts that he identified which differ between modern thought and that of ancient Israel are the concept of guilt and punishment and that of individuals and society. Modern thinkers usually linked reward or punishment as the result of implemented ideal norms, whereas in ancient Israel, adversity was understood as something already built into the evil deed (272). According to this Jewish line of thought, death was built into the essence of sin. Therefore, when Paul states that Jesus has been made to be our sin, it means that he has carried the consequence of the misfortune of those sins.

Pannenberg argued that modern thinkers must also consider the role of the individual in society in the Israelite understanding of guilt and expiation, wherein the reward or guilt of an individual has consequences for his entire society (Pannenberg 1966, 272). Pannenberg (1974b, 168) showed that "the life of the individual in Israel did not have a contrary meaning independent to the life of the nation." Pulling these two concepts together, he explained that the evil deeds of men, along with the misfortune they carried, had an impact on the individual and the entire society (Pannenberg 1966, 273). In other words, the evil deed had a type of independence from the doer. Moreover, he stated, "the transferability of guilt is the fundamental thought of the Israelite institution of the sin offering."[78] This is what Pannenberg meant by the concept of substitution, and it is this understanding, he insisted, that formed the foundation of the Israelite notion of expiation.

Ultimately, Pannenberg (1988, 171) viewed the vicarious death of Jesus as an "inclusive substitution," whereby he entered our sinful condition and shared our death in such a way as to change its significance for all humanity. This Jesus did by experiencing a moment of "exclusiveness" on the cross, which is why he cried out, "My God, my God, why have you forsaken me."[79]

---

from the outside ("Denn stellvertreter der menschheit ist er nicht"), but as one who represented all of humanity in himself as one.

77. "Verherrlichung, Verwandlung dieses unseres Lebens im Lichte der Herrlichkeit Gottes."

78. "Die übertragbarkeit der Schuld ist der Grundgedanke der Israelitischen Institution des Sündopfers."

79. Mark 15:34.

But Pannenberg (1974b, 178) argued that God remained in fellowship with Jesus on the cross, and it was this sustained connection that broke the power of death to separate men from God. He stated, "Through the death of Jesus the power of death to separate from God is removed." Therefore, although men still die, they do not have to do so in separation from God. Thereby, in the death of Jesus, the love of God is revealed (*im Tode Jesu die Liebe Gottes zur Welt offenbar*; p. 178).

3.4.5 Conclusion

For Pannenberg, the revelation of God in Jesus and humanity's destiny are closely related. Pannenberg contended that through the resurrection, we can conclude that Jesus is one in essence with God, but also that through the resurrection, Jesus had fulfilled the destiny of humanity, namely, to be raised from the dead. This life of resurrection, which is the destiny of humanity, has been fulfilled by Jesus both in his career and his death and resurrection. Therefore, one must consider both his office and fate together. He fundamentally disagreed with the *"munus triplex"* understanding of Jesus' office, for he believed it assigned the offices of king, prophet, and priest to Jesus based on his divinity rather than in light of his humanity. Instead, Pannenberg insisted that Jesus' vocation as a man was to call people to the kingdom, which gave them an openness to God and the future resurrection. Therefore, Jesus' proclamation granted eschatological salvation. This salvation meant the fulfillment of human destiny, which he claimed Jesus did through his resurrection and his proclamation by giving his hearers this openness towards God.

Regarding a theology of the cross, he insisted that we begin by linking Jesus' fate to his ambiguous career and acknowledge Jesus' acceptance of the consequences of his devotion to the mission of proclaiming the imminent kingdom of God. But it is the resurrection that brings the death of Jesus into perspective, for by this event, the salvific nature of the crucifixion comes to the fore. Here it is revealed that Jesus took the place of sinful humanity and died separated from God, as was ordained by God. Pannenberg pointed out that Jesus' death had universal significance since all men were shown to be blasphemers. Therefore, due to our communion with Jesus, which he extends to us, we no longer need to die alone or without hope because we may participate in the kingdom to come.

3.5 The Unity of the Person of Christ

3.5.1 Introduction

In the first section, Pannenberg derived the divinity of Jesus from the resurrection event. Afterward, he discussed the humanity of Jesus as revealed through his activities and fate. Finally, he investigated how these two concepts, the divinity and authentic humanity of Jesus, are interrelated. Pannenberg (1966, 291) showed that from the very beginning, Christian theology was compelled to state that Jesus was truly God and truly man, which is what the formula of Chalcedon sought to express. Kärkkäinen (2016, 44) and Migliore (2014, 177) show the most significant milestone in the development of classical Christology was the fourth ecumenical council of the official church held in Chalcedon in 451 AD. Due to the major disagreement between the Alexandria and Antioch schools (Migliore 2014, 176), the central theme under discussion was the humanity and divinity of Jesus Christ (Kärkkäinen 2016, 44). However, Pannenberg was concerned with the idea of two substances joining together to form one individual, as presented in the two-natures formula (Pannenberg 1966, 293). This problem, he argued, was inevitable for all Christologies from above, or as he called them, incarnational Christologies. This is because they already assume the two natures of Christ right from the outset, which means their discussions will inevitably emphasize either the unity of person in Christ or the humanity of Jesus. Rather than explaining the synthesis of two natures, he approached the issue of the unity of the person of Christ from a different angle. This section will examine how Pannenberg speaks about the unity of the divine and humanity in Christ and the consequences of such unity.

3.5.2 The Deadlock of the Two-Natures Formula

The Chalcedonian Creed confessed the divinity and humanity of Jesus to be unmixed, unchanged, indivisible, and inseparable in one person (Pannenberg 1966, 292). Thereby it attempted to preserve the uniqueness of both natures whilst maintaining the unity of a single person. Pannenberg found that the council at Chalcedon was concerned about the historical Jesus' true divinity and humanity; however, he argued that they did not make this concern clear enough through their formulation (291–92). He claimed that the true divinity and true humanity of Jesus Christ formed the foundation of Christian theology. Still, he was concerned by the concept of two substances joining together to form one individual, as presented in the two-natures formula (293). Pannenberg wrote, "The problem with the two natures dogma does not lie in the concepts of 'nature' (333). Rather the problem with the two natures doctrine lies in the expression of two natures as if they were on the same level."[80] For Schleiermacher, the idea of assigning one concept, such as the term "nature," to God and man was inappropriate because of God's "otherness." Likewise, Barth (2009b, 111) expressed a similar concern by stating that "oneness. . .is not at all self-evident, but inconceivable in itself." However, Pannenberg (1966, 293-94) was more open to the use of the term.

The issue for Pannenberg (1966, 333-34) was trying to explain the synthesis of two natures, one divine and one human, in such a way that it results in a single individual. He claimed that if the two natures are united, it will either form a third or the individuality of Jesus will be split. According to Pannenberg, the two-natures formula took the incarnation as the starting point for Christology, which was doomed to failure. In contrast to Weber (1962, 135-36), who argued that the Chalcedon formulation was the only appropriate mode of expression of the natures of Jesus, Pannenberg (1966, 295) warned that it was a theological compromise since rather than attempting to solve the problem of how the two natures united in Jesus Christ ("trägt die Kennzeichen eines Kompromisses") it merely synthesized the Alexandrian and Antiochene theologies. He argued that because both schools began their Christological formations with the incarnation, their conclusions were inevitable and that combining the two answers never solved the problem. Instead, it allowed more of the same answers, with different nuances, to the problem of how the two natures united in Christ. He pointed out that the Alexandrian theologians, who Stoicism heavily influenced, sought to explain the incarnation as the event whereby the divine Logos united himself with the human Jesus in such a way that the flesh of Jesus became the tool of the Logos, which compromised the real humanity of Jesus (295-96). He referred to their view as unification Christology (*Einigungschristologie*; p. 302). In response to this idea, the Antiochenes were more concerned about distinguishing the two complete natures to protect the divinity of Christ rather than to protect the unity of the two natures as insisted by the Alexandrians (296). However, Pannenberg showed that in this Antiochene Christology, the independence of the man Jesus was so heavily emphasized that it threatened the unity of God and man, effectively avoiding the unity question altogether (297). He called this "disjunction Christology" (*Trennungschristologie*, 302).

80. "Die Problematik der Zweinaturenlehre liegt nicht so sehr im Begriff "natur." Die Problematik der Zweinaturenlehre liegt vielmehr in der Rede von zwei Naturen, gleichsam auf derselben Ebene."

This conflict of the fifth century caused a dilemma (Pannenberg 1966, 299–300). The Antiochene position, which argued for independent beings uniting, the Logos and the completed man Jesus, cause a third being. In contrast, the Alexandrian position emphasized the unity of God and man and neglected the individuality of Jesus, making him a mere abstraction. Pannenberg argued that "the dilemma of both these Christological solutions is insurmountable as long as one develops Christology from the point of view of the incarnation, instead of culminating in the statement of the incarnation as its final sentence" (300).[81] Pannenberg understood that each of these two schools contained an element of truth; namely, the Alexandrian view highlighted the perfect unity between Jesus and God, whereas the Antiochene perspective maintained that the Logos assumed a real individual being, Jesus of Nazareth (300).

Nevertheless, he contended that these views would only have been able to solve the problem of God and man in Jesus if they approached the question from a different starting point than the incarnation (Pannenberg 1966, 300–301).[82] Because the Chalcedonian formula contains the elements of truth from both these views, he conceded that, although it does not provide a satisfactory answer to the problem, it forms the criteria that must be present in any acceptable Christological theory.[83] This criterion is that it must maintain the unity between God and man in Jesus and maintain his divinity and humanity. Pannenberg pointed out that after the Chalcedon formulation, the conflict between the unification Christology of the Alexandrians and the disjunction Christology of the Antiochenes reappeared in various forms (302–3). Additionally, he showed that conflicts among confessional churches had caused the break-away of the principles of modern life from the Christian faith altogether (Pannenberg 1976a, 360).

The inadequacies of the unification and disjunction Christologies also led to debates regarding the relationship between the attributes of the two natures. Pannenberg (1966, 306–7) pointed out that according to Alexandrian thought, the divine activity penetrated Jesus' human nature. In contrast, the Antiochenes kept the attributes of each nature separate, claiming that

---

81. "Das Dilemma dieser beiden christologischen Lösungswege ist unüberwindlich, solange man die Christologie vom Inkarnationsgedanken her entwickelt, statt sie umgekehrt in der Inkarnationsaussage als ihrem abschließenden Satz gipfeln zu lassen."

82. Because the Antiochene perspective recognized the real individual humanity of Jesus, Pannenberg (1966, 300–301) thought that it would have been less complex for them to assess Jesus from his historical human activities rather than from his incarnation.

83. Pannenberg (1966, 300–301) identified that this unresolved Christological debate caused the first real schism in Christianity which ultimately led to the conversion to Islam of previously Christian regions such as Syria, Palestine, and Egypt.

each nature could only communicate attributes to the person that belonged to them separately. Pannenberg believed that a mutual interpenetration of attributes was required for any unity of divinity and humanity to exist in Jesus.[84] He highlighted that Lutheran and Reformed theologians' views also differed regarding the communication of attributes across natures, particularly from the divine to human nature (309–11). Pannenberg once again assigned to the issue of starting Christology with the incarnation, which causes the inescapable dilemma (*Unentrinnbare Dilemma*) of maintaining the unity of person and the humanity of Jesus. He believed that as soon as one considers Jesus from the perspective of the incarnation, which occurred at Jesus' birth ("die Inkarnation Gottes in Jesus einen Anfang"; Pannenberg 1966, 310–11; 1968a, 108), then one is forced to either deify Jesus' humanity or one will be criticized for inadequately uniting of God with the man Jesus. Therefore, the dilemma of the communication of attributes cannot be avoided in the disjunction Christology or unification Christology due to their starting point, namely, the incarnation (Pannenberg 1966, 312–13). Pannenberg analyzed the more contemporary Christologies of Barth, Althaus, and Weber and highlighted how none of them can overcome this problem because they commence with the incarnation (311–12). Pannenberg argued against a gradual incarnation view to understand the relation between Jesus' divinity and humanity (316–17). He emphasized that the retroactive meaning of the resurrection as the confirmation of Jesus' pre-Easter activities and claims means that whatever is true about the person of Jesus, and his unity with God was true from the beginning.

Furthermore, Pannenberg (1966, 318–19) saw the limitations of Christologies that commence with the incarnation and the conflict between the unification Christology and disjunction Christology in the concept of *kenosis* (the self-emptying of Christ).[85] The Tubingen theologians, who maintained the unification tradition and, therefore, the Lutheran understanding of mutual interpenetration of attributes, argued that Jesus' divine glory was "concealed" during his earthly life, which, according to Pannenberg, threatened the actual historical reality of his humanness. In contrast to them, the Giessen theologians rejected the idea that Jesus concealed his divine attributes but rather affirmed an absolute renunciation of their use

---

84. The Cappadocians considered this unity to be a mixture whereby the divinity soaks Jesus' humanity as fire makes iron glow (Pannenberg 1966, 306).

85. The patristic theology was mostly concerned to maintain the pure divinity of Jesus for soteriological reasons, therefore, the church fathers considered Jesus' self-emptying as his taking on human flesh rather than a partial or complete relinquishment of his divine nature or attributes (Pannenberg 1966, 318).

during Jesus' earthly life, which compromised the unity of Jesus' humanity and divine nature (319–20).

Pannenberg (1966, 320) took issue with the nineteenth-century renewal of the kenosis doctrine, according to which it is neither the God-man nor the incarnate Logos but the divine Logos who humiliates himself. In other words, the divine Logos underwent a physical self-limitation in his divinity. According to this understanding, the Logos gave up his "relative attributes" of divinity, such as his omnipotence, omniscience, and omnipresence, but retained the "immanent perfections," such as holiness, love, and truth. However, Pannenberg contended that relinquishment of the "relative attributes" of divinity reduces the divinity of Jesus to such an extent that he is no longer divine (321). He believed, "Attributes that are essential to his divinity, cannot be missing even in his humiliation unless the humiliated were no longer God" (322).[86] Therefore, the nineteenth-century renewal of the kenosis doctrine could also not overcome the problem of incarnational Christology.

Pannenberg (1966, 323–30) also analyzed the more modern views of theologians such as Barth, Vogel, and Rahner. To the credit of these theologians, these modern continuations of the nineteenth-century kenosis doctrine excluded the idea of God relinquishing his divinity or any of his attributes during his self-emptying. Nevertheless, Pannenberg was not convinced by these new variations of the kenosis doctrine (Røsok 2017, 53–55). He was adamant that if God's self-humiliation to unity with humanity does not involve sacrificing some aspects of his divinity, then it compromises the concept of Jesus' real humanity because then the divine Logos dissolves the humanity of Jesus (Pannenberg 1966, 330–31). This idea, he continued, would not help to make the incarnation intelligible but would instead make Jesus a superman even though he modestly hides his glory. Alternatively, Jesus remains a "dual being" wherein divine glory and humble humanity co-exist without uniting. The only way that the kenotic Christology can maintain the integrity of Jesus' humanity, he argued, was to compromise God's unchanging character (331). For these Christologies, "the main point is the insight that the incarnation be thought of not as self-emptying but rather as self-realization of God" (Pannenberg 1975a, 172).[87] He proposed that by thinking of the incarnation as the self-realization of God, *der Selbstverwirklichung Gottes,* the one-sidedness of a Christology from below that focuses only on the humanity of Jesus can be prevented (175).

---

86. "Eigenschaften, die seiner Gottheit essentiell sind, können auch in der Erniedrigung nicht fehlen, es sei denn, daß der Erniedrigte nicht mehr Gott wäre."

87. "Den Angelpunkt bildet die Einsicht, daß die Inkarnation nicht als Selbstentäußerung, sondern als Selbstverwirklichung Gottes zu denken ist."

In contrast to the incarnational Christologies discussed, Pannenberg (1966, 332) emphasized that Jesus' unity with God cannot be established by dissecting the incarnation. Therefore, the debate between the unification and disjunction Christologies cannot be solved since both start from the wrong place. Rather, this unity can only be decided retrospectively from the perspective of Jesus' resurrection. He wrote, "Until his resurrection, the unity of Jesus with God was hidden, not only from the rest of humanity, but by all accounts, also from Jesus himself" (333).[88] The hiddenness of this truth, to others but also Jesus, safeguards the real humanity of Jesus. Pannenberg emphasized that approaching the incarnation as the conclusion rather than the beginning of Christology accomplishes what the incarnation Christologies could not do; namely, it manages to speak of the divine-human unity existing from the beginning of Jesus' life without compromising the real humanity of Jesus' activities (333–34). Pannenberg proclaimed, "What took place at the incarnation, came to full outworking in the resurrection of Jesus" (Pannenberg 1968a, 106). Therefore, Pannenberg (1977a, 322) summarized the incarnation as follows, "Out of his eternity, God has through the resurrection of Jesus, which was always present to his eternity, entered into a unity with this one man which was at first hidden. This unity illuminated Jesus' life in advance, but its basis and reality were revealed only by his resurrection." Consequently, Pannenberg did not consider Jesus to be the synthesis of two natures, one divine and one human, but rather as this man, Jesus is God (*als dieser Mensch ist Jesus Gott*; Pannenberg 1966, 334). Pannenberg avoided any speculation about the two natures and how they came together. Instead, he provided a broader picture by claiming that due to the resurrection, Jesus is one with God, which he has always been, and that as the man Jesus of Nazareth, Jesus is one with God. From the perspective of his resurrection, this man Jesus is not just man but is one with God and thus is himself God (*mit Gott eins und so selbst Gott*; 334).

3.5.3 Jesus' Personal Unity with God

When it comes to the unity between Jesus and God, Pannenberg worked from his understanding of the resurrection to the conclusion that there was a revelatory unity between them. This meant that the God revealed cannot be separated from Jesus through whom he was revealed, and anything said about God must conform to what has been revealed in Jesus. However, Pannenberg (1966, 335) pointed out that more can be said about the

---

88. "Bis zu seiner Auferstehung war die Einheit Jesu mit Gott verborgen, nicht nur den übrigen Menschen, sondern nach allem, auch für Jesus selbst."

internal uniqueness of this unity. As a result of the revelatory unity (*Offenbarungseinheit*) between Jesus and God, he contended that there was an essential unity (*Wesenseinheit*) wherein the eternal being of God and the totality of Jesus' person were connected. Furthermore, this essential unity can be presented more clearly as a unity of person (*Personeinheit*). By this, he meant how his divinity related to the humanity of his mission and fate.

Regarding what Jesus' deity meant for his human existence, Pannenberg began with Jesus' self-consciousness. He understood that an essential aspect of a person's personality is contained in their self-consciousness (*Selbstbewußtsein*); therefore, Jesus' self-consciousness was an important area of investigation to establish whether his unity with God was a personal unity (Pannenberg 1966, 336). Pannenberg maintained that because it was only revealed at the resurrection that Jesus is one in essence with God, this could not have taken place outside Jesus' pre-Easter life and consciousness (336–37). Furthermore, he continued, if Jesus did not have self-consciousness, that would make him less human since humanity typically has a form of knowledge about what constitutes his being a self, even if imperfect. Pannenberg showed that whoever does not have self-consciousness lives in self-contradiction, for it is essentially constitutive for a person to have a consciousness of himself. Therefore, he contended that Christology cannot ignore the self-consciousness of Jesus. The quest for the historical Jesus considered his self-consciousness the root of his claims to authority and the objective knowledge of his relation to God (337–38).

Pannenberg (1966, 338) warned that the self-consciousness of Jesus is not attainable through an investigation of the titles the gospels give him. He was adamant that the titles given to Jesus cannot be taken uncritically as a historical source of Jesus' authentic sayings. These were titles given to Jesus after the resurrection. He was also adamant that Jesus did not think of himself as the Messiah, the eschatological prophet, nor the Servant of God in terms of Isaiah 53, nor as the Son. Pannenberg agreed with Conzelmann (1973, 49) that the titles of Jesus are useless for investigating Jesus' self-consciousness.[89] Conversely, Pannenberg (1966, 338–45) was adamant that the most appropriate place to enquire about his self-consciousness was his activities, mission, and message shaped by his Jewish understanding of salvation and God.

Pannenberg (1966, 345) argued that Jesus' self-consciousness revealed his relatedness to the Father and not to the Logos, the Second Person of the Trinity. He stated that Jesus knew himself functionally in unity with

---

89. Pannenberg (1966, 339) pointed out that by placing conservative theology in conversation with historical-critical findings, the Protestants can learn from the Catholics, who did so with regards to the conservative titles given to Christ.

God's will (*Funktional mit Gottes Willen*) through his proclamation of the imminent kingdom of God and the entirety of his activity determined by his message. Therefore, one cannot understand the sonship of Jesus unless one starts with his relation to the Father. Pannenberg contended that "without the spirit of communion of the Father and the Son there is no knowledge of God and no knowledge of Christ" (Pannenberg 1975a, 164).[90] He believed this to be the issue with the incarnational Christologies that sought to explain the unity of God and man in Jesus by providing theories of its inner structure and how it came to be. He suggested that the issue of the unity of the man Jesus and the eternal Son of God cannot be answered directly (Pannenberg 1966, 346). Instead, the unity of the man Jesus and the Son of God results as a detour through Jesus' relation to the Father. Jesus showed himself to be the Son of the Father through his personal community (*Persongemeinschaft*) with the Father. The man Jesus showed himself to be identical to the Son of God indirectly (346).

Two concepts important to Pannenberg's description of Jesus' relation to the Father are his dedication and self-sacrifice, which he links to Jesus' behavior and fate. Pannenberg (1966, 346) emphasized that Jesus' mission was to call people into the imminent kingdom of God, which shaped his activities and message, and that his mission was confirmed by God through the resurrection. This showed that all of Jesus' activity was a dedication to God and his will. Additionally, Jesus' dedication took on a self-sacrificing nature through the fate that he suffered. "*So ist die Gottheit Jesu als Sohn vermittelt, begründet durch seine Hingabe an den Vater. Im Vollzug dieser Hingabe ist Jesus der Sohn*" (In this way, the divinity of Jesus as Son is conveyed, established through his devotion to the Father. In performing this devotion, Jesus is the Son) (347). Pannenberg (1994b, 373) proclaimed, "Only in this subordination to the rule of the one God is he the Son." Consequently, Pannenberg contended, along with Gogarten (1952, 242), that Jesus' Sonship is found in his humanity ("daß Jesus gerade in seinem Menschentum der Sohn Gottes ist"). Therefore, Jesus urged his followers to imitate his self-sacrificial dedication to God (Pannenberg 1991a, 33–34).

Instead of arguing for a specific view of the synthesis of the divine and human substances in Jesus, Pannenberg claimed that this man, Jesus, is the Son of God. He added a caveat that Jesus' identification as the Son of God was established by the resurrection and was not in Jesus' self-consciousness during his life (Pannenberg 1966, 348). Pannenberg (1991a, 31) went as far as to state that the doctrine of the Trinity seeks to explicitly communicate

---

90. "Ohne den Geist der Gemeinschaft des Vaters und des Sohnes gibt es keine Gotteserkenntnis und keine Christuserkenntnis."

that which was implicit in Jesus' dedication and relatedness to the Father during his earthly career.[91] Therefore, this is the approach to follow when arguing for the Trinity since it proves difficult to do from purely exegetical reasoning (*Exegetischer Argumentation*; Pannenberg 2003, 236). The distinctions and relations of the Trinity can only be known through the revelation of the Son and not, as in Origen, for example, through John's witness (Pannenberg 1991b, 273; 1969, 133–34).

Approaching the question of the relation of the divine and humanity through Jesus' life in this way, Pannenberg (1966, 349–51) suggested that he maintained the criterion of Chalcedon, namely, the integrity of Jesus' humanity along with the unity of God and man in Jesus. Pannenberg pointed out that, according to the Chalcedon formula, Jesus was described as an enhypostasis (*Enhypostasie*) in the Logos. In other words, his human nature could not be considered as an independent reality (hypostasis) of its own form of manifestation (person). This means that Jesus' humanity lacked a self-conscious personality and would be non-existent by itself. Therefore, the man Jesus has the basis of his existence (his hypostasis) not in his humanity but in the Logos. Pannenberg affirmed that there was truth in the formula, although he thought it necessary to avoid the negation of Jesus' human historical existence that it implied. Moreover, Jesus' unity with God is mediated through his self-sacrificial human dedication to God, which needs to be distinguished from the ontological dependence of Jesus' humanity upon the Logos.

Pannenberg (1966, 351) contended that a person is a relational concept, which means that due to Jesus' relation to the Father, which was characterized by his dedication to the Father, Jesus is identical to the eternal person of the Son of God. Therefore, the unity between God and man in Jesus is not known from his ontology but from his self-sacrificial dedication to God. Furthermore, this dedication stemmed from the dependence of Jesus' human existence, not on the Logos, but upon the Father (351). Pannenberg believed that Jesus did not live dependently upon the Son or Logos, which does not do justice to the historical features of the life of Jesus. Rather, he lived dependently on the Father, and by doing so, he showed himself to be one with the Son. Pannenberg argued that "his self-differentiation from God in obedience to the Father proves him as the Son" (Pannenberg 1977b, 91).[92] Pannenberg (1966, 351) warned that although Jesus was united with

---

91. Pannenberg (1977b, 87) contended that the resurrection of Jesus not only validated his sonship, but also the deity of the one he called Father. Without the resurrection the one he called Father would not be God ("Ohne Jesu Auferweckung wäre der von Jesus verkündigte Vater nicht Gott").

92. "Seine Selbstunterscheidung von Gott im Gehorsam gegen den Vater erweist

God through his self-sacrificial dedication, he remained distinct from the Father. Therefore, the Son demonstrates his deity through obedience (Pannenberg 2003, 239). Moreover, Jesus' enhypostasis in the Son of God means that he remained dependent upon the Father and claimed no independence from God (Pannenberg 1966, 362). Jesus' freedom consisted of doing God's will, his mission, and being in unity with God. His dedication to God's will and his mission excluded any freedom of choice and especially freedom from all sin (362). Pannenberg's point of view is summed up as follows: "In dedication to the Father, Jesus lives as the Son" (*In der Hingabe an den Vater lebt Jesus seine Personalität als Sohn*; p. 354).

3.5.4 The Lordship of Christ

The most significant implication of the unity of Jesus with God is a sharing in the lordship of God (Pannenberg 1966, 379–80). Pannenberg argued that Jesus' unity with God was established through the resurrection, and his personal unity was revealed in his dedication to the Father as Son; however, the effect thereof is Jesus' exaltation to participation in God's lordship. In light of the historical activities of Jesus, we see that Jesus did not proclaim his own lordship but the lordship of the Father. In this regard, Pannenberg (1966, 379) agreed with Ritschl (1902, 406) that the present reality of the lordship of Jesus Christ could also only be understood from the context of the whole of his earthly activity.

Pannenberg (1966, 380) indicated that the early Christians assigned the title of Messiah to Jesus post-resurrection and that this title was a reference to his lordship in the eschatological future, which they thought was imminent. However, as time progressed, a transition of thought occurred by which Jesus' present lordship (*gegenwärtige Herrschaft*) over the universe was seen as a hidden lordship (*verborgene Herrschaft*) that was distinguished from his revealed lordship (*offenbaren Herrschaftsausübung*), which is to be made manifest with his return (381). In other words, Christ's lordship should not be restricted to the future. Because God raised Jesus from the dead, which confirmed Jesus' claims to authority, the eschatological future had already started in Jesus (Pannenberg 1973, 70). Consequently, his lordship of the cosmos is already effective, albeit in a hidden form in heaven. However, Pannenberg (1966, 381–82) suggested that when the eschaton arrives fully, that lordship will become visible for all to see as he pronounces his judgment over the world and renews creation.[93] Therefore, the revealed

---

ihn als den Sohn."

93. Pannenberg (1966, 413) conceded that his Christological statements were only

lordship of Christ at his second coming is the necessary counterpart (*notwendige Gegenstück*) to the present hiddenness of his lordship (Pannenberg 1978a, 116). By his second coming, Jesus would bring redemptive history to a close (Pannenberg 1995, 82).

Pannenberg (1966, 383) disagreed with the Confession of Constantinople, which argued that Jesus would give his lordship over to the Father after his final judgment; instead, he insisted that the lordship of Jesus is contained within the lordship of the Father. To a certain extent, Pannenberg (383–84) agreed with Barth (1936c, 177) that "Jesus Christ is Himself the established kingdom of God," however, he specified that Jesus is only one with the lordship of the Father in the sense that he served the lordship of the Father in the total dedication of himself to that lordship. In other words, only due to his self-sacrificial dedication to the will of the Father does Pannenberg consider Jesus' lordship identical to the Father's. Pannenberg (2003, 240) suggested, "The Father not only begets the Son, but also entrusts his kingdom to him."

Therefore, Pannenberg (1966, 386) contended that Jesus rules over his church as Lord but that the full participation of Christians in his kingdom still belongs to the future. Pannenberg indicated that although the kingdom of God belongs to the future, it does already affect the present (*das seine Zukunft bereits jetzt die Gegenwart bestimmt*; Pannenberg 1977b, 91). For Schleiermacher (1822, 254–59, 263), the purpose of Jesus' mission was to find the kingdom of God among humanity, whereby through his prophetic office (*Profetische Ambt*), Jesus formed a social community (*Gemeinschaft*) around himself whom he called the kingdom of God. In other words, Jesus' mission was to establish the church, which he called the kingdom of God, because these people were brought into communion with God. In contrast to Schleiermacher, Pannenberg (1966, 387–88; 1988, 167) did not consider the kingdom of Christ and the church synonymous, for the church is a precursor to the kingdom of Christ, which is linked to the future. As such, the church is ruled by the exalted Lord through his Spirit and lives toward the future revelation of his kingdom on earth but is not itself the kingdom of Christ. Pannenberg wrote, "The Church is not the kingdom of God, but it is the body of Christ that grows in history towards the future of the kingdom of God" (Pannenberg 1978a, 116).[94] Pannenberg (1977c, 40; 2001, 203) contended that the acknowledgment of the lordship of Jesus and

---

metaphorical in meaning and carried a provisional character because all is yet to be revealed through the eschaton. For Pannenberg (1976a, 366) the quest for truth demands an awareness that theological assertions are provisional in character.

94. "Die Kirche ist nicht das Reich Gottes, aber sie ist der Leib Christi, der in der Geschichte wächst auf die Zukunft des Gottesreiches hin."

the uniqueness of the church as his body should lead to greater ecumenical openness (*ökumenischer Offenheit*). As a precursor, he argued that the church has the unique task of calling attention to the eschatological future of salvation (Pannenberg 1966, 388). He claimed that the church shares the mission of Jesus by dedicating itself to God through the proclamation of the kingdom of God and by submitting its behavior in both private and public to the lordship of Christ (389–90). Although Pannenberg argued for a separation between church and state, he nevertheless believed that the confession of the lordship of Jesus had political consequences (391–92).[95] For Pannenberg, no religion can ever contribute to its contemporary society unless the misguided privatization of religion is addressed (Pannenberg 1976a, 363). This conviction forms one of the central motivations of Pannenberg's entire Christological project.

According to Kärkkäinen (2016, 115), Pannenberg's reason for emphasizing a from below approach to Christology is that he believed that theology is a public discipline rather than the privatization of faith. Pannenberg (1985, 15) emphasized that if something is true, it must be the case not only for oneself but for everyone else. The freedom from sin through the Spirit of Christ impacts the entire person, not only in his private life but also in his economic and political relationships (*ökonomischen und politischen Beziehungen*; Pannenberg 1978a, 108). Pannenberg argued that even the hope of a future resurrection should not lead to the egoism of salvation for the individual (*Heilsegoismus des privaten Individuums*) but should lead to new life for all of humanity (*die ganze Menschheit*; Pannenberg 1974b, 180). He highlighted that Christian eschatology and its hope should not lead to escapism (*Weltflucht*) from the real world but should empower our present lives (*gegenwärtigen Lebens*; Pannenberg 1995, 72). Pannenberg (1978b, 26) believed that "this eschatological community is presently represented and symbolized through the community of believers."[96]

3.5.5 Conclusion

Pannenberg showed that Christian theology has always been compelled to say that Jesus is truly man and truly God. However, he argued extensively that any Christology that commences with the divinity of Jesus Christ, or

---

95. Pannenberg (1976a, 362) suggested that the origin of the secular idea that "God is dead" was due to the lack of dedication from Christians and their conformity to secular standards.

96. "Diese eschatologische Gemeinschaft ist gegenwärtig dargestellt und symbolisiert durch die Gemeinschaft der Glaubenden."

the incarnation, inevitably ends up in a position where it needs to explain how the two natures of Christ could co-exist in perfect unity whilst maintaining the integrity of his humanity. Pannenberg showed that these from above Christologies face the same issues when addressing the relationship between the attributes of both natures and the concept of kenosis. Rather than arguing for the unity of Christ and the integrity of his humanity with his back against the wall, he found that his approach was more adequate to explain these issues. Therefore, the answer lies in arguing from the resurrection to the incarnation and not the other way around.

From the resurrection, Pannenberg insisted that Jesus was the self-revelation of God. Therefore, he had a revelatory unity with the Father. This meant that the God revealed cannot be separated from Jesus through whom he was revealed, and anything said about God must conform to what has been revealed in Jesus. However, Pannenberg pointed out that more can be said about the internal uniqueness of this unity. As a result of the revelatory unity between Jesus and God, there was an essential unity wherein the eternal being of God and the totality of Jesus' person were connected. Furthermore, this essential unity can be presented more clearly as a unity of the person, by which he meant the way his divinity related to the humanity of his mission and fate. The unity of Jesus with God must not be approached from the angle of the relation between the Logos and the person of Jesus from Nazareth. Instead, it should be approached from the relatedness of Jesus with the Father. From this, Pannenberg concluded that, precisely due to his self-sacrificial dedication to the Father and his will, Jesus was shown to be the Son. Pannenberg was adamant that this approach kept the humanity of Jesus intact by limiting Jesus' self-consciousness to a vocation of dedication towards Israel's God rather than a self-awareness of his divinity. Consequently, Jesus shares in the lordship of the Father, which is the most telling indication of unity with the Father. The church then has the unique task of being the precursor to the kingdom of God.

3.6 Concluding Remarks

Pannenberg was resolute that the task of Christology must be based on historical facts rather than the preaching of the early church or contemporary experiences. In other words, he was concerned about what events caused the early church's preaching. Therefore, his method of Christology has Jesus' message and fate at its heart rather than the incarnation, as we find in the from above approaches. Additionally, although Christology and soteriology are inseparable, our need for salvation must not dictate who Jesus of

Nazareth was historically. The structure of his Christology followed the following sequence: (1) he dealt with the relationship of Jesus to God, (2) the fulfillment of human destiny through Jesus, and (3) the relationship of his divinity to his humanity.

First, Pannenberg addressed the issue of Jesus' relation to God, particularly to the God of Israel. This discussion was grounded on his investigation of the resurrection of Jesus. For Pannenberg, the pre-Easter claims to authority of Jesus are not a sufficient basis for faith in his divinity nor the grounds for considering his relation to God the Father. Rather, the resurrection formed the basis for faith in the deity of Christ. He argued that through the resurrection, God validated the pre-Easter claims of authority of Jesus, which means that Jesus' relation to God must be expressed as God's self-revelation. Moreover, Jesus was part of the essence of the God of Israel. He maintained that this was the case from the beginning of Jesus' existence by applying the conclusions reached from the resurrection. Therefore, the only appropriate way to speak about God's presence in Jesus is as revelatory presence.

Second, Pannenberg investigated the humanity of Jesus. He proposed that Jesus fulfilled human destiny through both his proclamatory career and fate. Jesus' vocation as a man was to call people to the imminent kingdom of God, which gave them an openness to God and the future resurrection. This, he argued, was eschatological salvation since it fulfilled humanity's destiny consisting of openness to God. Pannenberg also contended that through the resurrection, Jesus had fulfilled the destiny of humanity, namely, to be raised from the dead. Furthermore, when it came to the theology of the cross, he insisted that Jesus accepted his fate because of his devotion to the mission of proclaiming the imminent kingdom of God. But it is the resurrection that brings the cross of Jesus into perspective, and it is by this event that the salvific nature of the cross comes to the fore. Due to the resurrection, through which God affirmed the career of Jesus, Jesus was declared free from blasphemy, and those who accused him were confirmed to be the blasphemers. He showed that Jesus' death had a universal significance because all of humanity was shown to be blasphemers.

Third, Pannenberg examined the relationship between Jesus' divinity and humanity. He pointed out that the incarnational Christologies had difficulties articulating the relationship between the Logos and the human person, Jesus of Nazareth. These Christologies' attempts to describe the unity of the person whilst maintaining the integrity of Jesus' humanity are futile. Instead, Jesus had a self-consciousness about his mission and not his divinity. Therefore, Jesus never assigned any messianic titles to himself. As a human, Jesus lived into his mission with a self-sacrificial dedication through which he was shown to be the Son of God. In other words, Pannenberg believed one cannot answer the unity of the Son of God directly but must answer it from the perspective of his relation to the Father. Consequently, his sonship is established through his dedication to the Father and his will.

4

Critical Analysis of N.T. Wright's and Wolfhart Pannenberg's Christology

4.1 Introduction

THE GERMAN PHILOSOPHER FRIEDRICH Nietzsche is not often praised by conservative Evangelicals, especially given his pronouncement that "God is dead," which many have viewed as an onslaught on the compatibility between reason and religion (Chamberlain 2012). However, one aspect of his career that ought to be taken seriously is his understanding of the spirit of the times *(Zeitgeist)*. According to this, people can be sheeplike and mindlessly follow each other without any critical thought. People are susceptible to following the spirit of the times, that is, their day's leading philosophies and cultural norms (Goebel and Antrim 1899, 563). In a pre-Enlightenment world, people were criticized for not using their reason independently from institutions, especially the church (Kärkkäinen 2016, 73–74). Conversely, the Enlightenment has made skepticism and cynicism people's default posture. Applied to Christology, the pre-Enlightenment scholars were content to accept the church's dogma around Christ and therefore defaulted to a Christology from above. Contrariwise, treating the church's dogma around Christ as suspicious and thus preferring a Christology from below became the position of post-Enlightenment scholars. One group emphasizes trust and positivity towards Christian doctrine and creeds, whereas the other begins with skepticism and suspicion.

Similarly, there are two extremes when it comes to epistemology. One is a positivistic epistemology, which naively believes that historical facts can be objectively determined from a neutral position. The other, a post-modernistic epistemology, considers all knowledge as the person's interpretation and refutes any possibility of knowing external facts (Eddy 2009, loc. 406-8; McGrath 2009, loc. 2181-183). Both Wright and Pannenberg, however, would find themselves somewhere in the middle of that spectrum. Both acknowledged the folly of refuting the possibility of knowing external facts, as is evidenced by their Christological methods. And both would recognize that historical facts are interpreted through specific lenses and presuppositions, although Pannenberg would be closer to a positivistic epistemology than Wright. Whether they acknowledge it or not, most scholars become Christians before they become theologians, as shown by Macleod (2000, 20), which is also the case for Wright and Pannenberg. Wright comes from an Anglican tradition and Pannenberg from the Lutheran tradition, both of which have rich liturgical rituals. Therefore, both had a particular pair of lenses through which they interpreted the findings of their historical research, which shaped their conclusions and provided them with a strategy for coherency. Consequently, both scholars have strengths and weaknesses in their Christologies, which stem from their theological influences, traditions, and backgrounds.

In this chapter, a critical analysis of the main theories of Wright and Pannenberg's Christologies will be conducted based on the findings of chapters 2 and 3. It will address the subsidiary research question, namely, what might a critical analysis of the Christology of Wolfhart Pannenberg and N.T. Wright reveal? To do so, it will identify, define, and explore the strengths and weaknesses of these two Christologies by placing them in conversation with secondary sources and by engaging with Scripture. The strengths of these two Christologies will be applied to the Christocentric homiletic in chapter 6.

4.2 Strengths of N.T. Wright's Christology

4.2.1 Introduction

According to Wright (1998a, 54), his portrait of the historical Jesus has significant relevance for the life and mission of the contemporary church and, therefore, the world. He claims that various ministers and laypeople have testified that his description of Jesus and its consequences have enhanced their careers and Christian discipleship. It has made Jesus less abstract, relatable, and easier to imitate. This section will identify certain strengths of Wright's Christology that have led to his work being so well received by some. It is particularly interested in those strengths that will have significant implications for the Christocentric homiletic. It will also describe and explore these strengths by placing them in conversation with secondary sources and by engaging with Scripture.

4.2.2 Jesus' Story as Israel's Story

An apparent strength of Wright's work is the connections it allows us to make between Jesus and the Old Testament because of its emphasis on Jesus' Jewish context.[1] This emphasis on Jesus' Jewishness is not always found in other questers for the historical Jesus.[2] Some have sought to replace Jesus' Jewishness, instead conforming him to German ideologies, while others have attempted to replace the Jewish Jesus with the Christ of faith (Casey 1998, 96). However, Wright has gone to great lengths to maintain Jesus' Jewishness, which gives us fascinating links between Jesus and the Old Testament. The most prominent of these connections are linking Jesus to the Old Testament prophets, showing that Jesus was an Old Testament theologian, pointing out that Jesus' messiahship was the embodiment and fulfillment of Israel's story, that Jesus was the key to Israel's exile and restoration narrative, and that Jesus embodied the metaphorical symbols of YHWH's involvement in the world as revealed in the Old Testament.

First, Wright emphasizes that Jesus is the last of the Old Testament prophets. According to Wright, this is the foundation for understanding Jesus (Wright 1996a, 163). Like the prophets of old, Jesus came with a message from Israel's God, warning them of the consequences of their current conduct and inviting them to a different way. Wright contends that Jesus was modeling his career on John the Baptist and other Old Testament prophets such as Ezekiel, Jeremiah, Jonah, Amos, and, above all, Elijah (166–67). Not only does Wright link Jesus to the prophets of the Old Testament, but he presents a Jesus who thought theologically and who considered his reading of Israel's scriptures as a function of his prophetic role. Eddy (2009, loc. 432–35) rightly commends Wright for assigning Jesus the office of an

---

1. Snodgrass (2009, loc. 690–91) affirms Wright's efforts of providing a historical portrait of Jesus firmly planted within the Jewish world of the first century.

2. Eddy (2009, loc. 416–17) and Perrin (2011b, 128–29) state that one of the major strengths of Wright's work is his proficiency in second temple writings which has made good historical sense of Jesus in that context.

itinerate oracular and leadership prophet and for avoiding the temptation to play off the social and religious prophets against each other.

Likewise, Perrin (2011b, 129–30) commends Wright for depicting Jesus as someone familiar with the Jewish Scriptures and who thought theologically. Perrin shows that due to redaction criticism within historical Jesus studies, Old Testament quotations in the gospels have generally been thought of as theologically laden and therefore been considered improbable that they were used by Jesus himself (129). The idea that Jesus did not quote Old Testament texts, let alone think theologically through them, stemmed from the Bultmannian line of thought, according to which Jesus transcended Judaism (Watson 1997, 153–69). Consequently, because of Bultmann's influence, the more significant part of twentieth-century Jesus scholarship did not consider Jesus an Old Testament theologian (Perrin 2011b, 129–30). However, Wright has made a significant contribution to correcting this mistake. Eddy (2009, loc. 413–14) aptly points out that Wright's approach asks why Jesus should not be allowed to think as theologically creatively as the redaction and form critics assume the gospel writers were. Perrin (2011b, 130) writes, "I believe that it was above all Tom who granted this component of the Jesus tradition fresh historical explanatory power by seeing Jesus' reading of Scripture as a function of his prophetic role."

Second, Wright (1998b, 110–11) has made clear that first-century Jewish evidence demands that the title Messiah in the New Testament be interpreted according to its Jewish roots in Old Testament texts like the Psalms, Isaiah, and Daniel. In this way, Wright connects New Testament references to the Messiah to the Old Testament, a move that links Jesus and the Old Testament. In other words, Wright allows Old Testament categories to explain New Testament Christology (Kärkkäinen 2016, 27–28). Kärkkäinen shows that Wright, in particular, must be praised for his perpetual integration of the research on Judaism and its application to systematic disciplines (27–28). Wright's Old Testament understanding of the Messiah helps correct the improper view that the Messiah automatically meant the second Person of the Trinity. Choi (2011, 45) writes, "This is a critical point which we need to take into account since the Old Testament concept of the Messiah, who is attributed with divine qualities, would never make the statement that the Messiah would be God Himself."

It is moves like these that debunk criticisms like that of Casey (1998, 97) that Wright replaces the historical Jewish Jesus with the Christ of faith. Other critical scholars, such as Marsh (1998, 87), praise Wright for not being overly desperate to define Jesus in ways that orthodox theology would desire. Marsh writes about Wright, "He thus resists strongly the notion that his Jesus simply serves up what Christian theology wants to hear. Wright thus deserves credit for keeping the history-theology debate alive in the Quest." Furthermore, because Jesus identified himself as the Jewish Messiah, he identified himself with Israel. Marsh sums it up: "In a nutshell, Wright's position is this: 'Jesus is reconstituting Israel around himself' (78). Jesus was calling those around him to a 'new way of being Israel' and making a claim for the crucial role of his own person in Israel's reconstitution in this new way." In other words, as the Messiah, Jesus was claiming to be both the embodiment and fulfillment of the story of Israel (Perrin 2011b, 130). Jesus was fulfilling the climax of the redemptive story of the people of Israel. Consequently, Wright (1998d, 122) points out that because Jesus was believed to be the Messiah, he was also believed to be the *Kyrios*—the world ruler, as stated in Psalm 89 and Daniel 7—which provides another exciting opportunity to link Jesus with the rulers and kings of the Old Testament.

Third, Wright's kingdom of God threads, which originate from the Jewish scriptures, namely, the return from exile, YHWH's return to Zion, and the defeat of Israel's enemies, can all be very clearly linked to Jesus as the fulfillment of the Old Testament. The themes of exile and restoration are critical to Wright's presentation of Jesus and provide helpful connections between the Old Testament and the gospels. Perrin (2011b, 132) writes, "Indeed, I might be so bold to say that in bringing exile to the forefront, Tom has supplied the great missing link of modern Jesus studies, even, perhaps the missing link of New Testament theology." Perrin argues persuasively that Wright's description of Jesus as the embodiment and fulfillment of post-exile Israel is critical in the church's fight against Docetism (133–34). By bringing this to the forefront, the emphasis is placed on Jesus' career and not only his dying on the cross. Additionally, Jesus' story as Israel's story provides the foundation for an integrative biblical theology (134–35). In other words, Israel itself is the unifying thread between the Old Testament and New Testament theology. Perrin highlights that "for those inclined to undertake biblical theology through the lens of a narrative theology, Tom's paradigm grounds such a reading strategy in the historical Jesus himself and thereby provides hard backing, the gold standard of history" (134–35).

Jesus' story as Israel's story has further doctrinal implications. Perrin rightly points out that Jesus' story, as Israel's story, has soteriological and ecclesiological implications. Specifically, in the context of Wright's Jesus, soteriology takes on a communal nature (Perrin 2011b, 135–36). Perrin states, "By following him on this score, we are much better poised to advance ecclesiology not as an extraneous afterthought to the dogmatic enterprise, but as integral to it." The story of Israel and that of the early church is the same. Wright correctly claims that Jesus did not come to start the church because there already was one, Israel (Blomberg 2009, loc. 263–65). He came to reform Israel. Hays (2009, loc. 1996–997) observes, "Wright's construction of the historical Jesus does a great service for New Testament ethics by stressing the theme of continuity with Israel and Israel's heritage. Jesus was not rejecting or abolishing Israel; rather, he was proclaiming Israel's renewal and healing."

Fourth, Wright draws an essential link between the Jesus of the gospels and the metaphorical symbols of YHWH's involvement in the world, as revealed in the Old Testament. Wright (1998a, 47) contends that the early church utilized the language and imagery of Shekinah or Glory, Spirit, Law, Word or Logos, and Wisdom and developed them concerning Jesus. Additionally, the whole concept of monotheism and the Shema in the Old Testament can be linked to what Wright calls "Christological monotheism," as presented in Paul. Furthermore, he indicates that not only John but all four gospels use the Old Testament to tell the story of Jesus, whereby he is the living embodiment of Israel's God (Wright 2017a, 50). Hays (2011, 67) points out that Wright's reading of the Synoptic gospels goes a long way toward solving the persistent problem of the relationship between the Old Testament and the New Testament. Hays writes, "The Synoptic gospels, on Tom's reading, narrate a linear continuation of the storyline of Israel's national struggles and hopes. . .The New Testament then becomes, simply but profoundly, the story of God's restoration of his people Israel, and Jesus is 'the one to redeem Israel.'" Wright takes Jesus' Jewish context seriously, providing invaluable connections between the Old Testament Scriptures and Jesus himself.

4.2.3 *Homiletical Value of the Gospels*

Although the gospel stories are well known, Wright (2008b, 29–31; 2011c, 169) claims that the entire Western church, both Catholic and Protestant, has largely based itself on the epistles because they have not known what the gospels are for. He shows that the gospels have often been used to support a social gospel or as the foundation for Paul's soteriology. In opposition to these trends, Wright argues that the gospels reveal the salvific work of God.[3] Wright (2011c, 170), influenced by Ben Meyer, teaches that the gospels tell of a public figure called Jesus, who made a public announcement. The content of this concerned what Israel's God was doing in history. The

---

3. Wright (2009, loc. 3411–418) points out that he differs fundamentally with scholars such as Kähler and Johnson who argue that Christianity is unaffected by the validity of the gospels. Rather, for Wright, if the gospels are invalid, then Christianity is illegitimate.

Critical Analysis of N.T. Wright's and Wolfhart Pannenberg's Christology

public nature of Jesus' career that the gospels captured gives us access to Jesus' mindset and worldview as well as his actions from which to understand him better (171). Wright (2008b, 29) points out that the story all four gospels are telling is about the kingdom of God coming to earth through the public ministry, death, and resurrection of Jesus of Nazareth. Wright's assessment is commendable. Perrin (2011b, 133–34) sees that "so long as the meaning of Jesus' life retains only a vague connection to the meaning of his death, the gospels will continue to be regarded either as a catalog of assorted interesting things Jesus did or as the optional chips and dip leading up to the meat-and-potatoes main course of Pauline theology." This is how Wright answers the fifth question of the Third Quest: Why are the gospels what they are? He concludes that they are telling the story of Israel's God reclaiming the entire world in and through Jesus.

Moreover, Wright (2012a, 379) argues that this story of the kingdom of God is told as the climax of Israel's history in which their exile is ended, their sins forgiven, YHWH returns to Zion, and their enemies are defeated. He states, "Matthew, Mark, Luke and John, all in their very different ways, insist that the full meaning of Jesus is to be found precisely as the climax of the canon, the point where the large and complex story of Adam and Abraham, of Moses, David and the prophets all comes rushing together" (Wright 2011c, 175). Consequently, Casey's (1998, 100) argument that Wright interprets the gospels in a hermeneutical circle that seeks to replace the Jewish Jesus with the Christ of faith is not convincing because Wright goes to great lengths to connect the Jesus of the gospels with the larger narrative of the Old Testament. The gospels should stand at the center of the early church's missionary and theological life; a failure to understand what they are about is a failure to understand the drive of the early Christians (Wright 2012a, 381). The gospels, then, are all about how "God is becoming king" in and through Jesus (400).[4] Wright (2017c) goes so far as to state that unless the gospels are read like this, they are being falsified. He believes this is often the case when portions of the gospels are used as moralistic sermons or for abstract theology. Rather than reading it abstractly, Wright (2011c, 159) correctly points out that it should be read critically and historically, hence his phrase "critical realism."[5] In doing so, the church is safeguarded against

---

4. Wright (2017a, 53) engages with Hays (2016, 280) and argues by way of musical analogy that Jesus as the embodiment of YHWH in the gospels is the key in which the music is set, whereas the inauguration of the kingdom of God through the praxis, story, symbolic actions, death, and resurrection of Jesus is the tune of the music itself.

5. Newman (2009a, loc. 67–68) rightly points out that "by blending the epistemology of critical realism, the narratology of A.J. Greimas and a sophisticated notion of worldviews, Wright articulated an approach that symphoniously unites the polyphonic

deception and fantasy reflected in the type of sayings about Jesus that ends with the phrase "because my heart says so." In this way, understanding and preaching the gospels historically is the antidote to false fantasies about Jesus. Unless the church understands the historical nature of Jesus' career and fate as presented by the gospel writers, the preaching of the gospels will quickly revert to merely "Christ died for our sins" (172).

Wright's understanding of the gospels demands that they be used as lenses when reading Old Testament texts. Wright (2008b, 30–31) contends that after the Holocaust, there has been anxiety about potential anti-Jewish readings of the gospels, discouraging integration of the gospels with the Old Testament. However, he claims that nothing is gained historically nor exegetically by avoiding the Jewishness of the gospels and their claim to fulfill Jewish Old Testament hopes. Therefore, the gospels demand a deep integration with the Old Testament. Wright's high view of the gospels can be fundamentally seen in his historical approach, in which his attitude is one of trust towards the gospels, placing the burden of proof upon the skeptical scholars to prove the sayings and deeds of Jesus are inauthentic (Marsh 1998, 80; Moore 2003, 16).

Wright's historical understanding of the gospels, which takes Jesus' Jewishness seriously, has several benefits for contemporary preaching. First, it safeguards the church from preaching that treats the gospels as documents that seek to prove the deity of Jesus. Wright (2011c, 178–79) reminds us that "the gospels are not primarily written to convince their readers that Jesus of Nazareth is the second person of the Trinity." They are not talking about that. Choi (2011, 45) agrees, stating, "Indeed, even though there are clues which indicate Jesus' divinity, Christology according to the Synoptic gospels never goes as far as explicitly affirming the case." Instead, they are written to convince their audience that Jesus was inaugurating the kingdom of Yahweh on earth as in heaven. The gospels are about Jesus embodying Israel's God and about Jesus summing up the history of Israel in himself by fulfilling their destiny (Wright 2011c, 181). Wright correctly states that where an emphasis is placed on the divinity and humanity of Jesus, the gospels are de-Judaized and therefore misunderstood (181–82). "The gospels have a very high Christology, but this isn't about divinity in the abstract, but about *the God of Israel personally present and active*" (182). In a sense, asking the gospels whether Jesus was divine is a premature question (Wright 1998b, 108).

Second, it encourages the church to keep its theology of the kingdom of God and the cross together. Wright (2011c, 186–87) points out that "the

---

and many times discordant disciplines of literature, history and theology."

four gospels are quite clear that the kingdom and the cross go together, but much of the later Western church has found that conjunction very, very difficult, and has often played kingdom theology off against cross theology, because it's had one vision of reality about God making the world a better place and another vision of reality about God saving people from their sins, and never the twain shall meet." This division between the kingdom of God theology and the cross theology has often separated the gospels from Paul. Wright points out that scholars often emphasize the one whilst downplaying the other (188). However, "for the Evangelists, the kingdom is the project which is sealed, accomplished, by the cross, on the one hand, and the cross is the victory through which the kingdom is established, on the other" (192). This problem has a missiological consequence; if only one aspect is emphasized at the expense of the other, then the missional response will be either social ethics or saving souls (193).

Third, it urges preachers not to separate the resurrection from Jesus' kingdom mission. Wright (2011c, 198–99) highlights that the resurrection of Jesus cannot be separated from his kingdom of God-focused career and fate. He points out that "the resurrection is precisely the resurrection of the kingdom-bringer, the crucified kingdom-bringer, and that these elements are not left behind in the resurrection but rather fulfilled." This is an essential caveat because it prevents the church from falling into an escapist mindset. The gospels emphasized that the resurrection of Jesus affirmed his messiahship and declared that his death was the kingdom-bringing event, which means that the new creation has begun (199–201). Therefore, instead of waiting on earth until we go to heaven to be with Jesus, the church is summoned to implement this new creation on earth. In other words, as Wright puts it, "Jesus is alive again; therefore new creation has begun; therefore we have a job to do" (201).[6] These three major misreadings of the gospels, namely, focusing on the divinity and humanity of Jesus, choosing between a kingdom of God theology and a cross theology, and separating the resurrection from Jesus' kingdom mission, can be avoided if preachers take Wright's Christology seriously.

4.2.4 Recovery of the Practical Character of the Gospel

A significant strength of Wright's Christology is the practical implications for the contemporary church. The sixth question of the Third Quest is, "How does one's historical Jesus portrait relate to the contemporary church

6. There are hints of an over realised eschatology in Wright's presentation. For further discussion on this possible weakness refer to point 4.3.5 below.

and world?" In other words, what is the relevance of one's Christology to the twenty-first-century believer and his non-Christian contemporaries? According to Wright (1996a, 118), such contemporary reflection within the Third Quest has not been undertaken consistently. However, when it comes to Wright's work, this question is pondered throughout his corpus, and the implications are practical and detailed.

Hays (2009, loc. 1873–874) rightly argues that "every attempt to articulate a normative Christian ethic depends–whether explicitly or implicitly–on a particular construal of the figure of Jesus, along with some account of the message that he proclaimed." This is true of Wright's understanding of Jesus, especially regarding Jesus' death and resurrection. Hays (2011, 67) aptly points out that one of the strengths of Wright's presentation of Jesus is that it deepens our understanding in the sense that Jesus' death and resurrection were not only how God was removing the guilt of individuals but also part of God's large-scale plan to restore his people Israel and through them to bring salvation to the world. Although other historical theologians have contended that the death and resurrection of Jesus have clear implications for the church, for example, Calvin's schema of prophet, priest, and king, for Wright, this is a central notion. For him, the theology of the cross is only complete when it summons Jesus' followers to a "foot-washing" and "fruit-bearing" mission (Wright 2017c). Likewise, just as the resurrection meant mission for his followers then, it implies mission for his followers now (Wright 1998f, 141–42). He states that Jesus launched a new world order through the resurrection, a new reality within the space-time universe that he referred to as the kingdom of God (Wright 2008b, 31). The challenge for Jesus' followers is to be the means through whom Jesus continues to establish the kingdom of God on earth as in heaven (Wright 2011a, 220). From this perspective, recapturing the historical Jesus and his kingdom vision is central to a refreshed kingdom-focused missiology (Wright 2012a, 379).

Two overarching concepts by which we meet this objective are through being witnesses of the kingdom of God and by calling the world to account. First, this is done by bearing witness to the sovereign rule of Jesus (Wright 2011a, 225). The church is summoned to be witnesses of the kingdom of God holistically, namely, by praxis, symbol, and story. Wright (1998f, 152–53) cautions that this witnessing must not consist of hurling doctrines at people because God is only understood when the story, symbol, and praxis of our lives come together. In other words, the church must tell the story of Jesus' self-giving love and live it. We are witnesses of the kingdom of God through story by offering a meta-narrative that belongs to the entire world, a story by which everything in creation is understood (Goheen 2018, 336). Wright

(1991a, 54–55) is convinced Christology is not about certain abstract ideas but rather compels the followers of Jesus to perform the task given to them, namely, to live out the gospel publicly in this world.[7] Hays (2011, 53) sums up Wright's leaning, which he calls a Wrightian idiom: "true beliefs about Jesus cannot be separated from praxis that seeks to implement Jesus' kingdom agenda." Wright's Jesus demands his followers to live a certain way. Again, Hays (2009, loc. 1993–996) points out that:

> Wright's account of Jesus demonstrates that we cannot think of ethics apart from discipleship. We cannot ask in a vacuum what is good or right to do, nor can we be sufficiently guided by tables of rules or general ethical principles. Instead, we must ask what it means to become a follower of this particular man Jesus, to take up his agenda, to allow our praxis to be generated by the story that he told and lived.

One way we bear witness to the kingdom of God that Wright highlights is through our love for one another. Jesus challenges his followers to love one another in such a way that they reflect the glory of God. Wright argues from Philippians 2:5–11 that Paul's incarnational Christology explicitly appeals to the followers of Jesus to lay down their rights for one another (Wright 1991a, 50–53). The way to implement the victory of God over evil is not to embrace all kinds of human power, status, and authority but to give up our rights out of love for each other. Wright warns that insistence on our rights as Christians implies that someone other than the monotheistic God is being worshipped. To be the Messiah's people, Christians must imitate the Messiah in living lives of self-giving love (Wright 2017d). Wright (2017c) believes that this is how the glory and knowledge of God will cover the earth. Hays (2009, loc. 2032–36) points out that this, the call to community formation, is one of the most significant contributions that Wright's construction of Jesus brings to the table.

The second aspect of the church's vocation in this new creation is to be for the world what Jesus was for Israel and thereby call the world to account (Wright 2017c). Instead of privatizing their spirituality, the church is summoned to a path of mission to the world. Because the victory of God through Jesus on the cross was the ultimate defeat of evil, the church must not tolerate injustice, violence, or any other type of wickedness that still exists but should hold the world and its rulers to account (Wright 1998c, 53). In response, Hays (2009, loc. 2012–14) rightly praises Wright for reconstructing a Jesus who held a thoroughly anti-violence position. He states,

---

7. Johnson (2009, loc. 2832) points out that, for Wright, history has a normative function and therefore has serious implications for theology.

"Wright has also made a major contribution by highlighting Jesus' critique of violence. In Wright's construction, this is central to Jesus' message and mission."

Wright (2007b) points out in a sermon that the ascension of Jesus and his exaltation in heaven means that he is the rightful Lord of the world and, therefore, the church has the responsibility to pray for those in authority, to remind them of what their roles are, and to point out to them when they get it wrong. Because the dark powers have been defeated and Jesus is declared *Kyrios* of the world, his summons to his followers will inevitably have political consequences (Wright 2017b). Wright (2008c) preaches that the choice between spirituality and politics is a false one. Instead, God must be served in private and public.[8] He contends that serving God only in private leads to Gnosticism, escapism, and a safe and narcissistic spirituality, whereas serving God only in public becomes political posturing and heartless gestures. Christ's lordship and summons have implications for every household, community, country, and policy.[9] Hays (2011, 67) sums it up well:

> The Jesus who steps out of the pages of Tom's book is not an otherworldly, apolitical figure. He fits within a vivid political landscape of pragmatic collaborators, resistance fighters, would-be Messiahs and others struggling to sort out the national identity of a people trodden down by pagan powers but always dreaming that God would set them free and bring justice. Against this backdrop Jesus' prophetic proclamation of 'the kingdom of God' recovers its properly explosive political meaning.

Wright's Christianity is not what he calls a "pie-in-the-sky religion," according to which God prepares a pleasant, comfortable afterlife for us, called heaven, while we serve God merely privately in a spiritual sense (Wright 1998c, 53). Nor is it a religion that tolerates selfishness or focuses on individual emotions. He strongly contests that the church should hold itself accountable lest it becomes a privatized spirituality, conceited, or embraces

---

8. This is a vivid example of how Wright's Christology from below approach informs his sermons, particularly the application aspect of his sermons.

9. According to Wright (2016, 426–27), Dietrich Bonhoeffer personified this calling by standing up against the Nazi regime when he could have remained hidden in America. Cone (2011, 42) shows that even in America where the racial tensions were high, Bonhoeffer exemplified this aspect of being a Jesus follower by identifying with the black community and being heavily criticized for it. Bonhoeffer's Christology was also the driving force behind this conduct. For Bonhoeffer (2009, 323), as with Wright, Jesus holds the world to account through his church community.

some form of paganism (Wright 1991a, 51). Correspondingly, Wright calls Christianity a "kingdom-on-earth-as-it-is-in heaven" religion.

4.2.5 Jesus-centered God-language

Lastly, Wright's conclusion—that Jesus is the personification and embodiment of Israel's God—finds a way of speaking about Jesus as divine and providing a means to describe Israel's God. Wright (2015, 91–92) correctly points out that just as scholars need to learn a new way of speaking about Jesus' self-awareness, as being aware of a vocation rather than being the second Person of the Trinity, scholars must learn to speak about the identity of God in the light of this Christology. He writes, "Jesus' first followers found themselves not only (as it were) permitted to use God-language for Jesus but compelled to use Jesus-language for the one God" (Wright 2013, 1234). Moreover, the early Christians claimed that Israel's God had come in and through Jesus and had brought about the new creation. Wright takes this claim seriously.

Hays (2011, 75) points out that Wright and Barth agree that because of the incarnation, we need to rethink the meaning of the word *god*. Additionally, we need to reconfigure our understanding of God around Jesus, in whom God was surprisingly present rather than speculation or natural knowledge. Wright (1998a, 54) proposes that we think historically about Jesus as a young Jew with a somewhat irrational and risky vocation riding into Jerusalem with tears in his eyes, denouncing the temple, and dying on the cross at the hands of the pagans. Then, we re-center our understanding of the word "God" around that instead of taking our understanding of the word "God" and imposing that on Jesus. Wright's motivation for this approach is most clearly perceived in the Gifford Lectures. Wright (2019a, 2) points out that the ancient philosophers practiced "natural theology," that is, they used their observations of the natural world to conclude about the being and nature of God. According to Wright, natural theology is open to the challenge of public truth rather than restricted to private belief because whatever is said about God is open to public investigation. He argues in favor of defining God according to natural theology; however, he proposes that Jesus forms the center of this investigation. This is because Jesus was a human being at a specific place and time within the world of history, the world of space, time, and matter, in other words, the natural world. According to Wright (2008b, 29), one of the main points of the gospels is to reveal this "God" through Jesus of Nazareth, who comes, not as a tyrant but as one who restores genuine humanness through his coming kingdom.

Allowing Jesus to define God is an approach that seems faithful to the declaration of Colossians 1:15–20. Admittedly, this passage represents a high Christology; nevertheless, when Wright concludes that Jesus is divine through a from below approach to Christology, the natural next step is to think through what that means for God himself. Eddy (2009, loc. 656–57) observes, "Wright's model of Jesus, particularly the 'Yahweh embodied' element, points toward the presence of a high Christology historically rooted in Jesus' self-consciousness. Such a conclusion has not been a common deliverance within the history of the Quest." This idea of defining God through Jesus is also faithful to the notion of the incarnation, as Jeremias (2002, 1–17) reminds us that God became incarnate not in a text but in the flesh and blood of Jesus of Nazareth.

It seems, the default of Western evangelicals is mostly to think about Jesus in terms of the categories they've learned about God in the Old Testament. Wright (1996b, 411) correctly suggests that Western orthodoxy has regularly approached Christology with a detached and oppressive view of God that they have forced upon Jesus, a process that has resulted in a docetic Jesus. In other words, his humanity is compromised by beginning with an abstract understanding of his divinity. For example, Newman (2009b, loc. 3844–845) states that "without the deification of Jesus there would not be a Trinity; and, at least theoretically (if not also historically), Christianity ceases to be Christianity when Jesus is not confessed and worshipped as divine." Although Newman is correct in his assertion, the point is that we often seek to define Jesus in divine categories, but rarely do we seek to define God through what we've learned about Jesus. Consequently, Wright urges every generation of Christians to think long and hard about the real human being, Jesus Christ, because when we discover who Jesus was, we discover who God is (Dunn and Wright 2004, 15). Was this not what the early church did by its Christological adaption of the Shema? (Kugler 2020, 5). Wright's position can be summarized by a sermon remark he made at Wheaton College, "If you think you knew who God was, think again and look at Jesus" (Wright 2017e).

4.2.6 Conclusion

We have identified four helpful implications in answering the question of what relevance Wright's Christology has for the twenty-first-century church. First, Wright's Christology provides valuable connections between the Old Testament and Jesus as the fulfillment thereof. Second, Wright's Christology prescribes a manner of treating the gospels that takes seriously what they are fundamentally about; namely, the story of the kingdom of God coming to earth through the public ministry, death, and resurrection of Jesus of Nazareth. Or put it differently, Israel's God reclaiming the entire world in and through Jesus. Third, Wright's Christology is not a repetition of abstract ideas but has practical and political implications for the followers of Jesus. Wright argues that Jesus continues to establish the kingdom of God on earth as in heaven through his followers. He believes this is done through the witness of his followers in word and deed, holding this world, its rulers, and the church to account, and loving one another by laying down our rights for each other. Lastly, it provides Christians with a new perspective on speaking about God. Whereas there is a tendency among conservatives to define what God is like and then try to place Jesus within that definition, Wright describes what God is like by looking at the historical Jesus.

4.3 Weaknesses of N.T. Wright's Christology

4.3.1 Introduction

When there is a debate between two sides, the safest option to follow is to choose between the two options and join that side. One might even try to avoid the debate altogether, but the last thing one wants to do, if one wants to avoid conflict, is to make up and choose a third option in the middle of the two. The consequences of such a move will be criticism from both sides. Or, at best, one's opinion will be used as a battering ram by both sides against each other, but none will take one's side. This was the case for Albert Schweitzer during the first quest of the historical Jesus. According to Perrin (2011a, 10–12), Schweitzer's approach to historical Jesus studies did not follow the template of the liberal theologians on the one side or the conservatives on the other. Similarly, Wright has followed the same route, or *Autobahn*, as Schweitzer with his Christology. Perrin shows that neither the conservatives nor the liberals can claim Wright as their own (10–12). Therefore, his work has received explicit criticism from both sides, as seen by MacArthur (2020), but it has also been met with a type of "theological silence." Although not all criticisms against Wright's work are valid, this section identifies the weaknesses of Wright's Christology. It will describe and explore these weaknesses by placing them in conversation with secondary sources and by engaging with Scripture.

4.3.2 Avoidance of the Church's Traditional Confessions

As we have seen, Wright believes that history and theology belong together, especially when making a statement about Jesus Christ (Wright 1996a, 8–11; Borg and Wright 1999, 15–27).[10] However, in practice, Wright occasionally prioritizes history over faith in his hermeneutical process. Wright is concerned that without emphasizing history, we might create false portraits of Jesus. He writes, "That remains my main worry about the appeal to canon or tradition over against history. I believe in canon, and I believe in the Holy Spirit. But history has shown repeatedly that the church is well capable of misreading the canon, and that tradition can drift in many directions, some less than helpful, some decidedly destructive" (Wright 2011c, 163–64). In response, Hays (2011, 63) contends that "in several weighty passages he [Wright] seems to suggest that faith can obscure real history, or that hard-nosed history has a certain hermeneutical priority." So, although Wright states that theology and history are complementary in theory, in practice, he seems to prioritize history over theology. Or, as Hays puts it, he mostly brackets out Christian theological tradition.

This has led others, such as Evans (2009, loc. 2519–520), to suggest that Wright's work leans toward methodological naturalism.[11] Evans arrives at this suggestion because of Wright's (1996a, 652–53) insistence that those who tried to interpret Jesus through supernatural events are inadvertently trying to defend his deity and fall into the trap of Docetism, which denies the real humanity of Jesus. This criticism of Wright's prioritizing of history over theology, as pointed out by Hays (2011, 63–65), is persuasive, as seen from several examples.[12] First, Wright (1996a, 652–53) concludes that Jesus was aware of a vocation to symbolize the return of YHWH to Zion. But he emphatically declares that this self-awareness was not an awareness of being God in person in the same way a person knows they are hungry or thirsty. Wright criticized the view that Jesus had an awareness of being the second Person of the Trinity as pseudo-orthodoxy. By this, Wright demonstrates

---

10. Bock (2009, loc. 1388) highlights that Wright's approach is dedicated to the relationship between history and theology when so many other approaches seek to separate it.

11. Wright (2009, loc. 3360–368) suggests that his work does fall into such a category precisely because he endeavors to take the questions of the Enlightenment seriously.

12. Wright's critical realism epistemology rejects both historical positivism, which naively believes that historical facts can be objectively determined from a neutral position, as well as a post-modernistic epistemology, which considers all knowledge as the interpretation of the person and refutes any possibility of knowing external facts (Wright 1992, ch. 1; Eddy 2009, loc. 406–8; McGrath 2009, loc. 2181–83).

that he has placed a circle of wagons around his treatment of the evidence and that certain Christian theological traditions are left outside that circle.

Again, Wright states, "The Jesus I know in prayer, in the sacraments, in the faces of those in need, is the Jesus I meet in the historical evidence—including the New Testament, of course, but the New Testament read not so much as the church has told me to read it but as I read it with my historical consciousness fully operative" (Borg and Wright 1999, 26). Wright's adverse disposition towards church dogma and theological traditions can also be seen in his criticism of more orthodox Christological works such as Gaventa and Hays' (2008) *Seeking the Identity of Jesus: A Pilgrimage*. Wright claims that the "pilgrims had suspiciously clean feet" because it was not focused enough on history and presented a non-historical recovery of Jesus (Hays 2011, 54). In a sense, Wright follows Funk's (1996, 300) attempt to set Jesus free from institutional and creedal Christianity. McGrath (2009, loc. 2256–257) points out that, according to Wright, Protestant thinking about Jesus is defective, partly because of its inadequate understanding of the first-century Jewish context. Accordingly, Wright (2011e, 81) contends that "the Great Tradition has seriously and demonstrably distorted the gospels. Eager to explain who "God" really was, the church highlighted Christology; wanting to show that Jesus was divine, it read the gospels with that as the question; looking for Jesus' divinity, it ignored other central themes such as the kingdom of God."[13] Although one must concede that the church has got some things wrong through the ages, Wright's pervasive adverse position towards church dogma and traditions seems excessive.

At this point, one of the central concerns with Wright's work is that, as Hays (2011, 64–65) observes, Wright has not entirely escaped the "intellectual heritage of the liberal historicism" of the other quests for the historical Jesus. According to this stance, the church forces an oppressive and deceptive hermeneutical framework that needs to be bypassed to arrive at the real Jesus. Therefore, the church's traditions must be avoided in our interpretation of Jesus and replaced by a new historical consciousness. In this, Wright's practical application of his historical method prefers the academy's priorities more than the church's traditions (59). Correspondingly, Hays contends that the church describes history in a way that secularist history is bound to negate (78). Therefore, Wright's upbringing within the rich liturgical rituals of the church of England should support his understanding of Jesus as presented by the New Testament rather than be seen as a hindrance (71–73). This is true, especially considering McGrath's (2009, loc. 2153–54)

---

13. Eddy (2009, loc. 395–97) points out that modern Jesus studies have either leaned towards a perpetual skeptical approach or confessional fideism, however, Wright's work is an excellent example of an approach that questions both these approaches.

argument that "one of the most distinctive features of recent theology has been the recognition that there is no such thing as a view from nowhere; all theological and philosophical systems relate to historically mediated traditions." It was Meyer (1979, 253), who was one of Wright's most significant influences, who said it may be "in the tradition generated by Jesus that we discover what made him operate the way he did." Rather than keeping the church's dogma outside his circled wagons, Wright will adhere to his epistemology more succinctly if he admits that he has been heavily influenced by the Christian worldview and, consequently, gives theology a better seat at the table.[14]

Lastly, Hays (2011, 61) points out that Wright's reluctance to side with church tradition can also be seen in his reconstruction of Jesus from behind the gospels. Rather than using the gospels as the point of focus, Wright uses them as the windows through which he sees a Jesus beyond the portrait the gospels are painting. Additionally, the accessibility of the type of information needed for such a reconstruction is limited within the gospels themselves, which can result in all sorts of speculations. Wright (1998b, 106) states, "My project is in no obvious sense a 'New Testament Theology'. I have not so far expounded very much of the New Testament, and what I have written so far is not basically theology (I discuss things that may have happened within history, rather than things that may be true about some god or other)." Hays' point is well taken because this is what Wright does when he seeks to describe Jesus' mindset and intentions, which the gospels do not explicitly speak about. Consequently, this approach, with its disdain towards traditional Christian dogma, challenges a conventional understanding of the authority of scripture. By going behind the text, Wright sets his work up as a fifth gospel that seeks to displace the same texts it seeks to interpret (Hays 2011, 72–73). In Wright's defense, he differs from Borg, Crossan, and other questers for the historical Jesus in that he does not seek to contradict the gospels (73), nor does he claim that something in the gospels is merely legendary (57). Wright (2011e, 81) contends that he believes in the creeds but believes in the Jesus of the gospels more. However, Wright's ill-treatment of traditional Christian dogma, as observed in his attempt to go behind the gospels to arrive at Jesus, has far-reaching consequences, as seen in the following weakness.

---

14. Wright emphasizes the importance of history to Christianity and would agree with Crossan's (2000, 150–51) statement that the reconstruction of the historical Jesus is "a way of doing necessary open-heart surgery on Christianity itself."

4.3.3 The Omission of John

From a conservative evangelical perspective, Wright's historical reconstruction of Jesus must be criticized for its omission of the gospel of John. Thompson (2011, 25) aptly points out that Wright's Christological conclusions do not depend on any significant quotation or discussion from the gospel of John. Wright is aware of this critique of his work and defends his position with the argument that he aimed to participate in the debate of the historical Jesus according to the Synoptic tradition (Wright 1996a, xvi). Correspondingly, Thompson (2011, 26–27) shows that for Wright to follow this approach, his work had to resemble other Jesus scholars, such as Crossan (1991) and Sanders (1993), who walk in the footsteps of David Strauss by disqualifying John as a historical source.[15] Wright's main Christological work, *Jesus and the Victory of God (JVG)*, which is volume two in his *Christian Origins and the Question of God Series (COQG)*, only provides a portrait of the Synoptic gospels, which means his reconstruction is based on a threefold rather than fourfold gospel canon. Wessels (2006, 88–89) contends that the reason why John is often omitted from historical reconstructions of Jesus is twofold; first, John's gospel was written ten to fifteen years after the other gospels and is, therefore, further removed from the historical Jesus, and, second, John's goal in writing his account was not to merely present the details of Jesus' life historically but to show who Jesus truly was *(hy wou wys wie Jesus regtig was)* and the corresponding spiritual consequences. Because other scholars have labeled John as being theologically loaded and ahistorical, Wright finds it necessary to exclude it from his sources (Hays 2011, 61).

This omission is more intriguing because Wright does not dismiss John's Gospel as a credible historical source.[16] He argues "that to rule John out altogether a priori as a historical source is a mistake" (Wright 2009b, loc. 3423).[17] Part of the reason Wright excludes John from the core of his

---

15. Alison (2009, 58) points out that although scholars of the Jesus Seminar disprove the historicity of the gospel of John through their criteria of authenticity, Blomberg (2001) affirms the historicity of John through a similar process of authentication.

16. Wright (2004b) states, "It [John] gives the appearance of being written by someone who was a very close friend of Jesus, and who spent the rest of his life mulling over, more and more deeply, what Jesus had done and said and achieved, praying it through from every angle, and helping others to understand it."

17. Wright (1992, 410–12) contends that although John is a different type of book to the other Synoptic gospels, when compared to other sources such as the gospel of Thomas or Peter or the reconstructed source Q, it is closer to the Synoptics than not. It seems that he would agree with Robinson's (1985, 5) deduction that John is very near to the historical source but also the result of deep theological reflection.

Christology is because of his objective. Wright's goal is to respond to certain specific third quest key questions, which, in turn, are a response to the claims of Reimarus, namely, that the Christian faith must be based on who Jesus was before his crucifixion. In other words, Christianity must be based on Jesus' mindset, aims, and beliefs (Wright 1996a, 12). This confirms what Keck (1971, 18) argues: "It is not overstating the case to claim that all historical study of Jesus is a critical appropriation of [Reimarus'] view or a debate with it." For this reason, Wright relies heavily upon Meyer's (1979) *The Aims of Jesus* in his reconstruction. However, as pointed out by Thompson (2011, 28–29), the aims of Jesus were accomplished by good Friday, and therefore any Christology that focuses on that will not sufficiently include the resurrection of Jesus. Although Wright (2003) has discussed the resurrection extensively in other places, his magnum opus *Jesus and the Victory of God (JVG)*, presents Jesus without the resurrection (Hays 2011, 55). With this, he indicates that the resurrection belongs to the aftermath of Jesus' life rather than part of his historical existence. According to Hoskyns (1956, 35), for John, the Christ of faith and Jesus in the flesh was the same. Thompson (2011, 29–30) is correct in stating that the aftermath of Jesus' life, namely the resurrection, is part of who Jesus was historically and what his life was about. She states, "Because there is no Jesus without the resurrection, there is no historical Jesus without the resurrection." Therefore, a complete historical presentation of Jesus of Nazareth must include the aims and beliefs of Jesus and the aftermath of his life throughout the reconstruction. Again, perhaps it is because Wright is still bound to an intellectual heritage of the liberal historicism of the other quests, as shown by Hays (2011, 64–65), that he avoids investigating Jesus in light of the resurrection.

The omission of John's gospel is also disappointing, considering how John's presentation of Jesus overlaps with Wright's Jesus in ways the Synoptics do not (Perrin 2011a, 14). The gospel of John and Wright's Jesus, as presented in *Jesus and the Victory of God*, make very similar statements about Jesus' identity and mission. Thompson points out that Wright's Jesus, who believed that he should be and do for Israel and the world only that which YHWH himself could do, agrees with John's Jesus "who acts and speaks only as the Father tells him to, who claims his Father's prerogatives to heal on the Sabbath and to judge, and who does the work of God in giving life and raising the dead" (Thompson 2011, 34). Likewise, John's Jesus and that of Wright find a deep resonance regarding Jesus' aims, self-consciousness, and the purpose of his death (35). Correspondingly, Thompson points out that in certain areas, Wright could have taken the words from John directly (45). Thompson contends that some things within John's gospel might challenge some of Wright's arguments. First, according to John, Jesus made more frequent visits to Jerusalem than presented in Luke, which questions whether Jesus thought of his pilgrimage to Jerusalem as his final intended move to go there and die, as illustrated by Wright (31–32). This is Pannenberg's (1966, 251) position, who saw Jesus' fate as something that happened to him rather than something he intended to happen. Second, the idea that Jesus' actions in the temple symbolized its destruction as a form of judgment by YHWH at the hands of the Romans is challenged in John (Thompson 2011, 38–43). She argues that John indicates the restoration of the temple rather than its destruction. In other words, Jesus' statements about destruction reference himself, his death and resurrection rather than the actual temple. Rather than a symbol of destruction, she believes that, according to John's gospel, Jesus' temple action must be interpreted as an intention to purify the temple, in the tradition of the Maccabean martyrs (42–43).[18]

However, Thompson's challenges from John's gospel are unpersuasive. First, as Sanders (1985, 309–18) has shown, Jesus died because of his attitude towards the temple and his accompanying actions. He might have been to Jerusalem many times before, but this time he intended to bring the temple proceedings to a temporary halt by turning over tables. Therefore, one might easily conclude that he probably expected repercussions for his actions. In that way, at least, his final journey to Jerusalem was unique. Second, there are sufficient texts in John that indicate that Jesus is the replacement of the temple. Wright (2011d, 46–47) points out that "Jesus-as-temple upstaging the Jerusalem temple" is most certainly an apparent convergence of his work with the gospel of John. He contends that Jesus went to the Jerusalem festivals but that throughout the gospel account, he reinterpreted their meanings and applied them to himself.

Although these challenges of John's Gospel to Wright's conclusions can be easily overcome, the weakness remains, why did he not include more of it in his arguments? Especially considering the similarities and benefits that John's Gospel could have to Wright's thesis. Therefore, his work remains one based on a threefold gospel canon rather than a fourfold one. What makes this omission of John even more intriguing is that it contradicts Wright's historical methodology of including all the pieces of the puzzle in his process of hypothesis and verification. Regarding his methodology, Wright resists the temptation to be swept along by mainstream ideas, yet he excludes John from his research to be more accessible and credible to these critical scholars (Hays 2011, 61).

---

18. 2 Macc. 7:36–38; 4 Macc. 6:27–30; 17:20–24.

4.3.4 Silencing the Voices of the Evangelists

Although we might credit Wright for a coherent historical picture of Jesus, his interpretation of the gospels according to the meta-narrative of his hypothesis does seem to lead to an oversimplistic hermeneutic (Bock 2009, loc. 1399–1400). Johnson (2009, loc. 2811–812) rightly shows that the strength of Wright's model of hypothesis and validation leads to simplicity and clarity; however, that is also its downfall since simplicity is maintained at the cost of a more adequate interpretation of certain evidence. Because of this, Hays (2011, 61) correctly criticizes Wright for not paying sufficient attention to the literary and theological make-ups of the individual gospels and for not honoring their unique messages. In other words, Wright is so bent on proving his hypothesis that he does not allow each evangelist to articulate his distinctive theological witness. Hays argues, "The story in Wright's viewfinder is not exactly any of the specific stories told by the Evangelists; rather, it is a critically abstracted construct, the master meta-narrative of the Bible" (63). More specifically, it is heavily geared toward the second temple Judaism's exile and deliverance motif. Wright is not interested in finding these themes within the theology of the gospel writers but seeks to trace them back into the mind of Jesus himself (63). His hypothesis, namely, that Jesus proclaimed and enacted the kingdom of God, the return from exile, and the return of YHWH to Zion, has a major influence on how he construes the gospels' stories, indeed, to such an extent that the unique voices of the evangelists disappear (Hays 2011, 70; Bock 2009, loc. 1515–17). Hays (2011, 70) argues convincingly that the distinctiveness of the testimony of these writers is ignored by Wright's retelling of his description of Jesus. Again, Wright ignores the church's dogma and traditional theology in this regard and, unfortunately, negates the significant gains made by previous literary studies of the gospels (70).

One of the significant consequences of Wright's master narrative is its impact on his interpretation of gospel pericopes. For example, consider Wright's interpretation of Luke 15:11–32, the parable of the prodigal son (Snodgrass 2009, loc. 802). According to Wright (1996a, 125–31), this parable is a story of Israel's exile and return rather than the repentance of defiant individuals (Blomberg 2009, loc. 169–70). However, this is not a convincing conclusion. Hays (2011, 70–71) shows that this interpretation is incorrect for at least two reasons. First, Luke disagrees with Wright. Hays indicates that Luke places this story along with the other two parables, the lost sheep, and the lost coin, in the context of Jesus' exchange with the Pharisees and Scribes around the issue of Jesus' practice of eating with sinners (Luke 15:1–2). Therefore, the obvious conclusion is that Jesus speaks about mercy and forgiveness. The same conclusion is reached by scholars such as Stein (1992, 400), Bock (1994), Butler (2000, 252), and Edwards (2015, 431), all of whom indicate that the issue at hand was Jesus' association with sinners. Second, historical interpretations of this passage do not agree with Wright. As shown above, there seems to be a consensus among scholars around the context and meaning of Luke 15. Wright (1996a, 126) acknowledges this historical interpretation, "Years of scholarship have produced many commentaries on Luke and many books on the parables. But none that I have been able to consult has noted the feature which seems to me most striking and obvious." Hays (2011, 71) aptly contends that the reason for this is that it probably is not as obvious as Wright believes.

Another example is Wright's interpretation of Jesus' call to repentance. Keesmaat and Walsh (2011, 93) credit Wright for describing Jesus as a prophet, which necessitates some prophetic critique against injustice. However, they point out that wherever Jesus delivered such a prophetic critique or call to repentance, Wright almost exclusively interprets it in terms of violent revolutionary zeal (Wright 1996a, 241, 249, 290, 325, 384, 390, 404, 407, 417–19, 449–50, 569). Although they admit that this formed a critical part of Jesus' teaching ministry, they emphasize that very often, these prophetic critiques of violent nationalism were accompanied by a practical application. For instance, Matthew 5:38–48 and Luke 6:27–36 refer to a turning from violent agendas through turning the other cheek, praying for one's enemies, and being peacemakers. These calls also include the commands to give to whoever begs of one and not to refuse anyone who wants to borrow from one (Matt 5:42; Luke 6:35).

Furthermore, Keesmaat and Walsh (2011, 94) point out that many calls to repentance had nothing to do with Israel's violent revolutionary zeal. Keesmaat and Walsh aptly argue that if Jesus saw himself as part of the prophetic tradition, as Wright contends, then he would have followed their critique of Israel's socioeconomic sins on which the prophets focused (94).[19] Perrin (2011b, 139–40) likewise states that the ancient prophets used the term repentance to call Israel out of a broad range of sins such as idolatry, bribery, deceit, and the oppression of the outcast,[20] which is unlike the type of specialized repentance Wright's Jesus calls for; namely, the political call to abandon revolutionary zeal. However, as Keesmaat and Walsh (2011, 94)

19. On not caring for the outcasts, orphans and widows see Isa 1:23; 10:2; Jer 5:27–29; 7:5; 22:3–6; Ezek 22:7; Zech 7:8–14; Mal 3:5; regarding mercy and justice: Isa 5:7; Jer 22:13–17; Hos 12:7–8; Amos 5:7; 6:12; Mic 6:1–12; exploiting the poor and needy: Isa 3:14–15; 10:2; 32:7; 58:3; Jer 2:34; Ezek 22:29; Amos 2:6–7; 4:1; 5:11; 8:4–8; Job 24:9–14; Ps 37:14; 109:16.

20. Isa 1:27; Jer 9:5; Ezek 14:6.

point out, where Wright quotes from the prophets, he ignores the places where it speaks about justice and righteousness or where economic injustices are addressed.[21] The consequence is that Wright downplays such themes in the gospels as well.[22] Wright's treatment of the rich young ruler (Luke 18:15–30), Zacchaeus (Luke 19:1–10), as well as the parables of the sower and the tenants are examples of this (Keesmaat and Walsh 2011, 95–99; Snodgrass 2009, loc. 849–50).[23] In both the accounts of the rich young ruler and Zacchaeus, Wright downplays the economic injustice and the need to repent in his interpretation. [24]

In response, Wright (2011c, 175–76) defends the application of his meta-narrative template to interpret the gospels by stating that the canonical story is the big story of Scripture and that the gospel writers would urge us to do so. However, this seems to be an oversimplification of biblical hermeneutics. Johnson (2009, loc. 3045–49) sums it up well, "It will not do (to use one of Wright's favorite phrases) to assert that each of the Synoptic gospels 'more or less' tells the same story. That is obvious from their literary interdependence. But what is equally clear from a close reading of each of the gospels is that each gospel's own way of interpreting Jesus through Torah is distinctive."

4.3.5 Wright's Apocalyptic Eschatology

Wright's presentation of Jesus' eschatology is elegant; however, it raises some questions. Some have criticized Wright's view that the Jews still considered themselves in exile at the time of Jesus (Snodgrass 2009, loc. 696–97). For instance, Casey (1998, 99–100) argues strongly that this was not the case, stating, "At the time of Jesus, many Jews lived in Israel. Some lived permanently in Jerusalem. Jews came to Jerusalem from all over Israel and the diaspora for the major feasts. In the temple, the Tamid (daily offerings) was

---

21. Wright (2010, 227) did place more emphasis on the selling and redistribution of funds to the poor in a later work. In this he showed that in Acts 2 the disciples fulfilled this call given to the rich young ruler.

22. We see from Goodman (1982, 417–27) and Sanders (1992, 148–49) that economic injustice was a real issue in Jesus' time and the beneficiaries of the suppression of the poor were the temple industry.

23. Wright (2011f, 111–12) concedes that if he had to rewrite *Jesus and the Victory of God (JVG)*, he would have highlighted these economic issues.

24. Wright (2008d, 217–18; 2008e) has argued in different places for a paradigm shift with regards to the future global economic order, emphasizing how current economic structures are exploiting the poor. If he interpreted these parables in the way that Keesmaat and Walsh (2011, 96–99) point out, then he could have used Jesus' words to provide more weight to his arguments to change economic injustices.

sacrificed twice a day, a special symbol of God's presence with Israel." However, Casey's argument against Wright is not convincing. Wright (1998b, 111) points out that his usage of the term "exile" refers more to "a period of history with certain characteristic features, not a mere geographical reference." Snodgrass (2009, loc. 698–703) shows that Wright's view that the Jews of Jesus' day still thought of themselves as being in exile is, at worst, quite plausible. Snodgrass points out that even if the exile was over in Jesus' day, the effects were not, and the promises of YHWH had not been fulfilled (loc. 698–703). It might have been the Jews were enslaved people in their own land that God gave them (Neh 9:36; Ezra 9:8–9). Likewise, Evans (2009, loc. 933–1123) shows, through a survey of various second temple texts, that many Jews did consider themselves in exile during the time of Jesus.

The most questionable area of Wright's understanding of Jesus' eschatology was Jesus' expectations. Snodgrass (2009, loc. 705–6) writes, "Wright correctly focuses on the kingdom as present, but he reduces Jesus' message of judgment and his emphasis on the coming of the Son of Man in glory almost exclusively to references to the destruction of Jerusalem in 70 C.E." Although Wright does believe in the second coming of Christ, he chooses to focus on the destruction of Jerusalem and underemphasizes Jesus' return. Snodgrass sums it up well, "[Wright] is correct that Daniel speaks of the Son of Man's going to the Ancient of Days to receive a kingdom, but what happens then? The purpose of receiving the kingdom in Daniel is that the nations might serve the Son of Man in an everlasting kingdom" (loc. 898–902). The main issue with Wright's view of Jesus' eschatology is that, according to his account, the events of AD 70 seem to have been a final realization of Jesus' eschatological vision. Although Wright (1996a, 468–72) held an "already-but-not-yet" view of eschatology, according to his thesis, the "not yet" aspect of that view seemed to have been fulfilled by both the return of YHWH to Zion during his Jerusalem entry and the vindication of Jesus as Israel's prophet and Messiah through the occurrence of the 70AD events which he predicted (Eddy 2009, loc. 670–74). In other words, according to Wright, Jesus' eschatological prophecies were not references to the end of the age but to the fate of Jerusalem (Allison 2009c, loc. 1666–667). Wright (1996a, 635) points out that although there are references to Jesus' second coming in Luke's writings, they are not a major emphasis and are found only in Acts. Therefore, he writes, "It looks much more like a post-Easter innovation than a feature of Jesus' own teaching."

However, Wright's account is not persuasive for the following reasons. First is the present existence of evil. Eddy (2009, loc. 668–69) points out, "Despite Jesus' expectations and claims of the final defeat of evil in and through his kingdom mission, evil apparently remains as firmly ensconced in the very fabric of the cosmos as it ever was." If the kingdom of God had fully come with the events of 70AD, then the question remains, will evil ever be overcome? Hays (2009, loc. 2057–58) agrees, claiming that "the realized eschatology of Wright's account enhances the internal tension of the theodicy question virtually to the breaking point." Second, the temple's destruction in AD 70 as the climatic end of the exile and vindication of Jesus as Messiah and prophet is not convincing because it appears to be more a sign that the eschaton has started rather than fully come. The temple's destruction was not the eschatological end of exile itself but rather a sign that the eschaton was underway (Perrin 2011b, 144–45). Perrin writes, "But it does not seem to be the case that the destruction of the temple marked the end of exile–only that the return from exile was underway, even as a resurrected creation was slowly taking shape through the expanding impress of the preached kingdom." In other words, the events of 70AD indicated that the eschaton was on the way, implying that the exile stood to be reversed and the kingdom was both here and in the future.

In Wright's later works, *Simply Christian* (2006), *Surprised by Hope* (2008), and *After You Believe* (2010), he emphasizes the creational realities that the resurrection affirms, namely, the establishment of a new heaven and new earth. Wright (2010, ix) states, "The basic point is this: Christian life in the present, with its responsibilities and particular callings, is to be understood and shaped in relation to the final goal for which we have been made and redeemed." Although Wright (1996a, 217–18; 305; 322–23) does point to future events beyond 70AD, such as the final judgment and resurrection, he overemphasizes the destruction of Jerusalem by limiting Jesus' eschatological expectation to that event. One reason for Wright's disinterest in assigning a further future eschatology to Jesus' thinking is that many scholars have only emphasized that and have not done Jesus' Jewish context justice (Evans 2009, loc. 2420–421). In other words, these other scholars have not thought historically enough for Wright's liking. However, with Snodgrass (2009, loc. 710), we may very well ask, "Is the wrath of God limited to Roman swords?" Less poetically, is the coming of the Son of Man in glory limited to what happened in 70AD?

Finally, as Blomberg (2009, loc. 362–64) asks, how does Jesus' death on the cross, which according to Wright, brought about the turn of the ages, relate to his insistence that the exile only ended with the destruction of the temple in 70AD? Or, as Eddy (2009, loc. 606–7) puts it, if Jesus believed that he was taking Israel's judgment upon himself as the suffering servant, then why did he prophesy that Israel would again be judged and destroyed within a generation? Eddy sums it up well when he states, "If ancient Jews had a multidimensional view of the world as Wright recognizes, Jesus could have anticipated both a historical and a cosmic eschatology, both a (judgment upon 'this generation') and a not-so-near (the Parousia as classically understood) element of future expectation" (loc. 678–79). It would have benefited Wright's work significantly if he had placed a balanced emphasis on the destruction of Jerusalem in 70AD and future eschatology in the mind of Jesus. Admittedly, Jesus' reference to the catastrophic events in Jerusalem must have been part of his eschatology, and adding an emphasis on the future events does create confusion around which of Jesus' sayings refer to which event (Snodgrass 2009, loc. 716–18).

Nevertheless, a dual eschatology seems to be the best approach to deal with Jesus' apocalyptic language, especially when it comes to texts that refer to end-time eschatology.[25] Bock (2009, loc. 1521–524) agrees that dual eschatology seems to be a better fit, arguing for a two-phase return-from-exile language. He acknowledges that one phase referred to Jesus' historical context but that the other points to the future when all nations will be judged. Bock cleverly suggests that if Wright treats the destruction of Jerusalem in 70AD as a form of typology of what is to come, then his eschatology would remain distinct, yet he would move closer to critics (loc. 1620–631). Correspondingly, Blomberg (2009, loc. 282–84) points out that Wright's criterion of similarity and dissimilarity could have worked well to affirm the traditional understanding of the Parousia. There are links to this in traditional Jewish literature, yet Jesus expands it beyond that.[26]

4.3.6 Conclusion

Although we can commend Wright for taking history very seriously, it seems that he does not pay traditional Christian dogma the same compliment. For Wright, both history and theology belong at the same table, yet it appears that when faced with a decision, Wright opts for the way of the academy rather than the church's traditional dogma. Therefore, it is apparent that he wilfully brackets out some Christian theological traditions. Furthermore, his adverse position towards dogmatic traditions can further be observed insofar as he goes behind the text to explain what Jesus was like, in so doing creating a fifth gospel.

Wright's omission of the gospel of John from his portrait of Jesus is another indicator of his adverse position against tradition. This omission is unfortunate, especially if one considers that John's description of Jesus

---

25. Matt 8:11–13; 11:21; 12:41–42; 19:28–29; 20:20–28; Luke 22:29–30.
26. Also, this falls in line with the early church teaching on the topic (Acts 1:11; 1 Cor 15:51–57; 1 Thess 4:13–18; 2 Thess 2:1–8; Rev 19:11–21).

is complementary to Wright's in several ways. Another way Wright seems to distance himself from Christian dogmatic tradition is through his interpretations of the Synoptic gospels. Wright's hypothesis, namely, that Jesus proclaimed and enacted the kingdom of God, the return from exile, and the return of YHWH to Zion, has a noteworthy influence on how he interprets the gospels' stories. Although one might agree with his hypothesis in general, Wright errs in trying to force most of the gospels' material through that grid. This leads to an oversimplification of interpretation and certain incomplete conclusions. This was particularly observed through his treatment of certain parables and his interpretation of passages that call for repentance. Lastly, one can commend Wright for his dedication to placing Jesus within a Jewish eschatology. Although it seems highly probable that the Jews considered themselves in exile during the time of Jesus, we must question Wright's idea that all of this came to an end in 70AD. Although these events were significant, they are best interpreted as a sign that the eschaton has started rather than fully come.

4.4 Strengths of Wolfhart Pannenberg's Christology

4.4.1 Introduction

Pannenberg is one of the most esteemed theologians of the twentieth century. Some have listed Pannenberg in the same bracket as prominent theologians such as Karl Barth, Paul Tillich, and Karl Rahner, identifying him as one of the most significant progressive theologians in a transitional age (Canale 2001, 3). Above all, his Christological work significantly contributed to his international fame (Kärkkäinen 2016, 115). Pannenberg's universal historical emphasis and high regard for anthropology contribute to his unique presentation of a Christology from below.

This section identifies several strengths of Pannenberg's contribution to the field of Christology. Some are unique contributions, and others are perhaps not as exceptional but are relevant to this thesis. It will also describe and explore these strengths by placing them in conversation with secondary sources and by engaging with Scripture.

4.4.2 Anthropological Implications

A unique contribution that Pannenberg's Christology makes is its connection with anthropology. Branson and Roxburgh (2021, 117) define anthropology as "that body of work that seeks to provide an interpretive meaning for being a human being in the world" and show how Jesus is the ultimate revelation of what it means to be human. They argue that what it means to be human must come as a revelation from God and that God has revealed this through the incarnation (118). In other words, Jesus is not only the revelation of God to us but also reveals what it means to be human. Conversely, modern Enlightenment anthropology has sought to remove God from the equation: "The foundation had changed: society was now the fundament to be examined by new philosophical methods—empiricism, positivism, naturalism, humanism. In the light of this new foundation and its approaches to understanding, the presence of religion was to be explained (away) by the newly minted social sciences" (Ward 2009, 169). Pannenberg refused to go down this modern path of anthropology. He believed that Jesus' universal significance is grounded in the fact that Jesus showed what it means to be human. He argued that in the historical Jesus, humanity's essence and destiny had been revealed, thereby linking anthropology to Christology rather than removing Christ from the equation. This link manifested in three ways in Pannenberg's work.

First, Pannenberg (1966, 197) argued that the essence of man, what it means to be fully human, consists in openness for God. Therefore, belief in God is not a strange idea to the structure of a human being (Kärkkäinen 2016, 117). An awareness of God, albeit to various degrees, is a universal phenomenon that has only recently been challenged (Kilcrease and Ziegler 2018, 156). Pannenberg (1976b, 9–10) showed that the anthropology of his day, *Weltoffenheit* (cosmopolitanism), emphasized that man has an openness to the world and beyond. In Pannenberg's view, this is because "the family tree of modern anthropology points back towards Christian theology" (12). Although cosmopolitanism did not refer to God directly, Pannenberg contended that man's openness to the world and beyond implied man's openness to God (13). In other words, the idea of the eternal value of humanity was primarily due to the contribution of Christianity, which is embedded in Christ (Pannenberg 1977c, 14). Schwöbel (2005, 132) sums up Pannenberg's position: "God is the infinite horizon which is implicitly presupposed in every act of human self-transcendence." For Pannenberg, an openness to God forms part of humanity's essence, in other words, what it means to be human. Olsen (1986, 212) writes, "This means that God is the essence of man as man's transcendent 'destination'. God is not a being alien to man, but the goal in which alone his striving can find rest and his destiny be fulfilled." Peters (2014, 376–77) argues that this openness to God is God calling us to a relationship with him through the *Imago Dei*, which is our destiny and which Pannenberg defined in terms of Christ as the New Adam.

This openness for God plays a significant role in Pannenberg's understanding of Jesus' vocation. Pannenberg showed that this essence of humanity was revealed through the message of Jesus. Jesus' proclamation of the immanent rule of God gave humanity an openness to God *(Offenheit für Gott)* and God's future by creating an expectation of a future transformed world and the resurrection from the dead (Pannenberg 1966, 234). Therefore, Jesus' office was to call people into the kingdom of God and to impart salvation that consisted of an "openness for God." Pannenberg defined the idea that humanity has an openness to the world and beyond as an openness for God, which was foundational to the preaching of the historical Jesus. "This message calls all to find their fulfillment and reveals the fundamental openness of human beings to God" (Whapham 2017, 90–91).

Second, Jesus not only revealed the essence of humanity but also uncovered and fulfilled our destiny. Pannenberg (1966, 232–33) contended that Jesus' message of the imminent expectation of the kingdom of God provides one of the most significant understandings of humanity ever discovered. This message meant that the lordship of God was near, which summoned humanity out of its securities and uncovered the insufficiencies of this world to fulfill human destiny. Therefore, the ultimate human destiny can never be obtained during our earthly existence but is located in the future. Or, as Mattes (2017, 124) puts it, the ultimate goal of human striving is oneness with the infinite. Correspondingly, Pannenberg claimed that salvation is a concept that refers to the fulfillment of the ultimate human destiny for which human beings long. According to Pannenberg, people are driven by a focus on the future but are also reminded of the shortcomings of their present experience over their preferred future (Pannenberg 1978a, 104). Salvation is obtained when a man is united in his present with his past and future, which can only come after the resurrection from the dead (Pannenberg 1966, 197). The message of the nearness of God's lordship then revealed the destiny of humanity, to be united with the infinite through the resurrection of the dead, which is never fulfilled in this life (233).

However, in Jesus, the ultimate destiny of humanity, namely, our destiny to be raised from the dead, had been fulfilled (Pannenberg 1966, 195–96). Hazelton (2018, 115) writes, "Paul, Pannenberg asserts, described Jesus Christ as the eschatological form of humanity that in contrast to the previous Adamic humanity, obeys God, and overcomes mortality." This destiny is not only for the individual but extends to the whole of humanity because Jesus is the new Adam who has fulfilled the destiny of all humankind (Kärkkäinen 2016, 118). In other words, the revelation of God in Jesus

Critical Analysis of N.T. Wright's and Wolfhart Pannenberg's Christology   149

and the revelation of man's destiny are closely related.[27] Pannenberg (1966, 196) claimed that one must not separate the revelation of God in Jesus and the revelation of salvation for humanity. Consequently, humanity needs to come to Jesus and seek community with him, for he is the revelation of the future salvation *(Heilszukunft)* and can promise salvation directly (Pannenberg 1978a, 110).[28]

Third, Pannenberg (1966, 239–41) saw a close relationship between the love for God, forgiveness, and the love of neighbor. He suggested that Jesus' call to love one's neighbor and thereby create community also reveals another part of the essence of humanity, namely, their desire to seek community (240–41). Pannenberg (1976b, 59) stated, "*Die Menschen suchen Gemeinschaft*" (People seek community). Pannenberg (1966, 240) argued that the message that Jesus proclaimed, which announced the promise of salvation and the forgiveness of sins, empowered the hearer to love their neighbor. In this, the universal significance of Christ's activities became apparent since part of the essence and destiny of humanity is to strive for community (240–41). One of the most valuable aspects of this account is that it provides a useful approach to combatting the anthropology of modern individualism (Branson and Roxburgh 2021, 119–20). Pannenberg's statements about Jesus and what it means to be human have a universal or communal theme. In Jesus, we are shown that part of the essence of humanity is to have an openness to God, to desire community with others, and our destiny is to be raised from the dead in a universal resurrection, which should lead to new life for all of humanity (*die ganze Menschheit*; Pannenberg 1974b, 180).[29]

4.4.3 The Church's Call as a Precursor to the Kingdom

Branson and Roxburgh (2021, 121) point out that our praxis depends on our anthropology; likewise, Pannenberg's anthropological Christology has practical implications. Pannenberg's anthropological emphasis in his Christology, wherein Jesus is portrayed as the ultimate man, the new Adam, has

27. See Branson and Roxburgh (2021, 118).

28. Pannenberg (1978a, 105) held, "What occurred through Jesus Christ is not only for the Christians and their future significance but rather for the future of humanity generally."

29. Johnson (1982, 245–48), Medley (2013, 94) and MacDonald (2016, 75–77) suggest that Pannenberg's later work seems to imply that by approaching Christology from an anthropological perspective, according to which attention is given to humanity's connection to God in history, the chasm between the from below and from above Christologies might be crossed.

serious implications for the followers of Jesus. Pannenberg believed that because of Jesus' self-sacrificial dedication to the Father's will, he was exalted to participate in the lordship of God, which has implications for his disciples. Harvie (2008, 150) shows that Pannenberg's understanding of the kingdom of God is profoundly shaped by his understanding of Jesus of Nazareth's career, death, and resurrection. Pannenberg argued that Jesus' unity with God was established through the resurrection, his unity was revealed in his dedication to the Father as Son, and the effect thereof is Jesus' exaltation to participation in God's lordship. Consequently, Jesus rules over his church as Lord and will bring the kingdom of God to fulfillment in the future (Pannenberg 1966, 386). Harvie (2008, 156) states that "for both Moltmann and Pannenberg the Parousia of Christ brings the fulfillment of the kingdom of God." Although Pannenberg believed that the church cannot transform the world into the kingdom of God because of our fallen human nature, he nonetheless believed that the promise of God's future renewal should inspire and direct our conduct (Peters 2014, 370). Pannenberg (1966, 387–88; 1988, 167) did not consider the kingdom of God and the church synonymous, but the church is the precursor to the kingdom of Christ, which was linked to the future. The church then has the unique task of being the precursor to the future kingdom of God, which has practical implications for us.

Harvie (2008, 161) points out, "For Pannenberg, Jesus witnesses to the future kingdom in his proclamation. Both the earthly ministry of Jesus and his eschatological Parousia have ethical implications of Christian morality." In other words, the church's role as the precursor of the kingdom of God demands that their conduct indicate that they are a people of the kingdom. For example, one such implication is that the church shares in the Lord Jesus' mission. As a precursor, the church has the unique task of calling attention to the eschatological future of salvation (Pannenberg 1966, 388). The church shares the mission of Jesus by dedicating itself to God through the proclamation of the kingdom of God and by submitting its behavior in both private and public to the lordship of Christ (389–90).

Correspondingly, the church's role of acting as the precursor to the kingdom of God entails living for justice in all structures of human relationships, which, for Pannenberg, is the concrete form that the love demanded by the kingdom of God takes (Harvie 2008, 155). Being a follower of Pannenberg's Jesus requires love towards one's neighbor. Anyone who heard and believed Jesus' message about the nearness of the kingdom of God and who received the forgiveness of sins must conduct themselves in a particular manner towards others (Pannenberg 1966, 239). Pannenberg saw a close relationship between the love for God, forgiveness, and the love of neighbor (Mates 2017, 126). Pannenberg (1976a, 363) correctly emphasized that no religion can ever contribute to its contemporary society unless the misguided privatization of religion is addressed. The purpose of Pannenberg's rebuke of such a development is to keep the lordship of Jesus at the forefront and emphasize the church's mission as the precursor to the kingdom of God. The church's call to imitate Jesus' self-sacrificial dedication to the Father through accomplishing its mission has significant consequences for this world now and not only for the world to come. In other words, the idea of an escapist Christianity by which we only look forward to going to heaven without living lives that reflect the lordship of Christ is far removed from Pannenberg's Christology. For Pannenberg, the freedom from sin through the Spirit of Christ impacts the entire person, not only in his private life but also in his economic and political relationships (Pannenberg 1978a, 108).

Furthermore, being a precursor of the future kingdom of God has ecological implications for the church. Following Christ's example of self-sacrificial dedication to God has a positive impact on humanity and all of creation itself. Because Jesus is the new Adam, he reveals God's intentions for humanity and what it means to be created in the image of God (Kilner 2015, 124). Pannenberg believed that being created in God's image, and imitating Christ's example of what living as such means, necessitates responsibility for the well-being of the natural environment. Rise (2010, 227–28) explains that, for Pannenberg, becoming a follower of Jesus involves maturing to become conscious of the well-being of all that God has made. Moreover, Pannenberg (1977c, 40; 2001, 203) rightly believed that the acknowledgment of the lordship of Jesus and the uniqueness of the church as his body should lead to greater ecumenical openness. Schwöbel (2005, 132) points out that, for Pannenberg, disunity in the church is unacceptable and goes against the very calling of the church, namely, to be a foretaste of the kingdom of God. Pannenberg was called an ecumenist and was convinced that the best apologetic for the Christian faith in a secular culture is a visible unity of the Christian community (Mattes 2017, 137–40).

Loving people, as an implication of being a precursor of the future kingdom of God, also has potential repercussions for inter-faith dialogue. This is especially possible due to Pannenberg's Christian eschatology of the future kingdom. Pannenberg contended that even the hope of a future resurrection should not lead to the egoism of salvation for the individual but should lead to new life for all of humanity (Pannenberg 1974b, 180). Christian eschatology has far-reaching consequences and should lead to a restoration of life on earth. Winkler and Kärkkäinen (2011, 175–78) point out that Pannenberg's view that the church is the precursor to the future kingdom of God, which represents the eschatological community of God wherein all people will have fellowship with God, lays a foundation for inter-religious dialogue since "God wants to include everyone and everything in his eschatological fellowship." Consequently, the church's role of pointing to the future kingdom should urge them to live lives separate from the world's ways and encourage them to an inclusive mission to all of humanity.

4.4.4 Apologetic Nature

Pannenberg (1966, 22) made it clear even before he presented his historical findings of Jesus that the very task of Christology is to establish the Christian confessions about Jesus rather than merely repeat them. In other words, the field's focus should be on what can be known about his career and fate historically rather than rehearsing the Christian dogmatic confessions. It should therefore vindicate our confessions about his divinity from that perspective (Macleod 2000, 20). This approach addresses the Enlightenment challenge of not merely believing things without using one's independent reason. The apologetic nature of his work provides insightful language about Jesus with which one might engage an Enlightenment-affected audience. This is because his area of interest was primarily Enlightenment liberal Protestantism (Peters 2014, 368).

Pannenberg's view of the task of Christology sympathizes with Immanuel Kant's assertion that reason is the only form of valid knowledge and whatever opinions are based on faith are considered illusions that need to be "cleared up" (*Aufklärung*; Kärkkäinen 2016, 75–76). Hence, Pannenberg's approach makes it clear that faith cannot be based on faith but must be based on something that can be confirmed to be true repeatedly (Pannenberg 1974a, 140). Correspondingly, Kilcrease and Ziegler (2018, 156) argue that, for Pannenberg, theology is an intellectual endeavor. They write, "For Pannenberg, when understood properly, theology is a rational enterprise by its very nature. Not unlike the theology of Thomas Aquinas, Pannenberg believed that, for the dogmatic enterprise to be 'rational', practitioners must recognize the unity of all truth. It therefore seeks its own coherence with other forms of human knowledge." Pannenberg (1985, 15) was convinced that something is only true if it is true for everyone, regardless of whether everyone believes it. Therefore, the concepts of truth and universality formed the basis of his theological method. Chow (2018, 22) writes, "For Pannenberg, theology is a public discipline as it makes truth-claims about shared reality." Truth, especially when it comes to Jesus of Nazareth, must be grounded in history and have a universal significance to be worth pursuing.[30]

In response to this Enlightenment challenge, Pannenberg presents two very useful responses regarding the validity of Jesus' claims: his investigation of the resurrection and his description of Jesus as the revelatory presence of God. First, Pannenberg showed that the claims of Jesus needed to be confirmed by God, which occurred through the resurrection. Pannenberg (1966, 55–56) believed that Jesus' claim to authority comes in the form of a proleptic structure that anticipates a future verdict. The resurrection was that verdict. He was convinced that a historical investigation of the resurrection claims could validate that Jesus did rise from the dead (Peters 2014, 367). Pannenberg risked everything upon the historicity of the resurrection (MacDonald 2016, 74). Although certain scholars such as Wildman (2007, 287) consider a from below Christology that references the resurrection as suspect, Pannenberg's description of the two events on which he based his conclusion that the resurrection is historically probable, namely, the appearances of Jesus and the empty tomb tradition, is very persuasive.

Pannenberg (1966, 85–86) showed that at the time that Paul wrote 1 Corinthians 15, which speaks about the appearances of the resurrected Jesus to more than 500 people, many of those eyewitnesses were still alive (85–86). Consequently, this was Paul's way of providing an apologetic for these appearances by challenging his readers to confirm this event for themselves through conversation with these eyewitnesses. Macleod (2000, 25) aptly writes, "However impossible it may be for twentieth-century scholars to achieve certainty on events which took place 2000 years ago it was not impossible for those who lived through the events themselves." Likewise, Pannenberg (1994a, 327) aptly pointed out that if the empty tomb could not be established, then the preaching of the early church would not have lasted a day. In other words, an empty tomb is the assumption of the preaching of the early church's message about the resurrection of Jesus. However, the relationship between the empty tomb tradition and the tradition of appearances in Pannenberg's argument is most persuasive. He argued that the disciples returned independently to Galilee before they knew about an empty grave (Pannenberg 1966, 102–3). This means that the appearances of Jesus in Galilee did not happen because of their knowledge of an empty tomb. They had no predetermined expectation that knowledge of an empty tomb might have provided. Pannenberg (1994a, 328) rightly pointed out that "the Galilean appearances tradition alongside the Jerusalem grave tradition

---

30. It is because of this apologetic angle that Pannenberg was not willing to accept Jesus' claims to authority as final when many of his contemporaries did.

provides considerable weight for the verdict of the historical formation." According to his historical inquiry, the probability of the resurrection seemed the most convincing conclusion and the best explanation for the origin of Christianity (Pannenberg 1974a, 143). One also appreciates Pannenberg's contention that all conclusions drawn from a historical inquiry are never incontestable and should be revisited as discoveries are made (142–43). This posture provides further apologetic value in that one feels that he is honest in his conclusions.

Second, Pannenberg's (1966, 130–31) conclusion that Jesus is the revelatory presence of God, which includes an identity of essence, addresses the Enlightenment's requirement of reality in all statements. Pannenberg pointed out that the concept of revelation has become significant since the *Aufklärung* (Enlightenment), wherein the existence of God was no longer pre-supposed, and the experience of reality has become the ultimate foundation for dialogue (129). In this context, revelation has become the only credible basis for speaking about God. Therefore, only if God has revealed himself in the experience of reality can a correct knowledge of God be obtained. Consequently, as Canale (2001, 14) writes, "Pannenberg squarely removed the revelation experience from the classical interpretation of the supernatural order and placed it within the natural order. Within the natural order, Pannenberg situates revelation primarily within the realm of human history." Pannenberg was convinced that God could be known and spoken of because of his self-revelation through human history. Winkler and Kärkkäinen (2011, 155) state, "Ultimately, history matters so much for Pannenberg because it is not only the means of supporting his truth claims, but also the unfolding self-revelation of God for humanity." Therefore, for Pannenberg and his Heidelberg colleagues, history provides the medium and content of God's indirect revelation (Peters 2014, 368). Appealing to history is an effective way to engage with a post-Enlightenment society regarding the validity of Jesus' claims.

4.4.5 Critique of an Imaginary Contemporary Jesus

One strength of Pannenberg's Christology is his insistence on discovering who Jesus was historically rather than shaping a contemporary Jesus based on one's imagination. For Pannenberg, it made a significant difference whether one starts one's Christology with the historical Jesus or the kerygma of the early or contemporary church (Pannenberg 1966, 15). Centuries before Pannenberg, it was Calvin (1960, loc. 12886) who warned that unless the church understands who it is that they proclaim, they will be guilty of speaking of a name of which they know nothing. It is this notion against which Pannenberg's Christology guards us. Pannenberg contended that we can only understand who we are preaching about if we have studied Jesus historically. In other words, neither the early church's preaching nor the contemporary church should fundamentally be used to construct a portrait of Jesus.

Pannenberg (1966, 16) believed there is a continuity between the life and message of Jesus and the apostles' preaching; nevertheless, Christology must start with the historical Jesus himself. His reason for rejecting the early church's preaching about Jesus as the source for Christology is because if the church based its faith solely on the early church's preaching, then it based its faith on something that was itself a product of faith (17). Instead, he proposed that an understanding of the historical Jesus himself must support faith. Similarly, Pannenberg argued that faith should not solely rest on current Christian experience (*gegenwärtigen christlichen erfahrung*; p. 19). Moreover, historical research is how the contemporary and early church proclamation is legitimized *(legitimation des Kerygmas selbst)*.

Even though one might have good and pious intentions when speaking about Jesus, the risk exists that one becomes susceptible to self-delusion. The risk remains that one assigns characteristics to Jesus that he never claimed for himself. This problem is further elevated when such false views, regardless of how honorable, are proclaimed in the church. The consequence is an erroneous belief about Christ, which leads to disappointment when Jesus is trusted for certain outcomes based not on who he is but on self-delusion. These sorts of pious deductions can be seen in contemporary songs about Jesus, for example, where Jesus is identified as an emotion (Jesus Culture 2017).

A more severe distortion of who Christ is, which is based upon contemporary experience, can be seen in Richard Rohr's *The Universal Christ*. In this mystic work, Rohr (2019, loc. 9) goes as far as to dedicate his book to his dog, who was *Christ* for him. He writes, "I dedicate this book to my beloved fifteen-year-old black Lab, Venus, whom I had to release to God while beginning to write this book. Without any apology, lightweight theology, or fear of heresy, I can appropriately say that Venus was also Christ for me." One might shrug this notion off as preposterous, yet Rohr's work is Amazon's number one book in Christology and Christian Ethics (McClymond 2019). He has received much attention over the last few years and has acquired a large following among millennials (Falsani 2019). Especially those millennials who have found their childhood faith stale or those who have found Rohr's message more inclusive to their personal preferences. His work has been referred to as a fresh way of looking at Christianity, which has too often misunderstood Jesus' life and teachings due to cultural presuppositions, religious conflicts, and human egos (Garrett 2019, 18).

Rohr (2020) believes that the church has been preoccupied with Jesus and neglected to recognize Christ. Consequently, we have ended up with a sentimental personal religion rather than a universal, natural, and inclusive religion. He argues that by emphasizing Jesus above Christ, we once again created a story that is not big enough. However, if Jesus is studied and described historically, as Pannenberg suggests, then such contemporary reductionism of Jesus can be avoided. In contrast to Rohr, Pannenberg does not speculate about who Christ is apart from Jesus. Instead, Pannenberg shows through historical examination that Jesus has more significance than any other human being, particularly as revealed through the resurrection. Although Pannenberg affirms the pre-existence of the Second Person of the Trinity and the second coming of Christ, he never speculates who Christ is or was outside of Jesus of Nazareth. Therefore, Pannenberg's emphasis on who Jesus was historically is critical for our conversations about who Jesus is today and what his significance is for us (O'Collins 1967, 370).

4.4.6 Jesus' Relation to the Father

A significant strength of Pannenberg's presentation of Jesus is that he found an innovative way to describe the divinity of Jesus. Pannenberg argued that the resurrection affirmed the revelatory unity *(Offenbarungseinheit)* between Jesus and God; therefore, there was an essential unity *(Wesenseinheit)* wherein the eternal being of God and the totality of Jesus' person were connected. Furthermore, this essential unity can be presented more clearly as a unity of person *(Personeinheit)*, which can be deduced from Jesus' self-consciousness *(selbstbewußtsein*; Pannenberg 1966, 336). In other words, these notions were how Pannenberg spoke of Jesus' unity with God.

Pannenberg (1966, 338–45) was adamant that Jesus' activities, mission, and message, shaped by his Jewish understanding of salvation and God, hold the key to understanding his self-consciousness. Moreover, Pannenberg argued that Jesus' self-consciousness revealed his relatedness to the Father and not to the Logos, the Second Person of the Trinity (345). In other words, Jesus knew himself functionally in unity with God's will *(funktional mit Gottes Willen)* through his career, which was shaped around his proclamation of the imminent kingdom of God. Pannenberg believed that one cannot understand the sonship of Jesus unless one starts with his relation to the Father. He contended, "Without the spirit of communion of the Father and the Son there is no knowledge of God and no knowledge of Christ"

(Pannenberg 1975a, 164). Thus, Pannenberg was not interested in speculating about the inner construction of the divine and the humanity in Jesus. Or, to put it differently, his focus was Jesus' relation to the Father, which can be deduced from Jesus' self-consciousness as revealed by his public life, rather than speculating about the synthesis of the Logos and the human Jesus of Nazareth.

Pannenberg (1966, 346) proposed that the issue of the unity of the man Jesus and the eternal Son of God cannot be answered directly. Schwöbel (2005, 131) points out, "Pannenberg explores the possibility of asserting that the identity of Jesus with the Son of God is established indirectly through his relationship of absolute obedience to God the Father."[31] The unity of the man Jesus and the Son of God is a conclusion derived from Jesus' relation to the Father. Jesus showed himself to be the Son of the Father through his personal community *(Persongemeinschaft)* with the Father. Johnson (1982, 245) sums up, "Thus the unity of the man Jesus with the Logos is a dialectical one, established by way of a 'detour,' the detour of his dedication to the Father." McDermott (1974, 717) states that Pannenberg manages to speak about Jesus' relationship to the Father in more anthropological terms, namely, that their unity was, first and foremost, a functional unity wherein Jesus is distinct from the Father and subordinate to him. This relation between Jesus and the Father as the basis for the unity between himself and God is critical to understanding Pannenberg and is also one of his more significant contributions to the field of Christology (Johnson 1982, 244). Similarly, Peters (2014, 373) points out that the "key to Pannenberg's trinitarianism and key also to his doctrines of creation and anthropology is the dialectic of self-differentiation and unity between the Son and the Father."

Focusing on Jesus' relation to the Father rather than the Logos also impacted how Pannenberg viewed Jesus' kenosis. According to this view, Jesus' self-emptying was not of divine attributes but equality with the Father through his self-sacrificial dedication to the Father and his distinguishing himself from the Father (Kärkkäinen 2016, 117). Pannenberg used the ideas of self-distinction from the Father and Jesus' self-sacrificial dedication to the Father to argue for Jesus' divinity. Pannenberg declared the deity of Christ by emphasizing Jesus' self-distinction from the Father (Chiavone 2009, 263–64). Chiavone explains Pannenberg's reasoning here: "Christ distinguishes himself from the Father to establish the monarchy, which is the deity, of the Father, and thereby participates in that monarchy and deity."

---

31. This understanding is based on Pannenberg's anthropological presupposition that openness for God is essential to human nature (Schwöbel 2005, 132).

Christ participates in the deity of the Father by establishing it through his self-distinction. Chow (2018, 57) writes, "In sum, Pannenberg insists Jesus' divinity must be examined by his unity and self-distinction with the God of Israel." He also affirmed the sonship of Jesus by describing Jesus' relation to the Father in terms of his dedication and self-sacrifice, which he links to Jesus' behavior and fate.

Pannenberg (1966, 346) emphasized that Jesus' mission was to call people into the imminent kingdom of God, which shaped his activities and message, and that his mission was confirmed by God through the resurrection. This showed that all of Jesus' activity was a dedication to God and his will. Additionally, Jesus' dedication took on a self-sacrificing nature through the fate that he suffered. Pannenberg (1994b, 373) stated, "Only in this subordination to the rule of the one God is he the Son." Consequently, Pannenberg contended, along with Gogarten (1952, 242), that Jesus' sonship is found in his humanity. The Father and Son's relationship is revealed by Jesus' dedication to God through the proclamation of the Father's kingdom.

To summarize, Pannenberg claimed that this human, Jesus, is the Son of God instead of arguing about the synthesis of the divine and human substances in Jesus. However, Jesus' identification as the Son of God is not derived from Jesus' self-consciousness during his life but is confirmed by the resurrection (Pannenberg 1966, 348). Following this line of thought, Pannenberg (1991a, 31) went as far as to argue that the doctrine of the Trinity seeks to explicitly communicate that which was implicit in Jesus' dedication and relatedness to the Father during his earthly career. McDermott (1974, 718) sums up Pannenberg's position as, "Never formulate anything about the divinity of Jesus that is not based on a statement about the concrete unique relationship of the man Jesus to his Father and to his fellow man."

4.4.7 Conclusion

Pannenberg's universal historical approach to Christology and his anthropological emphasis led to distinct contributions to the field. Directly related to his approach are the connections that he made between Christology and anthropology, whereby he showed that humanity's essence consists of openness towards God, an openness that Jesus' proclamation of the nearness of the rule of God emphasized. Additionally, Jesus' fulfillment of humanity's destiny, namely, to be raised from the dead, empowered humanity to live into another destiny, namely, to be in community. And this anthropology has practical implications; specifically, Pannenberg's Christology reminds us of the church's vocation to live as a sign and foretaste of the future kingdom of God. Correspondingly, God requires certain conduct from those who call themselves followers of Jesus, which has implications for human relationships, ecumenical discussions, inter-religious conversations, and the stewardship of creation.

Pannenberg's approach also provides helpful language to engage with a post-Enlightenment culture regarding the historical validity of Jesus' claims. It appeals to history as the medium by which it affirms the deity of Christ, whether through an investigation of the resurrection or a description of Jesus as the self-revelation of God in history. This historically grounded approach assists the contemporary church in addressing certain Christological statements and ideas solely based on contemporary experience. It reminds us that Jesus cannot be what he never was historically. Lastly, Pannenberg gave us a fresh way to speak about the grounds of Jesus' divinity, this time not concerning the Logos but the relation to the Father.

4.5 Weaknesses of Wolfhart Pannenberg's Christology

4.5.1 Introduction

The influence on Pannenberg by Hegel's philosophy of history has resulted in a unique contribution to the field of Christology with various strengths. However, placing a high emphasis on a universal historical and anthropological approach to Christology brings certain weaknesses. Various scholars have esteemed Pannenberg's work, and one of the shreds of evidence of this admiration has been the interest shown by other scholars to engage critically with Pannenberg's work. In other words, the fact that so many scholars have engaged with Pannenberg's work over the last 50 years is a testament to the fact that his work is to be taken seriously. However, on closer investigation, there are certain inconsistencies in his approach, some omissions or underemphasis of critical issues, and a disparity between theory and practice. This section identifies the weaknesses of Pannenberg's Christology. It will describe and explore these weaknesses by placing them in conversation with secondary sources and by engaging with Scripture.

4.5.2 An Underestimation of the Cross

The first glaring weakness in Pannenberg's presentation of Jesus of Nazareth is his superficial handling of the events at Golgotha. Kärkkäinen (2016, 120) points out, "It has often been noted that Pannenberg so focuses on the resurrection that the cross does not play a crucial enough role in his

Christology. It is true that Pannenberg emphasizes resurrection and therefore places less emphasis on the cross." It must be noted that Pannenberg did affirm that there was a salvific element to Jesus' death on the cross and that it had universal implications. Pannenberg's view of the substitutionary nature of Jesus' death extended beyond Jews to humanity as a whole. His perspective on the cross can be summed up by the idea of inclusive substitution whereby in Jesus' death and resurrection, he acted as our substitute so that although we will die, we will not be abandoned, and we can look forward to a resurrected existence (120). Although Pannenberg should be praised for this presentation of a substitutionary meaning of the cross, there are several weaknesses in his presentation of the meaning of Jesus' death that devalue Jesus' accomplishment on the cross.

First, Pannenberg argued that Jesus' death was not premeditated but rather something that happened to him because of his career. Pannenberg (1988, 167; 1969, 133) believed that Jesus' death was not his primary mission but the consequence of his primary vocation, namely, to proclaim the imminent kingdom of God. By proclaiming the imminence of the kingdom of God, along with some ambiguous actions, Jesus was making the implicit claim that he was the mediator of the presence of God and; as a result, he was executed (Pannenberg 1966, 257–58; 1988, 167). Pannenberg went as far as to concede that Jesus' death was not a surprise to him but argued against any intentionality from Jesus' side. Pannenberg came to this position because he was convinced that the crucifixion must be interpreted considering Jesus' career. In doing so, he concluded that it resulted from his vocation of proclaiming the immanence of the kingdom of God. He emphasized that nothing meaningful can be said about Jesus' fate without consideration of the activities throughout the life of Jesus (Pannenberg 1966, 277). Ironically, although Pannenberg sought to interpret the crucifixion considering Jesus' career, he ignored Jesus' explicit teachings around what Jesus himself believed about his death. In a sense, Pannenberg tells us why Jesus died from a Roman and Jewish perspective, namely, because Jesus was a rebel and a blasphemer; however, he does not elaborate on why Jesus thought he would die. However, Schweitzer (2016, loc. 7183) aptly pointed out that Jesus did not go to Jerusalem that last fatal time to work but to die. The central symbolic action that confirms this suggestion is the Last Supper.[32]

Furthermore, Wright (1996a, 556–57) has shown that the Last Supper was a sort of Passover meal, celebrating the deliverance of Israel from the tyrant bondage of Egypt and that Jesus intended the meal to symbolize the new exodus that he was about to accomplish through his impending death.

---

32. Matt 26:17–19; Mark 14:12–16; Luke 22:7–15.

Wright points out that Jesus' symbolic actions and clarifying statements during the Last Supper strongly suggest that Jesus knew that he was about to die and that his death was part of the eschatological plan to usher in the kingdom of YHWH (559-62).[33] The parables around this event indicate that Jesus envisaged a great messianic battle, although radically redefined from the ruling Jewish expectation, after which the kingdom of YHWH was to come. This battle was against the real enemy, the Satan or Accuser that had infiltrated Israel (563-65). Moreover, it is not only the last supper and its accompanying riddles that Pannenberg ignored, but also Jesus' passion predictions.[34] All of the instances where Jesus spoke of his death strongly suggest that he expected his death to accomplish something and that although he was not surprised by it, it was more than something that merely happened to him because of his proclamation. The omission of why Jesus thought he needed to die leads to further weaknesses of Pannenberg's view on the meaning of the cross.

Second, although Pannenberg does affirm the substitutionary nature of Jesus' death and that it had an atoning nature, there is minimal mention of the *Christus Victor* motif in his discussion. Certain scholars have criticized Pannenberg's handling of Jesus' substitutionary atonement for sinful humanity, as Johnson (1982, 242) points out; however, his omission of Jesus' messianic battle causes more reason for concern. Kilcrease and Ziegler (2018, 160) indicate that Pannenberg does not advocate a vicarious satisfaction atonement exclusively because he believed that Jesus, as the new Adam, dealt with sin indirectly by inaugurating the new creation. In other words, based on his anthropological emphasis, according to which Jesus is the new Adam who fulfills the intentions of God in terms of what it means to be human, the old Adam who was enslaved to sin died with Christ on the cross. However, Pannenberg does not enter further into the notion that Christ took the messianic battle against evil upon himself on the cross, as shown convincingly by Wright (1996a, 563-65). Pannenberg omitted any thought around the messianic battle because he did not believe that Jesus thought of himself as the Jewish Messiah.

Third, Pannenberg's conclusion about the meaning of the cross from the perspective of the resurrection is insufficient. Pannenberg (1966, 252) was adamant that the meaning of the cross is only correctly deduced from the perspective of the resurrection because the resurrection of Jesus was an event that is easier to interpret than the meaning of the cross. Pannenberg

---

33. Matt 21:33-46; 22:34-40; 23:37-39; 26:6-13; Luke 12:49-50; 23:27-31; Mark 10:38-40.

34. Matt 16:21; 17:22; 26:31; 26:56; Mark 9:12; 10:45; 14:27; 14:41 Luke 18:31-33; 22:37.

(1968a, 107) believed that "Christology today (regardless of all confessional differences) should consider anew the fundamental importance of the resurrection of Jesus for all Christological statements."[35] Furthermore, he contended that "without the resurrection, there could be no salvific significance of the cross" (Pannenberg 1988, 170). Now, the initial critique must be raised against the idea that the resurrection is easier to interpret than the cross, especially since Jesus gave an impressive catalog of explanations, through symbols and words, of the meaning of the cross. It is curious that Pannenberg, who was so fixated on historical facts, would interpret the cross primarily through a unique supernatural event, which, according to him, not even Jesus expected, rather than interpreting it through a wide array of sayings and actions from Jesus. One senses that Pannenberg did not see all there is to see about the cross through these resurrection lenses.

Of course, if one ignores all that Jesus himself said about his death, in symbol and words, and reduces the reason for the crucifixion to a result of Jesus' imminent kingdom proclamation, according to which he was viewed to be a blasphemer, then one might conclude that the resurrection is the proof that Jesus wasn't a blasphemer. However, suppose the two points above are sound, namely, that Jesus intentionally died to bring forth God's eschatological plan and that he believed that he would engage in the great messianic battle against Satan on the cross. In that case, one must conclude that the resurrection also points towards the start of the new creation and the victory of God over evil. This underestimation of the cross could result from Pannenberg's position on the authority and inspiration of the Scriptures, a weakness to which we now turn.

4.5.3 Sceptical Treatment of the Scriptures

Pannenberg's treatment of scripture is problematic. Pannenberg goes behind the New Testament writings to construct his portrait of Jesus. As we have seen, the continuity between the kerygma of the early church and the life and message of Jesus was critical for Pannenberg because, on that premise, he built his argument that going behind the New Testament writers to find the historical Jesus is not only possible but necessary. Pannenberg (1966, 17) suggested that if the church based its faith solely on the early church's preaching, then it based its faith on something that was itself a product of faith. In contrast to this, and siding with Ebeling (1961, 46), he proposed

---

35. "Sollte die Christologie heute (unabhängig von allen konfessionellen Differenzen) die fundamentale Bedeutung der Auferstehung Jesu für alle christologishen Aussagen neu bedenken."

that faith must be supported by an understanding of the historical Jesus himself (*am historischen Jesus selbst*). Pannenberg believed that this historical understanding of Jesus could be obtained by going behind the New Testament text, by treating it as a historical source about Jesus himself rather than merely what was once believed and preached (Pannenberg 1966, 18).

This notion of going behind the New Testament texts as a necessity for a historical reconstruction of Jesus poses the question of Pannenberg's view on the authority of Scripture. Pannenberg opposed the Reformers' idea of a literal inspiration of the Scriptures and, therefore, the infallibility of every passage (Pannenberg 1997, 212–13; 1970, 4–5). He suggested that the Spirit of God infused the content of the apostolic gospel and, because the New Testament is the most authentic document of their proclamation, it is divinely inspired in that sense. In other words, the basis for the inspiration of Scripture is the gospel of Jesus Christ as proclaimed by the apostolic witnesses. This led him to conclude that the doctrine of the inspiration of Scripture can only be addressed after the doctrine of the person and work of Jesus Christ (Pannenberg 1997, 214).

This understanding of the inspiration of Scripture leads Pannenberg to reject certain passages about Jesus as mythical and legendary. It seems that he believed that the Holy Spirit inspired the Scriptures, yet in such a way that one can be selective regarding which parts are true. For example, Pannenberg solely based his investigation of the appearances of the resurrected Jesus on the writings of Paul because he believed the gospels' accounts were legendary. Pannenberg (1973, 23) thought that early Christianity was more prone to mythology than ancient Judaism because of its strict monotheism.[36] Additionally, Pannenberg's treatment of the virgin birth as mythical is another consequence of his view of the inspiration of Scripture. Pannenberg (1972, 71–77) referred to Jesus' virgin birth as the "legend of his virgin birth." He contended that the virgin birth legend began solely in the development of traditions through history (Pannenberg 1994b, 315–19). Moreover, he claimed that the virgin birth was unfamiliar to John and Paul and most likely invented by later theologians from the Hellenistic Jewish community who sought to elevate the person of Christ above other Old Testament characters. Hence, Luke and Matthew both included the notion of a virgin birth to communicate a theological point (Luke 1:26–38, Matt 1:18–25; Pannenberg 1966, 141–42). Moreover, Pannenberg believed that the virgin birth story was formed to preserve the idea of the incarnation

---

36. Macleod (2000, 20) points out that the most significant support for a from above Christology is that this is where the New Testament writers started. Perhaps Pannenberg's untrusting position toward the gospels' writers contributed to his emphasis that a Christology must be performed from below rather than from above.

against Gnostics. However, Pannenberg's most significant reason for rejecting the concept of a virgin birth is because he believed it compromised his understanding of the incarnation. He felt that the incarnation is better preserved through normal birth (145–46). Pannenberg claimed that the virgin birth account does not point to the incarnation but contradicts it because it implies that God created his Son in Mary, which meant that Jesus could not have been his Son in pre-existence (Pannenberg 1972, 63, 76). For Pannenberg, a virgin birth would mean that Christ was not pre-existent.

However, this treatment of the virgin birth idea is not convincing as Barth (1936b, 172–202) has shown that there is perfect unity between the incarnation of Jesus and the "sign" that points towards it, the virgin birth. Likewise, the idea that a normal birth preserves the pre-existence of Christ is questionable because one might conclude that God created his Son through Joseph in Mary. This would also compromise the pre-existence of Christ and pose problems regarding the sinlessness of Jesus Christ and, therefore, his sufficiency as a savior. Macleod (2000, 22) rightly points out that the virgin birth is about the beginning of the man Jesus of Nazareth and not the Son of God. Therefore, it is perfectly compatible with both the incarnation and the pre-existence of Christ. Additionally, if Jesus were born from two ordinary people, any union between Jesus and the Logos would have involved some form of Adoptionism or Nestorianism (22).

All of this points to Pannenberg's dissatisfactory understanding of the inspiration of Scripture, which makes his interpretation of Scripture inconsistent. He can believe in the historicity of the resurrection and even miracles, yet he calls the virgin birth a myth (Pannenberg 1966, 234–35). For Pannenberg, a historical study must have an openness to the supernatural and miracles (Kärkkäinen 2016, 116). Yet, it seems that Pannenberg chose which supernatural stories could be believed and which ones were myths. Macleod (2000, 40) rightly criticizes Pannenberg on this issue: "We cannot create a supernatural free zone from Virgin Birth to Crucifixion and then suddenly introduce a mega-miracle. It is only as the resurrection coheres with all that has gone before that it has any significance." Chiavone (2009, 248–50) also criticizes Pannenberg for this selective treatment of the Scriptures and points out that certain theological statements Pannenberg took at face value whilst rejecting others. He rigorously affirmed the historicity of the resurrection and the sayings of Jesus that affirm his distinctiveness from the Father, yet he denied the historicity of the virgin birth.[37]

---

37. Pannenberg differed significantly from Wright here, who opposes the idea of dismissing parts of the stories about Jesus as myth based on a predetermined criterion, choosing instead to include all the pieces of the puzzle (Hays 2011, 58).

Pannenberg's view of Scripture also accommodated other fields for doing theology. Pannenberg (1970, 3) opposed the idea of limiting the task of theology to the exposition of Scripture without investigating the claims of the other sciences. He was adamant that Christian theology must be placed in conversation with the secular world as it pursues truth because God has revealed himself not only in the Scriptures (Peters 2014, 367). Consequently, O'Collins (1967, 369) observes, "Certainly we have here a Christology based on a striking knowledge of Scripture, the Councils, the Fathers and a large range of theologians and philosophers, both ancient and modern. Its originality consists perhaps most of all in the way it understands Christ's role as Revealer." Pannenberg was convinced that God had revealed himself in other areas of history as well, not just in sacred history. Therefore, the truth can be obtained in other areas of knowledge as well, such as science, sociology, and anthropology (Winkler and Kärkkäinen 2011, 146–48; Fisher 2010, 45–46). But, as Kilcrease and Ziegler (2018, 162) point out, "in Pannenberg's rationalistic enterprise, the authority of Scripture and its true witness to the history of salvation cannot be trusted in an ultimate sense. Rather, all theological knowledge must conform to the canon of what Pannenberg views as universal human rationality. In this view, God must conform to the reason of humanity."[38]

4.5.4 Reluctance to Place Jesus within Jewish Categories

Pannenberg commented that it is crucial to place Jesus within his first-century Jewish context and to assess his relationship with Israel's God. He critiqued from above Christologies for not taking the actual historical context of Jesus seriously because of its neglect of Jesus' Jewish context (Pannenberg 1966, 28–29; 1970, 26–27). With the neglect of Jesus' relationship to Israel and the Old Testament, he argued further that even Jesus' death loses much of its significance within the from above approach. Furthermore, Pannenberg (1966, 30) warned that if Jesus' life and message are taken independently from an understanding of his relationship to Israel's God, then the history of Jesus will be inaccurate.[39] He insisted that Jesus' life, sayings, and fate be understood and evaluated in this context. Yet, when one examines

---

38. The idea that one can possess objective truth well beyond the Scriptures is questionable considering the role of the personal religious convictions of the theologian, as shown by Gregersen (2017, 20).

39. Pannenberg differed from Barth in terms of the relationship between the Jewish law and the gospel. Where the latter viewed the law and gospel intimately bound in Christ, the former believed the gospel replaced the temporary law (Scheuers 2015, 106).

Pannenberg's presentation of Jesus, one finds that he did not place Jesus in any Jewish categories, nor did he believe that Jesus thought of himself in any of these categories. While he opposed the Reformed concept of the threefold office of Christ *(munus Triplex)* at length, Pannenberg's refusal to at least place Jesus in the prophet category is alarming and inadequate because it seems to de-Judaize Jesus. Wright (1996a, 150–54) shows that although the writing prophets had ceased after Daniel, other prophets and prophecies of various sorts continued well into the first century.

Similarly, Webb (1991, 326–31) points out that there were as many as three different categories with which one might understand the prophets of this period. Wright (1996b, 407) highlights that Jesus was known as a prophet, spoke of himself as a prophet, and his career followed on from the prophetic work of John the Baptist.[40] As such, Jesus must be seen at a foundational level to have stood in the prophetic tradition of the Old Testament, bringing a word from Israel's God, and summoning her to a new path (Wright 1996a, 163). Moreover, Jesus was modeling his career on John the Baptist and other Old Testament prophets such as Ezekiel, Jeremiah, Jonah, Amos, and, above all, Elijah (166–67). The portrait of a prophet seems to be the clearest point upon which to ground a study of the historical Jesus. Sanders (1985, 237–41) correctly sums it up by claiming that Jesus saw himself as more than a prophet but never as less than one.

Likewise, Pannenberg argued that Jesus did not think of himself as the Messiah but that his followers assigned this title after his resurrection. He somewhat contentiously claimed that the Synoptic gospels projected the messianic office of the resurrected Christ back onto the historical Jesus to make his death seem premeditated (*planmäßig bedachten und vorausgesehenen*; Pannenberg 1966, 226). Pannenberg repeatedly contended that Jesus rejected the title of Messiah on earth but had been exalted to Lord and Messiah through the resurrection (132–33). In other words, the Son of God designation was given to Jesus after the resurrection as he was identified as the one who would come again in messianic lordship (152). However, the position that Jesus did not think of himself as the Jewish Messiah is not convincing. First, various people were regarded as Messiahs by certain Jewish societies before, during, and after Jesus' lifetime, and they presumably also regarded themselves as such (Wright 1996b, 409). Correspondingly, it would not have been strange for Jesus to regard himself as the Messiah within the first-century Jewish context. According to Mark 8:27–30, his

---

40. Matt 11:7–19; Luke 7:24–35; Mark 9:11–13; Luke 16:16; Mark 11:27–33; Matt 21:23–27; Luke 20:1–8.

followers did regard him as the Messiah before the resurrection, and Jesus seems to have accepted the title.

Furthermore, Jesus' kingdom pronouncement itself was a clue that he considered himself under a specific vocation assigned to the Messiah. According to the Qumran scrolls, the person who proclaims the arrival of the kingdom of YHWH is the Danielic Messiah (Wright 1996a, 530–32). Furthermore, Jesus' choosing of the twelve disciples who would constitute the renewed Israel likewise points to Jesus' belief that he was the Messiah as well as various sayings throughout his ministry, such as being the great shepherd (John 10:11), his comparisons to David (Mark 2:25) and Solomon (Matt 12:41), and his claims to be YHWH's anointed (Isa 61; p. 534–36).

Jesus claimed to be the Messiah through explicit words and symbolic actions. One such symbolic action was Jesus' action in the temple. Pannenberg (1966, 257–58) highlighted these events as ambiguous and identified them as one of the reasons why Jesus was crucified as a blasphemer. Still, he never thought of these actions as messianic. Jesus' actions in the temple[41] and the parables surrounding that event reveal Jesus' belief in his Messiahship. Wright (1996a, 485) points out that Jesus' temple action was his most obvious messianic act because the temple was one of the central symbols of royal vocation. The temple was linked to a long line of royalty in Israel's history. David planned it, Solomon built it, Hezekiah and Josiah reformed and restored it, and Zerubbabel was supposed to rebuild a new temple (Wright 2018, 299–300). Even the aspiring Messiahs had a close relation to the temple; they either cleansed it, rebuilt it, or intended to do so. Therefore, what one said about the temple was closely related to what was said about the Messiah. With that in mind, Wright's (1996a, 490–91) argument that through Jesus' temple action, he was claiming a kind of authority over the temple, which only belonged to the ruler of the temple, namely, Israel's king, proves to be very convincing. These actions were a royal claim, and this interpretation seems to be supported by the parables surrounding that event.[42]

Macleod (2000, 28–29) points to Pannenberg's skeptical approach to the Synoptic gospels as foundational to his reluctance to acknowledge that Jesus thought of himself as the Messiah. Macleod argues, "The historicity of Jesus' use of such titles is as well substantiated as the resurrection; equally indispensable to understanding the origin and life of the early church, particularly its worship of Jesus; and virtually indispensable to understanding

41. Matt 21:12–13; Mark 11:15–17; Luke 19:45–46; John 2:13–22.
42. Mark 14:58; Matt 26:61; John 2:19; Mark 11:23; Matt 21:23–27; Mark 11:27–33; Luke 20:1–8; Matt 21:33–46; Mark 12:1–12; Luke 20:9–19; Matt 22:15–22; Mark 12:13–17; Luke 20:20–26; Mark 12:35–37; Matt 22:41–45; Luke 20:41–44.

how a worship apparently so subversive of monotheism could so easily take hold in a Jewish matrix." Pannenberg contended that Jesus' claim to authority was contained within his vocation as the one who was to proclaim the imminence of God's kingdom. In that sense, he saw himself as the mediator of God's coming rule. However, if Pannenberg can believe that Jesus could claim such an authority that went beyond what a normal human might assign to himself, as Kärkkäinen (2016, 119) shows, why is it improbable that Jesus would have claimed the prophetic or messianic title?

4.5.5 *Critique of Chalcedon*

Although Pannenberg acknowledged the deity of Christ, he was reluctant to describe the relationship between the two natures of Jesus Christ. Additionally, when he did describe that relationship, his explanation was ambiguous to the point that it was no longer orthodox or in line with the Chalcedon creed.[43] Pannenberg (1977a, 322) summarized the incarnation as follows, "Out of his eternity, God has through the resurrection of Jesus, which was always present to his eternity, entered into a unity with this one man which was at first hidden. This unity illuminated Jesus' life in advance, but its basis and reality were revealed only by his resurrection." Consequently, he preferred not to speak of Jesus as the synthesis of two natures, one divine, and one human, but rather, "as this human, Jesus is God" (*als dieser Mensch ist Jesus Gott*; Pannenberg 1966, 334). From the perspective of his resurrection, this human Jesus is not just human but is one with God and thus is himself God (*mit Gott eins und so selbst Gott*; p. 334). Yet, Pannenberg also maintained that, although Jesus is God, he remained distinct from the Father, as can be observed through his obedience to the Father (Pannenberg 1966, 351; 2003, 239). In other words, Pannenberg both affirmed the deity of Jesus Christ and his distinctiveness from the Father. Yet, he refused to adequately address the next question: What is the relationship between the deity of Christ and his humanity? He extensively explained the relationship between the Father and the human Jesus; however, his conclusion that Jesus is God and yet distinct from the Father poses the question, what is going on in Jesus Christ?

Pannenberg criticized what he called the unification and disjunction Christologies that sought to address this question because he believed they

---

43. McDermott (1974, 718) writes, "Pannenberg is the mortal enemy of that interpretation of the two-natures doctrine according to which Christ is a compound (*zusammensetzung*) of two substances or principles; for him–and I concur–Jesus' humanity and divinity are two complementary, radically distinct, total aspects of his existence."

started their Christologies from above. In other words, they started their Christologies with the notion of the incarnation and sought to describe the relationship between the divine and the humanity of Jesus whilst staying within the parameters of the Chalcedonian creed, which confessed that the divinity and humanity of Jesus are unmixed, unchanged, indivisible, inseparable in one person (Pannenberg 1966, 292). However, Pannenberg contended that the Chalcedon formulation was a theological compromise because rather than attempting to solve the problem of how the two natures united in Jesus Christ (*trägt die Kennzeichen eines Kompromisses*), it merely synthesized the Alexandrian and Antiochene theologies (295). He argued that because both schools began their Christological formations with the incarnation, their conclusions were inevitable and that combining the two answers never solved the problem. But the question remains after Pannenberg arrives at the belief in the incarnation, why does he not proceed with the question of the unity between the divinity and humanity within Jesus himself? Pannenberg ends his Christology with the assertion that Jesus is God, that God entered into unity with this one human, Jesus of Nazareth, as confirmed by the resurrection. At this point, Chalcedon, as well as the disjunction and unification Christologies, commences.

Pannenberg could have viewed Chalcedon and these incarnational Christologies as extensions of his work rather than alternatives. McDermott (1974, 720) likewise is aware of this difference and is disappointed that Pannenberg did not further reflect on the personhood of Jesus from this point. He poses the question, "Pannenberg insists that the only divine Thou in Jesus' earthly life was the Father. Might we not conceive the eternal Son as the Father's communication of His own integrity and unity of life to Jesus' existence, which integrity and unity is the second divine hypostasis?" Surely Pannenberg's claim that there was unity between the Father and Jesus has further implications that must be reflected upon. Owen (1967, 59) likewise points out that after one considers the humanity of Jesus, the natural question that follows concerns the role of divinity within Jesus, which enabled him to live the way he did. Yet Pannenberg did not adequately address Jesus' relation to the Logos (Medley 2013, 94).

This reluctance to acknowledge and fully describe the relationship between the Logos and human Jesus leads one to conclude that the Logos was hardly ever-present and, as a result, Jesus' deification occurred in his humanity. Pannenberg's emphasis on the fact that Jesus' deity is confirmed and expressed through his self-distinction and self-sacrificial dedication to the Father indicates that he believed Jesus' divinity is found in his humanity. This notion is confirmed by Pannenberg's statement, "as this man, Jesus is God." This leads one to wonder whether Pannenberg really did believe in the incarnation. Macleod (2000, 37–39) points out that because Pannenberg found Jesus' deity in his humanity, along with the fact that Pannenberg's Jesus never claimed any titles, his conclusion seems to point towards the deification of a human. In Pannenberg's effort to preserve the full humanity of Jesus, which was motivated by his anthropological bent, he argued that Jesus' deity is located in his humanity, more specifically, in Jesus' subjecting and distinguishing himself from the Father (Kärkkäinen 2016, 117–18). Kärkkäinen shows the weakness of this approach, namely, "while Pannenberg's view helps avoid one of the major problems of the traditional incarnational model–that is, the robust affirmation of the true humanity of the incarnated Son–it may go too far in making the deity solely a matter of the humanity of Jesus and thus failing to establish a thick account of divinity" (118).

The second issue with Pannenberg's handling of the two natures of Christ is that in those instances where he did discuss the relationship between Jesus and the Logos, his views seem muddled. Chiavone (2009, 264–66) points out that Pannenberg only superficially adhered to the Chalcedon creed because when it comes to his handling of the human Jesus' relation to the Son or Logos, his assertions are too ambiguous to conclude that he was in line with orthodoxy. For instance, Pannenberg (1994b, 387–89) seems to have suggested a sort of divide between Jesus and the Logos based on Jesus' self-distinction with the Father. Only when Jesus' self-distinction from the Father becomes complete is he identified with the Logos, which only occurred after his death and resurrection. Pannenberg states, "The human nature of Jesus Christ shares, then, in the deity of the Logos, but only through the mediation of self-distinction from God" (388). And again, "In the death of Jesus the deity reached the extreme point of the self-distinction from the Father by which the Son is also related to the Father, so that even his humanity could not be held in death." Chiavone (2009, 265–66) observes that this would mean that Jesus was not fully divine during his career because Jesus only participated fully in the Logos during his death and resurrection. McDermott (1974, 711–13) similarly points out that, at times, it seems that Pannenberg's Jesus became divine only due to the resurrection. Other times, it appears that Jesus underwent a sort of progressive incarnation, which found its pinnacle in the resurrection. This leads Chiavone (2009, 268) to conclude, "At present, it seems that Pannenberg's Christology contains no single understanding of who the person of Christ is, no clear affirmation of his genuine, full deity, and no coherent account of his preexistence as the eternal Son. As such, it fails to measure up to Chalcedonian orthodoxy, and serves as a mark against Pannenberg's understanding of trinitarian unity." The issue with Pannenberg's discussion of the relationship between Jesus and God is not because Chalcedon's requirements aren't present but because it is mixed with various assertions that make his arguments non-coherent (269).

4.5.6 Conclusion

Pannenberg's Christology has many strengths related to his Christological approach, which has a significant universal historical emphasis and anthropological bent. However, this approach also leads to certain weaknesses in his Christology. His overemphasis on the resurrection led him to interpret the cross of Jesus only through the lens of the resurrection rather than taking Jesus' implicit and explicit words and symbolic actions seriously. For someone heavily bent on historical facts, it seems strange that he would interpret a historical event through the lenses of a unique supernatural event, namely, the resurrection. This drive towards historical validity was also why he never dealt with Jesus' messianic battle on the cross. Moreover, refraining from using Jesus' words and actions to interpret the crucifixion events points to another weakness of Pannenberg's Christology: his insufficient view of the authority of Scripture. Pannenberg's understanding of the authority of Scripture allowed him to decide which stories to believe and which to write off as myths. This, in turn, leads to an inconsistency in his interpretation of Scripture whereby certain events or words are valid, and others are mythical or legendary.

This is seen in Pannenberg's belief that Jesus did not refer to himself as a prophet, much less the Messiah. However, as we have seen, Jesus and his followers did regard him as a prophet, and Jesus' sayings and symbolic actions, specifically in the temple, point toward Jesus' self-understanding as the Jewish Messiah. Although Pannenberg was adamant that Jesus must be understood historically within the Jewish context, he denied Jesus the liberty of thinking of himself in Jewish categories that were very prominent in the first century. Lastly, although Pannenberg's Christology concluded that Jesus is God, it does so only in terms of his relationship with the Father. This is acceptable and even commendable for a Christology from below; however, his adverse position towards discussing the relationship between the Logos and the human Jesus is unnecessary, especially since these Christologies that deal with this notion begin where Pannenberg ends, namely, the incarnation. Correspondingly, when Pannenberg did speak about the two natures of Christ, he did so in an ambiguous manner that seems to have departed from orthodoxy.

4.6 Concluding Remarks

In this chapter, a critical analysis of the main theories of Wright and Pannenberg's Christologies was conducted based on the understanding obtained in chapters 2 and 3. The critical analysis of their work revealed various strengths that one can deduct from their Christologies, but also certain weaknesses. It identified, defined, and explored these strengths and weaknesses through conversation with various secondary sources and Scripture. Initially, the work of N.T. Wright was critically analyzed. It was shown that his work has various strengths that are commendable. His Christology provides helpful links between the Old Testament and Jesus as the fulfillment thereof. It prescribes a manner of treating the gospels that takes seriously what they are fundamentally about, namely, the telling of the story of the kingdom of God coming to earth through the public ministry, death, and resurrection of Jesus of Nazareth. Additionally, Wright's Christology has practical and political implications for the followers of Jesus; specifically, the witness of his followers in word and deed, holding this world, its rulers, and the church to account, and loving one another by laying down our rights for each other. Finally, Wright's account gives Christians a new perspective on speaking about God.

On the negative side, although Wright's epistemology allows for both theology and history to be taken seriously when they clash, Wright's default position is to choose history over theology. In other words, he wilfully brackets out Christian theological tradition and assumes an adverse position toward dogmatic traditions. This adverse stance against tradition can be seen in his omission of the gospel of John from his presentation. Another of Wright's weaknesses is his interpretations of the Synoptic gospels. Wright interprets the gospels' stories through the lenses of his hypothesis and, at times, forces the gospel's material through that grid. Finally, although we must praise Wright for placing Jesus within a Jewish eschatology, we must question Wright's notion that Jesus' eschatology should be limited to the Jerusalem events of 70AD.

Subsequently, a critical review of the Christology of Wolfhart Pannenberg was conducted. Like with Wright, certain strengths and weaknesses were identified through this process. On the positive side, Pannenberg's universal historical approach to Christology, with its anthropological emphasis, provides insightful connections between Christology and anthropology. He showed that Jesus has revealed the essence of humanity and fulfilled our destiny. From a practical perspective, Pannenberg's work points out that the church's vocation is to live as a sign and foretaste of the future kingdom of God. Hence, God demands certain conduct from those who call themselves followers of Jesus, which has implications for human relationships, ecumenical discussions, inter-religious conversations, and the stewardship of creation.

Additionally, Pannenberg's Christology provides helpful language to engage with both unbelievers and believers in an Enlightenment-inherited culture. It validated Jesus' claims to authority through a historical investigation of the resurrection and described Jesus as the self-revelation of God in history. This historically grounded approach safeguards the church from certain Christological statements and ideas that are solely based on contemporary experience. It challenges us not to speak about Jesus in ways that contradict who he was historically. Finally, Pannenberg gave us fresh language around the grounds of Jesus' divinity. He argued for Jesus' divinity based on his relation to the Father rather than his to the Logos, the Second Person of the Trinity.

Conversely, on the negative side, Pannenberg's work does contain certain issues. An emphasis on the resurrection of Jesus is central to Pannenberg's argument, which is commendable; however, this led him to interpret the cross of Jesus only through the lenses of the resurrection rather than taking Jesus' implicit and explicit words and symbolic actions seriously. This hesitancy to take Jesus' words and actions seriously points to another weakness of his Christology: his inadequate view of the authority of Scripture. Pannenberg's understanding of the authority of Scripture led to an inconsistency in his interpretation of Scripture, whereby certain events or words are valid, and others are mythical or legendary. Furthermore, although Pannenberg was adamant that Jesus must be understood historically within the Jewish context, he refused to describe Jesus within Jewish categories that were very prominent in the first century. Lastly, although Pannenberg's Christology concluded that Jesus is God, it does so only in terms of his relationship with the Father. He had an adverse stance towards discussing the relationship between Jesus and the Logos, which is unnecessary, especially since the Christologies that deal with this notion begin where Pannenberg ends, namely, the incarnation.

5

The Embedded Christology of the Christocentric Homiletic

5.1 Introduction

GOLDSWORTHY (2000, 121) INDICATES that the basic etymological meaning of expository is "to expose the meaning of the text." If that is the case, then the most fascinating expository sermon, which most preachers would have loved to hear, is the one the resurrected Jesus gave to some disciples on the road to Emmaus (Luke 24:13–35). This message left the disciples asking, "Did not our hearts burn within us while he talked to us on the road, while he opened to us the Scriptures?" (Luke 24:32, ESV). One might wonder what the content of that message was. Did Jesus merely retell some of the stories they had listened to since childhood? What made his teaching so profound that it left his audience deeply moved? Luke 24:27 tells us what the content of that message was; it states, "And beginning with Moses and all the Prophets, he interpreted to them in all the Scriptures the things concerning himself" (Luke 24:27, ESV). In this way, Jesus linked the Old Testament Scriptures to himself and thus, he unified the message of the Scriptures.

Chapell (2018b, 1–2) points out that this notion was further applied by the early church, who sought to unify the Scriptures around the redemptive work of Jesus Christ, which is what we now call the redemptive-historical approach. However, regrettably, it was not long after the early church period that this unified meta-narrative of the Scriptures led to all sorts of abuses whereby, through creative, allegorical, and questionable exegesis, Jesus was made to appear in every text of Scripture miraculously. Since those early days, the redemptive-historical approach, also called the Christocentric approach, has had a checkered story that ebbed and flowed in and out of mainstream hermeneutics and homiletics (Chapell 2018b, 1–3; Chow 2016, 115; Peppler 2012, 120). The Reformers, Luther and Calvin, sought to address these abuses by offering an alternative way to unify Scripture's message around the redemptive work of Christ. Luther suggested a law-gospel approach, whereas Calvin's work provided important inroads into understanding Scripture's unified redemptive message. Although unifying Scripture's message around Christ's redemptive work fueled the preaching of the Reformers, they had different battles to fight—justification by faith and the sacraments—which prevented them from further expounding how this unified message should shape our hermeneutics and homiletics.

Subsequently, the Dutch Reformers re-emphasized the importance of biblical theology, which sought to maintain and apply this unifying redemptive meta-narrative of Scripture, and this, in turn, influenced the Puritans, an influence that contributed to the great awakenings in America. The most recent of these Dutch Reformed scholars, who played a significant role in the current wave of redemptive-historic scholarship, was Geerhardus Vos. Sadly, biblical theology became the weapon of liberalism, which argued that just as the Old Testament points to Christ, who was beyond its expectations, in the same manner, a preacher could point to Christ beyond the message of the canon. Consequently, biblical theology became the enemy of conservative evangelicalism (Chapell 2018b, 1–3). However, around the 1960s and 1970s, certain conservative voices arose again, reminding the church of the necessity of using the grand meta-narrative of the Scriptures to interpret individual texts. This resurgence of the importance of biblical theology impacted homiletics, and scholars like Edmund Clowney and Sidney Greidanus developed preaching approaches that centered on this conviction.[1] Whereas biblical theology and its role in our preaching was pushed to the margins 50 years ago due to its abuse by liberalism, the pioneers of the modern development of the Christocentric approach, such as Clowney and Greidanus, have been instrumental in giving this movement the momentum needed to become one of the most significant preaching models today.[2]

---

1. Chou (2016, 115–16) provides six characteristics that summarize the modern Christocentric movement, namely, (1) it seeks to place each text in relation to Christ, (2) it emphasizes the unity of Scripture, (3) it emphasizes the theology of Scripture, especially Christology and the gospel, (4) it uses the grammatical-historical interpretation as its foundation, (5) it seeks to move beyond the grammatical-historical hermeneutic to link the text to the canonical context, (6) it emphasizes its Christian nature.

2. The influence of this approach is reflected in its implementation by prominent

This chapter will examine the Christocentric homiletic and its underlying Christology. It will commence with a literature review of the homiletical works of the pioneers of the approach—Edmund Clowney and Sidney Greidanus—as well as a contemporary representative in Bryan Chapell. These scholars' homiletical works and sermons will be analyzed, and their theological reasoning and practical guidance will be presented. Subsequently, this chapter identifies, describes, and explores the approach's shortcomings. The purpose of this chapter in the thesis is to gain an understanding of the Christocentric homiletic and its weaknesses in order to identify and examine its embedded Christology. This will assist in identifying ways in which the strengths of Wright and Pannenberg's from below Christologies might enrich and challenge the Christocentric homiletic in chapter 6.

5.2 Edmund Clowney: Redemptive-Historical Approach

5.2.1 Introduction

Edmund Clowney's ministry exceeded half a century, within which he served the church as a preacher, writer, pastor, theologian, and the first president of Westminster Theological Seminary.[3] Although he functioned in various roles, one constant in Clowney's ministry was his unwavering commitment to redemptive-historical preaching, which flows from a Christocentric biblical theology (Johnson 2009, 17–19). His Christocentric bent in preaching stemmed from a deep theological conviction that the story of the Bible ultimately finds its meaning in Jesus (Clowney 2013, 10–15). John Frame wrote, "Nobody had a deeper understanding of how all Scripture witnesses to Christ" (Clowney 2007, back cover). This commitment led to the fact that many now consider Clowney the most influential proponent of Christ-centred preaching in the twentieth century (Allen 2011, 43). Bryan Chapell, whose own Christocentric model will be assessed in this chapter, states, "Edmund Clowney is this generation's patriarch of redemptive-historical preaching" (Clowney 2003, loc. 4). This section will explore the theological basis and the practical application of Clowney's Christocentric

---

preachers such as Don Carson, Joel Nederhood, Sinclair Ferguson, John Piper, Steve Brown, James Montgomery Boice, Skip Ryan, Tony Merida, Jerry Bridges, Ray Ortlund, Joe Novenson, David Calhoun, Danny Akin, Ray Cortese, and Timothy Keller (Chapell 2018b, 2–3).

3. Current Westminster Theological Seminary president Lillback (2016, 6) states that even to this day, the Westminster Theological Seminary is proud to have sustained its advocacy of the Christocentric approach, which was laid upon the foundation of Clowney's work.

approach to preaching. It will also illustrate how Clowney applied his approach in sermon form.

5.2.2 *The Hermeneutic of the Redemptive-Historical Approach*

When it comes to Clowney's view of preaching, the weight, type, content, authority, and character are a natural response to a profound biblical theology. Allen (2011, 44) writes, "For Clowney, biblical theology does not merely inform Christ-centered preaching. Rather, Christ-centered peaching is the natural and inescapable result of a rightly ordered biblical theology." Although there are many different definitions of biblical theology, as pointed out by Clowney (2002, 10), his understanding of this concept was firmly shaped by Geerhardus Vos. In Clowney's flagship work on the theological basis for Christocentric preaching, *Preaching and Biblical Theology* (1961), he does not offer a definition himself but builds on the description given by Vos (Allen 2011, 44-45; Lee 2016, 71-72; Prince 2011, 89-90). Vos (1948, 13) argued that biblical theology is "that branch of exegetical theology which deals with the process of the self-revelation of God deposited in the Bible." In other words, he understood the Scriptures as the continuing self-revelation of God through different periods in history as determined by God's actions (Clowney 2002, 15). Clowney's understanding of the biblical theology that has so heavily influenced his preaching model was built on the definition of Vos.

Allen (2011, 45-49) points out that Clowney's biblical theology has three hermeneutical presuppositions: First, Clowney believed that the Bible consists of a progressive revelation wherein its message is systematically and progressively revealed. In other words, from the start of Genesis to the end of Revelation, God has chosen to manifest his revelation in various ways at various stages. However, these revelations should not be seen as independent from each other but as different scenes of the same grand narrative. In other words, these epochs build on each other; they bring clarity regarding what has gone before, just like any good screenplay. Clowney (2002, 75) contended that God's revelation unfolds in progressive epochs in the history of redemption, and the Scriptures tell us how it unfolded. As Allen (2011, 47) describes it, "The message runs from Genesis to Revelation, expanding in clarity, intensity, and perspicuity." Clowney (2002, 15) argued, "Biblical theology formulates the character and content of the progress of revelation in these periods, observing the expanding horizons from age to age. So understood, biblical theology is both legitimate and necessary." For Clowney, biblical theology is not only helpful but indispensable because it informs systematic theology. It safeguards the church from making incorrect deductions regarding certain topics in Scripture by keeping the whole narrative of the Bible central. Clowney (2007, xii–xiii) wrote, "Biblical theology follows the story of the Bible rather than the topics found in the Bible." For him, the central story that Scripture tells is the unfolding of the story of redemption.

Second, Clowney contended that the Scriptures have a consistent message because although it has many human authors, it has one divine author who sovereignly ensured that the message communicated is consistent. For Clowney, the Scriptures consist not only of progressive revelations, but these revelations tell a consistent story without contradictions. Clowney (2002, 15) proposed that God's revelation was given "in epochs determined by God's acts" and that there is unity in these successive eras because these progressive revelations were made by "one gracious design." Therefore, historical progression and theological unity of the Scriptures are essential (17). Clowney maintained that "biblical theology is a contradiction in terms unless the Bible presents a consistent message" (13). Therefore, anyone who seeks to interpret any part of the Bible must consider this unity, which for Clowney, is Jesus Christ.

Third, the Bible is completely Christ-centered in nature. Allen (2011, 47) recognizes that the notion of Christ as the fulfillment of Scripture's grand narrative is central to Clowney's biblical theology and forms the basis of his Christocentric approach to preaching. Clowney (2002, 74–75) contended that the epochs within which the unfolding progressive revelation of God has been revealed are united by Christ. For Clowney (1965, 7), one is not ready to preach any text of Scripture until it is viewed through the person of Christ. So, Lee (2016, 73) highlights, "Christ-centered biblical theology shows how every text is related to Christ in the redemptive-historical context." Therefore, Clowney (2003, loc. 87) believed that preachers who ignore redemptive history ignore the witness of the Holy Spirit about Jesus. Understanding Christ as the fulfillment of Scripture's meta-narrative leads to preaching that stems from the wisdom of God and the mind of Christ (Clowney 1965, 7). To interpret any text in relation to Christ takes God's progressive revelation and the overarching theme of the Bible seriously (Clowney 2003, loc. 98). Prince (2011, 91) writes, "Therefore, biblically faithful expository preaching has one essential message—Jesus Christ." Clowney differs from other expositors on this issue, such as Walter Kaizer, who only acknowledges Christ's presence in the Old Testament's prophecies about the coming Messiah. In contrast to this, for Clowney, based on Jesus' words in Luke 24:25–45, Christ is found in the entire Old Testament's message (Wiginton 2016, 43).[4] He believed that Jesus taught his disciples to understand the Jewish Scriptures in light of him (Clowney 2002, 30–31; 2003, loc. 539–624). According to Clowney (2003, loc. 76–87), the Pentateuch and the Old Testament are just as much about Jesus as the Gospels are. Therefore, Clowney concluded, "If all the Scriptures testify of Christ, Christ also is subject to the Scriptures" (Clowney 2002, 33). Allen (2011, 49) summarises Clowney's three presuppositions of biblical theology well with this statement, "The Bible is one book, not 66. This singular book has one continuous and ever-unfolding theme, and that progressively revealed theme is a person, Jesus Christ." These convictions about biblical theology naturally led Clowney to adopt Christocentric preaching as his preferred method of preaching.

Corresponding to his convictions about biblical theology, Clowney proposed a hermeneutical approach that consisted of two steps. The first step is to interpret the text in its immediate theological horizon[5] and then, subsequently, to interpret the text in the light of the entire revelation of God (Clowney 2002, 88). Clowney stressed that the second step must only be performed after the first. In other words, the text must be interpreted in its theological context and then, subsequently, it must be interpreted in light of God's overarching message of redemption. Allen (2011, 59–60) and Lee (2016, 74–75) emphasize that this first step is about understanding the text in terms of its immediate theological horizon and not only its immediate historical context. In other words, the first step of Clowney's hermeneutic is to understand the passage in its own context within its epoch.

After the text is understood in its immediate theological horizon, it must be interpreted in relation to God's total progressive revelation, which means that if it is an Old Testament text, it must be interpreted through the lenses of the New Testament. Clowney (2002, 88) contended that this step seeks to "relate the event of the text, by way of its proper interpretation in its own period, to the whole structure of redemptive history." Allen (2011, 61) clarifies, "In the second step, one looks to trace the projected, redemptive

---

4. Clowney (2003, loc. 98–243) argued that Christ is present as the Servant of and the Lord of the Covenant throughout the Bible. Clowney understood the term *Kyrios*, Lord, which is applied to Yahweh in the Old Testament, as pointing to Jesus Christ. Additionally, the righteous servant in the Old Testament prefigures the true Servant, Jesus Christ.

5. Clowney (2002, 89) contended that there were 6 great epochal periods through redemptive history: (1) the Edenic period, (2) the antediluvian period, (3) the Noachian epoch, (4) the patriarchal age, (5) the period from Moses to Christ, (6) the coming of Christ. Allen (2011, 60) pointed out that Clowney identified the period after the coming of Christ until the final consummation as the awaited age. Any texts after the coming of Christ period would fall within this theological horizon.

work of Christ from the point of foreshadowing in the Old Testament to its dawning in the New Testament." In this step, Clowney's three presuppositions of his biblical theology come into effect. Because the New Testament fully expounds on the redemptive work of Christ, Clowney believed the latter should clarify the earlier. Allen points out that at this point, Clowney departs from the conservative view that a text has one meaning, namely, the meaning assigned by the human author (75). Clowney instead argued for a dual meaning and dual authorship of a passage.[6]

5.2.3 The Homiletics of the Redemptive-Historical Approach

Along with the framework that guided his hermeneutics, Clowney provided practical tools for finding and preaching Christ from the Scriptures. Clowney's emphasis was mainly on how to find Christ in the Old Testament Scriptures because the New Testament explicitly refers to Jesus. The two tools Clowney relied on were symbolism and typology. According to Clowney (2002, 76), the Old Testament is filled with symbols that were fulfilled through the coming of Christ and his earthly career. Again, here we see two of Clowney's hermeneutical presuppositions at play: the progressive nature of Scripture and its continuity. Clowney contended that "symbols abound in Scripture, not incidentally, but because of the structure of the history of redemption which is at once organic and progressive" (101). Clowney's emphasis on the continuity of the theme of Scripture is also demonstrated through his understanding of these symbols. He argued, "It is evident, then, that symbolism is of particular importance in relating the revelation of the 'past ages' to the fulfillment in Christ" (101). Lee (2016, 77) shows that, for Clowney, "Both symbolism and typology are methods to show how Christ exists in the Old Testament as a type and appears in the New Testament as its antitype." In other words, God's progressive revelation, with its continuing unified message, provides the structure of symbolism. Clowney was adamant that finding types of Christ in the Old Testament must not be limited to those types that the New Testament writers point out. He wrote, "To conclude that we can never see a type where the New Testament does not identify it is to confess hermeneutical bankruptcy" (Clowney 2003, loc. 420–25). The progressive nature of Scripture and its continuity enables the church to continue to do this.

---

6. Allen (2011, 52) points out, "Biblical theology informed Clowney's exegesis and homiletics, therefore molding the nature of preaching itself." Ultimately, it was his biblical theology from which Clowney deduced the character of preaching and from which he drew the authority for preaching (Clowney 2002, 63, 73–74).

Clowney (2002, 100) contended that symbolism functions with a dual reference, which means it satisfies the event or person in the Old Testament and is subsequently fulfilled in Christ. Therefore, the symbol prefigures its ultimate fulfillment and reality in Christ. However, even though Clowney encouraged the church to continue in the footsteps of the early church by finding types of Christ in the Old Testament, he did propose a way to do so that might safeguard the interpretations of those who choose to do this.

When it comes to symbolism, Clowney provided several principles through which one might interpret the symbols in the Old Testament. First, he was adamant that the symbol is distinct from its reality. In other words, there must be a differentiation between the symbol and the reality it seeks to illustrate. Clowney (2002, 103–4) stated, "We should recognize that the symbol is distinct from that which it represents." Second, on the other hand, there must be a clear relationship between the symbol and its reality. For Clowney, this principle safeguards the church from absurd symbolic interpretations (104–5). Third, symbols are divinely determined in God's revelation. Because of this, the preacher should not be hesitant to connect the dots between Old Testament symbols and their New Testament fulfillment in Christ. Clowney proposed, "The symbolism of Scripture is communicated in word revelation, and its elements have rational meaning" (106). For Clowney, God placed symbolism in the Scripture for a reason; therefore, the interpretations need not be overly complicated. This, again, is possible because of the continuity and progressive revelation of God in the Scriptures.

Clowney (2002, 107) argued, "The interpreter of biblical symbols needs therefore to seek the meaning of the individual elements of symbolism in the context of scriptural use." Fourth, Clowney (2003, loc. 286–336) classifies symbols in terms of ceremonial symbols, official symbols, and historical symbols. Clowney wrote that ceremonial symbols in the Old Testament were mostly concerned with the notion of being clean or unclean (loc. 286). Official symbols are known as the symbolism of offices, such as kings, prophets, and priests (loc. 301). Regarding historical symbols, Clowney (loc. 316–17) wrote, "The Old Testament also discerns the symbolic aspect of historical events, especially as these reveal God's ongoing work of redemption." In other words, for Clowney, symbolism comes in various forms; it can be a sacrificial ritual that points to an Old Testament truth that points to Christ or, for example, King David's victory over Goliath. To explain the relationship between symbolism and typology, Clowney provided this figure:

Insert figure01

Figure 1. The relationship between symbolism and typology. Source: Clowney (2003, loc. 432)

Clowney (2003, loc. 432–45) explained that when symbolism appears in the Old Testament, that event or institution (E) symbolizes a truth in God's progressive revelation (T1). In turn, this truth (T1) will have its ultimate fulfillment in Christ (Tn) through the history of redemption and revelation. Preaching the fulfillment of truth in Christ gives the sermon its significance and authority. In contrast, if revealed truth (T1) is directly applied to sermons, that will result in moralism, and that sermon would be one that a person would expect in a Jewish Synagogue. Clowney contended that this type of preaching assumes we can get to the Father without the Son (loc. 439). A similar mistake, for Clowney, is when preachers apply a text allegorically to their hearers without placing it within its context. He considered both allegory and moralism inadequate messages to preach. Indeed, he dismissed allegory because "the preacher relying on allegory will try to explain a text by picking something in it and giving it an interpretation that is unrelated to the context or meaning" (loc. 464–66).

Lastly, there is typology. Clowney argued, "If there is symbolism in the account, we can rightly infer typology. If there is no symbolism, there can be no typology" (Clowney 2003, loc. 426–28). Lee (2016, 80) reflects, "Thus, to Clowney, typology begins with symbolism and ends with Christ's fulfillment." Clowney (1961, 110) explained that symbolism points to a revealed truth at a particular time in redemptive history, and typology references that same truth as it is fulfilled in Christ.

5.2.4 *The Redemptive-Historical Approach in Sermon Form*

Genesis 22:1–19

In Clowney's sermon on Genesis 22:1–19 entitled, "See What It Costs," Clowney (2003, loc. 1092–228) retells the story of God's testing of Abraham. He describes Abraham's ultimate test: the request to present Isaac as an offering. For Abraham, the boy was the seal of his faith up until that point; therefore, the cost was everything. Clowney describes the scenes between this request from God and the moment Abraham finally stretched out his hand. He invites his readers to enter the world of Abraham on this journey, to feel the weight of the request and the agony that Abraham must have endured. In this way, Clowney performs his first hermeneutical step, namely, to interpret the text in its own historical context and epoch. Yet, as Clowney points out, Abraham believed God's promises would not fail. Abraham's claim that "God himself will provide the lamb for the burnt offering, my son" (Gen. 22:8) proved prophetic. As Abraham stretched out his hand to kill his son, the angel of the Lord called out to Abraham and stayed his hand. And as Abraham looked up, there was a ram provided for the burnt offering, which replaced Isaac, his son.

Clowney (2003, loc. 1165–67) writes, "He [Isaac] was his by birth and his by redemption. The offering of the sheep symbolized not only consecration but atonement in the blood of a substitute." At this point, Clowney points to Abraham's experience as a picture of the Christian life. He claims, "The cost to Abraham was everything, yet as he clung to the Lord in faith, the cost was nothing" (loc. 1163–64). Similarly, all followers of Jesus are called to total commitment of faith which will cost us everything, yet trusting God in faith costs nothing. In this sense, Clowney's sermon is Theocentric. This is step 2 of his hermeneutical process because he places the story in the context of the whole canon. But he does make clear Christological connections. Clowney highlights that when God provided the ram, he spared Isaac but even more importantly, he showed Abraham that the price of redemption was too great for him to pay. Isaac was not a spotless lamb; therefore, another would have to take his place, symbolized by the ram. Because there is symbolism, Clowney feels at liberty to apply the method of typology. In doing so, he points out that the ram typifies the Lamb of God, who fulfilled God's redemption. Clowney concludes, "Not Isaac but the Lamb of God was the Sacrifice that the Father would provide" (loc. 1191–192). The story of the cost of redemption in Abraham's account points us to the Lamb of God, the Son, who paid the price for sinners on Calvary (loc. 1212–14).

Genesis 28:10–22

Clowney (2003, loc. 1230–1331) entitled his sermon on Genesis 28:10–22, "When God Came Down." He retells how Jacob deceived Isaac, infuriated Esau, and ultimately fled from Beersheba to Harran. On the way to Harran, Jacob fell asleep and dreamt of a stairway going up into heaven, with angels ascending and descending on it. Clowney points out that this was not a ladder that rested against the clouds but a Babbel-like structure reaching the heavens. Clowney emphasizes the gracious nature of God's calling by highlighting that God chose Jacob and not the first-born Esau. However, the climax of this story, according to Clowney, is that "God came down the stairway to stand over Jacob" (loc. 1264–65). Although the text does not explicitly state this, Clowney makes this deduction from Genesis 35:13, which states, "God went up from him at the place where he had talked with him" (NIV). The purpose of God's appearing to Jacob is to reinforce the promises God made in the past and to make new promises for the present and the future. This deduction fits Clowney's hermeneutical presuppositions, namely, that the Scriptures reveal God's revelation as a single continuous and progressive theme that reached its climax in Jesus Christ. Clowney applies this to the church with the encouraging words that "God's promises to us are no less sure"(loc. 1274). Bethel, then, is the house of the Lord that stands between the curse of Babbel and the promises of Pentecost (loc. 1287–288).

Clowney's Christological connections form the apex of the sermon. He does not suggest that the stairway, which connects heaven and earth, is representative of Christ, as a superficial Christocentric approach might. He does not argue that anything symbolizes Christ here; instead, he points to Christ's actual presence in this story. He argues that God who came down to Jacob was the second person of the Trinity, that this same person came down again to be born of Mary, and that he will come down again with his mighty angels at his second coming. Clowney uses the presence of the angels to argue for the presence of Christ in this scene because the angels were present at his incarnation and will be present at his second coming. To do this, Clowney moves forward to the words of Jesus to Nathanael in John 1:43–51. After amazing Nathanael, Jesus proclaims, "Truly, truly, I say to you, you will see heaven opened, and the angels of God ascending and descending on the Son of Man" (John 1:51, ESV). Clowney points out that this references Jacob's dream at Bethel. Based on his understanding of Bethel, he draws these conclusions:

> The Lord came down at Bethel. Since the Lord who came down was the Second Person of the Trinity, the person who reveals the Father, it is natural that Jesus would speak about the angels ascending from him at the bottom of the ladder, and coming down to him there. They did not ascend and descend in relation to Jacob but in relation to Jesus.

This sermon exemplifies how Clowney identifies Christ as Lord and servant of the covenant in the Old Testament (Clowney 2002, 100).

Joshua 5:13–15

"Meet the Captain" is what Clowney (2003, loc. 1549–636) entitled his sermon from Joshua 5:13–15. Clowney states that the historical context of this passage is significant because it finds itself at the start of a new epoch in the history of Israel. Here he is following his first hermeneutical step closely. Clowney retells how the Israelites had just passed through the Jordan and put the twelve commemorative stones in place to mark the passage through the water and how they renewed their covenant with God through circumcision and celebrating Passover. Clowney highlights that the Israelites were about to bring God's judgment upon Jericho because of their iniquities. They were going to be God's instrument through which He was about to pass judgment. Then, as Joshua stared at the intimidating walls of Jericho, a man approached with a drawn sword. Clowney explains that Joshua's request for information regarding allegiance was met with a strong reply, "I am the commander of the army of the Lord. Now I have come" (Joshua 5:14). Clowney argues that Joshua's posture of humility suggests his recognition that this was the Lord himself (loc. 1584–586). In other words, for Clowney, the commander of the army of the Lord is Christ himself and not someone else who symbolizes Christ.

Clowney states that now Christ is the ascended King of kings; however, throughout the Old Testament, Christ appeared as the angel of the Lord to deliver Israel and to bring judgment upon his adversaries. He writes, "The appearing of the Captain of the host of heaven was an appearing of the Son of God, who became incarnate when he was born of Mary" (Clowney 2003, loc. 1601–602). For Clowney, the reason Christ came to Jericho was to come against the dominion of evil which foreshadows Jesus' words in John 12:31, "Now is the judgment of this world; now will the ruler of this world be cast out." This was to foreshadow Jesus' great messianic battle. Although the commander of the army was Christ himself, his actions against Jericho symbolized his actions to come. In this sense, Clowney is using the progressive, unified, and Christ-centered nature of Scripture to shed light upon Jesus' career, death, and resurrection through this story. Again, Clowney points to the Old Testament character as an example for the church to imitate. This time he points to the reverent fear of Joshua before the Lord as a virtue worth pursuing. Furthermore, Clowney believes that the captain of the host of heaven was the one who brought down the walls of Jericho in judgment at the trumpet's call. Applying his message to the church, Clowney states that today the trumpet sounds with the gospel of Christ to which we must respond, and one day Christ shall return at the sound of the last trumpet. In doing so, Clowney views this story through New Testament lenses, which is his second hermeneutical step.

5.2.5 Conclusion

Clowney was convinced that Christocentric preaching stemmed from a correct biblical theology. For Clowney, this type of preaching was not a decision to be made but rather a consequence of a biblical theology according to which the Scriptures are seen as the continuing self-revelation of God through different periods in history as determined by God's actions. This biblical theology has certain presuppositions; namely, the Bible is seen as one book that reveals God's revelation as a single continuous and progressive theme that reached its climax in Jesus Christ. The consequence of these convictions about biblical theology naturally led Clowney to adopt a Christocentric preaching method. Clowney suggested a two-step hermeneutical approach, according to which a text must first be interpreted in its own historical context, placed within its epoch of redemptive history, and then in its canonical context, that is, God's total progressive revelation, which included the New Testament. In terms of his homiletical approach, Clowney emphasized two tools to preach Christ from the Old Testament: symbolism and typology.

5.3 Sidney Greidanus: Redemptive-Historical Christocentric Approach

5.3.1 Introduction

No other scholar has been a more influential proponent of the Christocentric approach to preaching at the start of the twenty-first century than Sidney Greidanus (Allen 2011, 84). Greidanus has presented a clearly articulated theology and carefully constructed methodology for Christocentric preaching through his various publications. Hence, some have referred to his work as generally representative of the Christocentric approach to preaching (Price 2018, 70). The starting point of Greidanus' commitment to Christ-centered preaching was a rebuke from a seasoned preacher after Greidanus delivered a sermon from the Old Testament. Greidanus (2004, 3) describes the event: "The gentleman said, 'I appreciated your sermon, Sid, but I wonder, could a Rabbi have preached your sermon in a synagogue?'" This changed the trajectory of Greidanus' approach to preaching. It was his book *Preaching Christ from the Old Testament: A Contemporary Hermeneutical Model* (1999) that became his flagship work on Christocentric preaching.[7] In this work, Greidanus presents the theology behind his redemptive-historical Christocentric method and his methodology around preaching Christ from the Old Testament (Greidanus 1999, loc. 73–75). This section will examine Greidanus' hermeneutical and homiletical approach and demonstrate how he applied his approach in sermon form.

---

7. This work originated from lectures Greidanus presented at Calvin Theological Seminary (Prince 2011, 103).

5.3.2 The Hermeneutic of the Redemptive-Historical Christocentric Approach

For Greidanus, preaching Christ from the Scriptures, particularly from the Old Testament, where he is not often explicitly mentioned, is not only acceptable but necessary. Greidanus (1999, loc. 141–55) contends that "the heart of apostolic preaching is Jesus Christ." By this, he means that the early church preached "the birth, ministry, death, resurrection, and exaltation of Jesus of Nazareth as the fulfillment of God's old covenant promises, his presence today in the Spirit, and his imminent return." Therefore, this is the benchmark for us to follow. Consequently, Greidanus believes that every passage, whether in the Old Testament or New Testament, must be understood in Christ, who is the climax of the Scriptures. For Greidanus, Christ is the center of the Bible, and therefore, the Old Testament must be interpreted through those lenses. He writes, "A person's view of the Old Testament is so decisive hermeneutically that it governs all subsequent interpretation" (loc. 568–69). This is because the Old Testament reveals God's redemptive acts, which reached their climax in Christ. He states, "Redemptive history is the mighty river that runs from the old covenant to the new and holds the two together (loc. 677–78)." Therefore, the Old Testament must be interpreted in light of Jesus. Greidanus is adamant that the Bible is one book; therefore, the Old Testament must be interpreted not only in its own historical and cultural context but also in the context of the New Testament, and since Christ is the apex of the New Testament, every text in the Old Testament must take him into account (loc. 719–23). This argument is firmly based on the progressive nature of redemptive history.[8]

Greidanus laments the fact that very little Christian preaching is done in the Old Testament, and when it is preached on, it is not seen through the lenses of Christ (Greidanus 1999, loc. 842–46).[9] Greidanus (1988, 103) refers to his interpretation model as "theological interpretation" since it concerns itself with the revelation of God about himself. However, he warns that interpreting the Old Testament through the lenses of Christ does not mean that it is done merely in a Theocentrical way, but specifically in a Christocentric manner. Lee (2016, 81) points out that Greidanus'

---

8. Greidanus (1999, loc. 724–25) writes, "The arrival of Jesus in the 'fullness of time' and God's final revelation in him calls for reading the Old Testament from the perspective of this final revelation."

9. Greidanus ascribes this to 3 possible sets of reasons, (1) the natural impulse to preach human-centered sermons, (2) concerns around forcing an interpretation upon the text, (3) the tendency to separate the Old and New Testaments (Greidanus 1999, loc. 507–10).

interpretive technique is somewhere between Calvin's Theocentric method because he interprets all texts in the light of redemptive history, and Luther's Christocentric method, due to his commitment to interpreting every text in the light of Christ.[10] Therefore, Greidanus (1999, loc. 2643) refers to his interpretive method as the redemptive-historical Christocentric method.

According to Greidanus' redemptive-historical Christocentric hermeneutic, there are two steps to follow in interpreting the Old Testament. First, any text must be interpreted in its historical-cultural context, which includes literary, historical, and Theocentric interpretations (Greidanus 1999, loc. 2652–680). The literary interpretation seeks to identify the text's genre and arrive at the meaning of the passage in its immediate context and the context of the book (loc. 2660–667). The historical interpretation seeks to understand the author's intended meaning of the text as intended for the original audience. This step includes the questions "who, to whom, when, where, and why?" For Greidanus, a critical question at this stage of interpretation is the "why" question because it reveals the passage's original relevance, which will help the contemporary preacher apply the passage to his context (loc. 2667–672). Subsequently, there is the Theocentric interpretation of the passage, which is concerned with what the text reveals about God and his will as he has revealed himself in history. While the historical context, especially the "why question," provides a helpful bridge for the contemporary preacher's application, the Theocentric interpretation provides the bridge to Christ (loc. 2673–680). Due to his commitment to this first step of interpretation, Greidanus does not consider his approach to be in opposition to the classic expositional approach but complementary (Allen 2011, 85). Admittedly, on the surface, Greidanus' method appears similar to the classic expositional approach; however, it differs in the fact that he leaves the door open for additional interpretations, as shown by Allen (2011, 111–14), which leads to step 2.

Second, the text must be interpreted in the context of the entire canon and redemptive history (Greidanus 1999, loc. 2680–682). Greidanus points out that because progressive revelation and redemptive history have moved on, interpretation of the Old Testament must take the New Testament seriously (loc. 2682). Greidanus (1988, 95) writes, "A holistic interpretation of biblical texts demands further that the interpreter see the message of the text not only in its immediate historical-cultural context, but also in the broadest possible context, that is, Scripture's teaching regarding history as a whole." He contends that Old Testament interpretations should not only

---

10. Gieschen (2017, 4) states, "Luther saw and proclaimed Christ from all the Scriptures, be they the four Gospels or the Epistles, but also Moses and the Prophets, the Psalms, and even Proverbs."

take the New Testament into account but Christ himself as the apex of the New Testament. Greidanus (1999, loc. 2643–645) writes:

> The Christocentric method complements the Theocentric method of interpreting the Old Testament by seeking to do justice to the fact that God's story of bringing his kingdom on earth is centered in Christ: Christ the center of redemptive history, Christ the center of the Scriptures.

In other words, in this step, the Theocentric interpretation question, "what does this passage reveal about God and his will?" moves to Christocentric questions, namely, "what does this text reveal about Christ?" and "what does it mean in the light of Christ?" (Greidanus 1999, loc. 2707–708). Therefore, Greidanus unashamedly holds to a *sensus plenior* view of biblical exegesis. Although he is not committed to the phrase, he nonetheless argues that the text may mean more than the author intended in the light of redemptive history (loc. 2715–716). In other words, the author wrote in his context based on what he knew at that stage, but God, being the ultimate author, knew what would come and how redemptive history would unfold. Therefore, Christ, who is the fulfillment of redemption, is already present in the Old Testament text. Greidanus' redemptive-historical Christocentric method is firmly established on these theological convictions.[11]

5.3.3 The Homiletics of the Redemptive-Historical Christocentric Approach

Greidanus (1999, loc. 126–38) points out that "preaching Christ" means different things to different people. For Greidanus, preaching Christ is not merely referencing Jesus' name in a sermon or identifying characters in the Old Testament, such as Yahweh, the Angel of the Lord, the commander of the Lord's armies, or Wisdom as Jesus (loc. 196–198). Instead, he defines Christ-centered preaching as "preaching sermons which authentically integrate the message of the text with the climax of God's revelation in the

---

11. Greidanus' commitment to honoring the Scriptures can be seen even in his critique of others that are also embedded in the redemptive-historical tradition. In his doctoral dissertation, *Sola Scriptura* (1970), Greidanus criticises the exemplary-redemptive-historical preaching of the Dutch Reformed in the 1930's and 1940's. He criticised these methods for (1) overemphasizing redemptive history above the historical context of the text, (2) becoming speculative around the details of God's progressive revelation, (3) focusing more on the past than the present, and (4) for ignoring human characters (Greidanus 1990, 13–14). However, by following his two steps, in the right order, Greidanus believes these issues can be overcome.

person, work, and/or teaching of Jesus Christ as revealed in the New Testament" (loc. 224–25).[12] Greidanus states, "More specifically, to preach Christ is to proclaim some facet of the person, work, or teaching of Jesus of Nazareth so that people may believe him, trust him, love him, and obey him" (loc. 201–2).[13] Greidanus' practical methodology of the redemptive-historical Christocentric interpretation method can be broken down into the following seven techniques or, as Greidanus categorizes them, "ways."

First, there is the way of redemptive-historical progression. For Greidanus, "Redemptive history is the bedrock for preaching Christ from the Old Testament" (loc. 2740). By redemptive history, Greidanus means the meta-narrative of the Bible. According to this meta-narrative, God's actions in bringing his kingdom to earth can be divided into four major movements: creation, redemption in the Old Testament age, redemption through Christ, and new creation (loc. 2733–737). Through redemptive-historical progression, one seeks to link Christ to Old Testament redemptive events that find their climax in him (loc. 2350). Greidanus argues that, in this way, every Old Testament text is seen in the context of God's redemptive history, which finds its fulfillment in Christ (loc. 2754–756). Therefore, the preacher must locate her text in the progression of redemptive history to make a move to Christ (loc. 2761–762). Greidanus provides an example of this critique using the David and Goliath story. Although one might interpret this story on a personal or national level, Greidanus argues for interpreting this story through the lens of Christ, which reflects Christ's victory over Satan (loc. 2762–788). Allen (2011, 94) points out that this way of redemptive-historical progression is the cornerstone of Greidanus' hermeneutic, and this is due to his conviction that Jesus is the climax of the Scriptures.

Second, there is the way of promise-fulfilment. As the title suggests, this way is focused on Old Testament promises and their fulfillment in

---

12. Greidanus (1999, loc. 225–73) believes that Christocentric preaching is essential today for the following reasons: (1) it is an essential ingredient for the accomplishment of our great commission. (2) The message itself demands that Christ be preached. (3) The life-giving nature of the message. (4) Christ is the only way of salvation. (5) Our audience is living in a post-Christian culture. Wiginton (2016, 55) suggests that this view opens many possible connections between Christ and the Old Testament.

13. Greidanus (1999, loc. 3269–72) lists ten steps to formulate a Christocentric sermon from a text. These are "1. Select a textual unit with an eye to congregational needs. 2. Read and reread the text in its literary context. 3. Outline the structure of the text. 4. Interpret the text in its own historical setting. 5. Formulate the text's theme and goal. 6. Understand the message in the contexts of canon and redemptive history. 7. Formulate the sermon theme and goal. 8. Select a suitable sermon form. 9. Prepare the sermon outline. 10. Write the sermon in oral style."

Christ.[14] Here, redemptive-historical progression forms the bedrock of Greidanus' promise-fulfillment method of preaching Christ from the Old Testament (Lee 2016, 84). Greidanus (1999, loc. 2817-828) provides two specific rules for interpreting the promises of the Old Testament that rely heavily upon this progression. First, God fulfilled his Old Testament promises progressively or in installments. Second, when the Old Testament promises are interpreted, one must move from the promise to its fulfillment in Christ and then back to the Old Testament passage. In other words, the Old Testament promises of God, particularly the messianic promises, were progressively fulfilled through Christ; therefore, Christ is already present in them as their future fulfillment.

Third, Greidanus advocates typology as a way to find Christ in the Old Testament. He points out that this approach has received the most criticism, especially because it can easily fall into typologizing (Greidanus 2018, 109). Greidanus (1999, loc. 2913-918) suspects that those skeptical scholars who operate from a historical-critical method inevitably reject typology because they reject the idea that God can work sovereignly in history. He writes, "For without the biblical teaching of God working sovereignly in history, typology is sheer nonsense" (loc. 2917). In addition to an outright rejection of typology based on a closed universe, skeptical scholars also associate typology with allegory, which Greidanus opposes. Prince (2011, 107) shows that Greidanus is particularly concerned about dissociating the Christocentric method with an allegorical one. Instead of making the text say what the interpreter wants, through allegory, Greidanus (1999, loc. 2919-920) contends that "typology, by contrast, is limited to discovering specific analogies along the axis of God's acts in redemptive history as revealed in Scripture." To avoid being guilty of eisegesis, Greidanus warns that certain conditions must steer the way of typology (loc. 2989-998). Greidanus has a particular appreciation for Clowney's boundaries regarding typology, namely, that there can only be typology if there is symbolism (Greidanus 2018, 109). However, he adds four essential conditions; namely, the type must be historical, which distinguishes it from allegory; it must be Theocentric, dealing with God's acts through human agency and events; it must present a substantial analogy along with its antitype; the relation between type and antitype must be characterized by escalation (Greidanus 1999, loc. 2989-998).

Fourth, and less controversial than typology, is the way of analogy. Greidanus (1999, loc. 3059-65) points out that contrary to typology,

14. Greidanus (1999, loc. 2803-15) points out that this approach has been scrutinized through the influence of Julius Wellhausen's distrust in the chronological patterns of the Old Testament and the acceptance of source criticism in seminaries throughout the 19th and 20th of centuries.

analogy does not claim to be a method of interpretation or exegesis but rather an approach to applying an Old Testament text to the contemporary church. Allen (2011, 102) highlights that, homiletically, analogy is communicated through "just as" or "like" phrases, which do not carry the same weight as typology. Dependent on the continuity of redemptive history, the process of analogy applies God's dealings with ancient Israel to the church. However, Greidanus is particularly interested not only in the application of Old Testament truths through analogy but in analogy itself as a method of preaching Christ from the Old Testament (Greidanus 1999, loc. 3066–67). Thus, the interpreter must examine the analogy between what God is, what he does, teaches and demands from Israel in the Old Testament, and what he is, does, teaches and demands from the church in Christ (loc. 3075–78).

Greidanus (1999, loc. 3117–3120) observes that where the first four ways of preaching Christ from the Old Testament are grounded in redemptive history, the following three ways are related to the history of revelation. So, Greidanus' fifth method focuses on longitudinal themes. Corresponding to the progressive nature of redemptive history, Greidanus contends that God's teaching about his redemptive plan is also progressive and, therefore, these themes need to be followed through to the New Testament to interpret its meaning for the contemporary church (loc. 3121–123). In other words, when encountering a passage, one needs to be concerned about what the text teaches about God's saving plan and how that idea is carried forward and ultimately fulfilled in Christ. Lee (2011, 88) points out that Greidanus does not seek to find only one theme in the Old Testament but many themes throughout. Greidanus (1999, loc. 3125–127) identifies the following as longitudinal themes: "The kingdom of God (reign and realm), the providence of God, covenant, the presence of God, the love of God, the grace of God, justice, redemption, law, sin and guilt offerings, God's concern for 'the poor', mediator, the Day of the Lord, and so on."

Sixth, Greidanus (1999, loc. 3153–58) lists the method of New Testament references. The New Testament authors also had the Old Testament to reference in their writings. Therefore, one can find paths to Christ from the Old Testament by following the New Testament authors. This may seem straightforward; nevertheless, Greidanus does warn that one is not at liberty to use the Old Testament exactly like the New Testament authors. He writes, "With other references, too, we must keep in mind that the New Testament authors do not intend to give us a definitive interpretation of Old Testament passages but use the Old Testament to support their own particular messages" (loc. 3156–157). In other words, because the New Testament writers were presenting a new revelation from God, their usage of the Old

Testament might differ from the original meaning the Old Testament writers intended (Allen 2011, 109).

Seventh, there is the way of contrast. Greidanus (1999, loc. 3190-199) points out that due to the progressive nature of revelation and redemptive history, it is inevitable that the Old and the New Testaments stand in contrast occasionally, which would include the ceremonial and civil laws of Israel. These texts should not be ignored but preached by using contrast. Greidanus (loc. 3200-201) writes, "The way of contrast clearly centers in Christ, for he is primarily responsible for any change between the messages of the Old Testament and those of the New." In other words, Christ is the reason for the contrast between the Old Testament rituals and laws and the New Testament. In this way, Greidanus agrees with Spurgeon that Christ is the solution to the Old Testament's problems (loc. 3207-208).

5.3.4 The Redemptive-Historical Christocentric Approach in Sermon Form

Daniel 3:1-30

An interesting homily that reveals Greidanus' Christocentric approach is Daniel 3:1-30, "Daniel's Friends in the Fiery Furnace" (Greidanus 2012, 171-86). In this sermon, he sets the stage for the story by recounting the last time we read about King Nebuchadnezzar. In doing so, Greidanus follows his first hermeneutical step by seeking to understand the story in its historical, cultural, and literary contexts. Greidanus shows that what preceded this narrative led to the promotion of Daniel as a ruler over the province of Babylon and his friends, Shadrach, Meshach, and Abednego, as administrators over that same province. Greidanus retells how, years later, and after much success, the king erected a statue of himself to make a name for himself and perhaps to defy the dream he had before. Thus, he invited all the officials across Babylonia to come to the statue's dedication and to worship before it. The consequence of not obeying this decree was death by a fiery furnace. After much elaboration on the details of the furnace, Greidanus points out that the admirable Shadrach, Meshach, and Abednego, being faithful monotheistic Jews, refused to bow down to the statue. This resulted in them being bound and thrown into the fiercely heated fiery furnace, much to the delight of the Chaldeans, who despised having Jews rule over them. This deduction again reveals Greidanus' commitment to understanding the passage in its own context.

Greidanus then paints the picture of the king looking inside the furnace in his rage, but to his surprise, he sees four unbound men walking around in the furnace, and the fourth had the appearance of "a son of the gods." This fourth person delivered the three from the fiery furnace, which once again, like before, left the king in awe. It is here where one would expect a Christocentric poster child like Greidanus to capitalize, yet surprisingly he does not make the obvious Christocentric connection. Greidanus (2012, 162) avoids the temptation to call the fourth person in the furnace the pre-incarnate Christ, which many commentators and preachers do; rather, he makes a more holistic Christocentric connection. Greidanus admits that this fourth person is the angel of God who is sent to deliver His people but does not imply that he is Christ. The Christocentric connection comes later in his sermon when he argues that just like this fourth divine person in the furnace, "Jesus came to save his people from the fire of hell and bring them into the kingdom of his Father" (183). This reflects Greidanus' commitment to viewing Old Testament passages through gospel lenses, which is his second hermeneutical step. In terms of tools, Greidanus primarily utilizes the way of historical-redemptive progression to preach Christ from this Old Testament passage as he seeks to show how this text reveals a redemptive event that ultimately finds its climax in Christ. In the application step of his sermon, Greidanus contends that the deliverance that Jesus brings is not only eschatological but also for today. We are called to imitate Shadrach, Meshach, and Abednego by being faithful to God, even while we are strangers in this world, and as we seek to do so, we can expect his help as we endure our fiery trials.

Ecclesiastes 1:1–11

Greidanus (2010, 101–11) commences his sermon, "No Gain from All Our Toil," with his first interpretive step, informing his readers of the Israelites' historical and cultural environment at that time. Greidanus shows how the Israelites experienced a change in their economic circumstances because they lived on the trade routes between Egypt and Europe/Asia; therefore, many pushed to accumulate wealth. Greidanus rightly points out that this scenario mirrors the current position of the West with its rampant materialism. He emphasizes the teacher's main point right from the start: all of life is vanity, which means vapor or a breath, something that is here one moment and gone the next. Greidanus believes that the imagery of a vapor speaks to the brevity and elusiveness of human life. Greidanus explains that "under the sun" means living without God in a closed universe. This word study again reflects Greidanus' dedication to his first hermeneutical step. Greidanus states that the main point of this text is the assertion that all of life is meaningless without God. In this sermon, Greidanus delves into the details of the text, verse by verse. Greidanus takes the literary context seriously and shows how the teacher formulated his argument, namely, that everything is vanity, including the pursuit of riches, from three different perspectives. These perspectives are the repetitive cycles of nature, the unsatisfactory nature of our senses, and the concept of history itself (96–98). It is all repetitive and ends up in dust. Elsewhere, Greidanus points out that one might use redemptive-historical progression at this point to preach Christ by showing that through Christ, God was doing something new in the world (96). Or, by using longitudinal themes, one might even preach Christ from this point by tracing the idea of laboring for nothing until we return to dust from the fall account and showing how Christ is the remedy (97–98).

Instead of using the redemptive-historical progression or longitudinal themes to preach Christ from the notion of the repetitive nature of life or the emptiness without Christ, Greidanus reverts to analogy as his chosen path to Christ. He points out that Christ, like the Ecclesiastes teacher, emphasized that nothing is to be gained without God. Jesus posed the question, "For what will it profit a man if he gains the whole world and forfeits his soul?" (Matt 16:26). Moreover, through the parable of the Rich Fool (Luke 12:16–21), Jesus warned against the futility of earthly possessions and called his audience towards a life that is rich towards God. Greidanus (2010, 111) writes, "Jesus' message is clear: We gain nothing if we store up treasures on earth. We gain nothing if we toil apart from God." Greidanus concludes by utilizing a contrast to point to Christ. He references Paul's statement in 1 Corinthians 15:58 to show that, in Christ, our labor is not in vain; it is not meaningless because it is not apart from God. Greidanus shows his gospel interpretive lenses in this sermon by placing the Old Testament story in conversation with these New Testament texts.

Leviticus 16:1–34

Greidanus (2021, 326–44) commences his sermon, "The Day of Atonement," by telling of Aaron's sons who were killed because they entered God's holy place inappropriately and how God warned Aaron, through Moses, not to do the same.[15] Greidanus employs the grammatical-historical approach at this stage as he shows how Lev 16:3–23 gives specific instructions

---

15. Leviticus 16 is considered by many to be the apex of the book of Leviticus, which is itself right at the centre of the Pentateuch (Greidanus 2021, 308).

for the high priest regarding the day of atonement so that he can avoid the same fate as Aaron's sons. In these verses, Greidanus points out that the high priest had to be washed, wear a special tunic, and make a sin offering for himself, whereafter he would make a sin offering as an atonement for the people. Greidanus elaborates on the two animals, the choice of which one is offered, and which one is used as the scapegoat. Then came the dangerous part; the high priest would have to enter the curtain and go into the holiest place (330). Greidanus expands on the detailed instructions given to the high priest for this risky entrance, including the sprinkling of the blood before the mercy seat and all the particulars of what followed up until the scapegoat was sent into the wilderness (335).

Greidanus finds this passage particularly easy to relate to Christ. He states that the New Testament often refers to this Day of Atonement and links it through typology to Christ and his redemptive work in at least four ways (Greidanus 2021, 338). First, he shows that the goat that was offered to atone for Israel's sin prefigured Christ, who gave his blood to atone for the sins of all who would believe in him.[16] Second, Greidanus points out that the scapegoat also prefigured Christ in the sense that he was innocent, yet the people's sins were laid upon him so he could carry them away into the wilderness (339).[17] Third, Greidanus writes, "The high priest Aaron who endangered his life to make atonement for himself and Israel prefigures Jesus Christ, who gave his life to make atonement for his people" (341).[18] Fourth, Greidanus shows that the tabernacle in which God dwelled pointed to Christ in whom God dwelled (342). In this sermon, there are only Christological connections and no practical application. Part of the reason for this is the nature of Mosaic law and its relevance to the Christian church (23).

5.3.5 Conclusion

For Greidanus, preaching Christ from the Scriptures is not only acceptable but necessary because Christ is the center of the Bible, and therefore the first Testament must be interpreted through Christological lenses. In other words, the Old Testament must be interpreted through the lenses of the New Testament, and every text must take Christ into account. Greidanus' hermeneutical method consists of two steps. The text must first be interpreted in its historical-cultural context, which includes the literary, historical, and

---

16. Matt 26:27–28; Rom 3:23–25; Eph 1:7; Heb 9:13–14.
17. Gal 3:13; 2 Cor 5:21; John 1:29; 1 John 3:5.
18. Heb 7:27; 8:1–2; 9:11–12, 26–28; 1 John 2:1.

Theocentric interpretations; then, the text must be interpreted in the contexts of the entire canon and redemptive history. Greidanus' tools to preach Christ from any text are impressive. He provides seven different ways to preach Christ from the Old Testament, namely, the way of redemptive-historical progression, the way of promise-fulfillment, typology, analogy, longitudinal themes, New Testament references, and the way of contrast.

5.4 Bryan Chapell: Christ-Centered Method

5.4.1 Introduction

Arguably the most well-known contemporary representative of the Christocentric method of preaching is Bryan Chapell.[19] Chapell, the former chancellor and president of Covenant Theological Seminary, has published various articles and books on the topic (Gibson and Kim 2018, xii). Prince (2011, 94) points out that Chapell's *Christ-Centered Preaching* (1994) has become the primary homiletics textbook at various seminaries. This work was produced on the back of the momentum provided to the Christocentric homiletic by Clowney, amongst others (Chapell 2004, 74). Although Chapell provides his nuances to the redemptive-historic approach, his work is firmly embedded in the works of some of the pioneers of the resurgence of this approach, namely, Clowney and Greidanus (Chapell 2018b, 2).[20] Chapell (2018a, loc. 202–3) summarizes his work with two words, "authority" and "redemption," the exact two words Prince (2011, 94) uses to describe Clowney's work. Chapell's work provides a unique contribution to the field and articulates a developed theological and homiletical basis for the redemptive-historical approach, which this section will now consider. This section will also show how Chapell applied his approach in sermon form.

5.4.2 *The Hermeneutic of the Christ-Centered Method*

As is customary to scholars involved in the resurgence of the Christocentric homiletic, Chapell's homiletic approach is also the result of a robust biblical

---

19. Chapell represented the redemptive-historic view in the recent publication *Homiletics and Hermeneutics* (2018), wherein the four most prominent contemporary preaching models were presented.

20. Like Greidanus, Chapell's interest in the Christocentric model was birthed out of his own personal experience as a pastor. He was preaching good sermons, but his people's lives were not empowered for change, until instead of preaching "try harder" messages, he reverted to redemptive-historical preaching.

theology. Chapell (2018b, 5) contends that the Scriptures tell the unfolding story of how a gracious God redeemed a fallen world through Christ to restore humanity and creation. The Scriptures reveal the necessity of this intervention and the details of God's redemptive plan. This larger narrative moves through different epochs, namely, "creation, fall, redemption, and final consummation" (5). Therefore, a text of Scripture cannot be understood merely in its historical and literary contexts but must also be interpreted in this broader redemptive context.

Chapell (2018b, 6–7) argues that the Scriptures do not only give historical facts and stories but are a progressive, organic, and redemptive revelation of God's nature and works. As such, Chapell's biblical theology is constructed on the following foundations. First, God's revelation is progressive, which means that the message of Scripture unfolds and progresses over time. This enables God's people to progress in their understanding of his nature and works, which becomes clearer over time. Second, God's revelation is organic, which indicates that the entire story is connected. Therefore, earlier sections lay the foundation to understand the latter portions, whilst the latter sections help clarify what went before. Third, the revelation of God is redemptive, telling the story of God's actions to redeem humanity from our fallen condition and world. Chapell states, "In this sense, the entire Bible is Christ-centered because Christ's redemptive work—in all of its incarnational, atoning, rising, interceding, and reigning dimensions—is the capstone of God's revelation of his dealings with his people" (7). Consequently, no portion of revelation can be understood in isolation from God's redemptive work through Christ.

Chapell (2018b, 7–8) admits that every text does not mention Christ, so our interpretation's goal should not be to force Christ upon a text but to observe where a particular passage stands in relation to Christ. In doing so, the interpreter imitates Jesus, who highlighted the redemptive nature of the Scriptures and their relation to himself on the road to Emmaus (8–9).[21] Clowney also used Jesus' interactions with the disciples on the road to Emmaus to argue for the Christ-centered nature of the Scriptures. However, Chapell contends that the transfiguration visually communicated what the Emmaus account conveyed verbally (9).[22] Chapell points out that Moses represented the law and Elijah represented the prophets, both of which point to Christ on the mount of transfiguration. He writes, "Thus, Jesus is the apex and culmination of Scripture's testimony" (9). In other words, the

---

21. Luke 24:27, 44; John 5:39, 46.
22. Matt 17.

prophets, apostles, and Jesus himself believed that all the Scriptures direct our attention to God's redeeming work in Christ.

Humanity's fallen condition plays an integral part in Chapell's hermeneutics and homiletics (Chapell 2018a, loc. 6475–6548). Although Chapell states that every text does not reference Christ, he contends that every text has a "fallen condition focus" that reveals humanity's need for redemption (Chapell 2018a, loc. 897; Wiginton 2016, 49). Chapell (2018a, loc. 895–97) defines this as follows: "The Fallen Condition Focus (FCF) is the mutual human condition that contemporary persons share with those to or about whom the text was written that requires the grace of the passage for God's people to glorify and enjoy him." Because of humanity's fallenness, we have failed to glorify God, and therefore we need God's redemption and grace to do so. By referencing 2 Timothy 3:16–17, Chapell argues that every biblical text has a purpose and has been included and designed by God to perfect us (loc. 879–82). Chapell writes, "[God] responds with the truths of Scripture that give us hope through facets of his grace that bear on aspects of our fallen condition revealed in every portion of His Word" (loc. 890–91). Elsewhere, he writes, "Every passage was written to bring glory to God by addressing some aspect(s) of our fallen condition that can be helped or healed by divine provision" (loc. 6521). Chapell is convinced that even if we understand the historical facts of a text unless the "FCF" is established, we have not truly understood the text (loc. 6525). Warren (1995, 253) emphasizes that Chapell's "fallen condition focus" is the primary theological notion shaping his Christ-centered preaching approach. For Chapell, faithful preaching indicates the FCF in the text, speaks to this issue of our fallenness and emphasizes the grace of God through Christ (Chapell 2018a, loc. 6492–493). All of this plays a role in Chapell's interpretive methods.

To interpret a passage, Chapell (2018a, loc. 1534–1618) suggests three principles: First, Chapell proposes that the original authorial intent is determined through using grammar and history (loc. 1534–566). By employing this method, the interpreter seeks to understand the author's message by analyzing the background and grammatical aspects of what they have written. Chapell calls upon Walter Kaiser to explain the extent of this principle. Kaiser (1981, 67) writes, "The grand object of grammatical and historical interpretation is to ascertain the *usus loquendi*, that is, the specific usage of words as employed by an individual writer and/or as prevalent in a particular age." Therefore, this first principle in biblical interpretation avoids interpreting the text through the context of the contemporary interpreter and allows the Scriptures to indicate their meaning (Chapell 2018a, loc. 1545). In other words, it is the literal interpretation of the writer within the literary and cultural context of the words used.

Second, the interpreter must observe the literary context (Chapell 2018a, loc. 1566–567). Chapell argues that the wording of the text must be understood in the broader context of its use, and therefore the literary circumstance is critical. He writes, "We determine literary contexts both by analyzing the concepts that surround a biblical statement and by identifying the type of literature in which the statement occurs" (loc. 1570–572). By this, he means that an interpreter must examine the chapters before and after the text to determine its meaning and establish the literature type in which the wording occurs (loc. 1572–583). Lee (2016, 102) points out that both of these steps function to determine the authorial intent of the passage. The first step is complemented by the second. Chapell (2018a, loc. 1583–584) contends that "many an error has been made by interpreting proverbs as promises, prophecy as history, parables as facts, and poetry as science." He is adamant that each genre must be interpreted according to the specific nature and purpose as determined by its context and authorial intent (loc. 1596–598).

Third, the interpreter must understand the passage in its redemptive context. In other words, for Chapell, an accurate assessment of the original authorial intent is not sufficient. Still, it must be completed by understanding the text in light of the entire meta-narrative of Scripture (Chapell 2018a, loc. 1598–1600). In this step, the interpreter should consider how the passage reveals the "meaning or need of redemption" (loc. 1600–1601). Chapell states, "Regard for context requires preachers to consider a text in the light of its purpose in the redemptive message that unfolds throughout all of Scripture" (loc. 1605–606). He warns that the details of a passage should not blind the interpreter from considering the redemptive context of the Bible (loc. 1612–613). Instead, one should imitate Paul, who always addressed issues by relating them to the redemptive work of God that found its apex in Christ (loc. 1610–611). To interpret every text redemptively, Chapell (2018b, 16–17) proposes that the interpreter asks these two questions: (1) "What does this text reflect of God's nature that provides redemption?" (2) "What does this text reflect of human nature that requires redemption?" He believes that in doing so, the interpreter approaches the text through gospel lenses which enables him to view the passage redemptively.

5.4.3 The Homiletics of the Christ-Centered Method

Chapell advocates preaching that places God's redemptive work through Christ at the forefront. He does so not only because it takes all three of his interpretive steps seriously but also because of its effect on the listener.

Chapell (2018b, 27) contends that redemptive-historical preaching avoids Pharisaic legalism, and it motivates the Christian to heartfelt obedience (27). For Chapell, the preacher can only call for certain moral behavior by relating it to the work of Jesus, without which the result will be legalism (4). Chapell affirms that because we are new creations in Christ and have the power of the Spirit, we can live obedient lives. However, he asks the question, why then do we still sin? To which he answers, "because we love it." Chapell writes, "Love for the sin is what kept us from employing the power we actually possess to resist it" (28).

Consequently, the only way our love for sin can be overcome is through greater love, a love for Christ.[23] He contends, "Overwhelming love based on an understanding of the sufficiency, efficacy, and majesty of his grace makes us willing and able to obey God" (Chapell 2018b, 28). Preaching on the grace of God thus raises the affections of the listeners, which motivates obedience. This renewed intense love for God then replaces the affections the listener has for their sin (28). Therefore, preaching must consistently point to God's redemptive work that culminates in Jesus' ministry. To preach redemptive-historical sermons, Chapell discusses three different scenarios that one might encounter as one approaches a text, namely, where Christ or his work is explicitly mentioned, where Christ or his work is typified, and where there is no direct reference to Christ.

First, there is what Chapell (2018b, 9–10) calls text disclosure. This relates to passages that explicitly relate to Christ or a facet of his redemptive work, such as a Gospel account or an epistle. In these cases, preaching Christ is relatively straightforward. It is important to remember, though, that preaching Christ is not only referencing his name but explaining an aspect of his redemptive action that the text uncovers. Chapell admits that those texts that explicitly reference Christ and his redemptive work are in the minority.

Second, Chapell points to type disclosure. This refers to those Old Testament texts where Christ and his redemptive work are typified. Chapell defines typology as follows: "the study of the correspondences between persons, events, and institutions that first appear in the Old Testament and persons, events, and institutions in the New Testament that more fully express salvation truths" (Chapell 2018b, 10). In applying typology, Chapell appears to be more careful than Greidanus in that Chapell limits the use of the types already pointed out by the New Testament writers, such as Adam, David, the exodus, Passover, and temple (10–11). As with the first scenario, text disclosure, type disclosure's use is also minimal.

---

23. Eph 3:16–20; Col 1:18.

Third, and most often, the preacher is confronted with texts that don't explicitly mention Christ, his saving work, nor typify him. In this instance, Chapell relies on context disclosure (Chapell 2018b, 11). He believes, "When neither text nor type discloses the Savior's work, a preacher must rely on context to develop the redemptive focus of a message" (11). In this method of preaching Christ, the preacher does not seek to insert Christ into the text illegitimately but instead aims to place the text within the grand narrative of God's redemptive actions as revealed throughout Scripture. Chapell (2018a, loc. 6698–6700) writes, "Christ-centered preaching rightly understood does not seek to discover where Christ is mentioned in every biblical text but to disclose where every text stands in relation to Christ."

To find out how the text relates to Christ, Chapell suggests that the preacher must look for the following four redemptive signals embedded in the text. First, Chapell (2018b, 12) points out that certain passages predict God's redemptive work through Christ by predicting his coming or work. He lists the messianic Psalms and texts from the prophetic and apocalyptic writings as examples of such predictions. He states that interpreting or preaching such Old Testament passages without assessing how they relate to Christ's work downplays the continuation of God's revelation throughout the Scriptures.

Second, other texts prepare the way to understand Christ's person and work. Chapell (2018b, 12–13) writes, "The inspired intention of some texts that do not specifically mention Jesus is to prepare the people of God to understand aspects of the person and/or work of Christ." By this, he means that certain Old Testament passages laid the foundation for us to understand Christ's activities better, such as the stories of the prophets, priests, and kings. Chapell points not only to persons in the Old Testament but also to events that fulfilled this function, such as the exodus, the Passover, and the sacrificial system, for instance.

Third, certain passages should be seen in the light of Christ's completed work of redemption. Chapell (2018b, 15) argues that "the truths of Scripture that do not anticipate or culminate in Christ's ministry must at least be preached as a consequence of his work, or we rip them from the context that identifies them with the Christian message." Here, Chapell specifically has instructions regarding moral conduct in mind. For Chapell, there is a danger in preaching imperatives in such a way that it makes it seem that divine acceptance is based upon obeying them (13–14). Rather, it must be shown that any obedience is the ultimate consequence of Christ's redemptive work rather than something we do in our own strength to obtain divine favor. Therefore, he warns that preaching on practices or faith that does not rest upon what God has done, or will do, for us redemptively through Christ leads to a sub-Christian human-centered faith (15). Based on this premise, he defines Christ-centered preaching as an act that "identifies the role of the text in the Bible's full testimony of God's gracious character, instruction, and actions, which are ultimately manifested in Christ" (15–16).

Fourth, Chapell (2018b, 16) points to the most used tool to construct Christ-centered sermons when Jesus is not explicitly mentioned, namely, by reflection. He writes, "When a text neither plainly predicts, prepares for, nor results from the Redeemer's work, then an expositor should simply explain how the text reflects key facets of the redemptive message" (16). This is where Chapell advocates for the application of gospel-centered lenses through which one asks what this text states about God's grace and humanity's need for redemption (16). As discussed above, Chapell is adamant that every text has a fallen condition focus (FCF) and therefore reflects some aspect of God's gracious redemptive action or humanity's need for redemption, which faithful preaching must highlight (Chapell 2018a, loc. 6492–493; Wiginton 2016, 51). So even though a text might not explicitly mention Christ or his work, the preacher can identify the FCF and consequently God's grace in the passage at hand through reflection. Prince (2011, 98) identifies that for Chapell, "The bridge between the world of the text and contemporary world lies in the mutual condition of fallenness and the need for grace."

5.4.4 The Christ-Centered Method in Sermon Form

Jeremiah 33:14–16

One of the paths Chapell suggests for finding Christ in a text that does not explicitly mention or typify Christ, or his work is by considering whether it predicts Christ or his work. In his sermon on Jeremiah 33:14–16, titled "Tinsel for Twigs," Chapell (2013, 123–41) does just that. After a short introduction of how it is typical of God "to make the forlorn glorious," Chapell breaks the implications of the passage up into three parts. First, Chapell argues that God uses the insignificant and failed. By following the first two steps of his hermeneutical process, Chapell explores the historical context of Jeremiah and shows that although Israel flourished under David and Solomon, because of Israel's sin, the Northern Kingdom fell to Assyria. Now Jeremiah was prophesying that Babylon would decimate Judah. The great tree has been cut down. But, from this stump, God was doing something new; namely, the savior of the world was going to come from it. Chapell writes concerning this branch, it is "the coming Messiah, Jesus Christ. The Savior of the world is going to come from this stump of a nation because God can drape the despised things of this world with his glory." Chapell applies this aspect of God's character to the church by encouraging it that God can use its failures for his glorious purposes (132).

Second, Chapell contends that God covers us with unfailing love. He points out that Israel's position was due to her sins and failures, which led to their punishment, yet God promised to give Israel One who would "execute justice and righteousness." Chapell proclaims, "Yet God promises to bring from this unfaithful people a branch who is Christ the Lord" (Chapell 2013, 133). From this prophecy, he encourages the church that God still loves those who are being disciplined for their sins. Third, Chapell suggests that God makes the appalling "shine with heaven's glory" by giving them his name and nature (136–40). It is at this point that Chapell inserts his strongest Christocentric connection. Chapell argues that God will not only give his people his name but also his nature. He points out that the very name given indicates that God will give his people righteousness that they could not provide for themselves through the Messiah. Chapell explains this passage in its redemptive context and writes, "By his work on the cross Jesus provides us with his righteous nature" (137). In other words, God intends to make us what he names us.

Considering this text, Chapell (2013, 125) concludes, "In this sense, Jeremiah's message becomes a bridge between our understanding of the gospel and the Old Testament people's anticipation of it." In this redemptive sermon, Chapell's two interpretive questions come to the fore, namely, what this text reveals about God and what it reveals about humanity's need for redemption. He answers these two questions in this sermon by showing that this passage indicates that God acts graciously towards humanity by using those who failed, covering the insignificant in love and giving the undeserved his nature. For Chapell, the meta-narrative of Scripture revolves around how a gracious God redeemed a fallen world through Christ to restore humanity and creation. This is evident in the sermon.

Numbers 20:1–13

A sermon in which Chapell (2013, 168–91) demonstrates how to preach Christ when he is not explicitly mentioned or typified, through reflection, is his message on Numbers 20:1–13 called "A First Repenter." Chapell (2018b, 16) shows that in applying the tool of reflection, the preacher explains how the text reflects a critical aspect of the redemptive message. So even though a text might not explicitly mention Christ or his work, through reflection, the preacher can identify the fallen condition focus (FCF) and, consequently, God's grace in the passage at hand. This is precisely what Chapell does in this sermon. Chapell commences with a brief introduction of the narrative's historical, cultural, and literary context. He elaborates on Israel's 40 years of wandering in the wilderness and its cause and points out that now they are ready to advance into the promised land but were grumbling because of a lack of water. After falling on his face before the Lord, Moses performed another display of bringing water from a rock in the desert. But this time, he overstepped a line with God, which led to God prohibiting Moses from entering the promised land (Num 20:12). This seems like an extremely harsh penalty, especially since Moses did so many things right. Yet, Moses did something so severe that God would not allow him to enter the promised land. Here is where Chapell discovers the fallen conditional focus of the text.

Chapell (2013, 181) explains the issue, "Moses disqualified himself from godly leadership by giving himself the status of prophet, priest, and king." He is quick to point out that the only person who can fulfill all three offices for God's people is Christ. Chapell explains that Moses operated as a self-proclaimed prophet by substituting the words God gave him with his own, he acted as a self-proclaimed priest by striking the rock without God's permission, and he acted illegitimately in the kingly office by assuming God's authority (179–81). However, this was not the last time God graciously used Moses, which leads to Chapell's Christocentric connection. Chapell uses his fallen conditional focus to emphasize the gracious redemptive nature of God, which can be most clearly perceived in the life of Christ. Chapell writes, "The passage points to Christ not by mystical mention but by reflecting aspects of our nature and God's that help to disclose the grace ultimately needed and provided in Christ" (168). Chapell indeed opposes biographical preaching because he believes this type of message only shows the characters' strengths (168–69). But such biographical preaching is not present in this sermon. Instead, throughout the sermon, Chapell shows Moses' failures as a leader, which he calls the fallen condition focus of the text. In light of this, Chapell shows the gracious character of God who provided for his people despite Moses' leadership issues and points out that, although Moses could not enter Canaan, God mightily used Moses for his purposes subsequently through the writing of the Pentateuch.

Daniel 5:1–31

In his sermon, "Loving Enough to Warn," Chapell (2014, 127–50) retells the story of how the party of Belshazzar, the successor of Nebuchadnezzar, was interrupted by the appearance of a detached hand that wrote a message on the palace wall. This, of course, led to the summons of Daniel to interpret the message and the revelation of the content of the message as one of judgment (128). Chapell emphasizes the importance of the passage's grammatical and literary context (130). He states that the previous chapters showed "God's faithful care for his people, his continuing provision for his people, his abiding presence among his people, and his willingness to deal graciously with those who humble themselves and repent." In chapter 5, Chapell contends that there is a different form of grace for us to be aware of, namely, that God judges the unrepentant (128). Chapell's assessment that God's judgment is gracious stems from his view of the nature of Scripture as a progressive, organic, and redemptive revelation of God's character and works.

Chapell reflects on the arrogance of Belshazzar, who, hiding behind his high walls, threw a party during wartime and used the holy vessels from Israel's temple to drink from. From this story, Chapell warns us that no human walls are high enough to prevent the wrath of God from being poured out on our sins (Chapell 2014, 132). Moreover, he points out that human achievement, reflected by Belshazzar's impressive wall, cannot cover our sins, nor does a simple knowledge of God (135–36). Chapell refers to the words of Romans 1:24 and writes, "The words remind us that sin is so awful that its worst punishment can simply be to let it run its course. God simply may let people have their way when they persist in sin" (145–46). Therefore, the consequences of our sins should cause us to grieve over them. But more than that, it should lead us to repentance (146). He points out that the writing on the wall is not only for Belshazzar but a warning for all of us. The consequences of sin are severe, as can be seen in the death of Jesus on the cross. However, Chapell encourages us that the blood of Christ does more than warn us against the severity of the consequences of sin (148). He writes, "It beckons sinners to be covered and cleansed by the crimson flow that God lovingly provides for all who truly repent. 'Come,' cries the blood, 'come away from your guilt and enter the forgiving, comforting, strengthening presence of the Savior (148). Therefore, Chapell concludes that God has graciously revealed the consequences of sin to us and the mercy of the Son that beacons us to return to Him (149). What is evident from the sermon is Chapell's ambition for heart transformation rather than only behavioral adjustment. He seeks to raise the affections of his listeners towards God and believes that the most effective way to do that is to reveal our need for redemption and God's gracious provision of that redemption. Moreover, because Christ is not explicitly mentioned in the text, Chapell uses reflection to find a path to Christ.

5.4.5 Conclusion

As with Clowney and Greidanus, Chapell's homiletic approach is also the result of a vigorous biblical theology. According to Chapell, the meta-narrative of Scripture, which grounds Christocentric preaching, concerns how a gracious God redeemed a fallen world through Christ to restore humanity and creation. Accordingly, Scripture is a progressive, organic, and redemptive revelation of God's nature and works. Consequently, Chapell argues that a text of Scripture cannot be understood merely in its historical and literary contexts but must also be interpreted in this broader redemptive context. Although he argues that not every text contains Christ, he contends that every text has a fallen condition focus, revealing humanity's need for redemption. Chapell's interpretation has three steps: understanding the original authorial intent as determined through his grammar and history, observing the literary context, and understanding the passage in its redemptive context. To interpret the passage redemptively, Chapell suggests two questions, (1) "What does this text reflect of God's nature that provides redemption?" (2) "What does this text reflect of human nature that requires redemption?" In terms of homiletics, Chapell suggests roadmaps to preach redemptive-historical sermons for all three scenarios one might encounter in a text, namely, where Christ or his work is explicitly mentioned, where Christ or his work is typified, and where there is no direct reference to Christ.

5.5 Shortcomings in Current Scholarship on Christocentric Homiletics

5.5.1 Introduction

Balance is essential in theology; for instance, one might emphasize God's holiness, purity, or righteousness but then negate God's grace, love, and mercy. The same phenomenon occurs in preaching models. Whether one follows the Christocentric approach, Christiconic approach, law-gospel method, or Theocentric approach, they all have shortcomings if applied unbalanced. Each model has its convictions of what biblical, God-honoring preaching looks like. What one can perceive from the discussion of the three

Christocentric scholars is that for them, Jesus Christ is the apex of God's progressive, organic, and redemptive revelation in Scripture and, therefore, if preaching is going to be faithful to the Bible, then it must find its focal point in the person, life, and teaching of Jesus Christ. However, if this model applies this conviction in an unbalanced manner, it can lead to repetitive sermons and, in a sense, numb itself to the spiritual needs of a congregation. Moreover, it can lead to sermons that overemphasize soteriology, that lack appropriate application, and elevate one person of the Trinity over the others. To a further discussion on these weaknesses, we now turn.

5.5.2 *Duplication of Sermon Goals*

The fact that the Christocentric approach perceives the Scriptures to be the unfolding progressive continuing revelation of God which finds its climax in Christ, has consequences not only for how the Scriptures are interpreted but also for the way sermons are formed. Carter (2018, 130) shows that all the Scripture points to salvation in Christ; scholars such as Goldsworthy (2018, 127) believe that our sermons should always be about Jesus and the redemption he has obtained for us. Because of the biblical theology behind the Christocentric method, for most of these scholars, preaching Christ in every sermon is not only a good option but a necessity. Sequiera (2018, 182) writes, "In my view, to preach any text of Scripture without showing how it sheds light on the person and work of Jesus Christ is to fail in our task as Christian shepherds." Likewise, Allen (2016) contends that "every sermon should feature Christ," and Greidanus (1999, loc. 2682) agrees, writing, "Therefore a Christian sermon on an Old Testament text will necessarily move on to the New Testament." In other words, every text must be presented in relation to Christ (Chou 2016, 115). This rightfully leads to Price (2018, 86) asking whether every sermon must contain Christ. Even if we agree about the nature of Scripture and the necessity of biblical theology in preaching, this is a valid question. Chapell's (2018b, 8) response to that question is that although Scripture does not command us to mention Jesus or his saving works in every sermon, why wouldn't we?[24]

One valid reason to avoid doing so is that this type of preaching duplicates sermon goals. Block (2018, 15–17) shows that sermons have many functions. It can encourage and build up, comfort, rebuke, and guide a church in terms of godly living, inform about God, his nature, character

---

24. Kuruvilla (2018, 30) responds to this question by arguing that we don't need to do this because most of the Bible does not do it and there is no biblical mandate to do so.

and works, and give hope. Although evangelistic sermons, which focus on Christ and his atoning works, are a valid sermon form, every sermon should not be evangelistic. Block rightly points out that just because a sermon does not mention Jesus or his redemptive works does not make it less Christian, even if the story of Scripture does find its climax in Christ. Poythress (2018, 54) argues that the principle of *Sola Scriptura* allows the preacher to use their God-given wisdom when preaching the whole counsel of God. He states that, within this principle, the preacher has the freedom, based on his circumstances, to use a wide array of styles if it remains within the boundaries of the whole counsel of God.

Price points out, "Although he [Greidanus] convincingly shows the importance of seeing Christ in the OT, it is a leap to argue that since Christ is present in the OT, Christ must be present in every single sermon from the OT." Instead of seeking to employ these different functions of preaching, the Christocentric method chooses to duplicate its function, namely, to speak about Jesus and his saving work. In other words, the Christocentric approach leads to preaching that functions on a general repetitive level, seeking to convey general canonical truths from every text (Price 2018, 84). Consequently, Gibson and Kim (2018, 162) conclude, "In Christ-centered preaching there is the risk that all sermons may sound the same and do not account for the biblical author's intentions." Kuruvilla's (2008, 139) review of Greidanus' work also points out this duplication of sermon goals. For instance, Kuruvilla shows that the sermon goals of Greidanus' sermons from Genesis 28:10–22; 39:1–23; 46:1–47 are all about God's promise of being with his people wherever they go. Although Greidanus sought to justify this repetition by claiming that these sermons were from the same book wherein the historical context was consistent, Price (2018, 85) convincingly points out that Greidanus' textual themes reveal a high level of generality and duplication.

Rather than reverting to the same function of preaching, which causes repetition, the sermon style should be decided upon through pastoral lenses based on the congregation's spiritual needs. Price (2018, 93) agrees, stating, "By using theological and pastoral discernment to draw from the best of each approach, preachers can let the fullness of the OT's message come through for contemporary listeners." York (2018, 201) illustrates from 2 Samuel what this would look like in practice. He argues that one should inform the congregation about the redemptive-historical context at various times, but not in every sermon. Moreover, one should preach Christ from 2 Samuel 7, which speaks about David's greater son, but one must refrain from preaching Christ from 2 Samuel 11 and instead address the dangers of adultery. In other words, the preacher or pastor should seek to have a balanced approach to preaching over the long term, wherein the whole counsel of God is proclaimed (Poythress 2018, 54).

Beale (2018, 88) indicates that this necessity of a balanced approach to preaching should make expository preaching the rule rather than a preferred method, whereby whole books of the Bible are preached through, and the whole counsel of God articulated. York (2018, 201) writes, "Like Scripture itself, we should evaluate our pastoral ministry as a whole rather than through the lens of any single sermon." This balance means that certain sermons will be Christ-centered whether there is an explicit mention of Christ in the text or not, but others will seek to fulfill some other function implicit in the text. Price (2018, 93) warns that one should refrain from attempting to do a Christocentric and a Theocentric sermon all in one. He argues that sermons become disorganized and disjointed in attempting to do so. Therefore, the emphasis should be placed on either the message of the text or how the text fits within redemptive history. In answering Chapell's question about preaching Christ, "why wouldn't you?" Langley (2018, 37) correctly points out that it may be because Christ was exalted in the singing, or his redemptive work was spoken on in last Sunday's sermon or will be in next week's sermon. We need to preach Christ regularly; however, there must be a healthy balance.

5.5.3 *Insufficient Application of Sermons*

Two strengths of the Christocentric approach are the consistent preaching of the gospel, which motivates the believer to obedience, and the dogged avoidance of moralistic human-centered sermons. However, like many things in the Christian faith, balance is critical. Because of its emphasis on God's redemptive actions through history and ultimately in Christ, which elevates the grace of God and the fallenness of humanity, Christocentric sermons often lack appropriate applications. Its bias towards preaching about the grace of God risks negating personal responsibility before God. It is concerned with the preaching of moralistic and legalistic sermons and therefore tends to avoid preaching about human obedience and good works. Chapell (2018a, loc. 4905–6) argues that "too much emphasis on duty, action, and 'What do you want me to do?' can leave the impression that sermon application is always about behavior change." Both Horton (1996, 5) and Greidanus (1999, loc. 987–99) warn against the applications that arise from atomistic preaching, which isolates a text from redemptive history.

This method is concerned with the heart and argues that the motivation for godliness comes from a transformed heart. Moreover, transformation is a deeper work than simply obeying rules. Chapell (2018a, loc. 4914-16) writes, "Transformation of conduct *and* heart are both legitimate aims of application." In other words, when Jesus and his saving works are consistently presented, our love for Him will exceed our love for sin, and we are thereby transformed.[25] The Christocentric method is committed to showing how the Scriptures point to Jesus and believe that by lifting up the savior, we are conformed to his image (Sequeira 2018, 193-94). However, in practice, it seems that the approach can place so much emphasis on the transformation of the heart that practical conduct is not adequately addressed. Gibson and Kim (2018, 162) raise this critique against Chapell's Christocentric method:

> Chapell seeks to guard against moralism/legalism. However, sermon application often becomes 'Jesus accomplished everything for us, we cannot obey on our own'; therefore, the unintended consequence may be that listeners do not need to bother trying.

In other words, a specific application from a particular text is not adequately made. Prince (2011, 136) and Price (2018, 81) indicate that both the Christocentric and non-Christocentric approaches are concerned with faithful application in their sermons but can differ in terms of their understanding and application of texts because of their different emphases. Price (2018, 80-84) makes a helpful comparison between Greidanus' Christocentric method and Kuruvilla's Christiconic approach[26] to illustrate the different emphases of the two approaches, which he summarizes in the following table.

Emphases of Greidanus' Christocentric Homiletic	Emphases of Kuruvilla's Christiconic Homiletic
Focus on the divine side of the divine-human relationship	Focus on the human side of the divine-human relationship
Christ as representative of God	Christ as representative of true humanity
Christocentric connections	Moral imperatives

25. Chapell (2018b, 14) is suspicious around preaching that requires obedience. He writes, "Divine love made conditional upon human obedience is mere legalism." However, the critics of the Christocentric homiletic do not question the unconditionality of God's love or the idea that salvation is through faith alone but do acknowledge that God requires his people to live a certain way and there are consequences to whether we do so or not (Kuruvilla 2018, 32-33).

26. Kuruvilla is heavily influence by E. D. Hirsch with regards to the application process of sermons (Price 2018, 82). For him, the application force lies within the pericope rather than from some theme developed somewhere in the rest of Scripture (Kuruvilla 2013, 137).

| Character of God | Human response |

Figure 2. A comparison between Greidanus and Kuruvilla's approaches. Source: Price (2018, 84).

The Christocentric method focuses on what the passage tells us about God; it portrays Christ as the representative of God, it seeks to make Christocentric connections by placing the text in conversation with the rest of the canon, and concentrates on God's character (especially his grace). Conversely, the non-Christocentric method emphasizes what the text conveys about humanity; it points to Christ as the true representative of humankind, seeks to emphasize the uniqueness of individual texts and their principles, and highlights our human response to divine commands. Based on these emphases, it is clear why the Christocentric approach can be criticized for not adequately applying the text to its contemporary listeners. But it also reveals that these two approaches are complementary rather than opposites, as correctly shown by Price (2018, 91–93), and should be applied as two different styles in the preacher's arsenal.[27]

The difference in emphases and sermon application between these two approaches can be illustrated in the David and Goliath story in 1 Samuel 17 (Stetzer 2013, 26–28). The application of the grammatical-historical approach is that, although we all face Goliath in different areas of life, such as unemployment, poverty, anxiety, or depression, we need to show courage like David and defeat these giants through faith (Lucado 2006, 2). In contrast to this, Christocentric scholars Woodhouse (2008, 535–36), Greidanus (1999, loc. 2763–2901) and Prince (2011, 137–38) argue that the application of this passage does not lie in the call for courage, but as an encouragement to trust the Lord's anointed, namely, Jesus Christ who, like David, won the victory over the ultimate enemy, Satan.[28] This application is consistent with the Christocentric approach's fundamental belief that the Bible is ultimately

---

27. Lillback (2016, 4), likewise, sees these two approaches as compatible. The one emphasizes Christ as the center of Scripture's redemptive message and the other considers Christ to be the goal of the Old Testament revelation. Welliver (2020, 3) finds it harder to synthesize these two approaches because he believes that they have different hermeneutical commitments. However, Lillback and Price's positions are more persuasive.

28. Another weakness of the Christocentric method's application process is its reluctance to use Old Testament characters as moral examples for the church to imitate. Where scholars from the grammatical-historical approach, such as Kuruvilla (2013, 242), consider biblical characters to be exemplars for believers (Rom 15:4; 1 Cor 10:6; 1 Tim 2:12–15; Heb 3:7–4:11; Jas 5:10–28), Christocentric scholars are averted to it (Greidanus 1999, loc. 524–34; 1988, 175–181; Prince 2011, 138; Clowney 1961, 79–82).

about Jesus and not me (Keller 2004). However, unless this approach is balanced and based on pastoral discernment, sermons will not adequately encourage, rebuke, correct, or train in righteousness.[29]

5.5.4 Overemphasis of Soteriology

Although soteriology must be emphasized, this ought not to be done at the expense of other important themes. Redemption is an essential notion in the Christocentric approach to preaching. Advocates of this method are convinced that the preacher must illustrate that the redemptive work of Christ is the apex and central idea of the Scriptures (Sequeira 2018, 182). The understanding that the redemptive work of Christ is the central idea of the Scriptures and, therefore, that it should be the central idea of our preaching can be seen in the writings of all three Christocentric scholars reviewed in this chapter. Clowney (1961, 78) wrote, "Biblical theology, then, serves to unlock the objective significance of the history of salvation. It focuses on the core of redemptive history in Christ." For Clowney, the main narrative that Scripture is telling is the unfolding of the story of redemption. Greidanus (1999, loc. 250–58) argues, "In a world dead in sin, alienated from God, headed for death, the life-giving message of Jesus Christ is so urgent that it simply must be told." For Greidanus, "Redemptive history is the bedrock for preaching Christ from the Old Testament" (loc. 2740).[30] The focus on redemption is particularly prevalent in the works of Chapell. Chapell (2018b, 5) contends that the Scriptures are telling the unfolding story of how a gracious God redeemed a fallen world through Christ to restore humanity and creation itself. Chapell argues, "In this sense, the entire Bible is Christ-centered because Christ's redemptive work—in all of its incarnational, atoning, rising, interceding, and reigning dimensions—is the capstone of God's revelation of his dealings with his people" (7) Therefore,

---

29. Although the lack of a robust application part of a sermon may seem insignificant, Chou (2016, 133) rightly points out that it hinders sanctification in two ways. One, in the deemphasizing of sanctification and Christlikeness in sermons and, two, in the omission of divine commands and requirements of the Christian life.

30. Peppler (2012, 120) points out that current and past Christocentric approaches fall into two categories: (1) "those who regard the life, teaching, and person of the Lord Jesus Christ as the locus of doctrinal formulation and proclamation" (for example Barth and Chapell) and (2) "those who hold that all of scripture must be read as revealing something about Jesus Christ and his saving work" (for instance Augustine and Goldsworthy).

the second question that Chapell asks of any text is, "What does this text reflect of human nature that requires redemption?" (15–16).[31]

Consequently, Gibson and Kim (2018, 159–60) ask, "Is redemption the point, purpose, and goal of every text?" Even if one agrees that, although Christ is not explicitly mentioned in every text, we can legitimately connect every passage with Christ through various ways and that it is beneficial to do so regularly, one must raise the question of why it almost always concerns Jesus' atoning sacrifice. Chou (2016, 133–34) writes, "Some warn Christocentric proponents are 'not Christ-centered enough' because they do not talk about Christ in His other roles outside of soteriology." Kuruvilla (2013, 259–60) likewise criticizes the Christocentric approach for ignoring the details of the text by being overly concerned with linking the text to New Testament soteriology. Moreover, according to this method, the gospel is often limited to substitutionary atonement. It depicts a lost and fallen humanity and an angry yet gracious God who sends and punishes his own Son to appease his wrath so that humanity may be reconciled to him. Price (2018, 80–81) shows that right at the core of the Christocentric approach is the prominence of Christ's passive obedience. It focuses on redemptive history, which emphasizes God's redemptive work towards his people, which reached its climax in Christ and therefore refers mostly to Christ's passive obedience. Horton (2011, 999) defines the passive obedience of Christ as a "term used to express Jesus Christ's suffering the penalty of sin and death on behalf of his people."

In contrast to this method, the more grammatically-historical approach focuses on the active obedience of Christ, whereby Christ becomes the model for us to imitate (Price 2018, 80–81). Again, Horton (2011, 991) describes the active obedience of Christ as a "term used to express Jesus Christ's fulfillment of the law on behalf of his people." The emphasis on Christ's passive obedience can be seen in the way he is referred to in Christocentric sermons, mostly as the one who died for our sins. For instance, in Greidanus' (2012, 183) sermon on Daniel 3:1–30, the Christological connection he makes is that the fourth divine person in the furnace is indicative of Jesus, who came to save his people from the fire of hell. So, when Chapell (2018b, 17) speaks about coming to the text with "gospel lenses," this is what he has in mind.[32] Piper (2019) states, "There is a preaching that almost never

---

31. Gibson and Kim (2018, 159–60) argue that this type of question can very easily lead to an individualistic Christianity which ignores the church community.

32. Langley (2018, 35) argues, "Even if redemption should be the privileged theological theme that governs preaching, let's be sure to name God as Redeemer and protect the gospel from harsh-Father-versus-kind-Son misunderstandings."

highlights the truth that Christ died not only to secure our forgiveness but to secure our sin-killing obedience."

Wilson (2018, 39) is correct when he argues that we need a redemptive paradigm that ventures beyond substitutionary atonement, as crucial as that is. He writes, "And sometimes deliverance is not only about being washed in the blood from Calvary; it is about being fed with bread from the bakery. Jesus fed the multitude until they were filled." Only focusing on Jesus' salvific death on the cross sells his career and the gospels short. Wright (1996a, 13–15) shows that one of the reasons why the first quest for the historical Jesus started was because of the Reformers' inadequate treatment of the gospels. According to this handling, all that needs to be known about Jesus is that he was born of a virgin, lived a sinless life, was crucified for our sins, and rose again from the dead. Although the gospel stories are well known, Wright (2008b, 29–31; 2011c, 169) claims that the entire Western church, both Catholic and Protestant, has largely based itself on the epistles because they have not known what the gospels are for and that the gospels have often been used to support a social gospel or conversely been used as the foundation for Paul's soteriology. This also seems to be the case with the Christocentric approach's heavy emphasis on substitutionary atonement.

5.5.5 Unbalanced Image of God

The doctrine of the Trinity is a complex tension within the Christian faith. Moreover, any preaching model that emphasizes one of the persons of the Trinity is bound to walk a fine line to avoid heresy. With its major emphasis on the redeeming work of Christ and Christ as the apex of the Scriptures, the Christocentric homiletic is in danger of creating an unbalanced view of the Godhead. However, Christocentric scholars do not see it that way. Clowney (1984, 246) argued that Christ-centered preaching is God-centered preaching because that is the way that God came to save. Likewise, Wellum (2018, 4) contends that the Christocentric approach is not anti-trinitarian and does not oppose the importance of the Trinity. He writes, "Instead, to be Christ-centered reminds us that in God's triune plan and work, there is a centrality to God the Son, and apart from him, we have no gospel and we cannot fully grasp the meaning of God's Word" (4). Similarly, Poythress (2018, 51–52) believes that Christ-centered and Trinity-centered interpretations are two sides of the same coin because the plan of the Father is outworked by the Son in the power of the Spirit. Therefore, Poythress argues, "Proper understanding of Christ naturally includes the Trinity. So, the approach we are considering might be called Trinity-centered preaching" (51–52).

Greidanus' (2018, 105) two-step interpretation process, as discussed earlier in this chapter, uses the Theocentric interpretation method as the foundation of the Christocentric interpretation. Along with their conviction that the Christocentric approach honors the doctrine of the Trinity, Christocentric scholars criticize the notion of Christo-monism. Christo-monism is the method of preaching only Christ incarnate, which ignores his pre-existence and preaching Christ separate from the context of the Trinity (Poythress 2018, 51). Beale (2018, 87), Poythress (2018, 51), and Greidanus (1999, loc. 2045) reject Christo-monism and consider that approach to be a threat to the doctrine of the Trinity. However, Seo (2019) correctly points out that "careless application or an improper understanding of the methodology can turn Christocentric preaching into Christo-monic preaching."

In practice, the Christocentric approach, although embedded in the doctrine of the Trinity, emphasizes one person, namely, Christ. For instance, Beale (2018, 87) argues that the New Testament is dominated by Christ rather than the Father or the Spirit; therefore, even when preaching from the Old Testament, which finds its fulfillment and climax in Christ, the preacher should focus on how the passage relates to the Son. Greidanus (2018, 105) states that it is difficult enough to preach Christ from all of Scripture, so why add the Spirit? For Greidanus, referencing all three persons of the Trinity in every sermon is an unnecessary burden to place upon the preacher, especially since Christ's redemptive work is part of the redemptive plan of the Trinity (Greidanus 1999, loc. 2105). Likewise, Peppler (2012, 125) proposed that if Jesus is "the image of the invisible God" (Col 1:15), then what we see in Jesus' person, words, and works are representative of that of the Trinity.

Nevertheless, the issue is that although the Christocentric approach acknowledges and is embedded in the doctrine of the Trinity, the person in the pew listening to this method will hear a disproportionate number of sermons about Christ compared to the Father or Holy Spirit. This can distort and confuse the image of the Trinity because focusing on one person can lead to the neglect of the other two persons (Chou 2016, 133). Price (2018, 87) legitimately asks, "If redemption is the work of the triune God, with every person of the Godhead actively involved in our redemption, why should the Son be prioritized over the Father and the Holy Spirit?" Likewise, Langley (2018, 35–36) and Kuruvilla (2018, 31) point out that the main character of Scripture is not Christ but the triune God, which speaks of his nature and work, and which should not be limited to only his grace and redemption.

Not communicating that the entire Trinity is involved in our redemption can lead to a distortion of the gospel, as shown by Chou (2016, 133), and a distortion of the nature of the Father. The redemptive story without the explicit involvement of the Father quickly becomes the story of poor Jesus taking the wrath of a disinterested, angry God upon himself in our place. It gives the impression that God so loved the world that he sent someone else to come and do his dirty work for him. It downplays the plan of Father and his sacrifice to bring that redemption about. Langley (2018, 35) aptly writes, "Even if redemption should be the privileged theological theme that governs preaching, let's be sure to name God as Redeemer and protect the gospel from harsh-Father-versus-kind-Son misunderstandings." Price (2018, 87) sums it up well when he argues that although it is correct to emphasize Christ in that he accomplished redemption for us, we should let our people know that the Father and Holy Spirit were actively involved in that process. Moreover, the Father and the Son glorify one another.[33]

5.5.6 Conclusion

From this discussion, it is evident that referring to redemptive history and its climax in Christ in every sermon tends to make sermons sound repetitive, which, instead of raising the affections of the audience, might have the converse effect. Perhaps the Christocentric method's greatest weakness is the lack of sermon application. Its desire to avoid moralistic sermons and its reluctance to do biographical preaching leads to sermons that sometimes have no practical application to one's life. Additionally, this method overemphasizes substitutionary atonement and rarely refers to other elements of Christ's atoning work. This significantly reduces the gospels' value in preaching and paints God the Father in an incorrect light. Lastly, although the approach criticizes Christo-monism, there is a real danger that the doctrine of the Trinity is undermined, and the other persons of the Trinity are not fairly presented.

5.6 Christocentric Homiletics' Embedded Christology

5.6.1 Introduction

Kärkkäinen (2016, 6) points out that the emphasis on a single Christology runs the danger of being one-dimensional in its understanding and

---

33. Block (2018, 11) also connects Christ to the Trinity and argues that when he preaches about YHWH from the Old Testament, he is preaching Christ. Therefore, he warns we should not fall into superficial typologizing and Christologizing of the Old Testament.

description of Jesus. In other words, the overreliance on one type of Christology can lead to hermeneutical and homiletical blind spots. The Christocentric method seeks to preach Christ in every sermon since he is the apex of Scripture. However, the issue is that there are different Christological lenses through which to approach and understand Jesus' person, life, and teaching. The two sides of this spectrum are called Christology from above and Christology from below. The conclusions about Jesus Christ that one seeks to bring into conversation with the rest of the Scriptures, if one follows the Christocentric approach, depends on the type of Christological lenses one looks through. For example, as Kärkkäinen points out, even Islam has its own "Christology" (3). Likewise, Allison (2009a, 80) shows that various New Testament texts reveal Jesus in two ways, namely, as a human being with human faculties and as someone divine. So, when Old Testament texts need to be interpreted through Christological lenses, the question remains, which Christological lenses are to be used? Migliore (2014, 170), writing about the New Testament writers' pictures of Christ, states, "Their portrayals of him as Savior and Lord are remarkably distinctive." Although the three scholars examined do not articulate which type of Christology undergird their homiletical approaches, one can confidently conclude which type they emphasize through observation.

5.6.2 Christology "from above"

To understand which method of Christology the Christocentric approach is based on, one must describe these methods. The from below Christology has been described at length in the thesis; therefore, attention will now be placed on the Christology from above. Kärkkäinen (2016, 4) describes the Christology from above approach as an analysis of Jesus, which finds its starting point in the New Testament's theological interpretation of Christ. This interpretation of Jesus is grounded upon a confession of faith in Jesus' divinity. Welker (2013, 75) highlights that the from above Christological method has the divine Christ, as confessed by the early church, as its point of departure. In other words, Christology from above takes the claims of the New Testament writers about Jesus' divinity at face value. It uses these claims as the foundation for all subsequent conclusions about Jesus.

Kärkkäinen (2016, 5) suggests that the from above method dominated the pre-Enlightenment period and that "the Christological tradition was simply an interpretation of the New Testament confession of faith in Christ and an attempt to express it in precise philosophical and theological terms."[34] Conversely, the Christology from below approach is an inquiry into the historical Jesus of Nazareth that seeks to investigate the historical and factual grounds of these Christological claims. Instead of arguing for it, the from above approach presupposes the divinity of Jesus.[35] Qin (2015, 39) suggests that Christology from above focuses on Jesus from an ontological perspective; that is, it perceives Jesus through his ontological identity rather than through his actions or words, which has been the position of most conservative theologians (Kärkkäinen 2016, 4–5).

5.6.3 A High View of the Scriptures

The Christology from below method has its roots in a post-Enlightenment phenomenon called historical criticism. From this perspective, one's portrait of Jesus cannot be based on the faith statements of the New Testament writers. In other words, if we do choose to place our faith in Jesus, it cannot be based on the faith of another but should rather be based on historical facts. Therefore, the from below approach of Christology seeks to paint a portrait of the historical Jesus by going behind the writings of the New Testament writers to investigate the historical and factual grounds of their Christological claims. As has been discussed above, Christology from above takes the claims of the New Testament writers at face value and uses these claims as the starting point of what can be known about Jesus. When we consider Clowney, Greidanus, and Chapell's posture towards Scripture, especially the New Testament and its claims, we see that they fall squarely within this category. All three have a very high view of the Scriptures and have formed their hermeneutical and homiletical approaches around their biblical theology. Clowney (2002, 75) argued that the Bible is God's unified and continual progressive revelation. For Clowney, the Scriptures consist not only of progressive revelations, but these revelations tell a consistent story without contradictions because it has a Divine author and was written by his "one gracious design" (15). Therefore, the Scriptures hold a historical progression and a theological unity. With Clowney, there is not a hint of historical criticism.

---

34. Kärkkäinen (2016, 5) argues that this was the dominant position in Christology before the Enlightenment. He states that the reason for that is that "there was no question about the historical reliability of the Gospel records."

35. An example of a statement that a Christology from above might commence with is "God acts, suffers, and triumphs in and through Jesus. In Jesus Christ we do not have less than God's very own presence in our humanity. In this person the eternal God suffers and acts for our salvation" (Migliore 2014, 183).

Similarly, Chapell (2018b, 6–7) contends that the Bible not only provides historical facts and stories but is a progressive, organic, and redemptive revelation of God's nature and works. This means that through the Scriptures, God's progressive revelation unfolds over time, wherein his revelation becomes clearer as time progresses. Therefore, earlier sections lay the foundation to understand the latter portions, whilst the latter sections help clarify what went before. Additionally, the revelation of God is redemptive, telling the story of God's actions to redeem humanity from our fallen condition and world.

Because all three scholars argue that Jesus is the apex of God's redemptive revelation in history, they not only believe that the New Testament, which tells us about Jesus' life, death, and resurrection, is to be trusted in its descriptions of Jesus but the New Testament should also be the lenses through which the Old Testament is interpreted. Greidanus is adamant that the Bible is one book. Therefore the Old Testament must be interpreted not only in its own historical and cultural context but also in the context of the New Testament (Greidanus 1999, loc. 719–23). The reliance these three scholars place upon the faith claims of the New Testament writers is indicative of a Christology from above.

5.6.4 Commence from a High Christology

The main consequence of this high view of Scripture is an acceptance and advocacy of the New Testament's claims about Jesus Christ. What the New Testament writers had to say about Jesus has such a significant impact on these three scholars that it became the lens through which they view the entire story of Scripture. In other words, not only do they believe the claims about Jesus in Scripture but contend that these claims should be used to understand the Old Testament. The New Testament's claims about Jesus then form part of the presuppositions of their biblical theology. For instance, Clowney (2002, 30–33; 2003, loc. 539–624) takes the words of Jesus on the Emmaus Road as presented by Luke in Luke 24:25–45 and concludes that Jesus is the main subject of all of Scripture. In other words, the law and prophets in the Old Testament are just as much about Jesus as the Gospels are. Likewise, Chapell (2018b, 9) argues from the transfiguration story in Matthew 17:1–13, without questioning the event's historical validity, that all the law and prophets in the Old Testament point to Jesus. He states, "Thus, Jesus is the apex and culmination of Scripture's testimony" (9). Therefore, Greidanus argues that the Old Testament should not only be interpreted in the light of the New Testament but in light of Jesus Christ, who is the apex of the New Testament. This Christocentric hermeneutic stems from a Christology from above. It takes, believes, and applies the claims of the New Testament writers regarding Jesus Christ.

When we put Christ as the apex of Scripture and the notion that the Bible is the progressive, continual, unified revelation of God, we arrive at where these scholars have landed, namely, that Jesus is the ultimate manifestation of God's revelation. Chapell (2018b, 7) writes, "The entire Bible is Christ centered because Christ's redemptive work—in all of its incarnational, atoning, rising, interceding, and reigning dimensions—is the capstone of God's revelation of his dealings with his people." Consequently, no portion of revelation can be understood in isolation from God's redemptive work through Christ. Clowney (2002, 74–75) contended that all periods within which the unfolding progressive revelation of God has been revealed are united by Christ. Therefore, he is the fulfillment of Scripture's metanarrative and the center of redemptive history. Correspondingly, Greidanus (1999, loc. 141–55) contends that just as the early church preached about Jesus' birth, career, death, and resurrection, because of who he is, we too must follow their example. These three scholars commence their hermeneutical and homiletical endeavors with the highest possible Christology. A Christology that emphatically affirms the divinity of Christ. They not only believe the claims of the New Testament writers, as is normative for a Christology from above but apply this Christology to their entire hermeneutical structure and preaching models.

5.6.5 *Six Key Questions of the Third Quest*

Now that we have assessed the Christocentric homiletic according to the criteria of the Christology from above method, we must consider it in light of the characteristics of a Christology from below. It is evident from the discussion above that these scholars are not interested in approaching the Bible with historical criticism. They see no need to verify the claims about Jesus that the New Testament writers made. Therefore, another way to assess their underlying Christology is to examine their response to some of the six key questions of the Third Quest for the historical Jesus. Six historical questions have emerged explicitly from the Third Quest, which, according to Wright (1998d, 107; 1996a, 90), all serious historians of the first century must consider if they are to construct a portrait of Jesus. These questions are, how does Jesus fit into first-century Judaism? What were his aims? Why did he die? How did the church come into being? Why are the gospels what they are? And how does the historical Jesus relate to the contemporary church and world?

First, scholars of the Third Quest for the historical Jesus take his Jewish context very seriously. With those who follow a Christology from below, like Wright, there tends to be a progression by first speaking about Jesus as a Jewish prophet, then the Jewish Messiah, then after the resurrection and ascension as the Lord and Savior of the world and other divine ways. This is not so much the case with Pannenberg, who acknowledged the importance of accounting for Jesus' Jewishness, yet never placed Jesus within first-century Jewish categories (see point 4.5.4 above). However, these Christocentric homileticians, although they connect Jesus to ancient Israel by considering him to be the climax of the story they are part of, rarely speak about Jesus in these Jewish categories. They would much rather speak of Jesus as the second person of the Trinity, as observed in Clowney's (2003, loc. 1287–1313) sermon on Genesis 28:10–22. And when they do speak of Jesus as the Messiah, they do so in a way that removes the Jewish sense of that title and replaces it with divine and universal implications. For example, Chapell (2013, 132) speaks of Jesus as the Messiah in his sermon on Jeremiah 33:14–16, writing, "the coming Messiah, Jesus Christ. The Savior of the world is going to come from this stump of a nation because God can drape the despised things of this world with his glory." Wright (1998b, 110–11) correctly opposes the use of the title Messiah as a means of referring to Jesus' divinity, which he argues stems from a de-Judaized Christian tradition.

Second, the Third Quest is interested in understanding Jesus' aims by addressing the question, what was he trying to accomplish within Judaism? Christology from below scholars pursue this question by going behind the New Testament writings to capture Jesus' self-understanding and vocation. Wright (1996a, 653) contends that Jesus did not "know" that he was God in the same way that he "knew" he was hungry or thirsty or tired, but he was aware of his vocation to do and be what only Israel's God did and was (Wright 1998a, 53). In contrast to this, Clowney (2003, loc. 111, 2705) argues that the same God who declared his covenant name, I am, to Moses through the burning bush is the same God who said, "Before Abraham was, I am" (John 8:58). For the Christocentric proponents assigning self-knowledge of divinity to Jesus is not farfetched.[36]

Third, for Christology from below scholars like Wright (2008b, 29) and Pannenberg (1966, 232), the emphasis of the gospels is on the kingdom

---

36. The third and fourth questions, namely, why did Jesus die and how did the church come into being are extensively addressed by the Christocentric scholars. Refer to 5.6.4 for further discussion on this point.

of God coming to earth through the public ministry, death, and resurrection of Jesus of Nazareth. Therefore, their primary function is not to convince us that Jesus is the second person of the Trinity (Wright 2011c, 178–79; Choi 2011, 45). Moreover, when the gospels are interpreted through the lenses of Jesus' divinity, the Jewish Jesus is replaced by the Christ of faith. Wright (2011c, 172) contends that the consequence of viewing the gospels as an apologetic for Jesus' divinity instead of understanding their presentation of the historical nature of Jesus' career and fate is preaching that merely reverts to "Christ died for our sins." The Christocentric method's obsession with soteriology, as shown by Kuruvilla (2013, 259–60), Chou (2016, 133–34), and Gibson and Kim (2018, 159–60), is indicative of their support of the former. Consequently, Gibson and Kim accuse the Christocentric homiletic of its lack of sermon application because sermons often conclude with Jesus accomplishing everything for us, so don't even bother trying (Gibson and Kim 2018,162).

Lastly, there is a vast difference between the Christocentric scholars and the Christology from below scholars on how the historical Jesus relates to the contemporary church and world. Whereas scholars such as Wright and Pannenberg contend that Jesus was representative of true humanity and, therefore, we are to imitate his life as we join in his movement, the Christocentric method emphasizes that Jesus was primarily representative of God, through whom God ultimately revealed himself. This point will be further elaborated on below.

5.6.6 Christ as Representative of God

Due to its historical focus, Christology from below focuses on the humanity of Jesus. This can also be seen in the six key questions that characterize the Third Quest for the historical Jesus, as discussed above. Therefore, unsurprisingly, one of the conclusions of such an endeavor is that Jesus is the ultimate representative of humanity. For instance, Pannenberg (1974b, 180) argued that in Jesus, the essence of humanity is revealed, namely, to have an openness to God and to desire community with others. Moreover, in Jesus, our human destiny is reflected, namely, to be raised from the dead in a universal resurrection, which should lead to new life for all of humanity (*die ganze Menschheit*). Pannenberg's anthropological view of Jesus leads him to conclude that Jesus shows what it means to be truly human, and that is conformity to the image of God (Col 1:15; Heb 2:6–9). Similarly, Wright (1996a, 245) contends that Jesus' kingdom announcement came in the form of invitation, welcome, challenge, and summons, which was an attempt to reform Israel through people who would follow Jesus' example of what it meant to be the people of God. Jesus' life is the model for the renewed Israel.

Conversely, the Christocentric approach tends to focus on Jesus as the representative of God rather than of humanity. Their biblical theology leads them to a particular understanding of the meta-narrative of Scripture, in which Christ is the representative of God. For Clowney (2002, 74–75), Greidanus (1988, 103), and Chapell (2018b, 7), the main overarching story that the Scriptures are telling is of God's unfolding progressive revelation, which reached its climax in Jesus Christ. As Chapell (2018b, 5) points out, the Scriptures are telling the unfolding story of how a gracious God redeemed a fallen world through Christ to restore humanity and creation itself. They reveal the necessity and details of God's redemptive plan, which reached its climax in Jesus Christ (Greidanus 1999, loc. 568–69). But this redemptive plan is part of the revelation of God's nature and works. Chapell (2018b, 7) writes, "[Christ] is the capstone of God's revelation of his dealings with his people." Likewise, Greidanus (1999, loc. 2643–645) contends that "the Christocentric method complements the Theocentric method of interpreting the Old Testament by seeking to do justice to the fact that God's story of bringing his kingdom on earth is centered in Christ." What transpired through Christ is the manifestation of the redemptive revelation of God himself.

It is for this reason that redemptive-historical scholars primarily view Jesus Christ as God's representative. Their biblical theology connects what they call redemptive history; therefore, instead of interpreting the gospels in isolation, they weave them into the grand story of what transpired before the coming of Jesus. Price (2018, 80–84) provides a helpful comparison between Greidanus' Christocentric method and Kuruvilla's Christiconic approach and points out that Kuruvilla's more traditional hermeneutical and homiletical approach emphasizes Christ as the representative of humanity; therefore we should seek to imitate him and pursue Christlikeness. On the contrary, Greidanus' approach primarily presents Christ as God's representative who came to fulfill God's redemptive purposes for humanity. Emphasizing Jesus as God's representative rather than humanity's is another connection between the Christocentric method and a Christology from above.

5.6.7 *Ontological Rather than Functional Focus*

The emphasis on Christ as the representative of God points to a more ontological perspective than a functional perspective. Christocentric scholars certainly focus on Jesus' works and words, but these are interpreted through the lenses of who he is, namely, the ultimate revelation of God in space and time. Qin (2015, 39) explains, "Regardless of what Jesus said and did, Jesus' 'ontological' identity implies that he was God incarnate even though mankind might not know this from the beginning." Moreover, he shows that a Christology from above focuses on Jesus from an ontological perspective; that is, it perceives Jesus through his ontological identity rather than through his actions or words (39).[37] In other words, an ontological perspective views Jesus according to his ontological identity as the ground of his works and words. Considering this, the Christocentric method can most certainly be linked to a Christology from above approach. For instance, this can be seen with Clowney, who locates Christ in the Old Testament stories, as seen from his sermons on Genesis 28:10–22 and Joshua 5:13–15. Clowney argues in these sermons that Christ himself visited Jacob on the way to Haran and that the commander of the Lord's armies who appeared to Joshua at Jericho also was Christ. For Christocentric scholars, speaking about Jesus only from what he did and said between his incarnation and death would be highly limiting, even demeaning. For them, Christ is the pre-existent Lord who was involved with the creation and is present in the Old Testament. Therefore, the law and prophets in the Old Testament are just as much about Jesus as the gospels are. This deduction can only be true if one defines Jesus ontologically rather than functionally.[38] Even though these scholars might use functional language, it still assumes ontological realities, namely, Christ's pre-existence and divinity. Their referencing of Jesus' words and works will most often be placed in the larger story of who Christ is, from the Old Testament through to the New. Wright (2011c, 172) makes the case that unless the church understands the historical nature of Jesus' career and fate, that is, from a functional perspective, as presented by the gospel writers, the preaching of the gospels will quickly revert to merely "Christ died for our sins." This is precisely the criticism against Christocentric preaching discussed in 5.5.4 and 5.5.5 above.

---

37. Conversely, Baker (2006, 77) and Qin (2015, 39) contend that Christology from below is functional in nature as it focuses on the functions of Jesus, namely, his words and deeds rather than his identity.

38. From above Christologies looks for Christ's divine presence in the Old Testament whereas from below Christologies places Christ into the historical narrative and trajectory of the Old Testament.

5.6.8 Conclusion

To suggest that every hermeneutical and homiletical model consciously chooses either a strictly Christology from above or from below would be an oversimplification. It is not so simple because the Christology embedded in such a model is mostly hidden, like lenses one puts on, and it might very well have connections to both sides of the Christological spectrum. In other words, a preaching model might use the type of lens that consists of a mixture of the characteristics of both Christologies. However, even without a clearly articulated declaration of the type of Christology behind a homiletical method, through observation, Christological connections can be identified from the type of Christology emphasized. From examining Clowney, Greidanus, and Chapell's work, it is evident that there are strong connections with the Christology from above approach to understanding and explaining Jesus Christ. This can be seen by their posture of faith in the validity of the Scriptures, particularly the New Testament. Consequently, they accept and advocate the New Testament writers' claims about Jesus Christ. They see no need to treat the Scriptures, nor the faith statements of the New Testament writers, with any suspicion. When examined through the criteria of the six key questions of the Third Quest for the historical Jesus, we also see their preference for a Christology from above rather than from below. Likewise, it is noted that where from below scholars, such as Pannenberg, emphasize Jesus as the representative of true humanity, the Christocentric scholars emphasize Jesus as the representative of God who has come into this world to redeem and restore it. This contributes to their focus on Jesus from an ontological rather than a functional perspective, as seen in Wright and Pannenberg. All of these emphases are indicative of a Christology from above.

5.7 Concluding Remarks

The modern development of the Christocentric approach has become a significant model in contemporary evangelical hermeneutics and homiletics. The works of Clowney and Greidanus have been instrumental in providing the foundation of this rejuvenated approach. Chapell's contribution has stood on the shoulders of their work and has been very influential in contemporary homiletics. This chapter commenced with a literature review of the works of the pioneers of the approach—Edmund Clowney and Sidney Greidanus—as well as their contemporary representative Bryan Chapell. The literature review of Clowney's work revealed that instead of choosing a homiletical model and having that influence one's interpretation of Scripture, Clowney's conviction about the nature and story of Scripture led to his preaching method. For Clowney, Scripture is one book that reveals God's revelation as a single continuous and progressive theme that reached its climax in Jesus Christ. Clowney suggested a two-step hermeneutical approach, in which a text must first be interpreted in its grammatical-historical context and then in the context of redemptive history. Clowney's homiletical approach suggested two tools to preach Christ from the Old Testament where he is not explicitly mentioned, namely, symbolism and typology.

Greidanus, likewise, believes that preaching Christ is not a luxury but a necessity because Christ is the center of the Bible. Therefore, Scripture, including the Old Testament, must be interpreted through those lenses. Like Clowney, Greidanus' hermeneutical method also consists of two steps; namely, the text must first be interpreted in its historical-cultural context, which includes the literary, historical, and Theocentric interpretations, and then the text must be interpreted in the contexts of the entire canon and redemptive history. Possibly Greidanus' most significant contribution to the Christocentric homiletic is his insightful seven ways of preaching Christ from the Old Testament, namely, the way of redemptive-historical progression, the way of promise-fulfillment, typology, analogy, the longitudinal themes, New Testament references, and the way of contrast.

As with Clowney and Greidanus, Chapell's biblical theology leads to his homiletical approach. For Chapell, the grand narrative of Scripture is about how a gracious God redeemed a fallen world through Christ to restore humanity and creation. Consequently, he argues that a text of Scripture cannot be understood merely in its historical and literary contexts but must also be interpreted in this broader redemptive context. Accordingly, he views Scripture as a progressive, organic, and redemptive revelation of God's nature and works. Chapell's hermeneutical method has three steps which consist of understanding the original authorial intent as determined through his grammar and history, observing the literary context, and understanding the text in its redemptive context. His homiletical method provides roadmaps to preach redemptive-historical sermons for all three scenarios one might encounter in a passage, namely, where Christ or his work is explicitly mentioned, Christ or his work is typified, and where there is no direct reference to Christ.

This chapter demonstrated that there are certain weaknesses to the Christocentric approach due to its specific convictions and emphases. Because of the Christocentric method's view of Scripture, they consistently emphasize the gospel of Jesus Christ, seeking to avoid moralistic sermons and to raise the listeners' affections toward God through which transformation can happen. However, on the other side of that emphasis, this can lead to repetitive sermons that have inadequate practical applications for the church. Sermons can be so focused on changing one's attitude that the behavioral change part is underemphasized. Finally, with its heavy emphasis on God's redemptive work through Christ, this approach risks overemphasizing one part of Christ's atoning work and overemphasizing one person of the Trinity. From this summary, Price's (2018, 91–93) conclusion that the Christocentric approach should be implemented alongside a grammatical-historical approach rather than be seen as dichotomous is very persuasive. For the Christocentric method, preaching Christ in every sermon is non-negotiable. Therefore, synthesizing this method with a grammatical-historical approach to make it more balanced would compromise its fundamental conviction. However, by employing a balanced Christology, in other words, a Christology from above and from below, the Christocentric method can find ways to overcome certain shortcomings.

Based on the understanding obtained from the literature review of these Christocentric scholars, their advocates, and opponents, this chapter identified, described, and explored the embedded Christology of the Christocentric approach. From examining Clowney, Greidanus, and Chapell's work, strong connections with the Christology from above approach were identified. These connections are their posture of faith in the validity of the Scriptures, particularly the New Testament, and the total acceptance and advocacy of the faith claims that the New Testament writers make about Jesus Christ. Moreover, their preference to refer to Jesus Christ in cosmic ways rather than Jewish categories, accompanied by a belief that Jesus had self-knowledge of his divinity and their primary treatment of the gospels within their larger meta-narrative can all be associated with a Christology from above. Because their model is embedded in this type of Christology, they focus more on Jesus from an ontological rather than a functional perspective and refer to Jesus primarily as a representative of God rather than humanity.

6

Implications for a Christocentric Homiletic

6.1 Introduction

THE CHRISTOCENTRIC METHOD IS built on a certain scriptural conviction, namely, that the Bible reveals God's revelation as a single continuous and progressive theme that reached its climax in Jesus Christ. It is the progressive, organic, and redemptive revelation of God's nature and works. These presuppositions shape the way Scripture is interpreted and what preaching looks like. Furthermore, these convictions regarding Scripture and Christ's function in it result in a substantial bias toward a Christology from above. Although it is an oversimplification to assume that all the shortcomings and strengths of a preaching model depend on its embedded Christology, this thesis suggests that another type of Christology will enrich and challenge the Christocentric method to address certain shortcomings and enhance some strengths because of its fresh perspective. This chapter aims to explore the implications of the strengths of Wright and Pannenberg's from below Christologies, as explored in the critical analysis performed in chapter 4, for the Christocentric homiletic.

The critical analysis of chapter 4 concluded that Wright and Pannenberg's Christologies provide invaluable links between the Old Testament and Jesus Christ. Their historical understanding and presentation of the story the gospels are telling, and its connection to the Old Testament provide significant homiletical value. It also showed that being a follower of

Jesus Christ has private, public, and political consequences. Their Christology challenges the church to obey its calling of being a sign and foretaste of God's kingdom. Their work not only shows what it means to be a follower of Jesus and his kingdom movement but also, more broadly, reveals the essence and destiny of humanity from the historical existence of Jesus Christ. Finally, it provides language to speak about God and Jesus in an apologetic and relevant manner.

This chapter will commence with an exploration of the implications of these strengths of Wright and Pannenberg's Christologies for the shortcomings of the Christocentric homiletic as identified in chapter 5. The Christocentric model's convictions and emphases have significant connections to a Christology from above, contributing to certain shortcomings. These shortcomings were identified as preaching sermons that can be repetitive and, in a sense, insensitive to the spiritual needs of a congregation. Furthermore, these sermons lack appropriate application, overemphasize soteriology, and elevate one person of the Trinity over the others. Since this thesis' main research question is around the implications of a critical analysis of Pannenberg and Wright's Christology for a Christocentric homiletic, this chapter will also identify and describe certain strengths of the Christocentric homiletic that Wright and Pannenberg's Christologies can enrich.

To conclude this chapter, examples will be provided to demonstrate what these implications might look like in sermon form. To do this, one sermon from Clowney, Greidanus, and Chapell from chapter 5 will be selected and adapted to reveal how these sermons could be different if they took these from below Christologies seriously.

6.2 Overcoming the Shortcomings of Christocentric Homiletics

6.2.1 Introduction

Kärkkäinen (2016, 6) rightfully states that any emphasis on a single Christology runs the danger of being one-dimensional in its understanding and description of Jesus. As we have seen, the Christocentric homiletic has significant connections to a Christology from above, which leads to certain hermeneutical and homiletical blind spots. Some of these shortcomings are the repetitive nature of their sermons, the scarcity of appropriate application, the overemphasis of soteriology at the expense of other important doctrines, and the elevation of one person of the Trinity over the others. It is unrealistic to assume that if the Christocentric homiletic incorporates a more balanced Christology, all its shortcomings will disappear. Nevertheless, there are certain implications Wright and Pannenberg's from below Christology will have on Christocentric homiletics' shortcomings, especially because of its embeddedness in the from above method. By expanding its foundational Christology with these two Christologies, the Christocentric approach can address some of its shortcomings without neglecting its major methodological convictions. This section will explore the implications of the strengths of Wright and Pannenberg's from below Christologies, as discussed in chapter 4, for the homiletical shortcomings of the Christocentric approach.

6.2.2 Creative Repertoire of Sermon Goals

A fundamental characteristic of the Christocentric homiletic is that every sermon should feature, in one way or another, the person and work of Jesus Christ (Goldsworthy 2018, 127; Sequeira 2018, 182; Allen 2016; Greidanus 1999, loc. 2682). Moreover, when Jesus is proclaimed, the emphasis is often placed upon the redemptive significance of his person and work. This stems from the biblical theology that undergirds the approach, which perceives Scripture to be the unfolding progressive continuing revelation of God which came to its culmination in Christ. Part of this revelation of God reflects his redemptive nature and purposes, which finds its climax in Christ. Hence, Chapell (2018b, 8) proposes that even though not all Scripture explicitly refers to Christ, why would we not always want to speak about Jesus and his saving works? In response, scholars such as Kuruvilla (2018, 30), Block (2018, 15–17), Poythress (2018, 54), and Price (2018, 84) point out that sermons have different functions; for instance, some encourage whilst others rebuke or warn. Therefore, for example, every sermon cannot be an evangelistic sermon, for when this is the case, there is a risk that preaching can become one-dimensional and malnutritional. Gibson and Kim (2018, 162) and Price (2018, 84–85) contend that because of this desire to preach Christ in every sermon, Christocentric preaching often communicates general canonical truths and operates with a high level of repetition and duplication. In other words, sermons sound monotonous and predictable. Conversely, rather than preaching Christ from every text, the pastor should be balanced and use his discernment and wisdom to decide when and from where to preach Christ.

One way to address this monotony is to interchangeably preach Christocentric and Theocentric sermons, as suggested by Price (2018, 93). This is a persuasive proposal because it can force the preacher to take the message of every text more seriously, it provides the opportunity to exercise different forms of preaching, and it gives the platform for a preacher to pastorally address the spiritual needs of the congregation. However, the Christocentric homiletic has concerns about non-redemptive historical preaching, most notably that it tends to lead to pharisaic moralism. It is more interested in the transformation of the listener than behavioral change, which is the risk the model perceives in Theocentric sermons. This transformation comes through growing in our love for the Triune God, which is fuelled by preaching that places the grace of God and the beauties of Christ on display. In other words, for both negative and positive reasons, the Christocentric homiletic is not interested in sharing the pulpit with a Theocentric approach, as Price suggests.

This is where the from below Christologies of Wright and Pannenberg can be very useful. By utilizing Wright and Pannenberg's findings, without negating their Pauline Christology, the Christocentric approach can remain true to its convictions of preaching Christ in every message but will gain a much broader repertoire from which to draw. This will allow them to take the gospels more seriously, preach sermons about the humanity of Christ, and pastorally address the congregation's spiritual needs. For example, Wright's Christology will inform the Christocentric preacher about Jesus' worldview, mindset, aim and beliefs, his ability to think theologically, his symbolic acts, and his vocation (Wright 1996a, 139; 1996b, 404). Under this notion of Jesus' mindset, the preacher can draw connections between the Old Testament and Jesus' habitual praxis, stories, symbolic acts, and the answers he gave to basic worldview questions. Correspondingly, the preacher can allude to Jesus' awareness of his vocation given to him by Israel's God to enact what the Old Testament promised God would accomplish by himself. According to Wright (1996a, 651), Jesus believed that Israel's God had called him to evoke and enact the tradition that YHWH would return to Zion and that he would share his throne. In other words, Jesus believed that his vocation was to do and be what only Israel's God did and was (Wright 1998a, 53). Hays (2011, 69) points out that although Wright followed a Christology from below approach, this self-knowledge of his vocation to enact YHWH in himself unexpectedly opens the door to a very high Christology, which makes it a very attractive prospect for the Christocentric homiletic. Incorporating the ideas of Jesus' mindset and vocation into their sermon repertoire, the Christocentric method can make fascinating connections to the Old Testament, which has staggering implications for the contemporary church.

Similarly, the Christocentric approach can, for example, incorporate Pannenberg's understanding of Jesus' self-sacrificial dedication to the Father to speak about Jesus' career and fate (Pannenberg 1966, 347). Pannenberg emphasized that Jesus' objective was to call people into the imminent kingdom of God, which shaped his activities and message. In other words, all of Jesus' activity was a dedication to God and his will (346). Pannenberg contended that Jesus knew himself functionally in unity with God's will (*funktional mit Gottes Willen*) through his career, which was shaped around his proclamation of the imminent kingdom of God (345). Additionally, Jesus' dedication took on a self-sacrificing nature through the fate that he suffered. By taking Pannenberg's contributions seriously, the Christocentric method can form sermons around the humanity and dedication of Jesus and his relationship with the Father.

Additionally, Pannenberg's Christology can provide the Christocentric homiletic with resources to speak about Jesus as the revelatory presence of Israel's God, as confirmed through the resurrection. Pannenberg (1966, 150) believed that the resurrection of Jesus was the revelatory event through which Jesus' unity with God's eternal essence was revealed. Pannenberg argued that through the resurrection, God validated the pre-Easter claims of the authority of Jesus, which means that Jesus' relation to God must be expressed as God's self-revelation (127–29). Using Pannenberg's views on the resurrection and its retrospective implications (*rückwirkenden bedeutung*), the Christocentric approach can affirm the validity of Jesus' claims and speak about Jesus' unity with God from the origin of his earthly life (139–40). This, undoubtedly, is a conviction that the Christocentric method holds; nevertheless, Pannenberg provides a fresh perspective that affirms that belief. This notion will connect well with the Christocentric homiletic's conviction that the unfolding progressive revelation of God throughout redemptive history is summed up and united by Christ (Clowney 2002, 74–75). In other words, Christ is the apex of God's revelation.

Messages incorporating Wright and Pannenberg's findings can be delivered in a descriptive manner in which the listener can listen, learn, and marvel at Jesus Christ. The Christocentric method excels at descriptive messages, hence the criticism from other homiletical approaches regarding the lack of application in Christocentric sermons. Descriptive messages that speak about these aspects of Jesus' life might very well function to raise the affections of the congregation in their process of transformation, especially if the Christocentric preacher balances his messages between Christ, who appeared as the commander of the Lord's armies to Joshua at Jericho, and the first century Jew Jesus of Nazareth who gained an understanding of his vocation by reading Daniel, Zechariah, the Psalter, and Isaiah (Wright 1996a, 597–601). The purpose of such descriptive messages is to assist the church in marveling at Jesus Christ.

Conversely, sermons incorporating Wright and Pannenberg's work might also be prescriptive, whereby the preacher can warn, rebuke, admonish, or call to action. For example, according to Wright, Jesus' kingdom announcement came in the form of an invitation to repent and believe (1996a, 247), a welcome to be part of the renewed Israel (274), a challenge to live like the renewed Israel according to the new covenant (275), and a summons to be his helpers and associates (298). Or, according to Pannenberg, Jesus urges his followers to imitate his self-sacrificial dedication to the Father (Pannenberg 1991a, 33–34). In staying with their conviction to preach Christ in every sermon, the Christocentric homiletic can incorporate the findings of Wright and Pannenberg's Christologies to form a more holistic approach to preaching, resulting in creative and pastoral sermons.

Finally, one type of sermon form that the Christocentric method tends to avoid is biographical sermons. This can be observed through the treatment of the David and Goliath story in 1 Samuel 17 (Stetzer 2013, 26–28). Where the grammatical-historical method encourages us to take courage through life's circumstances, the Christocentric method urges us to trust in Christ, who won the victory over the ultimate enemy, namely, Satan, sin, and death. Where scholars from the grammatical-historical approach, such as Kuruvilla (2013, 242), consider biblical characters to be exemplars for believers (Rom 15:4; 1 Cor 10:6; 1 Tim 2:12–15; Heb 3:7–4:11; Jas 5:10–28), Christocentric scholars are averted to biographical preaching (Greidanus 1999, loc. 524–34; 1988, 175–81; Prince 2011, 138; Clowney 1961, 79–82). The reason for their aversion to biographical preaching runs deeper than merely wanting to preach Christ, and therefore other characters are unimportant. For instance, Clowney demonstrated the difficulties of biographical preaching by using David as an example. He points out that many Sunday school lessons have been taught on the Goliath story (Clowney 2003, loc. 435–48). David is presented as the brave boy who defeated the giant, Goliath, with nothing more than a slingshot and some pebbles. However, this biographical approach runs into issues when it reaches David and Bathsheba. Although these are two extremes on the sliding scale of good and bad, for Clowney, the issue with biographical preaching arrives when the lines between good and bad become blurred. Clowney writes, "The real problem comes, however, when Bible characters seem to be commended for doing dreadful things" (loc. 450). For example, when Samuel cut king Agag to pieces before the Lord (1 Samuel 15).

Greidanus (1999, loc. 1866–880) argues that using the lives of biblical characters as positive or negative examples leads to moralizing. Price (2018, 84–85) shows, from Greidanus' treatment of Genesis 22, that he believes that by making biblical characters positive examples, we turn descriptive stories into prescriptive imperatives. In this case, Abraham's obedience and trust become requirements for righteousness. Chapell (2013, 168–69) likewise opposes biographical preaching because he believes this type of message only shows the characters' strengths. He points out that biographical preaching can be helpful if the characters' weaknesses are pointed out and their need for righteousness which comes only through Christ (Chapell 2018a, 7524–539). In other words, biographical preaching becomes acceptable if it aligns with his fallen condition focus (FCF) emphasis. For example, throughout his sermon on Numbers 20:1–13, Chapell (2013, 168–69) shows Moses' failures as a leader, which is what he calls the fallen condition focus of the text. Having identified this focus, Chapell shows the gracious character of God, who provided for his people despite Moses' leadership issues.

However, if biographical sermons are dismissed for these reasons, a very effective communication tool is left dormant. Chapell rightly states that our post-modern culture craves stories and refers to it as a "story- and image-oriented culture" (Chapell 2006a, 23; 2006b, 44). Biographical sermons convey messages through stories about biblical characters' lives that listeners can sometimes relate to and learn from. Wright (2011a, 87) points out that Jesus himself conveyed important truths through storytelling. He writes, "Jesus, as we saw, had one particular method of explaining what was going on. As part of his campaign, he told stories" (87). Storytelling should be an essential part of any preacher's arsenal, within which biographical sermons are vital.

This is where the from below Christology of Wright and Pannenberg, with its detailed description of Jesus' career, can add significant value. By incorporating aspects of their Christologies, the Christocentric homiletic can present biographical sermons focused on the life of Jesus Christ and, in that way, utilize this effective communication tool and diversify their approach. Moreover, by understanding who Jesus was historically, for example, as a prophet or the Jewish Messiah, the Christocentric method can relate the lives of other biblical characters to Jesus more effectively, both in how they foreshadow Jesus but also in where they fall short. Therefore, the historical findings of Wright and Pannenberg provide the Christocentric method with a more holistic approach to preaching, which, if implemented, can avoid repetitive sermons in terms of content and form.

6.2.3 Improved Application of Sermons

Hays (2009, loc. 1873–874) rightly contends that "every attempt to articulate a normative Christian ethic depends—whether explicitly or implicitly—on a particular construal of the figure of Jesus, along with some account of the message that he proclaimed." Christocentric homiletics' portrait of Christ is that he is the cornerstone of God's redemptive dealings with humanity (Chapell 2018b, 7). Consequently, as already discussed, the Christocentric approach places a significant emphasis on soteriology, especially substitutionary atonement. Because of its focus on God's redemptive actions through Christ, which promotes the state of fallenness of humanity and the gracious nature of God, the personal responsibility aspect is often neglected.

Proclaiming the grace of God through Christ is the primary concern of the Christocentric method's application because by declaring the beauties and riches of Christ and his redemptive work, the hearts of the listeners are motivated for godliness (Sequeira 2018, 193–94; Chapell 2018a, loc. 4914–916). The focus, then, is more on the transformation of the heart than behavioral change (Chapell 2018b, 14). Their picture of Christ and his central role in redemption leads to preaching that focuses on articulating the gospel as often as possible whilst simultaneously avoiding moralistic human-centered sermons. However, Gibson and Kim (2018, 162) rightfully state that these types of sermon applications leave the congregation with the idea that since Jesus graciously accomplished everything for us and because humanity is a fallen creature, why should we even bother trying? Likewise, Kuruvilla (2018, 32–33) highlights that although the grace of God as revealed through Jesus Christ is critical, we must acknowledge that God desires his people to live a certain way. Sermons that only focus on what Jesus has done for us on the cross without addressing what behavior God desires from his people can lead to an unhealthy privatization of faith and an escapist mentality in which the focus is only placed on our eternal destination.

The sermon application is perhaps where the Christologies of Wright and Pannenberg can offer the most significant contribution. Hays' assertion that our picture of Jesus shapes what we preach as normative Christian ethics can be perceived in Wright and Pannenberg. Their understanding of who Jesus was historically leads to inevitable practical implications for contemporary Christian life.[1] These two from below Christologies challenge the Christocentric method's application process and, if taken seriously, will significantly impact their application process. Wright's presentation of Jesus reveals that God was not simply removing the guilt of individuals through Jesus' death and resurrection but that it was part of God's larger plan to restore Israel and, through them, bring salvation to the world (Hays 2011, 67). Wright (2017c) famously declares that our soteriology is only complete

---

1. This is what the sixth question of the Third Quest for the historical Jesus seeks to address, namely, "How does one's historical Jesus portrait relate to the contemporary church and world?"

when it summons Jesus' followers to a foot-washing and fruit-bearing mission. His Christology concludes that through the resurrection of Jesus Christ, God has started the new creation, referred to as the kingdom of God, and therefore the followers of Jesus have a calling through which Jesus continues to establish the kingdom of God on earth (Wright 2008b, 31; 2011a, 220). Wright presents a Jesus who demands his disciples to implement his kingdom agenda through praxis, symbol, and story (Wright 2011a, 225; 1998f, 152–53). This means that a private belief in Jesus has public consequences. The followers of Jesus must be holistic witnesses of the kingdom of God by not only believing and telling the story of God's redemptive actions through Jesus but also by bearing witness to the kingdom through their lifestyles. They are to live out the gospel publicly and act as God's means by which heaven and earth interlock and overlap (Wright 2007b). Hays (2011, 53) states that, for Wright, "true beliefs about Jesus cannot be separated from praxis that seeks to implement Jesus' kingdom agenda."

For the Christocentric homiletic, this means that even sermons that emphasize the cross, substitutionary atonement, and the resurrection cannot merely end with "we are now at peace with God," as important as that is. The career, death, and resurrection of Jesus have not only private but also public consequences. The challenge that Wright's Christology poses to the Christocentric homiletic is not to separate the career of Jesus from his death and resurrection. Wright's Christology urges the Christocentric homiletic to ask what it means to be a follower of Jesus, to take up his agenda, and what it looks like when his story shapes our praxis.

More specifically, Wright's Christology has direct political consequences. According to Wright, part of the response Jesus demands from his disciples is to call the world to account (Wright 2017c). By this, Wright means that the church should stand up against all injustice, violence, and every other type of wickedness that exists in the world and hold its leaders to account (Wright 1998c, 53). Because Jesus is the *Kyrios* of the world, and Caesar is not, Jesus' lordship must affect every household, community, country, and policy. Wright's Christology does not lead to a "pie-in-the-sky religion," according to which God prepares our eternal dwelling, called heaven, while we serve God merely privately in a spiritual sense (53). Nor is it a religion that tolerates selfishness or focuses on individual emotions. The Christocentric approach's lack of sermon application and its strong emphasis on soteriology can easily lead to a privatized form of Christianity that concludes with Jesus loves me, died for me, and therefore I must only believe this to go to heaven. But this ignores Jesus' inauguration of the kingdom of God and his summons to his followers to imitate him in praxis, symbol, and story. Wright (1991a, 51) believes that the church should hold itself accountable, lest it becomes a privatized spirituality, conceited, or embraces some form of paganism. His Christology can safeguard the Christocentric homiletic in this regard.

Pannenberg's understanding of the kingdom of God differs from Wright's. Pannenberg contended that because of Jesus' self-sacrificial dedication to the Father, he now partakes in God's lordship and will bring God's kingdom to fulfillment in the future (Pannenberg 1966, 386). In other words, instead of implementing the already inaugurated kingdom of God, the church should act as the precursor to the kingdom of God (Pannenberg 1966, 387–88; 1988, 167). However, this summons to be a precursor to God's kingdom also has significant practical implications for how we direct our conduct. The church's role as the precursor of the kingdom of God demands that their behavior indicate that they are a people of the kingdom. Again, this summons should challenge the Christocentric method's aversion to behavioral change. For Pannenberg (1966, 388–90), being a precursor to the kingdom means that the church should continue Jesus' way of dedicating itself to the Father by announcing the message of the kingdom and by submitting its conduct in both private and public to the lordship of Christ. Like Wright, Pannenberg's Christology challenges the Christocentric homiletic to emphasize the faith's private and public aspects. Pannenberg (1976a, 363) warned that the privatization of religion is an enemy to practical displays of love towards society. Being a precursor to the kingdom, according to Pannenberg, means that the church lives for justice in all structures of relationships (Harvie 2008, 155). This implies loving our neighbors and maintaining certain conduct towards them (Pannenberg 1966, 239).

For Pannenberg, the implications of being a precursor of the kingdom of God extend beyond our moral conduct and relationships. It also has ecological implications for the church, whereby Jesus commissions us to preserve and protect creation itself. Rise (2010, 227–28) explains that, for Pannenberg, becoming a follower of Jesus involves maturing to become conscious of the well-being of all that God has made. Furthermore, Pannenberg (1977c, 40; 2001, 203) contended that living into its calling as a precursor of the kingdom will lead to greater ecumenical openness, which is the best apologetic for the Christian faith in a secular culture. Lastly, Pannenberg's Christology challenges the church to participate in interfaith dialogue because of the universal significance of the future kingdom of God.

Where the Christocentric homiletic's understanding of Jesus leads to sermons that emphasize the death of Jesus and lack practical applications, the Christologies of Wright and Pannenberg lead to an understanding of Jesus that makes practical realities unavoidable for followers of Jesus. By accepting the challenge of these Christologies, the Christocentric method can find ways to keep their sermons completely Christocentric yet have ample avenues to introduce practical applications. These applications can be as domestic as bearing fruit, joining Jesus on his mission in our neighborhoods, and participating in social justice. It can also be as universal as responding to global warming, climate change, CO_2 emissions issues, ecumenical relations or problems, and participating in inter-faith dialogue.

6.2.4 Emphasis on the Cross and the Kingdom

The biblical theology of Clowney (1961, 78), Greidanus (1999, loc. 250–58), and Chapell (2018b, 7) is built on the presupposition that the apex of the Scriptures is the redemptive work of God through Christ. Therefore, the Scriptures tell the story of how God graciously redeems and restores humanity and creation through Christ. Consequently, for the Christocentric homiletic, the notion of redemption is critical to every sermon in every text (Chapell 2018b, 15–16). Gibson and Kim (2018, 159–60) and Kuruvilla (2013, 259–60) criticize the Christocentric for this tendency because it surpasses the primary meaning of texts to link it to New Testament soteriology. Moreover, Chou (2016, 133–34) states that certain Christocentric preachers never speak about Christ outside his soteriology roles. Furthermore, the Christocentric method not only majors on soteriology but a specific perspective of soteriology, namely, substitutionary atonement. Price (2018, 80–81) suggests that due to its biblical theology, the Christocentric homiletic tends to emphasize Christ's passive obedience, which refers to his penal substitutionary sacrifice. Thus, many sermons end with Jesus dying on the cross to secure forgiveness for our sins but do not venture beyond that (Piper 2019).

However, the issue is that focusing merely on the salvific death of Jesus on the cross does not do justice to his entire career and what the gospels are predominantly about. For the Christocentric approach, the highlights of the gospels are that Jesus was born of a virgin, lived a perfect life, died on the cross for our sins to secure our forgiveness, and rose again from the dead as a sign that we have been pardoned. However, Wright (2008b, 29–31) indicates that reducing the gospels to these four points has been used throughout history to set up Paul's soteriology of substitutionary atonement. But when we read the gospels, we can see that God's redemption through Christ extends beyond substitutionary atonement. As Wright (2011c, 172) argues, unless the church understands the historical nature of Jesus' career and fate as presented by the gospel writers, the preaching of the gospels will easily revert to merely "Christ died for our sins" (172). Hence, with its historical understanding of the gospels, Wright's Christology from below can broaden the redemptive paradigm of the Christocentric method to preach sermons that focus both on Jesus' salvific death and the purpose of his career.

According to Wright (2008b, 29), the story that all four gospels are telling is about the kingdom of God coming to earth through the public ministry, death, and resurrection of Jesus of Nazareth. The gospels, then, are all about how "God is becoming king" in and through Jesus (Wright 2012a, 400). It tells the story of Israel's God reclaiming the entire world in and through Jesus. Moreover, this story of the kingdom of God is told as the climax of Israel's history in which their exile is ended, their sins are forgiven, YHWH returns to Zion, and their enemies are defeated (379). The gospels are about Jesus embodying Israel's God and summing up the history of Israel in himself by fulfilling her destiny (Wright 2011c, 181). Wright states, "The gospels have a very high Christology; but this isn't about divinity in the abstract, but about *the God of Israel personally present and active*" (182).

Wright's understanding of the gospels can assist the Christocentric homiletic to keep their theology of the cross and the kingdom together. Taking his presentation of the gospels seriously will safeguard the Christocentric homiletic from overemphasizing their soteriology. Too often, these two concepts, kingdom theology and cross theology, have been treated as alternatives that emphasize either God's work of renewing the world or God saving people from their sins (Wright 2011c, 186–88). In other words, scholars either focus on a kingdom theology and the gospels or a cross theology and Paul. The Christocentric homiletic, with its strong emphasis on soteriology and specifically substitutionary atonement, is no exception. However, these two notions belong together, and Wright's Christology is extremely helpful in holding them in proper balance. Wright contends that "for the Evangelists, the kingdom is the project which is sealed, accomplished, by the cross, on the one hand, and the cross is the victory through which the kingdom is established, on the other" (192).

Unless the Christocentric homiletic embraces a kingdom theology alongside its cross theology, the homiletical riches of the gospels will remain untapped. Because of its overemphasis on soteriology, it can reduce the gospels to a story about how and why Jesus died, but not how and why he lived. And for a Christocentric approach that seeks to preach Christ, such a shortcoming is glaring. Wright's work provides the Christocentric homiletic with an understanding of Jesus' aims, beliefs, symbolic actions, and vocation. Therefore, incorporating Wright's kingdom theology into its approach will enable the Christocentric method to deal with the events during Jesus' career. Because of their emphasis on the soteriological parts of Jesus' story, namely, his virgin birth, perfect life, death, and resurrection, and their aversion to moralistic preaching, certain sayings and teachings of Jesus can become inherently problematic for the Christocentric method. However, understanding Jesus' praxis, stories, and symbolic actions in light of his vocation will benefit the Christocentric approach.

Wright's understanding of the gospels, which emphasizes the importance of both a cross and kingdom theology, is surprisingly compatible with the Christocentric method for at least two reasons. First, Wright's understanding of the gospels demands intertextuality. He contends that "Matthew, Mark, Luke and John, all in their very different ways, insist that the full meaning of Jesus is to be found precisely as the climax of the canon, the point where the large and complex story of Adam and Abraham, of Moses, David and the prophets all comes rushing together" (Wright 2011c, 175). The Christocentric hermeneutic contends that the Scriptures are Christocentric precisely because Christ is the climax of its meta-narrative (Clowney 1961, 78; Greidanus 1999, loc. 250–58; Chapell 2018b, 7). Furthermore, like the Christocentric scholars, Wright's (2008b, 30–31) understanding of the gospels demands that they be used to interpret the Old Testament texts. He is adamant that nothing is gained exegetically or historically by avoiding the Jewishness of the gospels and their claim to fulfill Jewish Old Testament hopes. Second, as Marsh (1998, 80) and Moore (2003, 16) point out, Wright has a very high view of the gospels' integrity, even though he follows a from below approach and operates with a great deal of trust towards the gospels. This posture seems to fit the Christocentric approach's optimistic view of the Scriptures. Incorporating Wright's understanding of the gospels and thereby emphasizing both the kingdom and the cross will enable the Christocentric model to address the criticism that its redemptive paradigm is too narrow (Wilson 2018, 39).

The from below Christology of Wright connects the theology of the cross with the theology of the kingdom of God. These concepts are not only crucial in the context of soteriology but have a significant impact on missiology. Wright (2011c, 186–87) shows that large parts of the Western church have found it challenging to consolidate Jesus' penal substitutionary death on the cross with Jesus' kingdom of God-focused career. Scholars seem to find this convergence difficult to navigate; consequently, those who emphasize a cross-focused theology tend to believe that the primary purpose of missions is to preach the gospel so that sinners can receive salvation. Conversely, those who emphasize a kingdom of God theology can tend to argue that missions should be about the church being the instrument of God through whom he is making the world a better place. Wright points out that scholars often emphasize the one whilst downplaying the other (188). The problem is that if only one aspect is emphasized at the expense of the other, then the church's missional response will consist of either social ethics or saving souls (193).

Just as the Christocentric homiletic does not explicitly expound its Christology, it also does not elaborate on the type of missiology it endorses. Nevertheless, with its strong emphasis on preaching the gospel regularly, avoiding moralism, and its overemphasis on soteriology compared to other important doctrines, the approach can easily default to missiology, which is mostly only concerned with saving souls. In North America, where this new movement in Christocentric homiletics originated, there has been a significant shift in emphasis concerning missions. Corbett and Fikkert (2012, 43) show that before the twentieth-century North American evangelicals played a substantial role in caring for the poor's physical and spiritual needs. However, a shift occurred between 1900–1930 due to the conflict with the liberal theologians' social gospel. According to the social gospel movement, all humanitarian efforts were equated with ushering in God's kingdom. Corbett and Fikkert write, "As evangelicals tried to distance themselves from the social gospel movement, they ended up in largescale retreat from the front lines of poverty alleviation" (43). Historians have called this phenomenon the "Great Reversal." Importantly, Corbett and Fikkert point out that this great reversal by the evangelical church was fundamentally due to a change in theological position (43–44). This great reversal has fundamentally shaped the North American evangelical church's missional strategies and has often led to one-sided missiology. Corbett and Fikkert contend, "Often lacking an appreciation of the comprehensive implications of the kingdom of God, many missionaries have focused on evangelism to save people's souls but have sometimes neglected to 'make disciples of all nations'" (45).

The new movement of the Christocentric homiletic was birthed in that North American missiological context in the 1960s and so, by default, inherited this specific missiological focus. The approach's commitment to soteriology and the regular preaching of the gospel message is subtle evidence of this influence. Therefore, with its balance between cross and kingdom theology, Wright's Christology can provide the Christocentric method to form a more balanced structure for missions. For Wright (2012a, 381), we must allow the gospels to shape our perspective on mission because they stand at the center of the missionary and theological life of the early church. And according to Wright, the story that the gospels are telling emphasizes both the cross and the kingdom of God. The theology of the cross is only complete when it calls Jesus' followers to a "foot-washing" and "fruit-bearing" mission (Wright 2017c).

Consequently, the challenge for the church is to be the means through which Jesus continues to establish the kingdom of God on earth as in heaven (Wright 2011a, 220). In that sense, recapturing the historical Jesus and his kingdom vision is central to a refreshed kingdom-focused missiology (Wright 2012a, 379).[2] Consequently, the church has a job to do as a result of Jesus' life, death and resurrection, which involves both saving souls and social ethics. Thus, incorporating Wright's Christology will broaden the redemptive paradigm of the Christocentric method by linking a cross and kingdom theology and thereby unlocking the richness of the homiletical value of the gospels. Moreover, this will offer the Christocentric homiletic a balanced missiological framework which can result in preaching that is grounded in the reality of human experiences such as poverty and suffering.

6.2.5 A More Balanced Perspective of God

The Christocentric approach acknowledges the importance of the Trinity and does not perceive its method to be a threat to the doctrine of the Trinity. Clowney (1984, 246) and Wellum (2018, 4) contend that Christocentric preaching is God-centered because it conveys the plan of the Triune God who came to save humanity. Similarly, Poythress (2018, 51–52) and Greidanus (2018, 105) argue that the Christocentric interpretation of Scripture and a Trinity-centered interpretation are two sides of the same coin because the Christocentric method stands on the shoulders of the Theocentric hermeneutic. Apart from acknowledging the importance of the doctrine of the Trinity and the involvement of the entire Godhead in redemption, it also opposes Christo-monism because of its threat to the doctrine of the Trinity (Poythress 2018, 51; Greidanus 1999, loc. 2045). Although the Christocentric homiletic must be commended for these doctrinal convictions, in practice, their strong emphasis on Christ above the other persons of the Trinity can be problematic. The main issue with only preaching about Jesus is twofold. First, if the congregation does not hear about the Father and the Spirit's role in redemption, it can distort the image of the Trinity and the gospel itself (Chou 2016, 133). Second, if the entire involvement of the Trinity is not consistently communicated, then the portrait of the Father can get distorted. Unless the Triune God is seen as our redeemer, the gospel can easily become the story of the harsh Father and the kind Son (Langley 2018, 35).

---

2. Pannenberg's (1966, 388) work concludes that the church, as a precursor to the kingdom of God, has the unique task of calling attention to the eschatological future of salvation. In other words, the church shares the mission of Jesus by dedicating itself to God through the proclamation of the kingdom of God and by submitting its behaviour in both private and public to the lordship of Christ (389–90).

Wright's Christology can provide the Christocentric homiletic with language and resources that connect Jesus' life with God and describe God through what has been revealed in Jesus Christ. Wright's work draws attention to the fact that in Jesus Christ, God has ultimately been revealed; therefore, we should utilize what we have learned about Jesus historically to define God. This provides the Christocentric method with an opportunity to overcome the criticism of overemphasizing one person of the Trinity, even though they do not mean to do so doctrinally. Moreover, Wright's work poses a question to the Christocentric method: Now that you've gained a particular understanding of Jesus Christ and have communicated it to the congregation, what does this understanding tell you about God? Wright concludes that Jesus is the personification and embodiment of Israel's God, which provides a way of speaking about the identity of God in the light of his Christology. Where the Christocentric approach is comfortable with using God-language to speak about Jesus, Wright's Christology provides it with Jesus-language to speak about God. Langley (2018, 35–36) and Kuruvilla (2018, 31) remind us that the main character of the Scriptures is the triune God and that it tells us not only of his redemptive nature and works. Wright's work provides the Christocentric homiletic with a path from Christ-centered sermons to the triune God. Jeremias (2002, 1–17) rightly states that God became incarnate not in a text but in the flesh and blood of Jesus; therefore, Christ-centered sermons can be used to make a connection to who God is. Wright (1998a, 54) proposes that we think historically about Jesus, then, subsequently, we re-center our understanding of the word "God" around that as opposed to taking our understanding of the word "God" and imposing that on Jesus. For Wright, when we discover who Jesus was, we discover who God is (Dunn and Wright 2004, 15).

Furthermore, Wright's stance, which is summed up by this statement, "If you think you knew who God was, think again and look at Jesus" (Wright 2017e), can safeguard the Christocentric homiletic in two ways. First, it can guard the approach against practical Christo-monism that preaches Christ separate from the context of the Trinity, which the Christocentric approach can be susceptible to (Seo 2019). By incorporating Wright's challenge of seeking to define God from the life of Christ in its sermons, the Christocentric approach can align their conviction of the importance of the Trinity with their messages by making conclusions about God from the life of Jesus. Second, it can keep the reputation of the Father intact. Instead of being portrayed as a harsh Father who punishes the kind Son, Wright's work enables the Christocentric method to speak of God as the one who got his hands dirty in history. Wright (2008b, 29) emphasizes that one of the main points of the gospels is to reveal that through Jesus of Nazareth, God comes not as a tyrant but as the one who restores genuine humanness through his coming kingdom.

Pannenberg's Christology can also be particularly helpful to the Christocentric homiletic in finding ways to present a more balanced perspective of God. His work emphasizes the different types of unity that existed between Jesus and the Father throughout Jesus' life. Initially, he argued, there was a revelatory unity (*Offenbarungseinheit*) between Jesus and the Father, which was affirmed by Jesus' resurrection. This means that through Jesus, the God of Israel's self-revelation had become manifest. This, Pannenberg (1966, 127–29) argued, implies that Jesus belongs to the essence of God himself. Consequently, if God is revealed through Jesus, then God must only be defined by the Christ event, as Jesus belongs to his essence. Therefore, there was not only a revelatory unity but also an essential unity (*Wesenseinheit*) wherein the eternal being of God and the totality of Jesus' person were connected to form a unity of person (*Personeinheit*; p. 335). Like with Wright, Pannenberg's understanding of Jesus beckons the Christocentric homiletic not to consistently remove Jesus' personhood and works from that of God. Jesus is God's self-revelation in history; therefore, congregations must consistently be made aware that what we see Jesus doing is, in fact, what God is doing.

Furthermore, Pannenberg provides one more form of unity that can enable the Christocentric homiletic to present a more balanced view of God, namely, that Jesus was in functional unity with God's will (*funktional mit Gottes Willen*; p. 338–45). Pannenberg contended that Jesus' mission was to call people into the imminent kingdom of God, which shaped his activities and message, and that his mission was confirmed by God through the resurrection (346). This showed that all of Jesus' activity was a dedication to God and his will. In other words, Jesus' self-sacrificial dedication to the Father placed him in functional unity with the Father's will. This concept enables Christocentric homiletics to point to any of Jesus' speeches or deeds and make accurate conclusions about who God is.

Although the Christologies of Wright and Pannenberg do not venture into much detail regarding the relationship between Jesus and the Holy Spirit, they do emphasize the involvement of the entire Godhead in history through the life, death, and resurrection of Jesus of Nazareth. They provide the Christocentric homiletic with avenues to present a more balanced view of God by offering resources that link God to Jesus' life. By taking their work seriously, the Christocentric homiletic can find ways to speak about God more generally from the life of Jesus and can elaborate on the relationship between Jesus and the Father in greater depth. Even though Wright and Pannenberg's contributions will not provide the Christocentric method with a perfect trinitarian theology, it will provide resources to link God to Jesus' life and the means through which to explain the relationship between Jesus and the Father with greater clarity and depth.

6.2.6 Conclusion

In this section, the implications of Wright's and Pannenberg's Christologies on the shortcomings of the Christocentric homiletic were explored. It was noted that these shortcomings could be addressed by implementing the findings of Wright and Pannenberg. It is argued that these Christologies provide the Christocentric method with a more holistic approach to preaching sermons that will raise the congregation's affections toward Christ and address the congregation's spiritual needs in a descriptive and prescriptive manner. These two from below Christologies significantly contribute to the Christocentric method in terms of its application process. They challenge the Christocentric homiletics' application process by presenting Jesus in a way that demands private, public, and political commitment. Instead of merely using the sayings of Jesus to arrive at applications, Wright and Pannenberg's whole presentation of Jesus' career, death, and resurrection emphasizes the consequential private, public, and political implications for the church. They challenge the Christocentric homiletic to broaden its redemptive paradigm and propose a missional balance by integrating the theology of the cross and the theology of the kingdom, thereby restoring the homiletical value of the gospels to the Christocentric approach. Lastly, Wright and Pannenberg's work provides language that connects Jesus Christ with the Father so that God is not used to define Jesus, but rather the historical findings about Jesus are used to define who God is.

6.3 The Strengths of Christocentric Homiletics

6.3.1 Introduction

Although the Christocentric homiletic has certain hermeneutical and homiletical shortcomings, which stem from its significant connections to a Christology from above, it also has significant strengths. The Christocentric approach is one of the four most popular preaching methods in contemporary evangelical hermeneutics and homiletics (Gibson and Kim 2018, xii). This deduction proves true not only in academics but also in practical ministry. Various esteemed preachers, such as John Piper, James Montgomery Boice, Danny Akin, and Timothy Keller, have adopted this method. The assumption is that they have done so because this approach has certain homiletical strengths. This section will identify and describe certain main homiletical strengths of the approach. Subsequently, it will explore the implications of Wright and Pannenberg's from below Christologies in light of the strengths of Christocentric homiletics. As with the shortcomings, there are definite connections between the homiletical strengths of this approach and a Christology from above. Nevertheless, these two from below Christologies provide a new perspective that might enrich these strengths.

6.3.2 Preaching Christ from the Old Testament

Commenting on the importance of preaching the Old Testament, Kaiser (2003, 28) states, "To avoid it is to miss approximately three-fourths of what our Lord has to say to us today, whether we will hear it or not!" However, as Price (2018, 84) points out, the challenge for the preacher is to exposit the Old Testament, which is filled with ideas that are foreign to our contemporary Christian rituals, such as temple sacrifices, theocracy, and kingship, in ways that are meaningful today. The Christocentric approach helps bridge this gap between the story of ancient Israel and the New Testament church through their robust biblical theology and practical guidance regarding how to preach Christ from the Old Testament (Allen 2011, 112; Price 2018, 84).

Clowney (2003, loc. 432) provides two helpful tools by which to preach Christ from the Old Testament, namely, symbolism and typology. Clowney's methods carefully avoid moralism and allegory and emphasize that there can be no typology without symbolism. Additionally, his tools give interpreters and preachers the freedom to look for types of Christ in the Old Testament, even if New Testament writers did not identify them. Clowney wrote, "To conclude that we can never see a type where the New Testament does not identify it is to confess hermeneutical bankruptcy" (loc. 420–25). For the most part, the use of tools like typology must be safeguarded by certain conditions to avoid falling into allegory, as seen from Gentry's (2018, 96–97) approach. Therefore, Greidanus (2018, 109) has a particular appreciation for Clowney's boundaries regarding typology—namely, that there can only be typology if there is symbolism—but is more detailed in his approach.

Similarly, Greidanus provides seven ways of preaching Christ from the Old Testament. These are redemptive-historical progression, promise-fulfilment, typology, analogy, longitudinal themes, New Testament references, and contrast (Greidanus 2018, 108–10). Greidanus' toolkit is both carefully thought out and comprehensive.³ For this reason, even critics of the Christocentric method, such as Walter Kaiser, praise Greidanus' work (Greidanus 1999, cover page). His tools are carefully presented. For instance, Prince (2011, 107) shows that Greidanus is particularly concerned about disassociating the Christocentric method with an allegorical one. Instead of making the text say what the interpreter wants, through allegory, Greidanus (1999, loc. 2919–920) contends that "typology, by contrast, is limited to discovering specific analogies along the axis of God's acts in redemptive history as revealed in Scripture." His comprehensive tools leave a preacher with quiet confidence when approaching an Old Testament text. One of the valid criticisms against the Christocentric homiletic is the notion that sermons can become predictable and repetitive, leaving the congregation's spiritual needs unaddressed. However, Greidanus offers several tools a preacher can employ to keep her sermons creative and fresh.

Likewise, Chapell's (2018b, 9–16) approach prepares the preacher for different scenarios one might encounter when approaching the Old Testament. In this sense, Chapell's contribution acts as a kind of roadmap, which indicates which way to follow based on the scenario encountered in the text. He shows three different scenarios one might encounter as one comes to a text: where Christ or his work is explicitly mentioned, where Christ or his work is typified, and where there is no direct reference to Christ. His guidance on arriving at Christ when an Old Testament text does not explicitly reference Christ nor typify him is perhaps his most significant contribution to the preacher. In that case, he shows that certain passages predict Christ, others prepare the way for Christ, others reveal the consequences of his work, and others can be used to arrive at Christ through the process of reflection.⁴

This endeavor to connect the Old Testament and Jesus Christ is particularly compatible with Wright's Christology. Wright takes Jesus' Jewish context seriously and has gone to great lengths to maintain Jesus' Jewishness, providing invaluable connections between the Old Testament Scriptures and Jesus himself. Hays (2011, 67) shows that Wright's reading of

---

3. Charles Spurgeon is often quoted by Christocentric preachers as the example to imitate: "I have never yet found a text that has not got a road to Christ in it, and if I ever do find one that has not a road to Christ in it, I will make one; I will go over hedge and ditch but I would get at my Master, for the sermon cannot do any good unless there is a savor of Christ in it" (Stetzer 2013, 26). Greidanus, Clowney, and Chapell provide enough tools to preach Christ and stay on the road.

4. Poythress (2018, 47, 54) shows that using these tools to arrive at Christ from the Old Testament does not threaten the principle of *Sola Scriptura*, since within this principle there is freedom to employ various approaches and emphases in our endeavor to teach the whole counsel of God.

the gospels goes a long way toward solving the persistent problem of the relationship between the Old Testament and the New Testament. Although other post-Holocaust scholars have shied away from integrating the gospels with the Old Testament because of potential anti-Jewish readings of the gospels, Wright seeks to emphasize the Jewishness of Jesus in the gospels and its claim that Jesus fulfilled Old Testament Jewish expectations and hopes (Wright 2008b, 30–31). According to Hays (2009, loc. 1996–997) and Blomberg (2009, loc. 263–65), Wright's Christology presents a Jewish Jesus that did not reject or abolish Israel but sought to renew it; thereby, it stresses the continuation of Israel and Israel's redemptive history. Therefore, Wright's presentation of the Jewishness of the historical Jesus provides the Christocentric homiletic with the following specific links to preach Christ from the Old Testament.

First, according to Wright (1996a, 163–67), Jesus was fundamentally an itinerate oracular and leadership prophet, the last of the Old Testament prophets who modeled his career on John the Baptist as well as other Old Testament prophets such as Ezekiel, Jeremiah, Jonah, Amos, and, above all, Elijah. This notion allows the Christocentric homiletic to link these prophetic books to Jesus Christ in a way that shows how he fulfilled their prophecies and followed their example of warning Israel of the consequences of their current conduct and inviting them to a different way. Moreover, part of Wright's understanding of Jesus' prophetic role included Jesus' familiarity with the Old Testament and his ability to think theologically. This concept allows the Christocentric homiletic to think through how Jesus would have interpreted any Old Testament text in light of his proclamation and career.

Second, Wright (1998b, 110–11) emphasizes that Jesus was the Jewish Messiah. For Wright, Jesus' messiahship must be understood in terms of the Jewish texts, such as those found in the Psalms, Daniel, and Isaiah. By doing so, Wright connects the New Testament messianic references to Old Testament categories and allows this Jewish understanding of the Messiah to shape his Christology. Admittedly, this understanding will challenge the Christocentric method not to be too hasty to connect Jesus' messiahship with his divinity, as Chapell (2013, 123–41) does in his sermon on Jeremiah 33:14–16. The benefit of this Jewish interpretation of Jesus' messiahship to the Christocentric approach is that as the Messiah, Jesus was claiming to be both the embodiment and fulfillment of the story of Israel (Perrin 2011b, 130). Interpreting the messiahship of Jesus in Jewish categories will therefore allow the Christocentric homiletic to link the redemptive story of Israel to Jesus Christ more effectively.[5]

---

5. Wright (1998d, 122) contends that because Jesus was believed to be the

Third, Wright (1996b, 406) argues that the kingdom of God that Jesus proclaimed and inaugurated consisted of three threads, a return from exile, the return of YHWH to Zion, and the defeat of Israel's enemies. In other words, according to Wright's Christology, this is what Jesus believed was occurring in and through him, his work, and his imminent death. These three themes, prevalent throughout the Old Testament, can all be very clearly linked to Jesus as the fulfillment of the Old Testament. Moreover, the themes of exile and restoration are critical to Wright's presentation of Jesus and provide valuable connections for the Christocentric approach. Perrin (2011b, 132) writes, "Indeed, I might be so bold to say that in bringing exile to the forefront, Tom has supplied the great missing link of modern Jesus studies, even, perhaps the missing link of New Testament theology." By applying Wright's findings concerning the meaning of the kingdom of God, the Christocentric homiletic can use the concepts of Israel's exile, the return of YHWH to Zion, and the defeat of Israel's enemies to preach Christ from the Old Testament.

Fourth, Wright (2017a, 50) contends that all four Gospels are telling the story of Jesus, whereby he is the living embodiment of Israel's God. This is a conviction that Wright shares with the Christocentric approach. However, Wright argues further that the early church utilized the language and imagery of YHWH's involvement in the world as revealed in the Old Testament, namely, Shekinah or Glory, Spirit, Law, Word or Logos, and Wisdom and developed them concerning Jesus. These are very specific areas in which Jesus embodied Israel's God, which provides creative ways for the Christocentric method to speak of Jesus in this way.

6.3.3 Emphasizing the Whole Gospel

A significant strength of the Christocentric homiletic is its consistent presentation of the gospel message, which describes the redemptive works of God through Jesus Christ. Because Christ is central to the gospel message, this preaching method invariably presents the gospel in various ways (Poythress 2018, 55). Chou (2016, 116) points out that the Christocentric approach is also referred to as the gospel-centered approach.[6] Since texts are

---

Messiah, he was also believed to be the *Kyrios*—the world ruler as stated in Psalm 89 and Daniel 7—which provides another interesting opportunity to connect Jesus with the rulers and kings of the Old Testament.

6. Although the Christocentric approach does present the gospel regularly and even in creative ways, it does often limit the gospel to substitutionary atonement alone. Refer to the weaknesses (5.6.4) above.

placed within the grand narrative of Scripture, which reveals the redemptive actions of a gracious God, every text operates as a window into Christ and the gospel (Chapell 2018a, loc. 6699-6701).[7] By doing so, Prince (2011, 148) highlights that this allows every text to contribute to the richness of the gospel message.

Having the gospel message communicated regularly ensures that when unbelievers brave the doorway of the church, they will hear some aspect of the gospel. This is particularly relevant in countries that are still culturally Christian. Goldsworthy (2018, 126) writes, "We should rejoice in the common cause to honor the Bible as God's word, and in the desire to see Christ proclaimed in a way that will *make the offer of the Gospel to the whole world*" (italics mine). However, having the gospel message presented regularly also has significant benefits for believers. Prince (2018, 133) argues that when a believer "walks through the gospel door," it does not mean that they are no longer in need of grace or that this person should focus on merely keeping God's rules. Instead, the gospel message is critical to motivating obedience in the Christian life and, therefore, sanctification. Chapell (2005, 68-69) writes, "God's provision of saving, sustaining, and glorifying grace is the golden thread uniting all Christian Scripture and enabling all Christian faithfulness." Chapell (2018b, 23-28) reminds us that the reason why Christians continue to sin is not that we hate sin but because we love it. Therefore, by presenting the gospel message regularly, the love of sin in the human heart is replaced by a greater love, namely, a love for God. He writes, "So, if our love for sin is what gives it power in our lives, how do we displace love for sin? The plain answer is: with greater love. The gospel answer is: with a surpassing love for Christ (Eph 3:16-20; Col 1:18)" (28). This, Gibson and Kim (2018, 158) admit, gives us "an attractive solution for our sin problem." Therefore, neglecting Christ and the gospel in our preaching results in an unhealthy and insufficient diet for Christ's flock (Poythress 2018, 55).

Preaching Christ and the gospel regularly is one major area of difference between the Christocentric homiletics and the conservative, conventional expository preaching method precisely because the latter rejects a canonical *sensus plenior*. Kaiser (2003, 26) states that interpreting and preaching a text in light of the New Testament is "wrongheaded historically, logically, and biblically."[8] Therefore, an expository sermon on an Old Testament text

---

7. In fact, Chapell (2018a, loc. 6909-948) advocates that gospel lenses be used when we come to the Scriptures consisting of the question, "What does this text teach me about God and me?" In doing so, we will constantly be reminded of God's perfection and our need for grace, which makes the gospel message more appealing.

8. Prince (2011, 130-31) and Erickson (1993, 11) state that Walter Kaiser is considered to be gatekeeper of conservative orthodoxy in biblical interpretation and his works

that does not explicitly reveal or predict Christ will not mention Christ and, therefore, will not present the gospel. In response, Schreiner (2006, 26) writes, "If we only preach antecedent theology, we will not accurately divide the word of truth, nor will we bring the Lord's message to the people of our day." Moreover, Carson (1993, 23–28) and Prince (2011, 132) contend that preaching that expounds the Bible verse by verse without referencing Christ and his redemptive work displaces the gospel.[9]

Expository preaching is a helpful tradition, as shown by Poythress (2018, 54–55), but within the principle of *Sola Scriptura*, there is the freedom to choose many ways of teaching God's word. Rather than the be-all-end-all, expository preaching must be the foundation of a Christocentric approach. When this occurs, the gospel can be proclaimed in many creative ways. Prince (2011, 149) writes, "When exposition coaxes each passage to speak from the multiplicity of its contexts, human and divine, the hearers will see the gospel freshly in the diverse unfolding of the testimony of redemptive history." If this occurs, the same gospel can be preached from Judges and Romans, but from different perspectives (149).[10]

Nevertheless, one aspect of Christ's atoning work that the Christocentric homiletic tends to underemphasize compared to penal substitutionary atonement is the *Christus Victor* motif. In other words, the preaching method defaults to the blood-bought forgiveness aspect of Christ's atoning work but does not provide the same emphasis on Christ's triumph over the evil powers of the world. This is where the Christology of Wright can be of significant use to the Christocentric homiletic. Although some scholars, such as MacArthur (2020), have criticized Wright for not believing in penal substitutionary atonement, it is evident that he does. Wright (2006, 82–83) argues that the biblical penal substitution is that God punished sin through the representative flesh of the Messiah. On the cross, it is not only the wrath of God that was satisfied, but the love of God was satisfied (Wright 2007a). However, in his historical description of the meaning of Jesus' death, Wright's emphasis is placed on the *Christus Victor* aspect of Christ's atonement. Wright regards the *Christus Victor* motif as the overarching theory within

---

insist that Scripture can only have one meaning, namely, the human author intended meaning. He has been the most insistent and consistent advocate of this position.

9. Prince (2011, 132) and Moore (2010, 9–10) argue strongly that preaching that avoids Christ and the gospel is anti-Christian and resembles the preaching of the devil.

10. Chapell (2018a, loc. 6639–642) argues, "You do not explain what an acorn is—even if you say many true things about it (e.g., it is brown, has a cap, is found on the ground, is gathered by squirrels)—if you do not in some way relate it to an oak tree. In a similar sense, preachers cannot properly explain a seed (or portion) of biblical revelation, even if they say many true things about it, unless they relate it to the redeeming work of God that all Scripture ultimately purposes to disclose."

which the penal substitutionary atonement theory should be interpreted. Falconer (2017, 296) states that, for Wright, Jesus' victory over evil made the penal substitutionary element of Jesus' atoning death, by which our sins are forgiven, possible. Various passages in the New Testament support Wright's layout and presentation of this doctrine of atonement. Therefore, they can be a significant help to a Christocentric homiletic in articulating this aspect of Christ's atoning work.

Wright hypothesizes that, as the Messiah, Jesus was required to perform two crucial tasks, (1) cleanse, restore, and rebuild the temple, and (2) engage in the messianic battle and defeat the enemies of Israel (Wright 1996a, 604–6). Wright contends, through interpreting the Last Supper, Jesus' temple actions, and the teachings that surrounded these two events, that Jesus set out to accomplish these two tasks through his death. Wright argues that Jesus intended his sacrificial death to accomplish what the temple normally provided and ultimately to replace the temple. Moreover, he believes that Jesus drew on Isaiah 53 and, therefore, uniquely considered his death as part of the sacrificial system whereby the nation would be cleansed and purified. This event would usher in the new exodus, and this was how sins were to be forgiven.

Correspondingly, Wright (1996a, 605–7) contends that Jesus intended to fight the real enemy of Israel, not the Romans but the Accuser, Satan. Wright (2006, 87–88) believes that Jesus went into the heart of evil, took its total weight, and exhausted it. Moreover, this was the climax of Jesus' career, whereby he would decisively defeat evil through love (Wright 1996a, 610). For Jesus and the New Testament writers, his death is the victory over the bondage of evil that entangled Israel and the world, a victory that was confirmed through his resurrection (Wright 2019a, 9). In other words, Jesus' death was how the evil powers over this world were overthrown by the greater power, the revolutionary power of God's love. Through defeating evil, the new Passover took place, by which the creator had rescued humanity and the world from sin and death (Wright 2016, 348). Wright's robust presentation of the *Christus Victor* aspect of Christ's atoning work can provide the Christocentric method with a more holistic expression of the gospel. Implementing Wright's perspective on the atoning work of Christ will help to replace the love for sin with greater love, a love for God, by proclaiming the revolutionary power of God's love.

6.3.4 Avoiding Moralistic Sermons

According to the conservative expository preaching method, the preacher must expound on the text's historical, cultural, and literary contexts to ensure the authorial intent is understood. Subsequently, the principle of the author's message is drawn out and applied to the contemporary church. Kaiser (1981, 152) refers to this as "principalization," which, in his own words, is restating "the author's propositions, arguments, narrations, and illustrations in timeless truths with special focus on the application of those truths to the current needs of the Church and individual." This principalization excludes the use of the chronologically subsequent records, which means that the Old Testament must not be understood in the light of the New Testament. The issue with such expository preaching, or atomizing preaching as Horton (1996, 5) calls it, is that it ignores redemptive history and ultimately leads to moralistic preaching.[11]

Moralistic preaching's primary goal is ethics and behavioral change rather than transformation. Horton (2002, 123) argues, "The goal of so much preaching in both liberal and conservative churches is to make good people a bit better, instead of proclaiming from the biblical text the saving acts of God." Price (2011, 139) suggests that when the grand narrative of Scripture is ignored, the goal of preaching becomes personal ethics. Instead, the goal of preaching should be transformation. The Kaiser model, by itself, is insufficient as it informs people on how to behave rather than getting to the heart or emotions. It is the story of God's redemptive actions through Christ that is our hope for not only justification but also sanctification (139). Preaching that comes across as a commentary of the text, giving information only, results in head-knowledge rather than submission and obedience (Moore 2010, 12). Chapell (2018a, loc. 7143–145) proclaims, "Thus, instruction in biblical behavior barren of redemptive truth only wounds. Though it is offered as an antidote to sin, such preaching either promotes Pharisaism or prompts despair. Christ-centered preachers accept neither alternative."[12] In other words, expository preaching that seeks to find and apply the principle of a passage without any reference to subsequent events in the story tends to overlook the life, death, and resurrection of Jesus as the climax of the

---

11. The phenomena of moralistic preaching, with its various drawbacks, have become the constant diet of not only liberal churches but also many conservative churches (Price 2011, 133–34; Schreiner 2006, 21).

12. Goldsworthy (2000, 117–19) explains that the reason for this, which a preacher can either address or aid, is our human tendency to be legalistic, a tendency that lies at the heart of our sin.

Scriptures. In doing so, it does not consistently reference the gospel of God's grace and can lead to dry, lifeless moralism.

Chou (2016, 115) points out, "As opposed to morality, the Christocentric view desires to preach doctrine and theology, a theology of Christ and the gospel." By emphasizing Christ and the gospel in its sermons, the Christocentric homiletic tends to avoid moralistic sermons. It is correct to state that every sermon cannot be an evangelistic sermon and that the church needs the whole counsel of God to become more Christlike. However, as Goldsworthy (2018, 127) puts it, "Any application that is made apart from Christ tends to lead to legalism or moralism." This does not mean that there should not be any ethical and behavioral demands in preaching, but that they are grounded in the centrality of Christ's person and work. Poythress (2018, 48) contends, "There may be a spectrum of ways through which this centrality is wisely expressed and maintained." The main difference between moralistic preaching and preaching moral truths from the Bible is whether the meaning of the truth is contextualized by Jesus' person and work (Price 2011, 134).

Clowney (2003, loc. 425–32) suggests that if Old Testament truth is obtained through investigating the historical, cultural, and literary contexts, it cannot be applied in a straight line to the New Testament believer without showing how that truth is fulfilled in Christ; otherwise, such preaching will lead to moralism. Clowney (2007, 7–8) contends that because Jesus came and fulfilled the law, we, as Christians, can never look at the law in the same way.[13] Ultimately the Christocentric approach seeks to make more of the Scriptures rather than less. Chapell (2006b, 45) writes, "No Scripture is so limited in purpose as only to give us moral instruction or lifestyle correction."

Chapell (2018b, 4, 27) argues that a preacher can only call for certain moral behavior by relating it to the work of Jesus, without which the result will be legalism. A significant foundation from which Wright and Pannenberg's Christologies demand moral behavior is the resurrection of Christ. Therefore, these Christologies, with their major emphasis on the resurrection of Jesus, challenge the Christocentric homiletic to relate moral imperatives to the resurrection of Jesus specifically. For Wright, the

---

13. Price (2018, 91) provides a helpful description of the differences between the Christocentric homiletic of Sidney Greidanus and the Christiconic homiletic of Abraham Kuruvilla. He shows that where the Christocentric homiletic focuses on the divine side of the divine-human relationship, Christ as God's representative, Christocentric connections, and the character of God, the Christiconic homiletic places its emphasis on the human side of the divine-human relationship, Christ as humanity's representative, moral imperatives, and human response. Price (2018, 91–93) rightly proposes that these two approaches be joined in a preacher's arsenal, rather than divided.

challenge for Christians to live godly lives stems from the notion of the new creation launched through Jesus' resurrection. Wright (2008b, 31) contends that Jesus launched a new world order, a new reality within the space-time universe that he referred to as the kingdom of God through the resurrection. Consequently, the challenge for the church is to be the means through whom Jesus continues to establish the kingdom of God on earth as in heaven, which is done through being holistic witnesses of the kingdom of God and by holding the world to account (Wright 2011a, 220). The resurrection of Jesus forms the basis from which Christians, as new creations themselves, pursue Christlikeness.

Wright (1998e, 139) argues that the resurrection of Jesus is primarily about eschatology; it is about the dawning of the new creation, the renewal of the covenant, the end of the exile, and the forgiveness of sins which Jesus as the Messiah had accomplished not only for Israel but for the world. The resurrection is the sign of the launching of the new creation, which validated Jesus' messianic career and death; therefore, Jesus is the lord of the world and summons it to allegiance (Wright 2003, 660). Hence, the resurrection of Jesus cannot be separated from his kingdom of God-focused career and fate, a notion that prevents the church from falling into an escapist mindset (Wright 2011c, 198–99). Instead of "waiting on earth until we go to heaven to be with Jesus," the church is summoned to implement this new creation on earth. In other words, as Wright puts it, "Jesus is alive again; therefore, new creation has begun; therefore we have a job to do" (201). This entails living as witnesses of the kingdom of God holistically, namely, by praxis, symbol, and story and keeping the world to account. According to Greidanus (1999, loc. 2733–737), Scripture's meta-narrative can be divided into four major movements: creation, redemption in the Old Testament age, redemption through Christ, and new creation. By implementing Wright's understanding of new creation, the Christocentric homiletic can preach messages that relate imperatives with Christ's resurrection. This way, preaching is not moralistic in the sense that we should do things to become new creations—that would be moralism—rather, because we are new creations in and through Christ, we may live as true image-bearers. This would keep the imperatives in Greidanus' fourth major movement rather than trying to place them in movement three, which legalism does.

Similarly, Pannenberg's understanding of the resurrection reveals that the church should not seek to obey Jesus just because he is the risen Lord who demands allegiance or only because Jesus' resurrection is the start of new creation but also because Jesus secured our future resurrection, which should be transformative for the Christian. He argued that the hope of a future resurrection should not lead to the egoism of salvation for the individual (*Heilsegoismus des privaten Individuums*) but should lead to new life for all of humanity (*die ganze Menschheit*; Pannenberg 1974b, 180). Like Wright, he highlighted that Christian eschatology and the hope it provides should not lead to escapism (*Weltflucht*) from the real world but should empower our present lives (*gegenwärtigen Lebens*; Pannenberg 1995, 72). Both scholars, therefore, encourage the Christocentric homiletic not to preach moralistic sermons but imperatives in light of Christ's resurrection.

6.3.5 Strategies to Address Secular Culture

Modernity's disenchanted naturalistic worldview has significantly impacted Western culture and even the church (Mohler Jr 2016, 5–8).[14] Carter (2018, 129–30) argues that although evangelical hermeneutics have escaped total domination of higher criticism, it has not remained uninfluenced.[15] The entire Western university culture is dominated by an inherited Enlightenment naturalistic philosophy; therefore, anyone seeking education must do so in this context (Carter 2018, 130). So, as Carter points out, it is no surprise that biblical interpretation in many tertiary institutions has been limited to the confines of this naturalistic philosophy and its historical criticism (132). Mohler Jr (2016, 5) argues that the church must respond to this challenge of secularization through preaching. He points out that, historically, preaching has been the strategy of the church to challenge the opposition of culture from the time of Roman culture to the time of the Reformation (11–12).

In his book on preaching in a skeptical age, Keller (2015, loc. 123–305) addresses the question, "What is good preaching?" First, he argues that great preaching comes from love. By that, he means a love for the Scriptures and the listeners. A preacher must devote himself to handling the Scriptures accurately and find ways to speak to the hearts of people (loc. 196). Second, great preaching preaches Christ. Keller contends that 1 Corinthians 1:18–2:5 might be the most significant text on preaching in the Bible (loc. 196). In this text, Paul claimed to know nothing except Christ and him crucified. Keller points out that Paul only had the Old Testament at his disposal at the time of his writing, which indicates that in Paul's mind, Christ summed up the Old Testament (loc. 208). He writes, "For Paul, however, there is always

---

14. Mohler Jr (2016, 9) states that Western culture can be divided up into three intellectual periods, (1) the pre-Enlightenment period in which unbelief was considered impossible, (2) the post-Enlightenment period in which unbelief become possible, (3) the later modernity within which belief is considered impossible.

15. Clowney (1958, 19) named secularism as the greatest obstacle to the Christian mission.

one topic: Jesus. Wherever we go in the Bible, Jesus is the main subject" (loc. 208). Keller claims that this is the Christian preacher's power, not just to deliver informative sermons but to reveal and demonstrate the beauties of Christ.

Third, effective preaching in a skeptical age preaches to the cultural heart (Keller 2015, loc. 235). Considering the ideological and cultural changes that led to secularization, Keller again points to Paul as the model for addressing culture through preaching. He writes, "Paul uses the gospel to confront each culture with the idolatrous nature of its trusts and values" (loc. 247). To do so, Keller suggests two steps, the first being an exposition of culture's invisible beliefs. In doing so, the listener is helped to understand their culture and themselves.[16] Subsequently, the preacher should challenge culture's story and show that its longings are only fulfilled in Christ. This is what the Christocentric homiletic seeks to do, and, in that way, it provides a strategy for reaching a secular culture. Thus, the Christocentric homiletic provides a prophetic strategy that addresses secular culture and exposes its shortcomings. Chapell (2006b, 44) states that the reason why Christocentric preaching is so effective for an Enlightenment-impacted culture is that culture craves a story. He refers to this culture as a "story- and image-oriented culture" (Chapell 2006a, 23). However, Chapell warns that narrative preaching alone is insufficient to influence culture; instead, we need to be telling Christ's story, which is what redemptive-historical preaching seeks to do (40–41). Moreover, Chapell (2005, 67–68) shows that the Christocentric approach has received much attention recently because of this desire to address "the rise of cultural secularism."

Although the Christocentric method does well to address the secular culture prophetically, the Christologies of Wright and Pannenberg provide the impetus for the Christocentric homiletic to address specific key aspects of secular culture, namely, rationalism and its anthropology. First, the Christologies of Wright and Pannenberg supply historical tools with which the Christocentric homiletic may operate in apologetic spaces. Wright's (1996b, 410) presentation of Jesus as a young Jewish prophet proclaiming the story about YHWH returning to Zion as judge and redeemer and embodying that story through praxis and symbol provides an appealing option for the Christocentric method as an apologetic tool to address secular rationalism. It is intriguing because it appeals to the "story- and image-oriented culture" that Chapell (2006a, 23) refers to and relies on history to build its case. For Wright (1998a, 50), historical research is part of the church's

---

16. Mohler Jr (2016, 12) writes, "In a secular age, we can no longer rely on the luxury of having other cultural voices do the work of instilling our people with a Christian worldview."

God-given mandate and mission and has tremendous apologetic value in the Enlightenment-affected world. Moreover, Wright (2019a, 4) contends that history is real knowledge that follows the accepted methods of natural science. Therefore, Wright's work, which presents a historical story of how Jesus came to be worshipped by Jewish monotheists, can be a powerful tool for the Christocentric method to preach Christ-centered messages that appeal to a rationalist culture.

However, Pannenberg's work, in particular, has significant apologetic implications for the Christocentric homiletic. For Pannenberg (1966, 22), the task of Christology is not to repeat the Christological creeds of the church but to establish the Christian confessions about Jesus. In this sense, his work answers the Enlightenment challenge of not merely believing things without using one's independent mind. The apologetic nature of his work provides insightful language about Jesus with which one might engage a secular audience. Pannenberg found a way, by using historical inquiry, to confirm the deity of Christ without merely using statements of faith in the New Testament. Following his arguments and assertions, the Christocentric approach can rise against the Enlightenment challenge. Pannenberg affirmed the deity of Christ in two ways, namely, through an investigation of the resurrection and his description of Jesus as the revelatory presence of God. Pannenberg (1974, 143) provides an in-depth analysis of the empty tomb and the tradition of Jesus' appearances and concludes that the probability of the resurrection seemed the most convincing conclusion. From this conclusion, Pannenberg (1966, 129–31) argues further, by applying the implications of the resurrection retrospectively, that Jesus is the revelatory presence of God. By this, he means that God has revealed himself in the experience of reality; therefore, a correct knowledge of God can be obtained historically. Pannenberg was convinced that God could be known and spoken of because of his self-revelation through human history. Appealing to history is an effective way to engage with a rationalistic society regarding the validity of Jesus' claims.

Both Wright and Pannenberg used the shared reality of history to conclude that Jesus is, in fact, who he claimed to be. It follows that the Christocentric approach can quite simply incorporate certain arguments from Wright and Pannenberg's work as an apologetic strategy to address secular culture's rationalism. An example of this can be seen in Keller's (2016) sermon called *And if Christ Be Not Raised*. In this sermon, Keller, whom Clowney mentored, uses only two scholars to help him argue for the resurrection's historicity, namely, N.T. Wright and Wolfhart Pannenberg. He states that two scholars put the empty tomb, Jesus' appearances, and the successful start of Christianity together to present a very persuasive case for the resurrection, namely, Pannenberg and Wright. The Christocentric method can do this borrowing more frequently because of its significant compatibility between these two historical approaches. Both these Christologies from below provide language to speak about God and Jesus in a relatable, relevant, and apologetic way.

Second, the Christology of Pannenberg can provide the Christocentric method with resources and language to address secular, individualistic anthropology. One of the trademarks of cultural secularism is the attempt to remove God from worldview questions. An example of this is modern Enlightenment anthropology; the field that attempts to answer the questions of what it means to be human has moved beyond God. Modern anthropology places significantly more emphasis on the individual than on the community around the individual (Ward 2009, 169). In a sense, this has led to modern Western individualism (Branson and Roxburgh 2021, 119–20). On this front, one of the most valuable aspects of Pannenberg's Christology is that it provides a useful approach to combatting the exceptional anthropology of modern individualism from a Christocentric perspective.

Pannenberg argued from the life of Christ that the essence of humanity consists of openness to God and a desire for community. He contended that the essence of humanity, what it means to be fully human, consists of openness to God (Pannenberg 1966, 197). Pannenberg argued that the anthropology of his day, *Weltoffenheit* (cosmopolitanism), emphasized that humanity has an openness to the world and beyond (Pannenberg 1976b, 9–10). Pannenberg believed the openness to that which is beyond the world is the openness for God. Therefore, belief in God is not a strange idea to the structure of a human being (Kärkkäinen 2016, 117). This openness to God plays a significant role in Pannenberg's understanding of Jesus' vocation. Pannenberg showed that this essence of humanity was revealed through the message of Jesus. Jesus' proclamation of the immanent rule of God gave humanity an openness to God (Offenheit für Gott) and God's future by creating an expectation of a future transformed world and the resurrection from the dead (Pannenberg 1966, 234). Therefore, Jesus' office was to call people into the kingdom of God and to impart salvation to them, which consisted of an "openness for God." Additionally, Pannenberg suggested that another part of the essence of humanity is revealed through Jesus' call to love one's neighbor and thereby create community, namely, their desire to seek community (239–41). Pannenberg (1976b, 59) stated, "*Die Menschen suchen Gemeinschaft*" (People seek community). Pannenberg (1966, 240) believed that Jesus' call to love one's neighbor shows their need for community and empowered his hearers to do so. By incorporating the anthropological Christology of Pannenberg, the Christocentric homiletic intentionally advocates for communal Christian anthropology in a Christocentric manner.

Finally, Wright and Pannenberg's historical findings provide a safeguard against mythical statements about Jesus Christ that might alarm a disenchanted secular audience. When considering the Christocentric homiletic's past, it is evident that the approach is susceptible to allegorical or mythical statements about Christ if its guiding principles are not adequately applied (Chapell 2018b, 1–3). Even though Clowney, Greidanus, and Chapell all provide helpful guidelines around how to preach Christ from the Old Testament, there is the risk that their followers might misapply their approaches and end up with a presentation of Jesus Christ that is mythical.[17] For instance, because of the progressive nature of Scripture and its continuity, Clowney (2003, loc. 420–25) argued that finding types of Christ in the Old Testament must not be limited to those New Testament writers point out. Even though Clowney (2002, 100–107) does provide rules around typology, this opens the door for fictional interpretations of Scripture. Or, as another example, Chapell (2018b, 16) contends that reflection should be used to form sermons around Christ when Jesus is not explicitly mentioned. Again, Chapell provides some instruction, namely, that the process of reflection needs to ask what a text is telling us about God's gracious nature and our fallen nature (16). However, using reflection to speak about Christ when he is not mentioned in a text also opens the door for all sorts of creative and allegorical presentations of Christ. But, by applying the historical findings of Wright and Pannenberg about Jesus, the Christocentric method can ensure that it avoids mythical deductions about Jesus and, in that way, ensures that its prophetic, apologetic, and anthropological message is heard.

6.3.6 Conclusion

From this discussion, it is understandable why Christocentric preaching has become so popular in twenty-first-century homiletics, particularly in certain sections of the church. It not only provides a robust biblical theology but also provides practical ways in which to preach sermons that are faithful to God's redemptive story. Clowney, Greidanus, and Chapell provide different tools by which to preach Christ from the Old Testament that focus

---

17. Smith (2012, 164–66) suggests that potential pitfall of the Christocentric approach is that it might superimpose an unclear or ambiguous aspect of Christ upon another text. The gospels are not always straight forward to interpret, as can be seen in the discussion of N.T. Wright's Christology above. Therefore, if an incorrect assumption is made about Christ from the gospels, that can affect the way other texts are interpreted Christocentrically.

on the progressive and redemptive storyline of Scripture. Wright's Christology, which takes Jesus' Jewish context seriously, provides the Christocentric homiletics with further invaluable connections between the Old Testament Scriptures and Jesus. Furthermore, the Christocentric method must be praised for its commitment to preaching the gospel consistently due to its benefits to both unbelievers and believers. Wright's Christology, though, provides a robust presentation of the *Christus Victor* aspect of Christ's atonement and challenges the Christocentric method to a more holistic presentation of the gospel. Moreover, Wright and Pannenberg's Christologies view Christian imperatives in the light of Christ's resurrection, which provides an avenue for the Christocentric method to relate moral imperatives to Christ's person and work. Lastly, while the Christocentric approach is an effective method through which to address a secular culture prophetically, Wright's and especially Pannenberg's work provides resources through which to address secular culture's rationalism apologetically and through which to challenge modern individualistic anthropology.

6.4 Examples of Christocentric Sermons Using Christology from below

6.4.1 Introduction

Although the Christocentric method agrees that Christ is not found in every text in the Bible, it nonetheless proposes various tools through which a preacher can preach Christ even if he is not explicitly mentioned in a text. It is accustomed to many different paths to Christ, but what Wright's and Pannenberg's Christologies provide is a complementary yet distinct perspective on Christ. By taking these Christologies seriously, the Christocentric homiletic can add more arrows to its quiver. Drawing from these Christologies will equip the Christocentric method with more ways in which the preacher can address the spiritual needs of his congregation as they arise. This section will demonstrate what Christocentric sermons might look like if they incorporate the work of Wright and Pannenberg. It will use one sermon of each Clowney, Greidanus, and Chapell already presented in chapter 5 and will show how the sermons could be amended using Wright and Pannenberg's contributions.

6.4.2 An Adaptation of Clowney's Sermon on Joshua 5:13–15

Clowney (2003, loc. 1549–1636) starts his sermon called "Meet the Captain" by presenting the historical background of the narrative in Joshua 5:13–15. In keeping with his first hermeneutical step, Clowney tells of the journey of the Israelites through the Jordan, the twelve commemorative stones, Israel's renewed covenant with God through circumcision, and their celebration of Passover. Clowney proclaims that Israel was to be God's chosen instrument through which he would pass judgment on Jericho because of their wayward ways. Clowney then continues with the story and paints the picture of Joshua's encounter with the commander of the Lord's army, which enables him to move into his second hermeneutical step, namely, to interpret the text in the light of the entire revelation of God. Clowney reveals that the commander of the Lord's army is Christ, who came to Jericho to symbolize his future actions, namely, his great messianic battle against evil. In other words, the overthrown walls of Jericho are a picture of what Christ would do to evil. In his application process, Clowney calls for a posture of reverence towards Christ and an urge to respond to the trumpet of his gospel call.

In the presentation of the historical context of the text and the Christological reference to Christ and his eschatological battle against evil, Clowney treats various themes that Wright's findings could develop in helpful ways. Themes like the crossing of the Jordan, which simulates the crossing of the Red Sea, and the celebration of Passover commemorate the great Exodus whereby God delivered his people from the great tyrant in Egypt. Also, Clowney's idea of God using a person or people as an instrument of judgment on a wayward nation sets the stage for significant links to Wright's Jesus. These themes and Clowney's reference to Christ's battle with evil integrate seamlessly into Wright's understanding of Jesus' vocation. If the Christocentric homiletic took Wright's work seriously, it could be used at this junction to preach about Christ's vocation, which includes his victory over evil and the implications thereof for the church. Doing so can overcome the repetitive nature of Clowney's sermon and address its lack of application. A sermon incorporating Wright's Christology at this point could sound something like what follows.

The themes presented to us in this text resemble components that made up Jesus' self-understanding of his vocation. Yes, we can know something of Jesus' self-understanding of his vocation, not by psycho-analyzing him, but by observing his public career, by studying the first-century Jewish social-political context with all their aims, beliefs and expectations (which has become more readily available to us since the discovery of the dead sea scrolls at Qumran in 1947; Wessels 2006, 44), and by acknowledging that Jesus himself read the Old Testament theologically and applied it to his career and fate. When we do so, we see that the overarching story of first-century Judaism was one of exile and restoration. The Jewish people longed and hoped for the new Exodus (Wright 1996a, 576–77). The first aspect of Jesus' vocation referenced in this text is that he believed he was inaugurating God's kingdom. For Israel, this meant a return from exile, the forgiveness of sins, and the return of YHWH to Zion, which would lead to the defeat of Israel's enemies (Wright 1996b, 406). The best metaphor used by first-century Jews to describe this phenomenon was the new Exodus (Wright 1998f, 146). Jesus reaffirmed Israel's most basic hopes—namely, the return from exile, a return of YHWH to Zion, and the defeat of evil—but radically redefined them, claiming that these hopes were being realized through him.

Another aspect of Jesus' vocation, present in our text, is the idea that God uses a person or people as an instrument to judge. During the first century, there was a nationwide spread of revolutionary tendencies among various social classes of the people of Israel (Wright 1997, 372–73). This urge for revolution resulted from the agenda and influence of the Shammaite Pharisees who, out of zeal for the Torah, wanted to guard Israel against paganization and were, therefore, bent on a militant revolt to overthrow Roman rule (Wright 1996a, 384). This militant revolutionary agenda was also present in the one place where heaven and earth were supposed to meet, namely, the temple. But God sent Jesus as his instrument of judgment against this agenda. Jesus called for repentance, and when there was none, he pronounced judgment on an unrepentant Israel and predicted the destruction of the nation, Jerusalem, and the temple if they continued their current path of revolutionary zeal. His symbolic actions against the central symbol of Israel, the temple, were the climax of Jesus' prophetic career (415). Israel had become paganized; evil had infiltrated not only the pagan nations but even the nation of Israel, which is evidenced by the oppressive regime of the priestly order and the widespread violent revolutionary zeal (Wright 1996b, 406).

One other aspect of Jesus' vocation, which our text in Joshua foreshadows, is his messianic battle with evil. The Jewish Messiah had to partake in the messianic battle wherein he had to deliver Israel from her enemies (Wright 2018, 302–3). The Last Supper and the parables around that event reveal to us that Jesus envisaged a great messianic battle. Not with the pagan nations as Israel expected but with the real tyrant, Satan (Wright 1996a, 559–62). The Last Supper was a sort of Passover meal, celebrating the deliverance of Israel from the tyrant bondage of Egypt. But now Jesus intended the meal to symbolize the new Exodus he was about to accomplish through his impending death (556–57). Paradoxically, Jesus defeated evil by allowing it to do its worst to him, which launched the new Exodus, the kingdom of God in the world. Jesus went into the heart of evil, took its full weight, and exhausted it. He went into chaos to bring order, into death to bring new life; he defeated evil through love. The way of love would be the way of victory, the victory of God (610). For Jesus and the New Testament writers, his death was the victory over the bondage of evil that entangled Israel and the world, a victory that was confirmed through his resurrection (Wright 2019a, 9).

Just like Christ crushed the walls of Jericho, he crushed the head of the serpent. But, like Joshua and his companions, the church, too, must respond to the victory obtained by Christ. Joshua and the people of Israel had to conquer Jericho after Christ had demolished its impenetrable walls. Likewise, new creation has begun; therefore, the church has a job to do (Wright 2011c, 201). Because the victory of God through Jesus on the cross was the ultimate defeat of evil, we must not tolerate injustice, violence, or any other type of wickedness that still exists but should hold the world and its rulers accountable (Wright 1998c, 53).

6.4.3 An Adaptation of Greidanus' Sermon on Ecclesiastes 1:1–11

In his Christocentric sermon called "No Gain from All Our Toil," Greidanus (2010, 101–11) expertly lays out the historical and cultural foundation of the text. He shows that because of a change in economic circumstances related to increased trade between Africa, Europe, and Asia, many Israelites fell into the snare of pursuing materialistic wealth. In response, the teacher of Ecclesiastes' main point to address this vain pursuit is that life is brief and that without God, it is meaningless. It is meaningless because nothing on earth, not even wealth, can satisfy a human being apart from God. Greidanus provides three premises that support this central point: the repetitive cycles of nature, the unsatisfactory character of our senses, and the concept of history itself (96–98). These arguments all point to the same conclusion: without God, everything is a chasing after the wind, a brief repetition of unsatisfactory events. From this central point, Greidanus proceeds with his Christocentric shift. Using analogy, Greidanus points out that Jesus, like the teacher of Ecclesiastes, also proclaimed that life without God is meaningless. He shows that Jesus warned against the futility of earthly possessions and called his audience toward a life that is rich towards God (111).

This passage challenges modern anthropology that seeks to define humanity outside of God (Ward 2009, 169). Because the Christian understanding of anthropology is found in Christ, who is the ultimate revelation of what it means to be human, any passage in the Old or New Testament that refers to anthropology can be linked to Christ (Branson and Roxburgh 2021, 117). Wolfhart Pannenberg's anthropological, historical Christology can significantly contribute at this point. From a Christian perspective, humanity is limited in its ability to make a fair judgment about itself due to humanity's fallen state; therefore, we must look to God to define our anthropology, which he has done through the incarnation (118). For this reason, Greidanus makes his Christological connection to Christ's sayings about humanity's need for God. However, what Pannenberg could provide Greidanus at this point in the sermon are ways in which the whole life of Christ and not only his sayings define what it means to be human. A sermon that applies these insights might sound like what follows below.

Solomon was the writer of Ecclesiastes and was considered one of the wisest men who ever lived. Therefore, when he speaks to us about our humanity, we will do well to take heed. However, if ever there was someone who could ultimately define humanity and our needs, it is Jesus Christ. When we consider Jesus' career, death, and resurrection, we learn that in him, the essence of humanity has been revealed and humanity's destiny has been uncovered and fulfilled. First, Jesus revealed that the essence of man consists of openness to God (Pannenberg 1966, 234). Jesus' entire message was about the imminent kingdom of God; in other words that God's rule was closing in. This was meant to move humanity's gaze from themselves and place it on God and his future. The purpose of this message was to call forth something that is in every human being, namely, an openness to God. Secular anthropology affirms humanity's openness to this world and beyond it. There is a longing in the human heart for something transcendent, for something eternal, that forms part of our human essence. Although this does not refer to God directly, man's openness to the world and beyond implies man's openness to God (Pannenberg 1976b, 13). Olsen (1986, 212) writes, "This means that God is the essence of man as man's transcendent 'destination'. God is not a being alien to man, but the goal in which alone his striving can find rest and his destiny be fulfilled."

Second, beyond humanity's longing for God, Jesus revealed that another part of our essence is the need for human relationships, or more specifically, community (Pannenberg 1966, 239–41). Jesus revealed a close connection between loving God and loving people and that both are at the center of our humanity. Jesus' call to love our neighbors reveals our human need for community. Therefore, as the teacher of Ecclesiastes notes, human flourishing and fulfillment cannot be found in material possessions but in relationships, namely, our relationship with God and others.

Staying with the idea that nothing in this world can fully satisfy the human heart, Jesus revealed and fulfilled the ultimate destiny of humanity. Jesus' message of the imminence of the kingdom of God provides one of the most significant understandings of humanity ever discovered. It summoned humanity out of its securities and uncovered the insufficiencies of this world to fulfill human destiny. It pointed to the notion that the ultimate human destiny can never be obtained during our earthly existence but only in the future (Pannenberg 1966, 232–33). This message announced that the destiny of humanity is to be united with the infinite through the resurrection of the dead, something which is never fulfilled in this life (233). Nevertheless, this ultimate destiny to be raised from the dead has been fulfilled through Jesus Christ's resurrection (195–96). Because Christ rose from the dead, our destiny has been revealed. We, too, shall be raised from the dead and enter our destiny through which our ultimate satisfaction will be experienced.

The teacher of Ecclesiastes urges his audience not to pursue materialistic ideals, which is a meaningless endeavor, for the repetitive cycles of nature, our senses, and history itself testify that without God, everything is chasing after the wind. God has repeated and expanded this lesson for us through his Son. Through the life, death, and resurrection of Jesus Christ, we learn why pursuing materialistic aims is a chasing after the wind; namely, humanity has a capacity for God that nothing else can fill, and we need community. Loving God and loving people are not only commands Jesus gave us to obey, but they also reveal the very essence of what it means to be human (Matt 22:34–40). Therefore, if we want fulfilled lives, let us pursue these things. But know this, our ultimate fulfillment or destiny is beyond this world. Thus, "Set your minds on things that are above, not on things that are on earth" (Col 3:2).

6.4.4 An Adaptation of Chapell's Sermon on Jeremiah 33:14–16

In his sermon on Jeremiah 33:14–16 called "Tinsel for Twigs," Chapell (2013, 123–41) divides the text into three sections wherein he explains the text contextually and then links it to Jesus Christ. First, he highlights the idea that a branch will grow from the stump, indicating that God uses the insignificant and those who fail. From the time of David and Solomon, Chapell explains the historical context of Israel and Judah, including its sin and exile, up until the time of Jeremiah. In a Christocentric fashion, he argues that the branch to come is Jesus Christ, the Messiah and savior coming to a broken world to make all things new. He encourages the church that God can use its weaknesses for his glorious purposes. Second, by pointing to Israel's sins and failures and God's promise to use Israel for his purposes, Chapell contends that God lavishes us with unfailing love (132). Despite their shortcomings, God promised to give Israel one who would "execute justice and righteousness," namely, Christ (133). Third, Chapell indicates that God gives the unworthy his name and nature. He points out that the very name given indicates that God will give his people the righteousness that they could not provide for themselves and will give them his righteous nature through the Messiah (137).

The concept of *Sola Scriptura* allows for many ways to proclaim God's Word without overstepping any boundaries (Poythress 2018, 54–55). The advantage of this understanding is that the preacher can use this freedom to discern the congregation's spiritual needs. Rather than reverting to one function of preaching, which causes repetition, the sermon style can be decided upon through pastoral lenses. In this sermon, Chapell's two interpretive questions come to the fore, namely, what this text reveals about God and what it reveals about humanity's need for redemption. Chapell's emphasis on the fallen condition focus (FCF) throughout his sermons can make sermons sound repetitive. By incorporating the Christological contributions of Wright and Pannenberg, Chapell will have more tools to preach Christ with different sermon goals that can address congregational needs. A sermon drawing on Wright and Pannenberg to address this spiritual need might sound like the following.

Ancient Israel had two beliefs that formed the center of what it meant to be Jewish, namely, that there was only one true God, YHWH, and that he had chosen Israel to be his agents to bring forth his saving purposes in the world through the suffering and vindication of Israel (Wright 1991a, 46; 1998f, 148–49). Hence, the story told by Moses, the Psalms, and the Prophets point to how God would save the world through Israel and their Messiah (Wright 1998f, 148–49). At the time of Jeremiah, the Jews were still in exile, in a time of suffering brought about by their sin. But the Jews held on to the promise from God that he would cause life to sprout forth from barrenness, that he would vindicate his people and, through them, save the world. The expectation was that their vindication—their return from exile, the forgiveness of their sins, and the return of YHWH to Zion, which would lead to the defeat of Israel's enemies—would occur with the appearance of the Jewish Messiah (Wright 1996b, 406). Jesus came to fulfill these promises in and through his career and salvific death (Wright 1997, 365).

Through his life, death, and resurrection, this national expectation, which reached back as far as Jeremiah, was being fulfilled in a somewhat surprising fashion (Wright 1996a, 243). A catchphrase that sums up these expectations is the kingdom of God. The coming of the kingdom that Jesus envisaged was radically different from what his contemporaries imagined. The Jews expected a sudden violent revolution to overthrow the foreign Roman powers. On the contrary, Jesus announced that the kingdom of God would come like a seed that grows secretly. He came to reform Israel by establishing groups of followers who followed his praxis and vision of the way of being Israel and who would therefore be different from the others in their communities (276-77). This was how God's kingdom was to spread slowly. This was how the branch of hope would grow out of the dead stump Jeremiah speaks of, through the Messiah and his people.

But even the Messiah knew that for the kingdom of God to spread to the ends of the earth, he would need participants. Therefore, Jesus' kingdom announcement came as an invitation, welcome, challenge, and summons (Wright 1996a, 245). Jesus' message came with an invitation to repent of alternative agendas and to believe that God was acting climactically through him (262). Additionally, it offered strangers a welcome to be part of the renewed Israel (274). Jesus' welcome extended both to ordinary non-Pharisaic Jews and sinners, such as tax collectors and prostitutes (267). Jesus welcomed the unworthy to be used by God, as Jeremiah prophesied. His kingdom proclamation included a call and challenge to his audiences to live like the renewed Israel according to the new covenant (275). Moreover, with the invitation, welcome, and challenge, Jesus' kingdom story issued a summons to his hearers to be his helpers and associates (298). This way, the branch would spread to cover the world. This is how the Messiah continues to execute justice and righteousness.

What does this mean for us today? Jesus' kingdom pronouncement is made to us as well. The strategy through which God's redemptive branch spreads has not changed. Like in the first century, it comes with an invitation to repent and believe in the person and work of Jesus Christ. It comes with a welcome to all of us to join his kingdom movement regardless of our failures and shortcomings. It comes with the challenge to live the renewed kingdom people. This means that as the kingdom of God people, we submit our behavior, both private and public, to the lordship of Christ (Pannenberg 1966, 389-90). And finally, Jesus' kingdom story comes with a summons to join him on his mission. The summons for the church is to be the means through which Jesus continues to establish the kingdom of God on earth as in heaven (Wright 2011a, 220). The church is mandated to implement Jesus' kingdom agenda through preaching the gospel but also by living that gospel out in public (Wright 2011a, 225; 1998f, 152-53).

6.4.5 Conclusion

Incorporating the Christologies of Wright and Pannenberg into its homiletical method is beneficial to the Christocentric approach on various levels. It allows the Christocentric approach to remain faithful to its primary conviction, namely, to preach Christ in every sermon. Yet, it provides resources from which its sermon goals can be diversified, as observed in this section. In the adaptation of Clowney's sermon on Joshua 5:13–15, Wright's Christology enables the sermon to link the Old Testament with the New; it allows for a more detailed presentation of the *Christus Victor* element of Christ's atoning work and thereby presents another aspect of the gospel. In the adaptation of Greidanus' sermon on Ecclesiastes 1:1–11, Pannenberg's Christology provides Christocentric communal anthropology that counters modern individualistic anthropology. Finally, Chapell's sermon on Jeremiah 33:14–16 was adapted with the work of Wright and Pannenberg, which was utilized to connect Old Testament prophecy to Christ's career, death, and resurrection in such a way that a missional response seems appropriate. Like Clowney's adaptation, it links the Old Testament with the New, revealing the continuation of the meta-narrative and placing the listener in that story.

6.5 Concluding Remarks

This chapter commenced with an exploration of the implications of the strengths of Wright and Pannenberg's Christologies on the shortcomings of the Christocentric homiletic as identified in chapter 5. These shortcomings are that sermon goals are often duplicated, causing messages to sound repetitive, sermons often lack appropriate applications, soteriology is overemphasized—especially the substitutionary atonement theory—at the expense of other important doctrines such as sanctification or missiology, and Christ is emphasized at the expense of the Father and the Holy Spirit. Through this exploration, the following implications were identified and described: (1) the Christologies of Wright and Pannenberg provide the Christocentric method with a more holistic approach to form creative sermons with diverse sermon goals that are based on the spiritual needs of the congregation, without diverting from their main aim of preaching Christ. With their different Christological perspectives, they provide resources that might be drawn upon to address various congregational situations and provide the material to engage more in biographical sermons. (2) Wright and Pannenberg's presentation of Jesus calls for radical commitment to Jesus Christ and his kingdom in our private, public, and political lives. This is a significant challenge to the Christocentric method's application process. (3) It provides the link between cross and kingdom theology, enabling the Christocentric method to broaden its redemptive paradigm. This allows for sermons that deal with other important doctrines and human realities whilst remaining connected to Jesus' salvific work on the cross, especially missiology. (4) These Christologies closely associate Jesus with Israel's God and conclude that we do not use God to define Jesus but the other way around. This provides the Christocentric homiletic with avenues to present a more balanced view of God in their preaching.

It was noted that Wright and Pannenberg's Christologies not only have implications for the Christocentric approach's shortcomings but also for certain strengths. This chapter identified and described various strengths of the Christocentric method that can be enriched by the different perspectives that Wright and Pannenberg's Christologies provide. (1) It was noted that the Christocentric method is not only based on a robust biblical theology but also provides various practical paths to preach Christ from the Old Testament in several scenarios. Wright's Christology can add further invaluable connections between the Old Testament and Christ due to its extremely Jewish undertone. These include Jesus' office as an oracular and leadership prophet, his Jewish messiahship, his vocation of inaugurating the kingdom of God, and referring to Jesus as the embodiment of Israel's God. (2) The Christocentric homiletic rightfully emphasizes the importance of presenting the gospel regularly due to its benefits to both unbelievers and believers. Wright's detailed presentation of the *Christus Victor* aspect of Christ's atoning work challenges the Christocentric method to a more holistic presentation of the gospel and provides ample resources to do so. (3) The Christocentric method intentionally avoids moralistic sermons that either cause self-righteous pride or hopeless despair. To do so, it links all moral imperatives to Christ, which raises the affections of Christians toward God and results in lasting transformation. Wright and Pannenberg's Christologies, which place the resurrection of Jesus in a place of prominence, challenge the Christocentric method to preach imperatives in the light of Christ's resurrection specifically. (4) The Christocentric approach is an effective method through which to address a secular culture prophetically. Still, it can draw on the resources from Wright and especially Pannenberg's work to respond to secular culture's rationalism apologetically and its individualistic anthropology in a Christocentric fashion.

Finally, this chapter presented examples of what some of these implications could look like through adaptations of Clowney's, Greidanus', and Chapell's sermons. In the adaptation of Clowney's sermon on Joshua 5:13–15, Wright's Christology presents creative ways to link the Old Testament with the New and provides a detailed presentation of another aspect of the gospel, namely, the *Christus Victor* element of Christ's atoning work. In the adaptation of Greidanus' sermon on Ecclesiastes 1:1–11, Pannenberg's Christology provides Christocentric communal anthropology, which the Christocentric method can utilize to counter modern individualistic anthropology. Lastly, Chapell's sermon on Jeremiah 33:14–16 was adapted to address an assumed spiritual need in a congregation, namely, a need for encouragement in mission.

7

Conclusion

7.1 Review of Research

7.1.1 Objectives

THE MAIN OBJECTIVE OF this thesis was to answer the main research question, what are the implications of a critical analysis on the from below Christologies of Wright and Pannenberg for a Christocentric homiletic?

This problem required answering sub-ordinate questions, which resulted in five outcomes: (1) It investigated how N. T. Wright developed his historical Jewish-embedded Christology in light of the "Third Quest" for the historical Jesus. (2) It examined how Wolfhart Pannenberg developed his universal anthropological Christology in light of the "No Quest" and "New Quest" for the historical Jesus. (3) It critically analyzed the Christology of N. T. Wright and Wolfhart Pannenberg. (4) It identified and explored the embedded Christology of the North American modern development in Christocentric homiletics. (5) It identified and assessed the implications of the strengths of N. T. Wright and Wolfhart Pannenberg's Christologies on the Christocentric homiletic.

7.1.2 Design and Methodology

The nature of this research was a development from a literary type of theological research to a conceptual construction. The nature of the data involved was literary and without an empirical component. The design of this paper consisted of five literary tasks, which relate to the key questions. These tasks were as follows: (1) the first task examined the Christology of N.T. Wright, through a literary exploration of his Christological works, sermons, and the works of scholars who have engaged with him. (2) Similar to the first task, the second task investigated the Christology of Wolfhart Pannenberg through a literary investigation of his Christological works and the works of scholars who have engaged with him. Based on this literature review, the overarching tenets of their Christologies were considered and analyzed as well as the influences of other scholars upon them, their presuppositions, and Christological developments. (3) The third task was a critical analysis of the two Christologies wherein their strengths and weaknesses were identified, described, and assessed by placing them in conversation with secondary sources and by engaging with Scripture. The strengths of the two Christologies were applied to the Christocentric homiletic in task 5. Whilst literary, this task was predominantly conceptual, using conceptual analysis.

(4) This task engaged the literary works of current scholarship on the North American modern development in Christocentric homiletics. It examined the literary works and sermons of three of the most prominent representatives of the approach, Sidney Greidanus and Edmund Clowney, as well as a contemporary representative Bryan Chapell. This literature review identified and described their theological reasoning and practical guidance. A literature review was performed on the literary works of theologians who are opponents of the Christocentric homiletical approach, and its shortcomings were identified. Based on the literature review findings, this step performed a summary and analysis of the embedded Christology of the Christocentric homiletic. (5) The fifth task highlighted the implications of the from below Christologies of Wright and Pannenberg on a Christocentric homiletic through conceptual analysis. It applied the strengths of these Christologies to the Christocentric homiletic's shortcomings and relevant identified strengths. Here the implications for the shortcomings and strengths were assessed. On a practical level, this step demonstrated the implications for the Christocentric homiletic by providing sermon examples.

7.2 Summary of Research Findings

7.2.1 N.T. Wright's Christology

The Christology of Wright was examined through an investigation of his works and sermons on Christology. From this examination, it became evident that the most important influences on Wright's commitment to the historical inquiry process were Albert Schweitzer and Ben Meyer. Schweitzer imparted to Wright the conviction that the historical study of Jesus of Nazareth must place him firmly within an eschatological Jewishness, and Meyer taught him a unique way of approaching the study of the historical Jesus by placing the focus on the Jewish worldview of the first century, Jesus' mindset within that worldview, and, ultimately, Jesus' aims and beliefs. It became apparent that Wright belongs to the Third Quest for the historical Jesus and that he developed his Christology within the structure of the six key questions of the Third Quest, namely, how does Jesus fit into first-century Judaism? What were his aims? Why did he die? How did the church come into being? Why are the gospels what they are? And how does the historical Jesus relate to the contemporary church and world? Wright addresses these key questions through his hypothesis that Jesus was a Jewish eschatological prophet who believed that the climax of Israel's history, her return from exile, the return of YHWH to Zion, and the defeat of her enemies, was occurring in and through him, his work, and his imminent death on the cross.

First, Wright considered Jesus' mindset within the first-century Jewish worldview and concluded that Jesus saw himself as an "Oracular" and "Leadership" prophet through whose praxis, words, and symbolic acts the history of the Jewish nation was being brought to its climax. Jesus reaffirmed Israel's fundamental hopes—namely, the return from exile, a return of YHWH to Zion, and the defeat of evil—but radically redefined them, claiming that these hopes were being realized through him. Second, Wright discussed Jesus' aims and beliefs through an investigation of three significant events and their surrounding riddles, namely, Jesus' temple actions, the Last Supper, and his journey to Jerusalem. From these events, Wright concluded that Jesus considered himself the Jewish Messiah, the leader and focal point of Israel's return from exile. Jesus believed that through his death, the eschatological kingdom of YHWH would be ushered in and that his vocation was to do and be what only Israel's God did and was. Third, Wright examined the rise of early Christianity by seeking to understand how Jewish monotheists could ever worship Jesus as God. Wright established that this was due to one highly probable historical event, namely, the resurrection of Jesus. Wright concluded that, although early Jewish Christology believed that Jesus was somehow divine, they did so within the Jewish framework of monotheism.

7.2.2 Wolfhart Pannenberg's Christology

From examining Pannenberg's Christological works, it became clear that he believed that the task of Christology is to describe who Jesus was based on historical facts rather than merely repeating the Christological creeds. It was noted that Pannenberg made his Christological contribution during the "No Quest" and "New Quest" periods, which means that he was confronted with the dialogue of whether to start one's Christology with the preaching of the early church or with Jesus himself. Pannenberg utilized the "No Quest's" idea that there was continuity between the life and message of Jesus and the kerygma of the early church and the "New Quest's" notion that the early church's preaching needed to be demythologized. It was discovered that by doing this, Pannenberg reconstructed a portrait of Jesus by going behind the New Testament writers to get to the historical Jesus. Additionally, he ensured that our need for salvation did not dictate his historical conclusions about Jesus of Nazareth, even though Christology and soteriology are inseparable. From the literary investigation of his Christological works it became evident that he structured his Christology in the following sequence: (1) he dealt with the relationship of Jesus to God, (2) the fulfillment of human destiny through Jesus, (3) the relationship of his divinity to his humanity.

First, Pannenberg addressed the issue of Jesus' relation to Israel's God and argued that through the resurrection, God validated the pre-Easter claims of authority of Jesus. It became clear that, for Pannenberg, Jesus' relation to Israel's God must be viewed through the lenses of the resurrection. Fundamentally, the resurrection formed the basis for any faith in the deity of Christ. Pannenberg retrospectively applied the consequences of the resurrection and concluded that because God validated Jesus' claims to authority, Jesus' relation to God must be expressed as God's self-revelation. This insight led Pannenberg to refer to Jesus as part of God's essence; therefore, the only appropriate way to speak about God's presence in Jesus is as revelatory presence. Second, Pannenberg investigated the humanity of Jesus by considering Jesus' office and fate. It was noted that Pannenberg did not have high regard for the "*munus triplex*" understanding of Jesus' office because he believed it assigned the offices of king, prophet, and priest to Jesus based on his divinity rather than his humanity. Rather, he preferred to speak of Jesus' office as a vocation, according to which he was to call people to the kingdom, which gave them an openness to God and the future resurrection.

From this vocation, Pannenberg suggested that Jesus' proclamatory career and fate revealed the essence of humanity, namely, an openness to God and community, and fulfilled humanity's ultimate destiny, namely, to be raised from the dead. Third, Pannenberg examined the relationship between Jesus' divinity and humanity. It became clear that Pannenberg was adamant to show that any Christology that commences with the divinity of Jesus Christ, or the incarnation, inevitably ends up in a problematic position where it needs to explain how the two natures of Christ could co-exist in perfect unity whilst maintaining the integrity of his humanity. Pannenberg emphasized that Jesus' unity with God cannot be established by dissecting the incarnation. He believed that he bypassed this problem by speaking about Jesus' relation to the Father rather than speculating about the two natures of Jesus Christ. Therefore, for Pannenberg, the unity of Jesus with God must not be approached from the angle of the relation between the Logos and the person of Jesus from Nazareth. Instead, it should be approached from the relatedness of Jesus with the Father. He contended that through Jesus' self-sacrificial dedication to the Father, Jesus was shown to be the Son of God.

7.2.3 A Critical Analysis of Wright and Pannenberg's Christologies

The critical analysis of Wright and Pannenberg's Christologies placed their work in conversation with various secondary sources and Scripture. Through this critical analysis, it became evident that various strengths can be deduced from their Christologies, but also certain weaknesses. The strengths and weaknesses were identified, defined, and assessed. On the positive side, Wright's Christology stems from various commendable historical methods wherein he locates Jesus right in the heart of the first-century Jewish context. Consequently, his Christology provides helpful links between the Old Testament and Jesus as the fulfillment thereof. Additionally, he provides significant homiletical value to the gospels through his robust presentation of what the gospels are fundamentally about, namely, the telling of the story of the kingdom of God coming to earth through the public ministry, death, and resurrection of Jesus of Nazareth. It became evident that a significant strength of Wright's Christology is the notion that being a follower of Jesus has practical and political implications, namely, the church is called to bear witness in word and deed, to hold this world, its rulers, and the church to account, and to love one another by laying down our rights for each other. Finally, Wright's work challenges the church to define God through Jesus Christ and not the other way around. In that, he provides a new perspective on speaking about God. Conversely, it was noted that Wright's Christology also has certain shortcomings; namely, it wilfully brackets out some Christian theological traditions, it omits the gospel of John from his presentation of Jesus, and Wright's hypothesis, namely, that Jesus proclaimed and enacted the kingdom of God, the return from exile, and the return of YHWH to Zion, has a noteworthy influence on how he interprets the gospels' stories, and his apocalyptic eschatology is questionable, especially his interpretation of the historical events of 70AD.

The critical analysis revealed various strengths in Pannenberg's Christology; namely, its anthropological emphasis makes distinct contributions to the field. Pannenberg's anthropological universal Christology makes insightful connections between Christology and anthropology. He showed that Jesus had revealed the essence of humanity, namely, an openness for God, and fulfilled our destiny to be raised from the dead. Like Wright, it is evident that Pannenberg's Christology concludes with practical implications for the followers of Jesus, namely, that the church's vocation is to live as a sign and foretaste of the future kingdom of God. For Pannenberg, this means that Christians should conduct themselves in a certain way, which has implications for human relationships, ecumenical discussions, inter-religious conversations, and the stewardship of creation. Another significant strength observed in Pannenberg's Christology is its pervasive apologetic nature. It provides historically grounded apologetic language that addresses Enlightenment-impacted culture whilst simultaneously challenging the Christological statements and ideas of the contemporary church that are solely based on experience. Finally, Pannenberg's work provides a fresh way of speaking about the grounds of Jesus' divinity, namely, in relation to the Father.

Certain weaknesses also became evident in Pannenberg's Christology, most notably, his underestimation of the cross, according to which Jesus' execution was merely an event that happened as a result of his career, his skeptical treatment of the Scriptures whereby certain significant events were considered mythical, Pannenberg's reluctance to place Jesus within Jewish categories, his major critiques of Chalcedon.

7.2.4 *The Embedded Christology of the Christocentric Homiletic*

It was noted that the modern development of the Christocentric approach had become a significant model in contemporary evangelical hermeneutics and homiletics. Clowney, Greidanus, and Chapell's works have been

Conclusion

instrumental in providing the foundation of this rejuvenated approach. Through the literature review of the theological works and sermons of the pioneers of the approach—Edmund Clowney and Sidney Greidanus—and their contemporary representative in Bryan Chapell, it became apparent that the Christocentric homiletic stems from a robust biblical theology. Moreover, it was noted that this biblical theology has certain presuppositions, namely, that the Bible is one book that reveals God's revelation as a single continuous and progressive theme that reaches its climax in Jesus Christ. The Scriptures are continual, progressive, and Christocentric. For these scholars, the implication of their biblical theology necessitates a Christocentric preaching method. Additionally, it became evident that all three scholars provide thorough practical guidance regarding how to form Christocentric sermons from anywhere in the Bible.

Clowney's homiletical approach revealed two tools through which to preach Christ from the Old Testament where Christ is not explicitly mentioned, namely, symbolism and typology. Similarly, it became evident that Greidanus' most significant contribution to the Christocentric homiletic is his carefully thought-out seven ways of preaching Christ from the Old Testament, namely, the way of redemptive-historical progression, the way of promise-fulfillment, typology, analogy, the longitudinal themes, New Testament references, and the way of contrast. Like his predecessors, it was noted that Chapell's homiletical method provides roadmaps to preach redemptive-historical sermons for all three scenarios one might encounter in a passage, namely, where Christ or his work is explicitly mentioned, where Christ or his work is typified, and where there is no direct reference to Christ. It became apparent that these practical steps to preach Christ from anywhere in the Bible were well received in the field of hermeneutics and homiletics.

Engaging with secondary sources and Scripture made it clear that there are certain shortcomings to the Christocentric approach, some of which can be traced to its sole emphasis on the Christology from above. These shortcomings, namely, that sermon goals are often duplicated, causing messages to sound repetitive, sermons often lack appropriate applications, soteriology is overemphasized—especially the substitutionary atonement theory—at the expense of other important doctrines, and Christ is emphasized at the expense of the Father and the Holy Spirit, were placed in conversation with the strengths of Wright and Pannenberg's Christologies in chapter 6.

Subsequently, this chapter identified, described, and assessed the embedded Christology of the Christocentric approach. It was noted that although these scholars do not explicitly mention their preferred method of Christology, one can safely deduce that the Christocentric homiletic has strong connections with the Christology from above approach for understanding and explaining Jesus Christ. This conclusion was based on their posture of faith in the validity of the Scriptures, the total acceptance and advocacy of the faith claims of the New Testament writers, their preference to refer to Jesus Christ in cosmic ways rather than Jewish categories, their acknowledgment of Jesus' self-knowledge of his divinity, and their focus on Jesus from an ontological perspective rather than a functional perspective.

7.2.5 Implications for a Christocentric Homiletic

Through an exploration of the implications of the strengths of Wright and Pannenberg's Christologies on the shortcomings of the Christocentric homiletic, I concluded that these Christologies: (1) Provide the Christocentric method with a holistic approach to forming creative sermons with diverse sermon goals that are based on the spiritual needs of the congregation. These contributions can be made in sermon content—descriptive and prescriptive—and form, such as biographical sermons. (2) They challenge the Christocentric homiletics' application process by presenting Jesus in a way that demands private, public, and political commitment. The Jesus presented by these two Christologies confronts the unintended consequence of Christocentric preaching, namely, that because Jesus accomplished everything for us and we cannot obey because of our fallen condition, we should not even bother trying. Instead of being content with the spiritual privatization of faith, these two Christologies demand being a practical follower of Jesus.

(3) Wright and Pannenberg's Christologies can broaden the redemptive paradigm of the Christocentric method by linking the theology of the cross and kingdom theology. This maximizes the homiletical value of the gospels and offers a balanced framework for missions that focus on both evangelism and social issues. It was noted that the new movement of the Christocentric homiletic was birthed in the cultural and historical context of the "Great Reversal" and, therefore, these two Christologies can provide the Christocentric method with a more balanced structure for missions. Consequently, from such a balanced missiological framework, the Christocentric homiletic can ground their sermons in the reality of human experiences such as poverty and suffering. (4) They provide the Christocentric homiletic with avenues to present a more balanced view of God by offering resources that link God to Jesus' life and provide means through which to explain the relationship of Jesus with the Father better, which safeguards the Father's reputation. It was noted that by applying these two Christologies,

the Christocentric method could be enriched and challenged without diverting from its primary aim of preaching Christ.

It became apparent that these two from below Christologies, if taken seriously, have implications for certain strengths of the Christocentric method: (1) The Christocentric method has an impressive ability to preach Christ from the Old Testament by providing various paths to Christ. However, these two historically based Christologies, with their deeply Jewish undertones, especially that of Wright's, provide various specific links to the Old Testament that provide a fresh strategy to preach Christ from the Old Testament. (2) The Christocentric homiletic has a noble ambition to consistently preach the gospel due to its benefits to both unbelievers and believers. But, due to its focus on substitutionary atonement in its presentation of the gospel, Wright's robust presentation of the *Christus Victor* aspect of Christ's atoning work can provide the Christocentric method with a more holistic presentation of the gospel.

(3) The Christocentric method has an unwavering commitment to avoiding moralistic sermons that leads to self-righteousness or despair by relating all imperatives to Christ. Wright and Pannenberg's strong emphasis on the resurrection of Jesus Christ as the start of the Christian movement challenges the Christocentric method to consider the connection between moral imperatives and Christ's work in light of the resurrection. (4) The Christocentric approach effectively addresses secular culture prophetically by addressing culture and exposing its lies. Wright and especially Pannenberg's work provides the apologetic and anthropological resources to address two key aspects of secular culture, namely, rationalism and modern individualistic anthropology. By applying the findings of these two Christologies, the Christocentric method can address secular culture not only prophetically but can speak to secular culture's rationalism apologetically and challenge its modern individualistic anthropology.

7.3 Contribution of This Research

This thesis has contributed to the field of Christology by engaging with and placing Wright and Pannenberg's Christologies in conversation. It did this by identifying the strengths and weaknesses of both approaches. These strengths provide a helpful structure that promotes the use of their from below Christologies in the church. Too often, the Christology from above method has been heavily favored by the neglect of the from below approach. However, the strengths of the Christology of Wright and Pannenberg provide a way to speak about the humanity of Jesus without denying his deity.

Identifying and articulating the embedded Christology of the Christocentric homiletic is another significant contribution of this thesis. Although the favored Christology behind a preaching model may be implicit, this thesis identified and described several strong connections between the Christocentric homiletic and the Christology from above approach. These characteristics ultimately offer any preaching model the criteria for assessing whether one Christological approach is overemphasized compared to another.

Connecting the implications of Christology on homiletics is another contribution that this thesis provides. More specifically, the implications of Wright and Pannenberg's from below Christologies on the Christocentric method. This unique perspective might contribute to the current dialogue on Christocentric preaching by pointing to Christology to solve important issues. This thesis makes a significant contribution to what it means to preach Christ today.

7.4 Recommended Topics for Further Theological Research

(1) Implications of N.T. Wright's Christology on modern missions.

(2) A Comparative study of how Paul informs N.T. Wright and Wolfhart Pannenberg's eschatology.

(3) Implications of N.T. Wright and Wolfhart Pannenberg's Christologies on the Christiconic Homiletic.

Bibliography

Allen, Jason K. "The Christ-centered Homiletics of Edmund Clowney and Sidney Greidanus in Contrast with the Human Author-centered Hermeneutic of Walter Kaiser." PhD diss., Southern Baptist Theological Seminary, 2011.
———. "Eight Tips for Beginning Preachers." https://jasonkallen.com/2016/05/eight-tips-for-beginning-preachers/, 2016.
Allison, Dale C., Jr. *Constructing Jesus: Memory and Imagination*. Grand Rapids: Baker Academic, 2009b.
———. *The Historical Christ and the Theological Jesus*. Grand Rapids: Eerdmans, 2009a.
———. "Jesus & the Victory of Apocalyptic." In *Jesus and the Restoration of Israel: A Critical Assessment of N.T. Wright's Jesus and the Victory of God*, edited by Carey C. Newman, Chapter 7. Downers Grove, IL: InterVarsity. Kindle edition, 2009c.
Althaus, Paul. *Der Christliche Wahrheit*. 6th ed. Gütersloh: Bertelsmann, 1962.
———. *Die Wahrheit des kirchlichen Osterglaubens: Einspruch gegen Emanuel Hirsch*. Gütersloh: Bertelsmann, 1940.
Baker, W. R. "The Chalcedon Definition, Pauline Christology, and the Postmodern Challenge of "from below" Christology." *Stone-Campbell Journal* 9 (2006) 77–97.
Barth, Karl. *The Doctrine of the Word of God*. Vol. 1.1 of *Church Dogmatics*. Translated by G. T. Thomson. Edinburgh: T. & T. Clark, 1936a.
———. *The Doctrine of the Word of God*. Vol. 1.2 of *Church Dogmatics*, edited by G. W. Bromiley and T. F. Torrance. Translated by G. T. Thomson and Harold Knight. Edinburgh: T. & T. Clark, 1936b.
———. *The Doctrine of God*. Vol. 2.2 of *Church Dogmatics*, edited by G. W. Bromiley and T. F. Torrance. Translated by GW Bromiley and J. C. Campbell. Edinburgh: T. & T. Clark, 1936c.
———. *The Doctrine of Reconciliation*. Vol. 4.1 of *Church Dogmatics*, edited by G. W. Bromiley and T. F. Torrance. Translated by G. W. Bromiley. London: T. & T. Clark, 2009a.
———. *The Doctrine of Reconciliation*. Vol. 4.2 of *Church Dogmatics*, edited by G. W. Bromiley and T. F. Torrance. Translated by G. W. Bromiley. London: T. & T. Clark, 2009b.
Bauckham, Richard J. *Jesus and the God of Israel: God Crucified and Other Studies on the New Testament's Christology of Divine Identity*. Rev. ed. Milton Keynes, UK: Paternoster, 2008.

———. "Jesus' Demonstration in the Temple." In *Law and Religion: Essays on the Place of the Law in Israel and Early Christianity*, edited by Barnabas Lindars, 72–89. Cambridge: James Clarke, 1988.

———. "Paul's Christology of Divine Identity." https://www.ntslibrary.com/Pauls%20Christology%20of%20Divine%20Identity.pdf, 2002.

Beale, G.K. "Preaching Christ from the Old Testament: A Review of Elliot Johnson and Vern Poythress." *Southern Baptist Journal of Theology* 22.3 (2018) 85–92.

Berniker, Eli, and David E. McNabb. "Dialectical Inquiry: A Structured Qualitative Research Method." *Qualitative Report* 11 (2006) 643–64.

Block, Daniel I. "Christotelic Preaching: A Plea for Hermeneutical Integrity and Missional Passion." *Southern Baptist Journal of Theology* 22.3 (2018) 7–34.

Blomberg, Craig L. *The Historical Reliability of John's Gospel: Issues and Commentary*. Downers Grove, IL: InterVarsity, 2001.

———. "The Wright Stuff: A Critical Overview of *Jesus and the Victory of God*." In *Jesus and the Restoration of Israel: A Critical Assessment of N.T. Wright's Jesus and the Victory of God*, edited by Carey C. Newman, Chapter 2. Downers Grove, IL: InterVarsity. Kindle edition, 2009.

Bock, Darrell L. *Luke*. The IVP New Testament Commentary Series. Downers Grove, IL: InterVarsity, 1994.

———. "The Trial & Death of Jesus in N.T. Wright's *Jesus and the Victory of God*." In *Jesus and the Restoration of Israel: A Critical Assessment of N.T. Wright's Jesus and the Victory of God*, edited by Carey C. Newman, Chapter 6. Downers Grove, IL: InterVarsity. Kindle edition, 2009.

Bonhoeffer, Dietrich. *Berlin: 1932–1933*. Edited by Larry Rasmussen. Dietrich Bonhoeffer Works 12. Translated by Isabel Best and David Higgins. Minneapolis: Fortress, 2009.

Borg, Marcus J. *Jesus in Contemporary Scholarship*. Valley Forge: Trinity, 1994.

Borg, Marcus J., and Nicholas T. Wright. *The Meaning of Jesus: Two Visions*. San Francisco: Harper San Francisco, 1999.

Bornkamm, Gunther. *Jesus of Nazareth*. Translated by Irene McLuskey, Fraser McLuskey and James M. Robinson. Minneapolis: Fortress, 1995.

Branson, Mark L., and Alan J. Roxburgh. *Leadership, God's Agency, & Disruptions: Confronting Modernity's Wager*. Eugene, OR: Cascade Books, 2021

Brunner, Emil. *The Mediator: A Study of the Central Doctrine of the Christian Faith*. 6th ed. Translated by Olive Wyon. London: Lutterworth, 1949.

Butler, Trent C. *Luke*. Holman New Testament Commentary. Nashville: Broadman & Holman, 2000.

Bultmann, Rudolf. "A Reply to the Thesis of J. Schniewind." In *Kerygma and Myth: A Theological Debate*, edited by Hans W. Bartsch, 102–123. Translated by Reginald H. Fuller. London: SPCK, 1953.

Caird, George B. *Jesus and the Jewish Nation*. London: Athlone, 1965.

Calvin, John. *Institutes of the Christian Religion: Volume 1*, edited by John T. McNeill. Translated by Ford L. Battles. Louisville: Westminster John Knox. Kindle edition, 1960.

Canale, Fernando L. *Back to Revelation-Inspiration: Searching for the Cognitive Foundation of Christian Theology in a Postmodern World*. New York: University Press of America, 2001.

Carson, D. A. *The Cross and Christian Ministry: Leadership Lessons from 1 Corinthians.* Grand Rapids: Baker Academic, 1993.

Carter, Craig A. "Preaching Christ from the Old Testament: A Response to Daniel Block, Elliott Johnson and Vern Poythress." *Southern Baptist Journal of Theology* 22.3 (2018) 129–41.

Casey, Maurice. "Where Wright Is Wrong: A Critical Review of N.T. Wright's *Jesus and the Victory of God*." *Journal for the Study of the New Testament* 69 (1998) 95–103.

Chamberlain, Lesley. "The Political Message of Nietzsche's 'God Is Dead.'" https://www.theguardian.com/commentisfree/belief/2012/feb/07/political-message-nietzsche-god-is-dead, 2012.

Chapell, Bryan. *Christ-Centered Preaching: Redeeming the Expository Sermon.* 3rd ed. Grand Rapids: Baker Academic. Kindle edition, 2018a.

———. *Christ-Centered Sermons: Models of Redemptive Preaching.* Grand Rapids: Baker Academic, 2013.

———. "The Future of Expository Preaching." *Presbyterion* 30.2 (2004) 65–80.

———. *The Gospel According to Daniel: A Christ-Centered Approach.* Grand Rapids: Baker Academic, 2014.

———. "Here We Stand: Rooted in Grace for Reformation and Transformation." *Presbyterion* 31.2 (2005) 65–71.

———. "Preaching His Story: Narrative Paths, Problems and Promise." *Journal of the Evangelical Homiletics Society* 6.1 (2006a) 23–43.

———. "Redemptive-Historic View." In *Homiletics and Hermeneutics: Four Views on Preaching Today*, edited by Scott M. Gibson and Matthew D. Kim, 1–29. Grand Rapids: Baker Academic, 2018b.

———. "The Story of the Gospel Applied to Exposition." *Journal of the Evangelical Homiletics Society* 6 (2006b) 44–54.

Chiavone, Michael L. *The One God: A Critically Developed Evangelical Doctrine of Trinitarian Unity.* Eugene, OR: Pickwick Publications, 2009.

Chilton, Bruce D. *The Kingdom of God in the Teaching of Jesus.* London: SPCK, 1984.

———. *The Temple of Jesus: His Sacrificial Program within a Cultural History of Sacrifice.* University Park: Pennsylvania State University Press, 1992.

Choi, Sungho. *The Messianic Kingship of Jesus: A Study of Christology and Redemptive History in Matthew's Gospel with Special Reference to the Royal-Enthronement Psalms.* Eugene, OR: Wipf & Stock, 2011.

Corbett, S and Fikkert, B. *When Helping Hurts: How to Alleviate Poverty without Hurting the Poor. . .and Yourself.* 2nd ed. Chicago: Moody, 2012.

Chou, Abner. "The Christocentric Hermeneutic." https://www.youtube.com/watch?v=2H1LHFJv5ZE, 2022.

———. "A Hermeneutical Evaluation of the Christocentric Hermeneutic." *Master's Seminary Journal* 27.2 (2016) 113–39.

———. "Real Thick Meaning and Preaching Christ from the Old Testament." *Southern Baptist Journal of Theology* 22.3 (2018) 143–55.

Chow, Kevin. "Evaluation of Pannenberg's Self-distinction of the Father and Son." Masters thesis, Singapore Bible College, 2018.

Cilliers, Johan H. *A Space for Grace: Towards an Aesthetics of Preaching.* Stellenbosch: SUN Press, 2016.

Clowney, Edmund P. *How Jesus Transforms the Ten Commandments.* Phillipsburg, NJ: P&R, 2007.

———. *Preaching and Biblical Theology*. 1977. Reprint, Phillipsburg: P&R, 2002.

———. "Preaching Christ." *Christianity Today* 9.12 (1965) 5–7.

———. *Preaching Christ in All of Scripture*. Wheaton, IL: Crossway, 2003.

———. "Preaching the Word of the Lord: Cornelius van Till, V.D.M." *Westminster Theological Journal* 46 (1984) 233–53.

———. "Secularism and the Christian Mission." *Westminster Theological Journal* 21 (1958) 19–57.

———. *The Unfolding Mystery: Discovering Christ in the Old Testament*. 2nd ed. Phillipsburg: P&R, 2013.

Cone, James H. *The Cross and the Lynching Tree*. Maryknoll, NY: Orbis, 2011.

Conzelmann, Hans. *Jesus: The Classic Article from RGG expanded and updated*, edited by John Reumann. Translated by Raymond J. Lord. Philadelphia: Fortress, 1973.

Crossan, John D. *The Historical Jesus: The Life of a Mediterranean Jewish Peasant*. San Francisco: HarperSanFrancisco, 1991.

———. *Jesus: A Revolutionary Biography*. HarperCollins e-books, 1994.

———. *A Long Way from Tipperary: A Memoir*. San Francisco: HarperSanFrancisco, 2000.

———. *Who Killed Jesus? Exposing the Roots of Anti-Semitism in the Gospel Story of the Death of Jesus*. San Francisco: HarperSanFrancisco, 1996.

Davies, William D. *The Gospel and the Land: Early Christianity and Jewish Territorial Doctrine*. Berkeley: University of California Press, 1968.

Diem, Hermann. *Dogmatics*. Translated by Harold Knight. Philadelphia: Westminster, 1959.

Downing, Gerald F. *Cynics and Christian Origins*. Edinburgh: T.& T. Clark, 1992.

Dunn, James G., and Nicolas T. Wright. "An Evening Conversation on Jesus and Paul with James D.G. Dunn and N.T. Wright." https://ntwrightpage.com/2016/05/09/an-evening-conversation-on-jesus-and-paul/, 2004.

Eaton, Michael. "This has not been done in a corner S1.1." https://www.michaeleaton.org/the-real-jesus, 2022.

Ebeling, Gerhard. *The Nature of Faith*. Translated by Ronald G. Smith. Philadelphia: Fortress, 1961.

Eddy, Paul R. "The (W)Right Jesus: Eschatological Prophet, Israel's Messiah, Yahweh Embodied." In *Jesus and the Restoration of Israel: A Critical Assessment of N.T. Wright's Jesus and the Victory of God*, edited by Carey C. Newman, Chapter 3. Downers Grove, IL: InterVarsity. Kindle edition, 2009.

Edwards, James R. *The Gospel according to Luke*. Pillar New Testament Commentary. Grand Rapids: Eerdmans, 2015.

Elert, Werner. *Der Christliche Glaube: Grundlinien der Lutherischen Dogmatik*. 4th ed. Hamburg: Furche, 1956.

Evans, Craig A. *Fabricating Jesus: How Modern Scholars Distort the Gospel*. Downers Grove, IL: InterVarsity, 2006.

———. "Jesus & the Continuing Exile of Israel." In *Jesus and the Restoration of Israel: A Critical Assessment of N.T. Wright's Jesus and the Victory of God*, edited by Carey C. Newman, Chapter 5. Downers Grove, IL: InterVarsity. Kindle edition, 2009.

Evans, Stephen C. "Methodological Naturalism in Historical Biblical Scholarship." In *Jesus and the Restoration of Israel: A Critical Assessment of N.T. Wright's Jesus and the Victory of God*, edited by Carey C. Newman, Chapter 10. Downers Grove, IL: InterVarsity. Kindle edition, 2009.

Falconer, Robert D. "*Crux Sola est Nostra Theologia*: Luther's Theology of Atonement and its Development in Recent Theology on the Cross of Christ." https://www.researchgate.net/publication/321168266_Crux_Sola_est_Nostra_Theologia_Luther's_Theology_of_Atonement_and_its_Development_in_Recent_Theology_on_the_Cross_of_Christ, 2017.

———. "A Theological and Biblical Examination of the Synthesis of Penal Substitution and Christus Victor Motifs: Implications for African Metaphysics." PhD diss., South African Theological Seminary, 2013.

Falsani, Cathleen. "For Millennials, Mysticism Shows a Path to Their Home Faiths." *National Catholic Reporter*, April 24, 2019. https://www.ncronline.org/news/people/millennials-mysticism-shows-path-their-home-faiths.

Fee, Gordon. *Pauline Christology: An Exegetical-Theological Study*. Grand Rapids: Baker Academic, 2007.

Fisher, Christopher L. *Human Significance in Theology and the Natural Sciences: An Ecumenical Perspective with Reference to Pannenberg, Rahner, and Zizioulas*. Eugene, OR: Pickwick Publications, 2010.

Freyne, Sean. *Galilee, Jesus, and the Gospels: Literary Approaches and Historical Investigations*. Philadelphia: Fortress, 1988.

Funk, Robert W. *Honest to Jesus: Jesus for a New Millennium*. San Francisco: HarperSanFrancisco, 1996.

Funk, Robert W., Bernard B. Scott, and James R. Butts. *The Parables of Jesus: Red Letter Edition*. The Jesus Seminar. Sonoma: Polebridge, 1988.

Funk, Robert W., Roy W. Hoover, and the Jesus Seminar. *The Five Gospels: The Search for the Authentic Words of Jesus*. New York: Macmillan, 1993.

Garrett, Lynn. "The Search for Meaning: New Books Offer Answers to the Big Questions for Those Leery of Traditional Religions." *Publishers Weekly* 266.12 (2019) 17–21.

Gaventa, Beverly R., and Richard B. Hays, eds. *Seeking the Identity of Jesus: A Pilgrimage*. Grand Rapids: Eerdmans, 2008.

Gibson, Scott M., and Matthew D. Kim, eds. *Homiletics and Hermeneutics: Four Views on Preaching Today*. Grand Rapids: Baker Academic, 2018.

Gieschen, Charles A. "All Scripture Is Pure Christ: Luther's Christocentric Interpretation in the Context of Reformation Exegesis." *Concordia Theological Quarterly* 81 (2017) 3–17.

Goebel, Heinrich, and Ernest Antrim. "Friedrich Nietzsche's *Uebermensch*." *Monist* 9 (1899) 563–71.

Gogarten, Friedrich. *Der Mensch zwischen Gott und Welt*. Heidelberg: Lambert Schneider, 1952.

———. *Die Verkündiging Jesu Christi: Grundlagen und Aufgabe*. Heidelberg: Lambert Schneider, 1948.

Goheen, Michael W. *The Church and Its Vocation: Leslie Newbigin's Missionary Ecclesiology*. Grand Rapids: Baker Academic, 2018.

Goldsworthy, Graeme. "How do we preach Christ from the Old Testament? A Response to Daniel Block, Elliott Johnson, and Vern Poythress." *Southern Baptist Journal of Theology* 22.3 (2018) 117–28.

———. *Preaching the Whole Bible as Christian Scripture: The Application of Biblical Theology to Expository Preaching*. Grand Rapids: Eerdmans, 2000.

Goodman, Martin. "The First Jewish Revolt: Social Conflict and the Problem of Debt." *Journal of Jewish Studies* 33 (1982) 417–27.

Grass, Hans. *Ostergeschehen und Osterberichte*. 2nd ed. Göttingen: Vandenhoeck & Ruprecht, 1962.

Gregersen, Niels H. "J. Wentzel van Huyssteen and Interdisciplinary Theology." In *Human Origins and the Image of God: Essays in Honour of J. Wentzel van Huyssteen*, edited by Christopher Lilley and Daniel J. Pedersen, 14–47. Grand Rapids: Eerdmans, 2017.

Greidanus, Sidney. *The Modern Preacher and the Ancient Text: Interpreting and Preaching Biblical Literature*. Grand Rapids: Eerdmans, 1988.

———. *Preaching Christ from Daniel: Foundations for Expository Sermons*. Grand Rapids: Eerdmans, 2012.

———. *Preaching Christ from Ecclesiastes: Foundations for Expository Sermons*. Grand Rapids: Eerdmans, 2010.

———. *Preaching Christ from Leviticus: Foundations for Expository Sermons*. Grand Rapids: Eerdmans, 2021.

———. "Preaching Christ from the Old Testament." *Bibliotheca Sacra* 161 (2004) 3–13.

———. *Preaching Christ from the Old Testament: A Contemporary Hermeneutical Method*. Grand Rapids: Eerdmans. Kindle edition, 1999.

———. "Redemptive History and Preaching." *Pro Rege* 19.2 (1990) 9–18.

———. "Reflections on Preaching Christ from the Old Testament." *Southern Baptist Journal of Theology* 22.3 (2018) 103–15.

———. *Sola Scriptura: Problems and Principles in Preaching Historical Texts*. 1970. Reprint, Eugene, OR: Wipf & Stock, 2001.

Gussmann, Wilhelm. *Quellen und Forschungen zur Geschichte des Augsburgischen Glaubensbekenntnisses*. Berlin: Teubner, 1911.

Harvie, Timothy. "Living the Future: The Kingdom of God in the Theologies of Jürgen Moltmann and Wolfhart Pannenberg." *International Journal of Systematic Theology* 10.2 (2008) 149–64.

Hays, Richard B. "The Corrected Jesus." *First Things* (1994). https://www.firstthings.com/article/1994/05/the-corrected-jesus.

———. *Echoes of Scripture in the Gospels*. Waco: Baylor University Press, 2016.

———. "Knowing Jesus: Story, History and the Question of Truth." In *Jesus, Paul and the People of God: A Theological Dialogue with N.T. Wright*, edited by Nicholas Perrin and Richard B. Hays, 51–78. London: SPCK, 2011.

———. "Victory over Violence: The Significance of N.T. Wright's *Jesus for New Testament Ethics*." In *Jesus and the Restoration of Israel: A Critical Assessment of N.T. Wright's Jesus and the Victory of God*, edited by Carey C. Newman, Chapter 8. Downers Grove, IL: InterVarsity. Kindle edition, 2009.

Herrmann, Wilhelm. "Der geschichtliche Christus: Der Grund unseres Glaubens." *Zeitschrift für Theologie und Kirche* 2 (1892) 232–73.

Herzog, William R., II. *Jesus, Justice, and the Reign of God: A Ministry of Liberation*. Louisville: Westminster John Knox, 2000.

Horsley, Richard A., with John S. Hanson. *Bandits, Prophets, and Messiahs: Popular Movements at the Time of Jesus*. Minneapolis: Winston, 1985.

Horton, Michael. *A Better Way: Rediscovering the Drama of God-Centered Worship*. Grand Rapids: Baker, 2002.

———. *The Christian Faith: A Systematic Theology for Pilgrims on the Way*. Grand Rapids: Zondervan, 2011.

———. "What Are We Looking for in the Bible?" *Modern Reformation Magazine* 5.3 (1996) 1–6.
Hurtado, Larry W. *Lord Jesus Christ: Devotion to Jesus in Earliest Christianity*. Grand Rapids: Eerdmans, 2003.
Jaspers, Karl. *Die grossen Philosophen: Volume 1*. Munich: Piper, 1957.
Jeremias, Joachim. *Jesus and the Message of the New Testament*. Edited by K. C. Hanson. Fortress Classics in Biblical Studies. Minneapolis: Fortress, 2002.
Jesus Culture. "Jesus Culture—Love Has a Name (Live) ft. Kim Walker-Smith." https://www.youtube.com/watch?v=ZO-3dj33k-I, 2017.
Johnson, Dennis E. *Heralds of the King*. Wheaton, IL: Crossway, 2009.
Johnson, Elizabeth A. "The Ongoing Christology of Wolfhart Pannenberg." *Horizons* 9(2) (1982) 237–50.
Johnson, Luke T. "A Historiographical Response to Wright's Jesus." In *Jesus and the Restoration of Israel: A Critical Assessment of N.T. Wright's Jesus and the Victory of God*, edited by Carey C. Newman, Chapter 11. Downers Grove, IL: InterVarsity. Kindle edition, 2009.
———. *The Real Jesus: The Misguided Quest for the Historical Jesus and the Truth of the Traditional Gospels*. San Francisco: Harper San Francisco, 1996.
Jonker, Willie D. *Christus, die Middelaar*. Cape Town: Nasionale Boekdrukkery, 1977.
Kähler, Martin. *The So-called Historical Jesus and the Historic, Biblical Christ*, edited by Carl E. Braaten. Translated by Carl E. Braaten. Philadelphia: Fortress, 1964.
Kaiser, Walter. *Preaching and Teaching from the Old Testament: A Guide for the Church*. Grand Rapids: Baker, 2003.
———. *Toward an Exegetical Theology: Biblical Exegesis for Preaching and Teaching*. Grand Rapids: Baker, 1981.
Kant, Immanuel. *Religion Within the Limits of Reason Alone*. 2nd ed. Translated by Theodore M. Greene and Hoyt H. Hudson. New York: Harper & Row, 1960.
Kärkkäinen, Veli-Matti. *Christology: A global introduction*. 2nd ed. Grand Rapids: Baker Academic, 2016.
Keesmaat, Sylvia C., and Brian J. Walsh. "Outside of a Small Circle of Friends: Jesus and the Justice of God." In *Jesus, Paul and the People of God: A Theological Dialogue with N.T. Wright*, edited by Nicholas Perrin and Richard B. Hays, 85–111. London: SPCK, 2011.
Keller, Timothy J. "And if Christ be not Raised." https://gospelinlife.com/downloads/and-if-christ-be-not-raised-5454/, 2006.
———. *Preaching: Communicating Faith in a Skeptical Age*. London: Hodder & Stoughton. Kindle version, 2015.
———. "Preaching in a Post-Modern City: A Case Study: I." https://westerfunk.net/archives/theology/Tim%20Keller%20on%20Preaching%20in%20a%20Post-Modern%20City%20-%203/, 2004.
Kilcrease, Jack D., and Roland Ziegler. *The Doctrine of Atonement: From Luther to Forde*. Eugene, OR: Wipf & Stock, 2018.
Kilner, John F. *Dignity and Destiny: Humanity in the Image of God*. Grand Rapids: Eerdmans, 2015.
Koch, Gerhard. *Die Auferstehung Jesu Christi*. Tübingen: Mohr Siebeck, 1959.
Kugler, Chris. "Judaism/Hellenism in Early Christology: Prepositional Metaphysics and Middle Platonic Intermediary Doctrine." *Journal for the Study of the New Testament* 43 (2020) 214–25.

Künneth, Walter. *Glauben an Jesus? Die Begegnung der Christologie mit der modernen Existenz*. Hamburg: Wittig, 1962.

———. *The Theology of the Resurrection*. Translated by James W. Leitch. St. Louis: Concordia, 1965.

Kuruvilla, Abraham. "Christiconic Interpretation." *Bibliotheca Sacra* 173(2) (2016) 131–46.

———. *Privilege the Text!: A Theological Hermeneutic for Preaching*. Chicago: Moody, 2013.

———. "Response to Bryan Chapell." In *Homiletics and Hermeneutics: Four Views on preaching today*, edited by Scott M. Gibson and Matthew D. Kim, 30–34. Grand Rapids: Baker Academic, 2018.

———. "Review of *Preaching Christ from Genesis* by Sidney Greidanus." *Journal of the Evangelical Homiletics Society* 8.1 (2008) 137–40.

Lang, Bernhard. "The Roots of the Eucharist in Jesus' Praxis." *Society of Biblical Literature* 128 (1992) 467–72.

Langley, Kenneth. "Response to Bryan Chapell." In *Homiletics and Hermeneutics: Four Views on Preaching Today*, edited by Scott M. Gibson and Matthew D. Kim, 35–37. Grand Rapids: Baker Academic, 2018.

Lee, Hongkil. "Christ-saturated Preaching: A Hermeneutical and Homiletical Analysis of Christ-centered Preaching and Its Implications." PhD diss., Southern Baptist Theological Seminary, 2016.

Leipoldt, Johannes. "Zu den Auferstehungsgeschichten." *Theologische Literaturzeitung* 73 (1948) 737–42.

Lewis, Gordon R., and Bruce C. Demarest. *Integrative Theology*. Grand Rapids: Zondervan, 1996.

Lillback, Peter A, ed. *Seeing Christ in All of Scripture: Hermeneutics at Westminster Theological Seminary*. Philadelphia: Westminster Seminary Press, 2016.

Lucado, Max. *Facing Your Giants: A David and Goliath Story for Everyday People*. Nashville: Nelson, 2006.

MacArthur, John. "NT Wright Is NT Wrong!—John MacArthur." https://www.youtube.com/watch?v=Q8AxadepsWs, 2020.

MacDonald, Benjamin M. "Waiting for God: An Examination and Critique of Prolepsis in the Theology of Wolfhart Pannenberg." Master's thesis, Acadia Divinity College, 2016.

Mack, Burton L. *A Myth of Innocence: Mark and Christian Origins*. Philadelphia: Fortress, 1988.

Macleod, Donald. "The Christology of Wolfhart Pannenberg." *Themelios* 25.2 (2000) 19–41.

Marheineke, Philipp. *Die Grundlehren der christlichen Dogmatik als Wissenschaft*. 2nd ed. Berlin: Duneker & Humbolt, 1827.

Marsh, Clive. "Theological History? N.T Wright's Jesus and the Victory of God." *Journal for the Study of the New Testament* 69 (1998) 77–94.

Mattes, Mark C. *The Role of Justification in Contemporary Theology*. Edited by Paul Rorem. Minneapolis: Fortress, 2017.

McClymond, Michael. "Everything is Christ-and Other Muddled Messages from Richard Rohr." https://www.thegospelcoalition.org/reviews/universal-christ-richard-rohr/, 2019.

McDermott, Brian O. "Pannenberg's Resurrection Christology: A Critique." *Theological Studies* 35 (1974) 711–21.

McGrath, Alister E. "Reality, Symbol & History: Theological Reflections on N.T. Wright's portrayal of Jesus." In *Jesus and the Restoration of Israel: A Critical Assessment of N.T. Wright's Jesus and the Victory of God,* edited by Carey C. Newman, Chapter 9. Downers Grove, IL: InterVarsity. Kindle edition, 2009.

Medley, George III. "The Inspiration of God and Wolfhart Pannenberg's field theory of information." *Zygon* 48 (2013) 93–106.

Meier, John P. *A Marginal Jew: Rethinking the Historical Jesus.* New York: Doubleday, 1994.

Meyer, Ben F. *The Aims of Jesus.* 1979. Reprint, Eugene, OR: Wipf & Stock, 2002.

———. *Christus Faber: The Master-Builder and the House of God.* Allison Park, PA: Pickwick Publications, 1992.

Migliore, Daniel L. *Faith seeking understanding: An introduction to Christian Theology.* 3rd ed. Grand Rapids: Eerdmans, 2014.

Moltmann, Jürgen. *The Crucified God.* 40th Anniversary ed. Minneapolis: Fortress, 2015.

Moore, Andrew. "Who Are the Liberals Now? History, Science, and Christology in N.T. Wright and Alister McGrath." *Anglican Evangelical Journal for Theology and Mission* 20.1 (2003) 9–24.

Moore, Russell D. "Preaching Like the Devil." *Touchstone* 3 (2010) 9–12.

Neill Stephen C., and Nicholas T. Wright. *The Interpretation of the New Testament, 1861–1986.* Oxford: Oxford University Press, 1988.

Newman, Carey C. "From (Wright's) Jesus to (the Church's) Christ: Can We Get There from Here?" In *Jesus and the Restoration of Israel: A Critical Assessment of N.T. Wright's Jesus and the Victory of God,* Chapter 14. Downers Grove, IL: InterVarsity. Kindle edition, 2009b.

———., ed. "Right Reading, Reading Wright." In *Jesus and the Restoration of Israel: A Critical Assessment of N.T. Wright's Jesus and the Victory of God,* Chapter 1. Downers Grove, IL: InterVarsity. Kindle edition, 2009a.

O'Collins, G. G. "The Christology of Wolfhart Pannenberg." *Religious Studies* 3 (1967) 369–76.

Olsen, Roger E. "The Human Self-realization of God: Hegelian Elements in Pannenberg's Christology." *Perspective in Religious Studies* 13 (1986) 207–23.

Osborne, Grant R. *The Hermeneutical Spiral: A Comprehensive Introduction to Biblical Interpretation.* Wheaton, IL: IVP Academic, 2006.

Owen, J.M. "Christology and History." *Reformed Theological Review* 26.2 (1967) 54–64.

———. "First Look at Pannenberg's Christology." *Reformed Theological Review* 25.2 (1966) 52–64.

Pannenberg, Wolfhart. *Anthropology in Theological Perspective.* Translated by Matthew J. O'Connell. Philadelphia: Westminster, 1985.

———. *The Apostles Creed: In the Light of Today's Questions.* Translated by Margaret Kohl. London: SCM, 1972.

———. "Die Auferstehung Jesu: Historie und Theologie." *Zeitschrift für Theologie und Kirche* 91 (1994a) 318–28.

———. "Die Auferstehung Jesu und die Zukunft des Menschen." *Kirche und Dogmatik* 24 (1978a) 104–17.

———. "Die Aufgabe christlicher Eschatologie." *Zeitschrift für Theologie und Kirche* 92 (1995) 71–82.

———. *Basic Questions in Theology: Collected Essays, Volume 1.* Translated by George H. Kehm. Philadelphia: Fortress, 1970.

———. *Die Bestimmung des Menschen: Menschsein, Erwählung und Geschichte.* Göttingen: Vandenhoeck & Ruprecht, 1978b.

———. "The Christian Vision of God: The New Discussion on the Trinitarian Doctrine." *Asbury Theological Journal* 46.2 (1991a) 27–36.

———. *Christliche Spiritualität: Theologische Aspekte.* Göttingen: Vandenhoeck & Ruprecht, 1986.

———. "Christologie und Theologie." *Kirche und Dogmatik* 21 (1975a) 159–75.

———. "Constructive and Critical Functions of Christian Eschatology." *Harvard Theological Review* 77(2) (1984) 119–39.

———. "The Contribution of Christianity to the Modern World." *CrossCurrents* 25 (1976a) 357–66.

———. "Dogmatische Erwägungen zur Auferstehung Jesu." *Kirche und Dogmatik* 14 (1968a) 105–18.

———. "Die Einzigkeit Jesu Christi und die Einheit der Kirche. Anmerkungen zu der Erklärung der vatikanischen Glaubenskongregation Dominus Jesus." *Kirche und Dogmatik* 47 (2001) 203–09.

———. "Eternity, Time, and Space." *Zygon* 40 (2005) 97–106.

———. "Eternity, Time, and the Trinitarian God." *Dialogue: A Journal of Theology* 39.1 (2000) 9–14.

———. "Geschichtliche Offenbarung Gottes und ewige Trinität." *Kirche und Dogmatik* 49 (2003) 236–46.

———. "God's Presence in History." *Christian Century* 98 (1981) 260–63.

———. "Der Gott der Geschichte: Der trinitarische Gott und die Wahrheit der Geschichte." *Kirche und Dogmatik* 23 (1977b) 76–92.

———. *Grundzüge der Christologie.* 2nd ed. Gütersloh: Gütersloher, 1966.

———. "History and the Reality of the Resurrection." In *Resurrection Reconsidered*, edited by Gavin D'Costa, 62–72. Oxford: Oneworld, 1996.

———. *Human Nature, Election, and History.* Philadelphia: Westminster, 1977c.

———. *The Idea of God and Human Freedom.* Translated by R. A. Wilson. Philadelphia: The Westminster, 1973.

———. "Jesu Geschichte und unsere Geschichte." *Radius* (1960). Reprint, Munich: Kaiser, 1975b.

———. *Jesus—God and Man.* 2nd ed. Translated by Lewis L. Wilkins and Duane A. Priebe. Philadelphia: The Westminster, 1977a.

———. "Jesus' History and Our History." Translated by Ted Peters. *Perspectives in Religious Studies* 1.2 (1974a) 139–47.

———. *Jesus-God and Man.* SCM, 2002.

———. *Offenbarung als Geschichte.* Göttingen: Vandenhoeck und Ruprecht, 1982.

———. *Revelation as History.* Translated by David Granskou. New York: Macmillan, 1968b.

———. *Systematic Theology: Volume 1.* Translated by Geoffrey W. Bromiley. Grand Rapids: Eerdmans, 1991b.

———. *Systematic Theology: Volume 2.* Translated by Geoffrey W. Bromiley. Grand Rapids: Eerdmans, 1994b.

———. "Theological Table Talk: On the Inspiration of Scripture." *Theology Today* 52 (1997) 212–15.
———. *Theology and the Kingdom of God*. Philadelphia: Westminster, 1969.
———. "A Theology of the Cross." *Word and World* 8 (1988) 162–72.
———. "Tod und Auferstehung in der Sicht christlicher Dogmatik." *Kirche und Dogmatik* 20 (1974b) 167–80.
———. *Was ist der Mensch? Die Anthropologie der Gegenwart im Lichte der Theologie*. Göttingen: Hubert, 1976b.
———. *What Is Truth?* Translated by George H. Kehm. Philadelphia: Fortress, 1971.
Pearson, Birger A. "The Gospel According to the Jesus Seminar." *Religion* 25 (1995) 317–38.
Pelikan, Jaroslav. *Jesus through the Centuries: His Place in the History of Culture*. New Haven: Yale University Press, 1985.
Peppler, Christopher. "The Christocentric Principle: A Jesus-Centered Hermeneutic." *Conspectus* 13 (2012) 117–35.
Perrin, Nicolas. "Introduction." In *Jesus, Paul and the People of God: A Theological Dialogue with N.T. Wright*, edited by Nicholas Perrin and Richard B. Hays, 8–21. London: SPCK, 2011a.
———. "Jesus' Eschatology and Kingdom Ethics: Ever the Twain Shall Meet." In *Jesus, Paul and the People of God: A Theological Dialogue with N.T. Wright*, edited by Nicholas Perrin and Richard B. Hays, 122–48. London: SPCK, 2011b.
Peters, Ted. "In Memoriam: Wolfhart Pannenberg (1928–2014)." *Dialog: A Journal of Theology* 53 (2014) 365–83.
Piper, John. "Two Dangers in 'Gospel-Centered' Preaching." https://www.youtube.com/watch?v=5PcmDFhQx6o, 2019.
Poythress, Vern S. "Christocentric Preaching." *Southern Baptist Journal of Theology* 22.3 (2018) 47–66.
Price, Eric S. "Comparing Sidney Greidanus and Abraham Kuruvilla on Preaching Christ from the Old Testament." *Trinity Journal* 39 (2018) 69–93.
Prince, David E. "The Necessity of a Christocentric Kingdom-focused Model of Expository preaching." PhD diss., Southern Baptist Theological Seminary, 2011.
Qin, Daniel. "The Starting Point of Christology: From Below or from Above? Part II." *Asian Journal of Pentecostal Studies* 18 (2015) 39–51.
Rise, Svein. "Creation and Redemption in Pannenberg with a View to the Ecological Perspective." *Worldviews* 14 (2010) 216–31.
Ritschl, Albrecht. *The Christian Doctrine of Justification and Reconciliation: The Positive Development of the Doctrine*, edited by H. R. Mackintosh and A. B. Macaulay. 2nd ed. Translated by H. R. Mackintosh. Edinburgh: T. & T. Clark, 1902.
Rohr, Richard. *The Universal Christ: How a forgotten reality can change everything we see, hope for and believe*. New York: Convergent. Kindle edition, 2019.
Røsok, Ingvild. "The Kenosis of Christ Revisited: The Relational Perspective of Karl Rahner." *Heythrop Journal* 58 (2017) 51–63.
Sanders, Ed P. *The Historical Figure of Jesus*. London: Penguin, 1993.
———. *Jesus and Judaism*. Philadelphia: Fortress, 1985.
———. *Judaism: Practice and Belief 63 BCE–66 CE*. London: SCM, 1992.
———. *Paul, the Law, and the Jewish People*. Philadelphia: Fortress, 1983.

Scheuers, Timothy R. "Law and Gospel in the Theologies of Wolfhart Pannenberg and Karl Barth: A Comparative Study." *Mid-America Journal of Theology* 26 (2015) 105–29.

Schleiermacher, Friedrich D. *The Christian Faith*, edited by H. R. Mackintosh and J. S. Stewart. 2nd ed. Translated by H. R. Mackintosh. Edinburgh: T. & T. Clark, 1928.

———. *Der Christliche Glaube nach den Grundsätzen der evangelischen Kirche*. Berlin: Reimer, 1822.

Schreiner, Thomas R. "Preaching and Biblical Theology." *Southern Baptist Journal of Theology* 10 (2006) 20–29.

Schweitzer, Albert. *The Quest for the Historical Jesus*. Translated by F. C. Burkitt. Jovian. Kindle version, 2016.

Schwöbel, Christoph. "Wolfhart Pannenberg." In *The Modern Theologians: An Introduction to Christian Theology since 1918*, edited by David F. Ford and Rachel Muers, 129–46. 3rd ed. Oxford: Blackwell, 2005.

Seeberg, Reinhold. *Christliche Dogmatik*. 2nd ed. Erlangen: Deichert, 1924.

Seo, Kyeongmin. "Christomonism: A Pitfall of Christocentric Preaching." https://preachingsource.com/blog/christomonism-a-pitfall-of-christocentric-preaching/, 2019.

Sequeira, Aubrey. "Preaching Christ from the Old Testament: A Response to Daniel Block, Elliott Johnson, and Vern Poythress." *Southern Baptist Journal of Theology* 22.3 (2018) 181–95.

Smith, Kevin G. "The Christocentric Principle: Promise, Pitfalls, and Proposal." *Conspectus* 13 (2012) 157–70.

Snodgrass, Klyne R. "Reading and Overreading the Parables in *Jesus and the Victory of God*." In *Jesus and the Restoration of Israel: A Critical Assessment of N.T. Wright's Jesus and the Victory of God*, edited by Carey C. Newman, Chapter 4. Downers Grove, IL: InterVarsity. Kindle edition, 2009.

Stein, Robert H. *Luke*. New American Commentary. Nashville: Broadman & Holman, 1992.

Stetzer, Ed, ed. *Christ-Centered Preaching & Teaching*. Nashville: LifeWay, 2013.

Thiselton, Anthony C. *Understanding Pannenberg: Landmark Theologian of the Twentieth Century*. Cascade Companions. Eugene, OR: Cascade, 2018.

Thompson, Marianne M. "*Jesus and the Victory of God* Meets the Gospel of John." In *Jesus, Paul and the People of God: A Theological Dialogue with N.T. Wright*, edited by Nicholas Perrin and Richard B. Hays, 23–46. London: SPCK, 2011.

Tillich, Paul J. *Reason and Revelation, Being and God*. Vol. 1 of *Systematic Theology*. Chicago: University of Chicago Press, 1957.

Tilling, Chris. *Paul's Divine Christology*. Tübingen: Mohr Siebeck, 2012.

Tupper, Frank E. "Christology of Wolfhart Pannenberg." *Review & Expositor* 71 (1974) 59–73.

Vogel, Heinrich. *Christologie I*. Munich: Kaiser, 1949.

Von Campenhausen, Hans. *Tradition und Leben: Kräfte der Kirchengeschichte*. Tübingen: Mohr Siebeck, 1960.

Vos, Geerhardus. *Biblical Theology*. Grand Rapids: Eerdmans, 1948.

Wainwright, Geoffrey. *For Our Salvation: Two Approaches to the Work of Christ*. Grand Rapids: Eerdmans, 1997.

Ward, Graham. *The Politics of Discipleship: Becoming Postmaterial Citizens*. Edited by James K Smith. Grand Rapids: Baker Academic, 2009.

Warren, Timothy S. "A Review of Christ-Centered Preaching: Redeeming the Expository Sermon, by Bryan Chapell." Bibliotheca Sacra 152(606) (1995) 252–53.

Webb, Robert L. *John the Baptizer and Prophet: A Socio-Historical Study.* Journal for the Study of the New Testament Sheffield: JSOT, 1991.

Weber, Otto. *Grundlagen der Dogmatik.* 2nd ed. Neukirchen-Vluyn: Neukirchener Verlag, 1962.

Welker, Michael. *God the Revealed: Christology.* Translated by Douglas Stott. Grand Rapids: Eerdmans, 2013.

Welliver, Jesse. "Fortifying a Christocentric Homiletic through the Concept of Covenant Consciousness in the Preaching Theology of Gerard van Groningen." PhD diss., Southeastern Baptist Theological Seminary, 2020.

Wellum, Stephen J. "Editorial: Preaching the Glory of Christ from a 'Whole Bible.'" *Southern Baptist Journal of Theology* 22.3 (2018) 3–6.

Wessels, Francois. *Wie was Jesus Regtig? Oor die historiese Jesus.* Epping: ABC Boekdrukkers, 2006.

Whapham, Theodore J. *The Unity of Theology: The Contribution of Wolfhart Pannenberg.* Minneapolis: Fortress, 2017.

Wiginton, Daniel I. "Training Congregants at First Baptist Church of Matawan, New Jersey, to study the Bible in a Christocentric manner." PhD diss., The Southern Baptist Theological Seminary, 2016.

Wildman, Wesley J. "Basic Christological Distinctions." *Theology Today* 64 (2007) 285–304.

Williams, Rowan. *Christ the heart of creation.* Great Britain: Bloomsbury, 2018.

Winkler, Lewis E., and Veli-Matti Kärkkäinen. *Contemporary Muslim and Christian Responses to Religious Plurality: Wolfhart Pannenberg in Dialogue with Abdulaziz Sachedina.* Eugene, OR: Pickwick Publications, 2011.

Witherington, Ben, III. *The Jesus Quest: The Third Search for the Jew of Nazareth.* Downers Grove, IL: InterVarsity, 1995.

Woodhouse, John. *1 Samuel: Looking for a Leader.* Wheaton, IL: Crossway, 2008.

Wright, N. T. *After You Believe: Why Christian Character Matters.* New York: HarperCollins, 2010.

———. *The Challenge of Jesus: Rediscovering Who Jesus Was and Is.* Downers Grove, IL: Intervarsity, 2015.

———. "Christian Origins and the Resurrection of Jesus: The Resurrection of Jesus as a Historical Problem." *Sewanee Theological Review* 41.2 (1998d) 107–23.

———. *The Climax of the Covenant: Christ and the Law in Pauline Theology.* London: T. & T. Clark, 1991b.

———. *The Day the Revolution Began: Reconsidering the Meaning of Jesus' Crucifixion.* New York: HarperCollins, 2016.

———. "Doing Justice to Jesus: A Response to J. D. Crossan, 'What Victory? What God?'" *Scottish Journal of Theology* 50 (1997) 359–79.

———. "Early Traditions and the Origin of Christianity." *Sewanee Theological Review* 41 (1998e) 125–40.

———. "Economy and Business: Debate on the Queen's Speech." https://empireremixed.com/2008/12/09/economy-and-business-debate-on-the-queens-speech-monday-december-8-2008/, 2008e.

———. *Evil and the Justice of God.* London: SPCK, 2006.

———. "God in Private and Public." https://ntwrightpage.com/2016/03/30/god-in-private-and-public/, 2008c.

———. "Grave Matters: Take away the Resurrection and the Center of Christianity Collapses." *Christianity Today* April 6, (1998c) 51–53.

———. "The Historical Jesus and Christian Theology." *Sewanee Theological Review* 39 (1996b) 404–12.

———. *How God Became King: The Forgotten Story of the Gospels*. New York: HarperCollins, 2012b.

———. "Imagining the Kingdom: Mission and Theology in Early Christianity." *Scottish Journal of Theology* 65 (2012a) 379–401.

———. "In Grateful Dialogue: A Response." In *Jesus and the Restoration of Israel: A Critical Assessment of N.T. Wright's Jesus and the Victory of God*, edited by Carey C. Newman, Chapter 13. Downers Grove, IL: InterVarsity. Kindle edition, 2009b.

———. "Jesus and the Identity of God." *Ex Auditu* (1998a) 42–56.

———. *Jesus and the victory of God*. Vol. 2 of *Christian Origins and the Question of God*. Minneapolis: Fortress, 1996a.

———. "Jesus in Space, Time, and History: Natural Theology and the Challenge of Talking about God." *Crux* 55.4 (2019a) 2–11.

———. "Jesus in the Perfect Storm." https://ntwrightpage.com/2016/03/30/jesus-in-the-perfect-storm/, 2011b.

———. "Jesus' Resurrection and Christian Origins." *Stimulus* 16.1 (2008a) 41–50.

———. "Job 42." https://www.youtube.com/watch?v=GLOzo7pct9Y, 2017e.

———. *John for Everyone, Part 1: Chapters 1–10*. London: SPCK, 2004b.

———. "Kingdom Come: The Public Meaning of the Gospels." *Christian Century* 125.12 (2008b) 29–34.

———. "Living in God's Future–Now!" https://ntwrightpage.com/2016/03/30/living-in-gods-future-now/, 2009a.

———. *Luke for Everyone*. 2nd ed. London: SPCK, 2004a.

———. "Messianic Grammar? A Response to Matthew V. Novenson, *The Grammar of Messianism: An Ancient Jewish Political Idiom and Its Users*." *Expository Times* 129 (2018) 295–302.

———. *The New Testament and the People of God*. Vol. 1 of *Christian Origins and the Question of God*. London: SPCK, 1992.

———. "The New Testament in Its World: How History Can Revitalize Faith." https://www.youtube.com/watch?v=ccWTtNLs-YA, 2019b.

———. "On Earth as in Heaven." https://ntwrightpage.com/2016/03/30/on-earth-as-in-heaven/, 2007b.

———. "One God, One Lord, One People: Incarnational Christology for a Church in a Pagan Environment." *Ex Auditu* 7 (1991a) 45–58.

———. *Paul and the Faithfulness of God*. Vol. 4 of *Christian Origins and the Question of God*. London: SPCK, 2013.

———. "Pictures, Stories, and the Cross: Where Do the Echoes Lead?" *Journal of Theological Interpretation* 11.1 (2017a) 49–68.

———. "Response to Marianne Meye Thompson." In *Jesus, Paul and the People of God: A Theological Dialogue with N.T. Wright*, edited by Nicholas Perrin and Richard B. Hays, 46–48. London: SPCK, 2011d.

———. "Response to Nicholas Perrin." In *Jesus, Paul and the People of God: A Theological Dialogue with N.T. Wright*, edited by Nicholas Perrin and Richard B. Hays, 148–50. London: SPCK, 2011g.

———. "Response to Richard Hays." In *Jesus, Paul and the People of God: A Theological Dialogue with N.T. Wright*, edited by Nicholas Perrin and Richard B. Hays, 78–82. London: SPCK, 2011e.

———. "Response to Sylvia Keesmaat and Brian Walsh." In *Jesus, Paul and the People of God: A Theological Dialogue with N.T. Wright*, edited by Nicholas Perrin and Richard B. Hays, 111–13. London: SPCK, 2011f.

———. "Resurrecting Old Arguments: Responding to Four Essays." *Journal for the Study of the Historical Jesus* 3 (2005) 209–231.

———. "The Resurrection and the Postmodern Dilemma." *Sewanee Theological Review* 41.2 (1998f) 141–56.

———. "Resurrection in Q?" In *Christology, Controversy and Community: New Testament Essays in Honour of David R Catchpole*, edited by David G. Horrell and Christopher M. Tuckett, 85–98. Novum Testamentum Supplements 99. Leiden: Brill, 2000.

———. *The Resurrection of the Son of God*. Rev. ed. Vol. 3 of *Christian Origins and the Question of God*. Minneapolis: Fortress, 2003.

———. "The Royal Revolution: Fresh Perspectives on the Cross." https://www.youtube.com/watch?v=XOq2hQLqNPs, 2017b.

———. "Saving the World, Revealing the Glory: Atonement Then and Now." https://www.abc.net.au/religion/saving-the-world-revealing-the-glory-atonement-then-and-now/10095866, 2017c.

———. "Simply Christian." https://www.youtube.com/watch?v=omAwWJEyYJo, 2017d.

———. *Simply Jesus: Who He Was, What He Did, Why It Matters*. London: SPCK, 2011a.

———. *Surprised by Hope*. New York: HarperCollins, 2008d.

———. "Theology, History and Jesus: A Response to Maurice Casey and Clive Marsh." *Journal for the Study of the New Testament* 69 (1998b) 105–12.

———. "Whence and Whither Historical Jesus Studies in the Life of the Church?" In *Jesus, Paul and the People of God: A Theological Dialogue with N.T. Wright*, edited by Nicholas Perrin and Richard B. Hays, 154–212. London: SPCK, 2011c.

———. "The Word of the Cross." https://ntwrightpage.com/2016/03/30/the-word-of-the-cross/, 2007a.

York, Hershael W. "Reflections on Preaching Christ from the Old Testament." *Southern Baptist Journal of Theology* 22.3 (2018) 197–204.

www.ingramcontent.com/pod-product-compliance
Lightning Source LLC
Chambersburg PA
CBHW071157300426
44113CB00009B/1234